AUTODESK® REVIT® ARCHITECTURE 2013

ESSENTIALS

James Vandezande
Phil Read
Eddy Krygiel

John Wiley & Sons, Inc.

Senior Acquisitions Editor: Willem Knibbe
Development Editor: Sara Barry
Technical Editor: Adam Thomas
Production Editor: Eric Charbonneau
Copy Editor: Tiffany Taylor
Editorial Manager: Pete Gaughan
Production Manager: Tim Tate
Vice President and Executive Group Publisher: Richard Swadley
Vice President and Publisher: Neil Edde
Book Designer: Happenstance Type-O-Rama
Compositor: Jeff Lytle, Happenstance Type-O-Rama
Proofreader: Kim Wimpsett
Indexer: Ted Laux
Project Coordinator, Cover: Katherine Crocker
Cover Designer: Ryan Sneed
Cover Image: SOM | ©Hayes Davidson

Published simultaneously in Canada
ISBN: 978-1-118-24478-4 (pbk)
ISBN: 978-1-118-33325-9 (ebk)
ISBN: 978-1-118-33042-5 (ebk)
ISBN: 978-1-118-33107-1 (ebk)

Library of Congress Control Number: 2012933631

10 9 8 7 6 5 4 3 2 1

Dear Reader,

Thank you for choosing *Autodesk Revit Architecture 2013 Essentials*. This book is part of a family of premium-quality Sybex books, all of which are written by outstanding authors who combine practical experience with a gift for teaching.

Sybex was founded in 1976. More than 30 years later, we're still committed to producing consistently exceptional books. With each of our titles, we're working hard to set a new standard for the industry. From the paper we print on to the authors we work with, our goal is to bring you the best books available.

I hope you see all that reflected in these pages. I'd be very interested to hear your comments and get your feedback on how we're doing. Feel free to let me know what you think about this or any other Sybex book by sending me an email at `nedde@wiley.com`. If you think you've found a technical error in this book, please visit `http://sybex.custhelp.com`. Customer feedback is critical to our efforts at Sybex.

Best regards,

Neil Edde
Vice President and Publisher
Sybex, an Imprint of Wiley

For Stephen. Stay focused and achieve your dreams.

—James

Justine: You're a peace-loving Kiwi and mother who insists on handgun lessons and a concealed carry permit. I don't understand all the contradictions in the previous sentence, but the upside is I get to have friends like Eddy and James.

Harrison: High school is upon you. The most amazing careers haven't even been created yet. The trick? Studying in order to become an entrepreneur—not just an employee.

Millicent: As soon as Carol Bartz pens her biography, we're going to stand in line to buy it. Until then, there's always Ayn Rand and Jane Austen—neither of which would ever suggest you settle for the 99%.

Jasper: Stubbornness is a virtue and the world certainly needs more people who refuse to believe in the impossible (such as airplanes, atom-splitting, and personal computers). But arguing about bedtime isn't one of those things.

—Phil

For Zoë and Maya

—Eddy

Acknowledgments

Ah, the acknowledgments. While the fame and glory of writing a book is almost entirely consumed by the egos of the authors, it takes so much more effort and so many more people than the three of us to make this book happen. Writing and publishing a book, like designing a building, is the effort of a team; without their hard work and willingness to correct a lot of mistakes (made by us), this book would never have happened.

To that end, first we'd like to thank the fine folks on the Autodesk® Revit® Architecture team because without their excellent software we wouldn't have a topic to write about. While it's not possible to name them all, the work of the product designers, quality assurance team, and all the others doesn't go unrecognized or unappreciated. Thank you, gals and guys, for taking a tough job and doing it with a great attitude. Thank you to the development team for putting up with all of our continued requests to make the product better.

Second, a big thank you to the team at Sybex. They dot our i's, cross our t's, and add spaces to words like a-lot. Beyond the sheer complications of good English grammar, they also help us stay focused, make sure what we write makes sense to more than just us, and help us keep the pace through the winter months of the authoring season. So, thank you to Sara for being brave enough to be the first person to read our prose and help make it better for the second and third versions. Thanks also to our copy editor, Tiffany Taylor, for being that critical set of eyes looking into the details and for, well, editing the copy. Thank you to Pete for keeping us on track during the holidays, weekends, evenings, and all the other times we should be writing but are doing less important things like tending to our families. And as always, a special thanks to Willem for putting up with what we are regularly told is a very high-maintenance authoring team. You guys and gals are great.

—James Vandezande, Phil Read, Eddy Krygiel

About the Authors

James Vandezande is a registered architect and a principal at HOK in New York City, where he is a director of firm-wide BIM. After graduating from the New York Institute of Technology in 1995, he worked in residential and small commercial architecture firms performing services ranging from estimating to computer modeling to construction administration. In 1999, he landed at SOM and transformed his technology skills into a 10-year span as a digital design manager. In this capacity, he pioneered the implementation of BIM on such projects as One World Trade Center, a.k.a. Freedom Tower. James has been using Revit since version 3.1 and has lectured at many industry events. He is a cofounder and president of the NYC Revit Users Group (`http://nyc-rug.com`) and has been an adjunct lecturing professor at NYU.

Phil Read holds degrees in communications and architecture, as well as a master's degree in architecture. After working in both civil engineering and architecture, he downloaded Revit version 1.0 (at the suggestion of an ArchiCAD reseller) and was hooked. Less than a year later, he began working for Revit Technology and soon after as an Autodesk project implementation specialist, where he had the honor and pleasure of working with some of the most remarkable people and design firms around the world. He's a regular speaker, blogger, and tweeter and relishes the role of change agent as long as it makes sound business sense. Presently back in startup mode, Phil is one of the driving forces behind M-SIX and VEO—the world's first fully integrated, cloud-based platform for the visualization, construction, and operations of buildings.

Eddy Krygiel is a senior project architect, a LEED Accredited Professional, and an Autodesk Authorized Author at HNTB Architects headquartered in Kansas City, Missouri. He has been using Revit since version 5.1 to complete projects ranging from single-family residences and historic remodels to 1.12-million-square-foot office buildings. Eddy is responsible for implementing BIM at his firm and also consults for other architecture and contracting firms around the country looking to implement BIM. He has been teaching Revit to practicing architects and architectural students in the Kansas City area and has lectured around the nation on the use of BIM in the construction industry. He also lives in the first LEED house in KCMO, which he designed using Revit. Eddy coauthors the *Mastering Autodesk Revit Architecture* series with Phil Read and James Vandezande.

Contents at a Glance

Contents

Chapter 3 Walls and Curtain Walls 57

Chapter 4 Floors, Roofs, and Ceilings 91

Foreword

I'd like you to think about two significant numbers: 12 and 10. Revit Architecture will turn 12 years old in the coming year, possibly while you are reading this book. Our baby is almost a teenager. This year also marks the 10-year anniversary of Autodesk acquiring Revit Technology Corporation. Double-digits. These two events have had a significant impact on my professional life and thinking about the importance of these numbers put me in a contemplative mood. It seems appropriate to spend a bit of time reflecting on the origins of this tool and describe a small portion of the history of Revit from my personal perspective, as well as some of the factors that influenced where we are now.

Change was Coming

The basic tenants of Building Information Modeling (BIM) and parametric building modeling have been discussed for 30 years. So why did it take so long for the AEC industry to get there? I believe the high-tech software industry and AEC industry were uniquely aligned over the past 12 years and, in the context of larger macroeconomic conditions like economic booms and recessions, helped catalyze the changes we see today. Over that time period, conditions were right for the inception, formation, and strengthening of the ideas and technologies inside of Revit and for the development of the larger concept of BIM.

There were significant reasons why the AEC industry *should* have been primed for change 12 years ago in the late 1990's. The United States had come out of the recession from earlier in the decade. The construction industry was booming. There was a boom time surrounding high technology and the Internet. There had been dramatic increases in computational power and networking. Adoption of CAD was increasing dramatically in architectural firms. There were other solutions on the market that offered 3d modeling and building-specific modeling capabilities. The typical construction documentation process was tedious and error-prone. The typical design-bid-build construction process was inefficient and costly. Was that enough to cause the architectural design industry to change? Quite simply, no. The industry was simply not ready for dramatic process and technical change from a business, design process, or technology adoption standpoint. The AEC industry is not known for moving quickly….

The factors listed above did not change the AEC industry overnight, but they did start to sow the seeds. A contributing factor in the evolution towards what we now understand as BIM can be found in the early history of Revit. The early history tells a story of how small teams, a clear vision, a little bit of venture capital money, and a large amount of luck can contribute towards building an innovative software product.

There Are People Who Do

In 1999 I was happily working as a design architect who also happened to be interested in technology. Over time, I started reading *WIRED* and *Fast Company* more than *Architectural Record.* In Silicon Valley and the San Francisco Bay Area, venture capital money was flowing. A change was also happening on the east coast, friends of mine had started to take jobs at software startups. I noticed they seemed to spend a good deal of time playing foosball….

I joined a small startup software company called Charles River Software in October of 1999 and was one of the first architects hired to work on a new parametric building modeler, code named Perspective. At that point the software could do little more than draw walls and place windows. The roof tool was just a rough sketch on a whiteboard and the column tool had just come online. It crashed when you clicked the button. There were a lot of crashes in those days. We had no shipping product, no customers, and did not even have a name for the company or the product (the name Revit came later). My expectations of playing foosball in a fun startup environment had vanished. There was a lot of work to do.

In retrospect, the most important things we had were a product vision and a small group of people who knew how to get things done. The software development team was literally a group of physicists and rocket scientists. Impressive. They had experience building parametric modeling applications and maintaining a high level of bi-directional associativity (hard math and logic problems). The marketing team proved to be quite adept. The quality assurance, product design, and technical support teams were from the AEC industry. The management team believed in the power of small teams and in accountability. They also knew how to ruthlessly prioritize and force a level of critical thinking. The team learned how to get things done and deliver results, because they had to, our survival depended on it.

As an impressionable novice in the realm of software development I learned a great deal from the early Revit management team. Two books that informed their thinking were *Crossing the Chasm* by Geoffrey Moore and *Rules for Revolutionaries* by Guy Kawasaki. They were popular in the late 1990's and are still good entry points into the field today. I dug them out of my basement to help write this foreword.

"Great teams are usually small – under fifty in total head count…"

Guy Kawasaki, Rules for Revolutionaries

In April of 2000, I helped ship a crappy product (to paraphrase Guy Kawasaki). Revit 1.0 was launched at the AIA Convention in Philadelphia. It could only draw walls, roofs, floors, and ceilings. There were only 14 creation commands and they all fit on the screen at one time. It was insanely hard to build your own windows and doors. Performance was horrible. Our baby was not perfect, far from it, but the fundamental concepts of the parametric building model were all there. The hardest part was convincing ourselves we were ready to ship. We had to learn it was ok to not be perfect.

> *"Revolutionary products don't fail because they are shipped too early; they fail because they are not revised fast enough."*
>
> Guy Kawasaki, Rules for Revolutionaries

Iterating and Innovating in a Recession

> *"It turns out our attitude toward technology adoption becomes significant any time we are introducing products that require us to change our current mode of behavior or to modify other products and services we rely on. In academic terms, such products are called* discontinuous innovations. *The contrasting term,* continuous innovations, *refers to the normal upgrading of products that does not require us to change behavior."*
>
> Geoffrey Moore, Crossing the Chasm

Geoffrey A. Moore's book *Crossing the Chasm* is one of the must-reads when attempting to deliver innovative products and services to a market. He introduces the "Technology Adoption Life Cycle" which divides up customers into segments like Innovators, Early Adopters, Early Majority, and Late Majority, following a traditional bell-curve. The first thing any new product needs to do is identify and work with the Innovators and Early Adopters in the industry.

The next 2 years from 2000 to 2002 were spent iterating and revising, designing and developing the first few versions of Revit. The things we had during that time were a vision, and, most importantly, a small set of customers that definitely fit the mold of Innovators and Early Adopters. These customers believed in the vision and were not afraid to stick their necks out and try our software, and they were vocal in telling us what did and did not work. Ideas were tried and rapidly improved or discarded.

"Listen to what your early adopters say about your product and improve it accordingly because while better is the enemy of good enough, better... better be coming."

GUY KAWASAKI, RULES FOR REVOLUTIONARIES

By the fall of 2001, we still did not have very many customers and the economy at that time was not doing well. The Internet boom was over and the United States was in another recession. Companies that sold pet food online had started to fail. Quite frankly, times were tough. Money was tight and it was not clear what the future would bring. We dug in, continued to listen and work with our customers and produce more versions. There was a remarkable sense of creativity and camaraderie in our second-rate office building in Boston as we designed, built, tested, and supported a young product. The simplistic way this is portrayed below does have a kernel of truth:

"A lousy building and lousy furniture are necessary because suffering is good for revolutionaries. It builds cohesiveness; it creates a sense of urgency; and it focuses the team on what's important: shipping! If you are ever recruited by a team that claims to be revolutionary and see beautiful, matched Herman Miller furniture, run do not walk, from the interview. On the other hand, if you see a lousy building, lousy furniture, but fantastically creative workspaces, then sign up immediately."

GUY KAWASAKI, RULES FOR REVOLUTIONARIES

During this timeframe from 2000-2002, the team built the main features of Revit as a parametric building modeler and created the seeds of a discontinuous innovation and a disruptive technology, as defined by Clay Christensen below:

*"**Disruptive technologies** bring to a market a very different value proposition than had been available previously. Generally, disruptive technologies underperform established products in mainstream markets. But they have other features that a few fringe (and generally new) customers value. Products based on disruptive technologies are typically cheaper, simpler, smaller, and, frequently more convenient to use."*

CLAY CHRISTENSEN, THE INNOVATOR'S DILEMMA

It was not apparent to us at that time, but the core features of Revit that are the most disruptive and technologically innovative were developed during this timeframe. Perhaps there is some correlation between the squeeze of the tech bust in the early 2000's and the effect it might have had on a small team of software engineers and architects hunkered down in an ugly office building outside of Boston. Interestingly, there are now publications that discuss how major innovations are more likely to happen in recessions. Probably a good thing we did not spend those years playing foosball.

"Consider the year 2001, by all accounts a rough year. It was clear that the Internet bubble had burst. The Nasdaq index was down close to 30% — and that was before the Sept. 11 terrorist attacks. But was it a bad year for disruption? Quite the contrary. In 2001, [there were] at least a dozen specific disruptive developments in the U.S. alone."

SCOTT D. ANTHONY AND LESLIE FEINZAIG, INNOVATING DURING A RECESSION

Nurturing a Young Technology

The business environment continued to prove challenging in the early 2000's. Revit needed a sales channel and customers. The saving grace came on April 1, 2002, when Revit Technology Corporation was acquired by Autodesk, Inc. There were now opportunities to continue nurturing a young technology and start utilizing the global reach of the Autodesk organization.

The 7 years since the acquisition were spent nurturing and developing the product and the underlying platform. An investment was made by forward-looking industry executives inside Autodesk, not just in the acquisition of a small startup, but in the development of a new platform for the AEC industry. During that time, the expanded Revit product development team, also known as the "The Factory" continued to develop software. Customers were listened to; features were added and refined; support, sales and marketing organizations were exposed to the newly acquired product.

It is difficult to prove exactly when, but at some point along the way Revit Architecture "crossed the chasm" and started to be deployed in the larger market of Early Majority customers. Many products and services fail to make the treacherous crossing.

There were still large challenges to overcome. The product needed to be turned into a platform. Teams started to work on what are now Revit Structure and Revit MEP. Large customers needed to be supported. A large number of creative and passionate people started working on Revit. Forward-looking executives started to articulate the ideas we now know as Building Information Modeling.

I feel and extremely fortunate and honored to work with many creative, passionate people in the Autodesk organization, as well as many leading architectural and engineering firms. One of the project teams I am still grateful to have worked with was the original World Trade Center Tower 1 team at Skidmore Owings & Merrill. James, Phil, and I spent many a long evening working with a talented large team on this effort.

So, where are we now?

We are now living in a BIM-enabled world where technologies like Revit are have helped enable larger process and business related changes. The small experimental software project from 12 years ago has been nurtured and supported. It has matured over time into the current Revit Architecture 2013. The number of new firms and individuals starting to use Revit is still increasing rapidly.

Concepts like BIM are larger than any technology and, when combined with other trends like Integrated Project Delivery (IPD), are helping the AEC industry to change very quickly, more quickly than any time in the last 10-15 years. It is important to understand BIM as a larger construct than just Revit.

So how can we help more professionals in the industry understand the implications, complications and context of their design decisions as early as possible? My colleagues in The Factory are also helping by continuing to deliver new versions of Revit. The process used to design, develop and test each release is thoughtful and rigorous. The teams working on these problems are professional and work closely with users. If you are interested in learning more about this process I recommend you visit the "Inside the Factory" blog (`http://insidethefactory.typepad.com`). I am confident that our talented team of software designers and developers will continue to work with users in the field and, collectively, we can create better tools for the industry.

Revit is being implemented in mainstream architecture and engineering firms worldwide, and books like this one are instrumental in helping people make the transition from CAD to BIM. I applaud James, Phil and Eddy for the dedication, time and effort they have contributed to the multiple versions of this book.

I've been fortunate enough to work with each of the esteemed authors of this book during my professional career. Phil Read and I are long-time friends, colleagues and collaborators. We both share a deep love of design and geometry and in fact we used to challenge each other with "geometry smackdowns" to solve a hard modeling problems. Phil has this great ability to solve problems at an intuitive, almost subconscious level. He calls these "two beers and a cheeseburger" moments. James Vandezande and I have worked together for almost as long. We had the honor of working together on a very unique project in New York City. I've always admired James' uncanny ability to remain simply unflappable in high-stress situations. This is the guy you want next to you when things go south. Eddy and I worked together when his firm was working on another hard geometry problem with a local Boston firm. He also was a great source of knowledge as we started to move into the area of sustainable design. They are experts not just in the software, but more importantly in the process shift that is BIM.

So, what is next?

Ten years ago, the environment was right for a few software visionaries to see the market opportunity in the AEC industry. Eight years ago, the challenging times of the last recession influenced the critical formation of a new technology. Five years ago, the environment was right for a strengthened technology to be piloted by more firms and used on significant projects like Skidmore Owens and Merrill's World Trade Center Tower 1, (aka the Freedom Tower). During that same time period the larger concept of BIM was formed and is now a generally recognized as where the industry is headed.

So what is next? What pressures, market conditions and opportunities do we see in the current day? Here are two pressures affecting both the AEC and high-tech industry:

Economic Pressures

We are in the midst of a massive global economic downturn, some say the worst recession we have seen in a lifetime. What does this mean for the AEC industry and for how we think about technology? How can the design teams work more effectively together and provide more value to their clients and owners? How can design teams produce a better built environment in these times? How can they use the tools we have more effectively, foster deeper insight into our designs and ultimately make better design decisions?

Revit was conceived of as a platform for managing change and coordinating documents but as people get past the building modeling part of BIM, they realize the middle letter of BIM stands for 'Information'. The data in the Revit model can help design teams make better decisions earlier in the process. We see firms using the building information model not just for coordinated documentation, but to perform efficiency calculations and "what-if" scenarios for their clients. As design teams become more conversant in the tools and more design data is added to the model, the relative value of the model increases. This can help not only the core design team, but also the larger team including the owner and contractor, especially when used in conjunction with Integrated Project Delivery (IPD). Between the basics of coordinated documentation, improved building insight, and sharing of valuable information with the extended design team, investing in BIM seems to make sense, even in the current downturn.

Environmental Pressures

We are also in the midst of severe environmental changes and have come to a collective realization that the way we use energy and our natural resources is not sustainable. We know our buildings have an enormous impact in terms of energy usage during construction and operation of a given building. Can we better understand how our current building stock is performing and where energy is being used today? Can we propose thoughtful and strategic modifications to existing buildings? Can we work to make our new designs more sustainable and energy-conscious?

Once again, the middle letter of BIM stands for 'Information'. As government officials and the general population become more aware of the impact buildings have on the environment, one might expect a renewed interest in energy-efficient design. The same information latent in the building model can be used to better understand and predict how a building will perform, through both whole building energy analysis and more detailed, specific analysis. This is where I've been spending a great deal of time over the last few years. My teams have implemented new building-performance features in Revit and have also created separate new programs like the Project Vasari Technology Preview to test out new ideas and connect more closely to computing resources available via cloud computing. If you are interested in finding out more, please visit `http://www.autodesk.com/green` or `http://labs.autodesk.com/utilities/vasari`.

So, what does the future look like? From a technology and software design standpoint, I can't help but wonder what the world will look like in another 5-10 years. Given the current economic and political climate, perhaps there is another round of increased innovation on the horizon? Only time will tell. Revit has certainly been a core part of advances in the industry over the past 12 years and we look forward to working with you and other architects and engineers to design better tools for the AEC industry in the future.

All the best,
Matt Jezyk
Senior Manager
AEC Conceptual Design Products
Autodesk, Inc.
March 2012

Matt Jezyk is Senior Product Manager, AEC Conceptual Design Products. Matt has been in the Architecture and Engineering industry for 16 years and has spent the past 12 years developing Autodesk Revit. He was one of the original architects hired by Revit Technology Corporation and helped build what is now Revit Architecture and Revit Structure. He is experienced in building parametric and geometric modeling tools on the Revit platform.

Recently, Matt has focused on emerging markets and technology. His groups have designed and developed new parametric modeling and integrated energy analysis features. Most recently, he has lead the team working Project Vasari, a new technology preview available on Autodesk Labs.

Introduction

Welcome to **Autodesk Revit** Architecture 2013 **Essentials**, based on the Revit Architecture 2013 release.

When we authors first sat down to learn Revit Architecture (eons ago), each of us was put into a room with a trainer (for James and Eddy, that was Phil), and over the course of four days, we clicked through all the buttons and functionality to learn the software. Once initiated, we walked away with some answers, some questions, and a general understanding of what Revit Architecture does and how we could use it to leverage building design, documentation, and construction.

Our aim with this book is to replicate that training experience. The book is divided into training "days" with the idea that each chapter should take you a couple of hours to complete and four chapters equal a full day of training. Once you've made it through the book, in the final two chapters we offer a half day's worth of tips and tricks to help you leverage those skills on real projects.

When we sat down to plan this book, we looked to serve the needs of individuals who were fresh to Revit Architecture as well as those who had taken training so long ago they needed a solid refresher. We hope you will find that our efforts to meet that need were successful. We designed the book in a nonlinear fashion with the intention that the chapters would be freestanding, so the reader could take almost any chapter and learn its topics rather than having to work through the book from beginning to end.

We wanted to write a book that is as much about architectural design and practice as it is about software. Architecture is a way of looking at the world and the methods that inspire creatively solving the problems of the built world. The book follows real-life workflows and scenarios and is full of practical examples that explain how to leverage the tools within Revit Architecture. We hope you'll agree that we've succeeded.

Who Should Read This Book

This book is written for architects, designers, students, and anyone else who needs their first exposure to Revit Architecture or has had an initial introduction and wants a refresher on the program's core features and functionality. It's for architects (and those who'd like to be) of any generation—you don't need to be a computer wizard to understand or appreciate the content. We've designed the book to follow real project workflows and processes to help make the tools easy to follow, and the chapters are full of handy tips to make Revit Architecture easy to leverage. This book can also be used to help prepare for Autodesk's Certified Associate and Certified Professional exams. For more information on certification, please visit `www.autodesk.com/certification`.

What You Will Learn

This book is designed to help you grasp the basics of Revit Architecture using real-world examples and techniques you'll use in everyday design and documentation. We'll explain the Revit Architecture interface and help you find the tools you need as well as help you understand how the application is structured. From there we'll show you how to create and modify the primary components in a building design. We'll show you how to take a preliminary model and add layers of intelligence to help analyze and augment your designs. We'll demonstrate how to create robust and accurate documentation and then guide you through the construction process.

As you are already aware, BIM is more than just a change in software; it's a change in architectural workflow and culture. To take full advantage of both BIM and Revit Architecture in your office structure, you'll have to make some changes to your practice. We've designed the book around an ideal, integrated workflow to aid in this transition.

Once you've mastered the content in each chapter, we include a section called "The Essentials and Beyond" where you can continue to hone your skills by taking on more challenging exercises.

What You Will See

In Revit 2013, Autodesk has taken a slight divergence in the user interface. There are now two flavors of Revit: A "one-box" solution that has Revit Architecture, Structure, and MEP inside the same application and the Revit Architecture you're used to. There are some small differences between the applications; Revit Architecture has a Home tab as the first tab. In Revit, it's called the Home tab. In Revit, the Mass & Site tab is not visible by default while it is in Revit Architecture.

We want the reader to be aware that we have based the book and the screen captures on Revit—the combined version. If you notice those small differences, we apologize as it would be very confusing to base the book on both applications noting all the small differences along the way. However, whichever version you have, we feel you'll still be able to follow the lessons with the chapters of this book with ease.

What You Need

To leverage the full capacity of this book, we highly recommend that you have a copy of Revit Architecture installed on a computer strong enough to handle it. To download the trial version of Revit Architecture, go to `www.autodesk.com/revitarchitecture`, where you'll also find complete system requirements for running Revit Architecture.

From a software standpoint, the exercises in this book are designed to be lightweight and not computationally intensive. This way, you avoid long wait times to open and save files and perform certain tasks. That said, keep in mind that the Autodesk-recommended computer specs for Revit Architecture are far more than what you need to do the exercises in this book but are *exactly* what you need to work on a project using Revit Architecture.

If you're working from a 32-bit OS, you'll need the following:

- Microsoft Windows 7 32-bit Enterprise, Ultimate, Professional, or Home Premium edition, Microsoft Windows Vista 32-bit (SP2 or later) Enterprise, Ultimate, Business, or Home Premium edition, or Microsoft Windows XP (SP2 or later) Professional or Home edition
- For Microsoft Windows 7 32-bit or Microsoft Windows Vista 32-bit: Intel Pentium 4 or AMD Athlon dual core processor, 3.0 GHz (or higher) with SSE2 technology
- For Microsoft Windows XP: Intel Pentium 4 or AMD Athlon dual core, 1.6 GHz (or higher) with SSE2 technology
- 4 GB RAM
- 5 GB free disk space
- 1,280 × 1,024 monitor with true color
- Display adapter capable of 24-bit color for basic graphics, 256 MB DirectX 10-capable graphics card with Shader Model 3 for advanced graphics
- Microsoft Internet Explorer 7.0 (or later)
- Microsoft Mouse-compliant pointing device
- Download or installation from DVD9
- Internet connectivity for license registration

If you're working from a 64-bit version (which is preferred for project work because of how much RAM you can leverage), you'll need the following:

- Microsoft Windows 7 64-bit Enterprise, Ultimate, Professional, or Home Premium edition, Microsoft Windows Vista 64-bit (SP2 or later) Enterprise, Ultimate, Business, or Home Premium edition, or Microsoft Windows XP Professional x64 edition (SP2 or later)
- For Windows 7 64-bit or Windows Vista 64-bit: Intel Core i5-2300 quad-core processor (2.8 GHz, 6 MB cache) or equivalent AMD processor.
- For Windows XP Professional x64: Intel Pentium 4 or AMD Athlon dual core, 1.6 GHz (or higher) with SSE2 technology
- 8 GB RAM
- 5 GB free disk space
- 1,680 x 1,050 monitor with true color
- Display adapter capable of 24-bit color for basic graphics; 256 MB DirectX 10-capable graphics card with Shader Model 3 for advanced graphics
- Microsoft Internet Explorer 7.0 (or later)
- Microsoft Mouse-compliant pointing device
- Download or installation from DVD9
- Internet connectivity for license registration

What Is Covered in This Book

Revit Architecture is a building information modeling (BIM) application that has quickly emerged as the forerunner in the design industry. Revit Architecture is as much a change in workflow (if you come from a 2D or CAD environment) as it is a change in software. In this book, we'll focus on using real-world workflows and examples to guide you through learning the basics of Revit Architecture 2013—the *Essentials*.

Autodesk Revit Architecture 2013 Essentials is organized to provide you with the knowledge needed to gain experience in many different facets of the software. The book is broken down into 14 chapters, which represent the content you would cover if you were to attend a three- or four-day training class.

Day 1

This section is designed to be an introduction to the software, the user interface, and the basic components that you will use every day.

Chapter 1, "Introducing the Autodesk Revit Architecture Interface," introduces to you the user interface and gets you acquainted with the tools and technology—the workflow—behind the software.

Chapter 2, "Schematic Design," introduces you to situations that would happen on a real project; say, a designer has given you a sketch and now you need to take this basic building design and model it.

Chapter 3, "Walls and Curtain Walls," helps you build on that initial learning by establishing some of the basic building blocks in architecture: walls.

Chapter 4, "Floors, Roofs, and Ceilings," rounds out the first day of training by introducing you to the other basic building blocks: floors, roofs, and ceilings. By the end of the first four chapters, you will know how easy it is to create a building form; apply walls, floors, roofs, and ceilings to that form; and easily quantify how much space and area are in your designs.

Day 2

With the basic building forms established, you spend day 2 of training augmenting that form with components that help building form interact with reality. These components are what we interact with every day—things like stairs, windows, doors—and help establish the design.

Chapter 5, "Stairs, Ramps, and Railings," begins by explaining the basics of stairs, ramps, and railings. These core components are versatile and using them can be a bit tricky, so we'll guide you through the process of creating several types of stairs and railings.

Chapter 6, "Adding Families," shows you how to add a core element to your project: families. You use families to create most of your content, and Revit Architecture by default comes with a robust supply.

Chapter 7, "Modifying Families," shows you how to take these families, modify them, or create your own, making the library of your content limitless.

Finally, in Chapter 8, "Groups and Phasing," you'll learn techniques for taking families and repeating them in the model in ways you can use to augment your design.

Day 3

With two days of training under your belt, you'll have most of the tools you need to create building designs in Revit Architecture. What we will focus on for the next four chapters is taking that design and documenting it so you can share the building design with owners, contractors, or anyone on your project team.

Chapter 9, "Rooms and Color Fill Plans," shows you how to add room elements to your spaces, assign information to them, and create colorful diagrams based on space, department, or any other variable you need.

Chapter 10, "Worksharing," discusses how to take your Revit Architecture file into a multiperson working environment. Worksharing allows several people within your office or project team to work on the same Revit Architecture file simultaneously.

In Chapter 11, "Details and Annotations," we focus on adding annotation to explain your designs. You'll learn how to add detail to your model in the form of dimensions, text, keynotes, and tags, and how to embellish your 3D model with additional detailing.

Chapter 12, "Creating Drawing Sets," shows you how to take all this information and place those drawings and views onto sheets so they can be printed and distributed to your project stakeholders.

Day 4

The final two chapters in this book are designed to build on the skills you have just learned and give you some additional resources to leverage your new talent.

Chapter 13, "Workflow and Site Modeling," provides the basics on how to take your office from a CAD environment to one that works with BIM. This chapter explores tools for every level of the project team—from the new staff to project managers. Understanding the process and workflow will be key to the success of your first Revit Architecture project.

The final chapter, Chapter 14, "Tips, Tricks, and Troubleshooting," is chock-full of useful tips and tricks, and you'll learn how to troubleshoot your Revit Architecture project.

The *Essentials* Series

The *Essentials* series from Sybex provides outstanding instruction for readers who are just beginning to develop their professional skills. Every *Essentials* book includes these features:

- Skill-based instruction with chapters organized around projects rather than abstract concepts or subjects
- Suggestions for additional exercises at the end of each chapter, where you can practice and extend your skills
- Digital files (via download) so you can work through the project tutorials yourself. Please check the book's web page at `www.sybex.com/go/revit2013essentials` for the companion downloads.

Note: Should you choose to browse the book's companion web page, it will look like a site to purchase the book—which it is. But if you pan down just a bit, you'll see three gray tabs. The third one is the book's companion downloads.

Contacting the Authors

We welcome your feedback and comments. You can find the three of us on our blog, `www.architecture-tech.com`; on Facebook at Mastering Revit, or via email at `MasteringRevit@architecture-tech.com`. We hope you enjoy the book.

CHAPTER 1

Introducing the Autodesk Revit Architecture Interface

After one decade in the architecture, engineering, and construction (AEC) space, the Autodesk® Revit® Architecture software continues to be unique in its holistic building information modeling (BIM) approach to design integration. Sure, there are other BIM-ish tools that allow you to design in 3D. And 10 years ago, 3D might have been a differentiator, but today 3D is a commodity!

Revit Architecture provides the unique ability to design, manage, and document your project information from within a single file—something no other BIM tool allows you to do. Because all your data resides in a single project file, you can work in virtually any view to edit your model—plan, section, elevation, 3D, sheets, details, and even a schedule. To begin the journey in learning Revit Architecture, we'll help you become comfortable with the user interface and the basic principles of a Revit Architecture project.

In this chapter, you learn the following skills:

- **Understanding the interface**
- **Understanding the interface workflow**
- **Using common modifying tools**

Understanding the Interface

The user interface (UI) of Revit Architecture is similar to other Autodesk products such as the Autodesk® AutoCAD®, Autodesk® Inventor, and Autodesk® 3ds Max® products. You might also notice that it's similar to Windows-based applications such as Microsoft Word and Mindjet's MindManager. All of these applications are based on the "ribbon" concept: toolbars are placed on tabs in a tab bar, or *ribbon*, and are contextually updated based on the content on which you're working. We'll cover the most critical aspects of the UI in this section, but we won't provide an exhaustive review of all toolbars and commands. You'll gain experience with the common tools as you read the chapters and exercises in this book.

Figure 1.1 shows the Revit Architecture UI. To illustrate some different project views, we've tiled four different view windows: Plan, Elevation, 3D, and Camera.

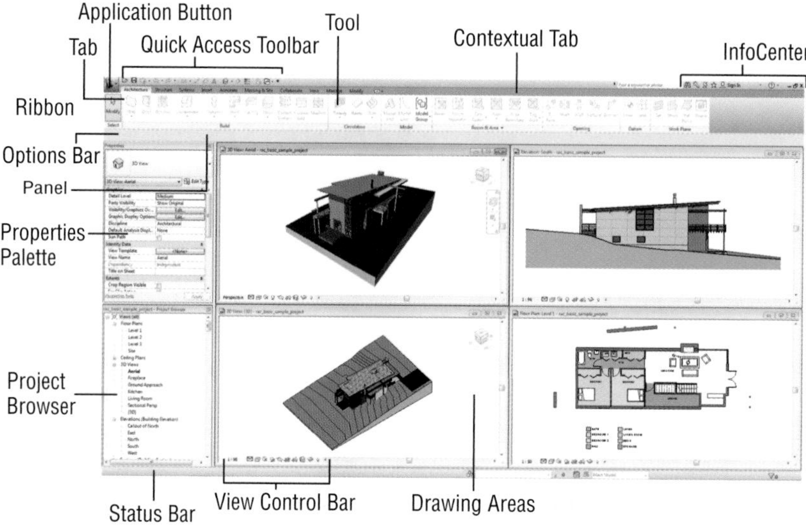

FIGURE 1.1: Revit Architecture user interface

Let's begin by examining a few important parts of the UI. As you progress through this book, you'll gradually become more familiar with the other basic parts of the UI.

Properties Palette

The Properties palette is a floating palette that can remain open while you work in the model. The palette can be docked on either side of your screen, or it can be moved to a second monitor. You can open the Properties palette in one of three ways:

- Click the Properties icon in the Properties panel of the Modify tab in the ribbon.
- Select Properties from the right-click context menu.
- Press Ctrl+1 on your keyboard, as you would in AutoCAD.

As shown in Figure 1.2, the Properties palette contains the Type Selector at the top of the palette. When you're placing elements or swapping types of elements you've already placed in the model, the palette must be open to access the Type Selector.

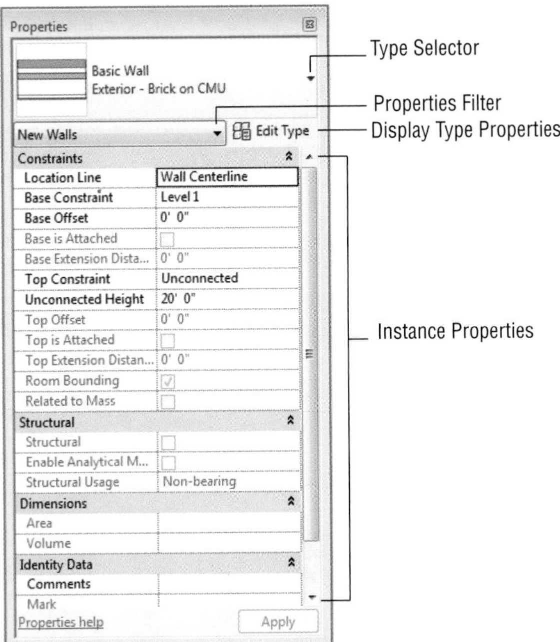

FIGURE 1.2: The Properties palette allows you to set instance parameters for building elements and views.

When no elements are selected, the Properties palette displays the properties of the active view. If you need to change settings for the current view, simply make the changes in the Properties palette, and the view will be updated. For views, you may not even need to use the Apply button to submit the changes.

Finally, you can also use the Properties palette as a filtering method for selected elements. When you select a large number of disparate objects, the drop-down list below the Type Selector displays the total number of selected elements. Open the list, and you'll see the elements listed per category, as shown in Figure 1.3. Select one of the categories to modify the parameters for the respective elements. This is different from the Filter tool in that the entire selection set is maintained, allowing you to perform multiple modifying actions without reselecting elements.

Project Browser

The Project Browser (Figure 1.4) is a virtual folder tree of all the views, legends, schedules, sheets, families, groups, and links in your Revit Architecture project. You can collapse and expand the tree by selecting the + or – icon. Open any view listed in the Project Browser simply by double-clicking it.

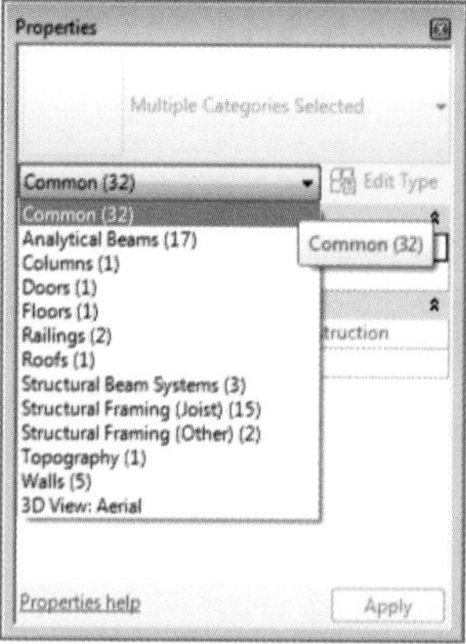

FIGURE 1.3: Use the Properties palette to filter selection sets.

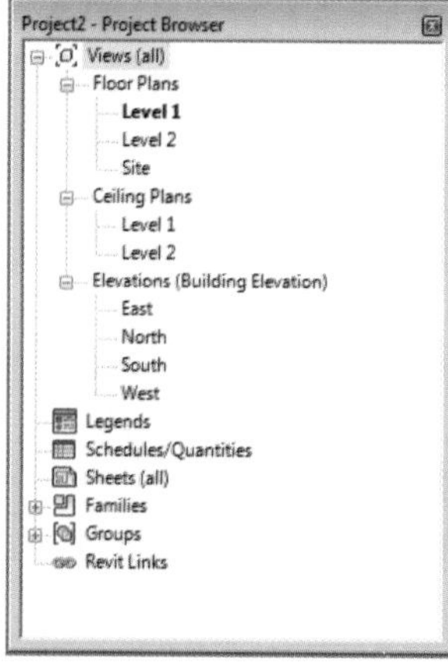

FIGURE 1.4: Project Browser

The Project Browser can also be filtered and grouped into folders based on any combination of user-defined parameters. To access the type properties of the Project Browser, right-click Views at the top of the tree, and select Type Properties. Select any of the items in the Type drop-down list or duplicate one to create your own.

Status Bar

The status bar provides useful information about commands and selected elements (Figure 1.5). In addition to the worksets and design options toolbars, the status bar displays information about keyboard shortcut commands and lists what object you've selected. It's also particularly useful for identifying when you're about to select a chain of elements.

FIGURE 1.5: The status bar is located at the bottom of the Revit Architecture application window.

View Control Bar

The View Control Bar is at the bottom of every view. It displays different icons depending on the type of view in which you're working (Figure 1.6).

FIGURE 1.6: The View Control Bar gives you quick access to commonly used view properties.

From left to right, you have Scale, Detail Level, Visual Style, Sun Path (On/Off), Shadows (On/Off), Rendering Show/Hide (only in 3D views), Crop On/Off, Show/Hide Crop, Lock 3D View (only in 3D views), Temporary Hide/Isolate, and Reveal Hidden Elements. Note that some of these buttons access view properties that you can also set in the Properties palette.

ViewCube

As one of several navigation aids in Revit Architecture, you'll find the ViewCube in 3D views. You can orbit your model by clicking and dragging anywhere on the ViewCube. You can also click any face, corner, or edge of the ViewCube to orient your view.

Hovering over the ViewCube reveals the Home option (the little house above the ViewCube), which brings you back to your home view. Right-clicking the ViewCube opens a menu that allows you to set, recall, and orient your view, as shown in Figure 1.7.

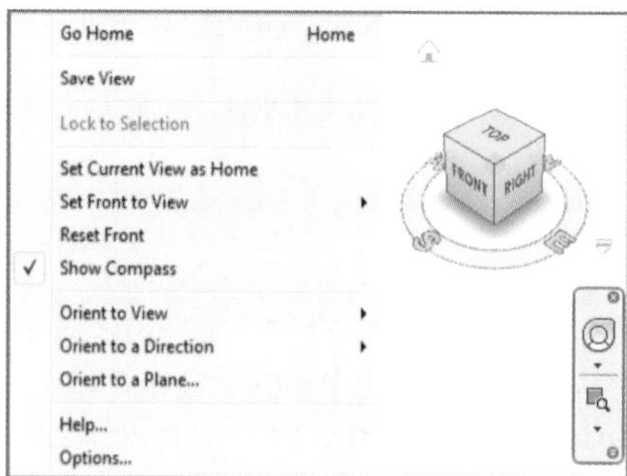

FIGURE 1.7: Right-click the ViewCube to access more view-orientation options.

Options Bar

The Options Bar is a context-sensitive area that gives you feedback as you create and modify content. This is an important UI feature when you're creating model content. For example, when you use the Wall command, the Options Bar displays settings for the height, location line, offset, and chain-modeling options, as shown in Figure 1.8. Even when you place annotations, the Options Bar provides you with choices for leaders and other additional context.

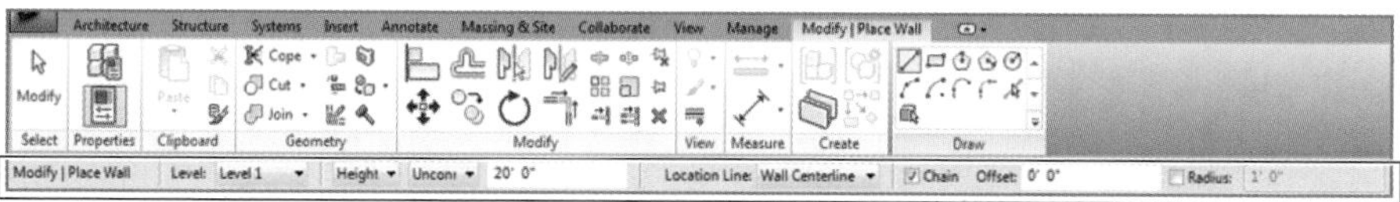

FIGURE 1.8: The Options Bar provides immediate input of options related to a selected object or command.

Understanding the Interface Workflow

In this section, we'll dive into the workflow of the Revit Architecture interface with some basic modeling exercises. These lessons can be applied to just about every tool and function throughout the program.

Activating a command in Revit Architecture is a simple and repeatable process that takes you from a tool in the ribbon to options and properties and into the drawing window to begin placing an element. In the following exercise, you'll create a simple layout of walls using some critical components of the UI as well as a few common modifying tools.

Creating a Simple Layout

Begin by downloading the file `c01-Interface-start.rvt` from this book's companion web page: `www.sybex.com/go/revit2013essentials`. You can open a Revit Architecture project file by dragging it directly into the application or by using the Open command from the Application menu. You can even double-click a Revit Architecture file, but be aware that if you have more than one version of Revit Architecture installed on your computer, the file will open in the last version of Revit Architecture you used.

Once the project file is open, notice in the Project Browser that the active view is {3D}. This is the default 3D view, which you can always access by clicking the icon in the Quick Access toolbar (QAT; it looks like a little house). Note that the view name of the active view is always shown as bold in the Project Browser.

Let's begin by placing some walls on some predetermined points in a plan view:

1. In the Project Browser, locate the Floor Plans category, expand it, and double-click Level 1. This opens the Level 1 floor plan view.
2. From the ribbon, select the Architecture tab, and click the Wall tool.
3. In the Options Bar located just below the ribbon, change Height to Level 2 and set Location Line to Finish Face: Exterior. Also make sure the Chain option is checked.
4. At the top of the Properties palette, you see the Type Selector. Click it to change the wall type to Basic Wall: Exterior - Brick on Mtl. Stud. Also find the parameter named Top Offset and change the value to 3′-0″ (1000 mm).

   Before you begin modeling, notice the Draw panel in the ribbon (Figure 1.9). You can choose from a variety of geometry options as you create 3D and 2D elements in the drawing area.

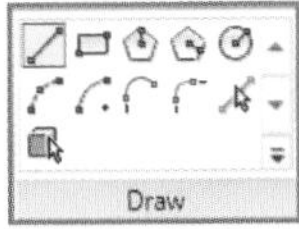

FIGURE 1.9: **Select geometry options from the Draw panel in the ribbon.**

5. You're now ready to begin modeling wall segments. In the drawing area, click through each of the layout markers from 1 through 6. Note how you can use automatic snapping to accurately locate the start and end of each segment. At point 3, place your mouse pointer near the middle of the circle to use the center snap point.

6. After you click the last wall segment at point 6, press the Esc key once to stop adding new walls. Notice that the Wall command is still active and you can continue adding new walls if you choose. You can even change the wall type, options, and properties before continuing.

7. Press the Esc key again to return to the Modify state. You can also click the Modify button at the left end of the ribbon.

Your layout of walls should look like Figure 1.10.

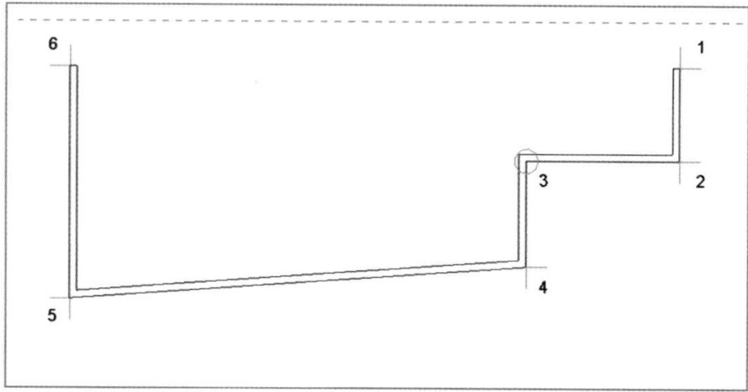

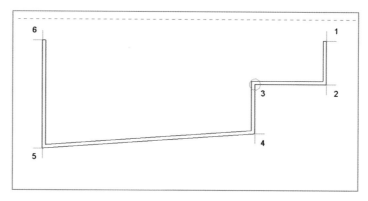

FIGURE 1.10: Your first layout of walls in a plan view

Using Filter, Mirror, and Trim/Extend

As you continue the exercise, you'll use a few common modifying tools to further develop the layout of walls. You'll also learn how to select and filter elements in the model. Let's begin by mirroring part of the layout and connecting the corners with the Trim tool:

1. Using the mouse pointer, click and drag a window from the lower left to the upper right to select only the wall segments running east-west, as shown in Figure 1.11.

2. You'll probably have more than just walls when you use this method of selection. To reduce the selection to only walls, click the Filter button in the ribbon, and clear all the check boxes except Walls, as shown in Figure 1.12.

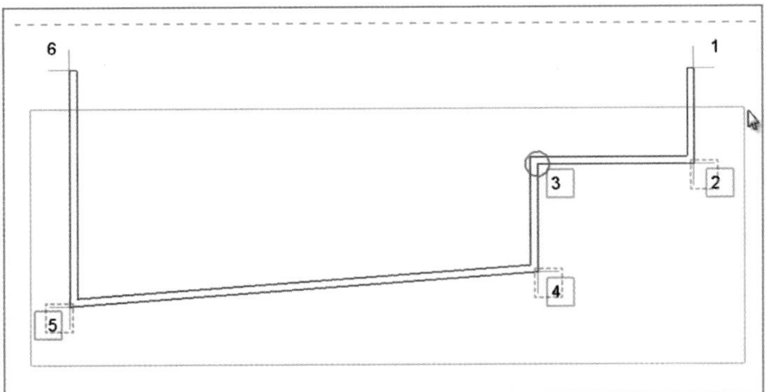

FIGURE 1.11: Drag the cursor from left to right to select some of the walls.

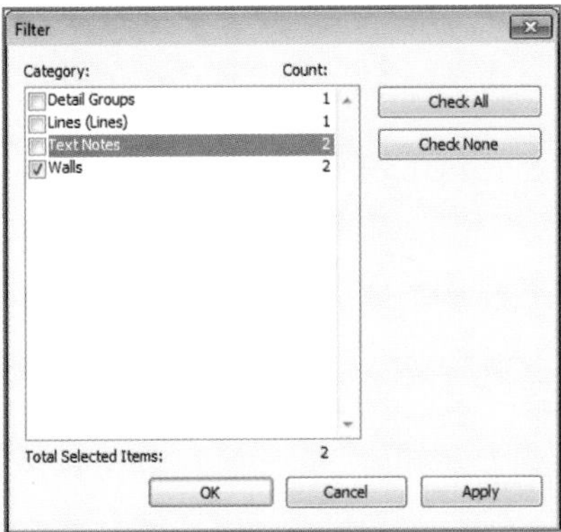

FIGURE 1.12: Filter your selection to include only walls.

3. From the Modify tab in the ribbon, click the Mirror – Pick Axis tool, and then click the dashed line representing the reference plane in the plan view. Mirrored copies of the selected walls appear opposite the reference plane, as shown in Figure 1.13.

4. Again from the Modify tab in the ribbon, click the Trim/Extend To Corner tool. In the plan view, pick each of the north-south walls and then the respective wall that was mirrored in the previous step. The resulting closed perimeter wall should look like the image in Figure 1.14.

5. Save your project file before continuing to the next exercise.

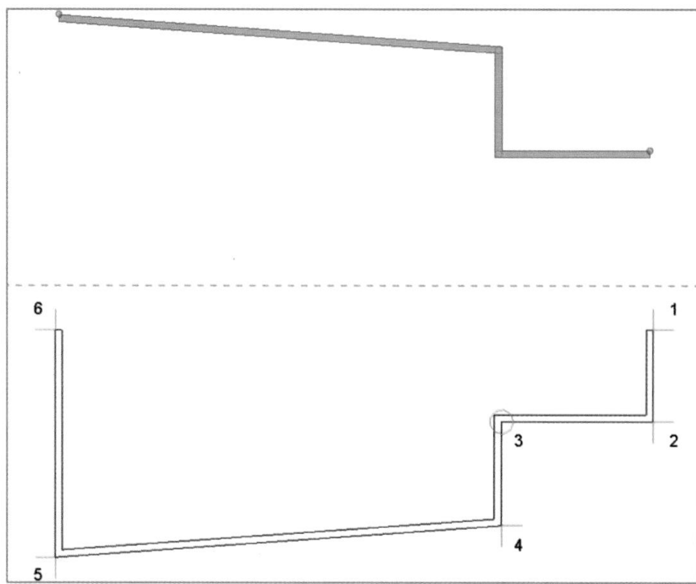

FIGURE 1.13: Mirrored copies of the selected walls

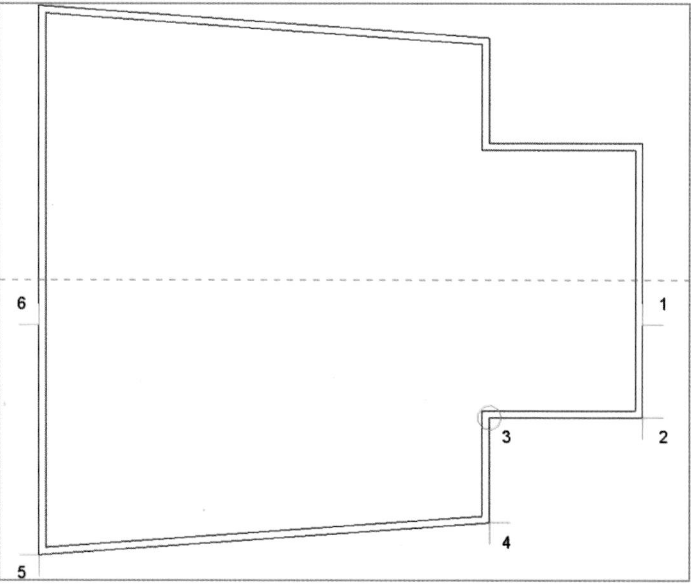

FIGURE 1.14: Use the Trim/Extend To Corner tool to complete the perimeter walls.

Adjusting Datums

In Revit Architecture, project datums consist of reference planes, grids, and levels. These elements are usually only visible in a 2D view, but they establish control of all model elements in your file. In the next exercise, you'll examine how levels affect the modeled elements and how you can adjust their graphic representation in a 2D view:

Building Elevation (shown in parentheses) is a type of elevation view. You can create more view types for elevations, sections, details, and other views as necessary.

1. In the Project Browser, locate the Elevations (Building Elevation) category, and double-click the South view. You may need to click the + symbol to expand the tree.
2. Zoom in to the right side of the view, and you see the graphic representation of the levels that are defined in this project (Level 1 and Level 2). Select the level line, and notice that both the name of the level and the elevation turn blue. This indicates that they can be directly edited.
3. Click the elevation value for Level 2, and change it from 10´-0˝ (3000 mm) to 15´-0˝ (4500 mm). Notice how the walls you created in the first exercise maintain their relationship with Level 2 because you specified that datum in the Options Bar before placing the walls.

   Let's suppose you want to modify the design and add a third level along with a roof. You need to add two more levels and adjust the heights of the exterior walls. We'll show you two different methods for creating new levels.

You might also notice that the top offset is maintained relative to the changes of the level. This value can be found in the Properties palette.

4. Go to the Architecture tab in the ribbon, and find the Datum panel. Click the Level command, and make sure the Make Plan View check box is selected in the Options Bar. Click in the elevation view exactly 10´-0˝ (3000 mm) above the left end of Level 2, using the temporary dimension as a guide. Notice the end of the new level snaps into alignment with the end of the existing level. Click the end of the level above the right end of Level 2 to complete the command.

   If you need to adjust the elevation or the name of the level you just created, select the level, click the elevation value, change it to 25´-0˝ (7500 mm), and make sure the name is Level 3. Next you'll create another level by copying an existing one.

Remember that you can zoom and pan with the mouse while other commands are active. You might need to do this to complete the Level command.

5. Select Level 3 in the elevation view, and click the Copy tool on the Modify tab in the ribbon. Click anywhere in the elevation to specify a start point for the Copy command, and place the mouse pointer in

the upward (90$) direction. Type **12´-0˝** (**3600 mm**), and then press Enter to complete the command. Note that you can also press and hold the Shift key to force Copy or Move commands to operate in 90-degree increments.

> **You can also start the Copy tool first, pick the level, and then press Enter to complete the selection process and start the command.**

6. Select the newest level, and change the name to **Roof**. Also make sure the elevation value is 37´-0˝ (11100 mm).

   Note that when you copied the last level, a corresponding floor plan wasn't created. This is indicated by the graphic level symbol being black instead of blue. You can double-click the blue level markers to activate the associated plan view of that level. In addition, you can double-click any blue view symbol such as a section, an elevation, or a callout.

7. From the View tab in the ribbon, find the Create panel, click Plan Views, and then click Floor Plan (Figure 1.15). By default, you'll only see levels that don't already have floor plans created. In this case, you see Roof. Select Floor Plan from the list, and click OK.

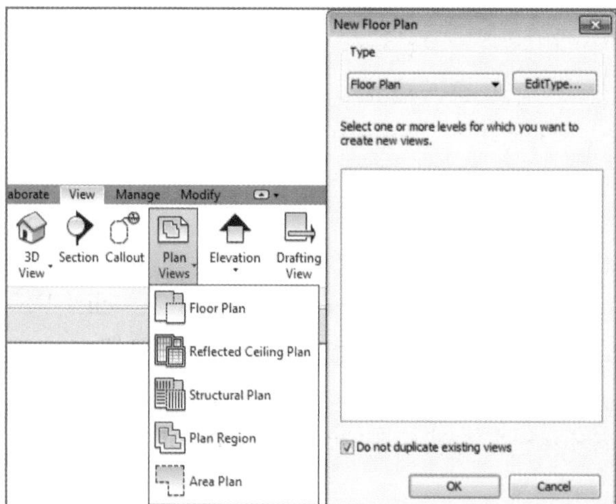

FIGURE 1.15: Use the View tab in the ribbon to create new floor plans.

The new floor plan for the Roof level is activated, so you need to switch back to another view to continue the exercises. Go to the View tab in the ribbon, locate the Windows panel, and then click Switch Windows, as shown in Figure 1.16.

8. Save your project file before continuing to the next exercise.

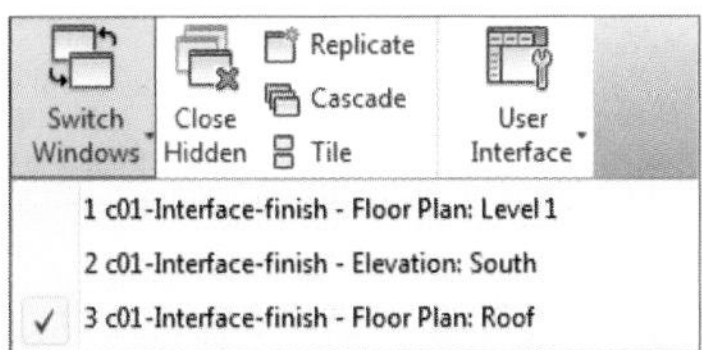

FIGURE 1.16: Use the Switch Windows command to see what views you've activated.

The Switch Windows tool is used so often that it's also located in the QAT by default.

You might notice as you continue to work through the chapter exercises in this book that many views are opened as you activate plans, sections, elevations, schedules, and so on. Having too many windows open at one time may affect the performance of Revit Architecture, so be sure to close some view windows when you don't need them anymore. There is also a Close Hidden Windows command in the View tab of the ribbon and the QAT; use this command to close all but the active window. If you have more than one project open, this command leaves open only one view from each project.

Changing Element Types

Next you'll change the properties for some of the elements you've already created using the Properties palette. You'll also change some walls from one type to another. In the previous exercise, you created additional levels, thus increasing the overall desired height of your building. In the following steps, you'll adjust the top constraint of the exterior walls and swap a few walls for a curtain wall type:

1. Activate the default 3D view. Remember, you can click Default 3D View in the QAT or double-click the {3D} view in the Project Browser.
2. Click the Close Hidden Views button in the QAT, and then activate the South view under Elevations (Building Elevation) in the Project Browser.
3. From the View tab in the ribbon, locate the Windows panel, and then click the Tile button. You should now see the two active views (default 3D view and South elevation) side by side.
4. In either view, find the Navigation bar, click the drop-down arrow under the Zoom icon, and then click Zoom All To Fit, as shown in Figure 1.17.

   In the 3D view, you need to select all the walls to change the properties. To do this, you must use the *chain-select* method.

Use the chain-select method on anything from walls to lines in sketches to detail lines.

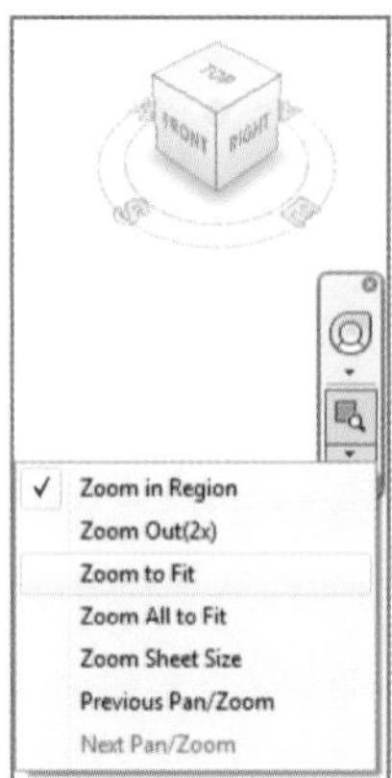

FIGURE 1.17: Use Zoom All To Fit when you're using tiled windows.

5. Place and hold the mouse pointer over one of the walls. Press the Tab key once. The status bar should indicate "Chain of walls or lines." Click to select the chain of walls. You should see an indication in the Properties palette that eight walls have been selected, as shown in Figure 1.18.

6. In the Properties palette, find the parameter Top Constraint. Change the value to Up To Level: Roof, and then click Apply. Notice how the walls all change height in both the 3D view and the elevation view. Also note how the offset is maintained relative to the level of the top constraint (Figure 1.19).

   In the final steps of this exercise, you'll change a few wall segments from one wall type to another. Making these kinds of changes in Revit Architecture is similar to changing the font of a sentence in Microsoft Word, where you select the sentence and then choose a different font from the font selector.

7. In the 3D view, select the wall at the west (left) side of the layout. Press and hold the Ctrl key, and select the wall segment at the east (right) side as well (Figure 1.20).

8. At the top of the Properties palette is the Type Selector. Click it to open the list of available wall types in the project. Scroll down to the bottom of the list, and select the type Curtain Wall: Exterior Glazing. You may get a warning when you make this change; if so, just select Unjoin Walls or whatever the recommended action is. Your result should look like Figure 1.21.

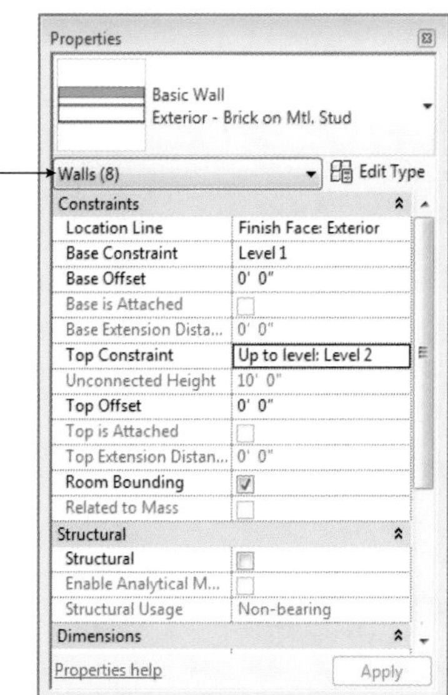

FIGURE 1.18: The number of selected items can be seen in the Properties palette.

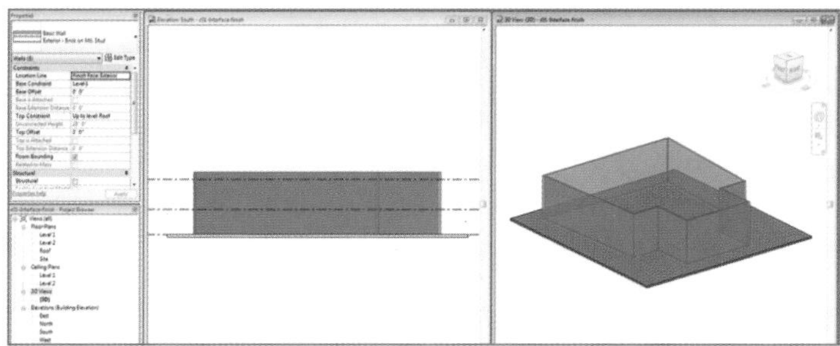

FIGURE 1.19: Tiled windows show the result of modifying the top constraints of the walls.

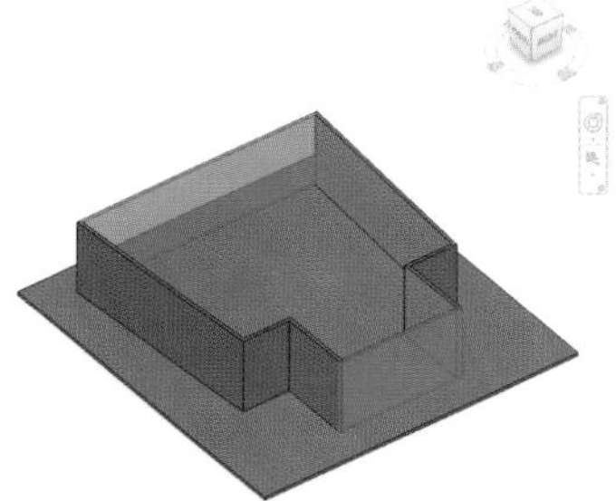

FIGURE 1.20: Use the Ctrl key to manually select multiple items in your model.

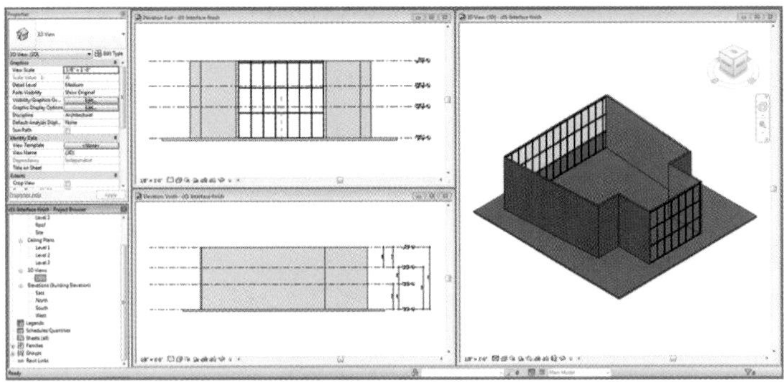

FIGURE 1.21: Wall segments have been changed to a different type.

9. Remember to save your project file before continuing with subsequent lessons.

Using Common Modifying Tools

Now that you've been introduced to the basic workflow of the Revit Architecture user interface, we'll examine some common tools used to modify your designs. These exercises won't expose you to every available tool; rather, they're designed to introduce you to the ones you'll most likely use every day.

You'll be guided through a series of exercises that show how to create a simple interior layout, continuing use of the project file from the previous section. In these exercises, you'll learn how to effectively copy, move, and rotate elements as well as create basic constraints to preserve design intent. You'll also learn how to use dimension strings not just as annotations but also as interactive modifying tools.

Using Dimensions for Modifying Designs

The Function parameter of a wall helps define its default height options. For example, an Interior wall defaults to the level above, whereas an Exterior wall is set to unconnected height.

In this exercise, you'll create a simple layout of interior partitions to explore the use of dimensions in establishing and preserving your design intent. Follow these steps:

1. Activate the Level 1 Interior floor plan from the Project Browser.
2. From the Architecture tab in the ribbon, click the Wall tool and then change the wall type to Interior - Partition Type A2.
3. In the Options Bar, set the Location Line to Finish Face: Interior. In the Properties palette, make sure Top Offset is set to 0.

4. In the Draw panel in the ribbon, click the Pick Lines icon, as shown in Figure 1.22, and then click each of the red lines indicated in the floor plan.

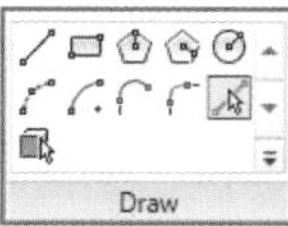

FIGURE 1.22: Use the Pick Lines mode to add walls using layout lines or other guiding elements.

5. With the Wall command still active, change Location Line to Wall Centerline and switch the Draw mode back to Line.

6. Draw two walls inside the area at the right of the layout, as shown in Figure 1.23. Note that you may need to press the Esc key once at the end of each segment to continue the command for the next segment. Don't worry about exact placement of these walls; you'll get to that next.

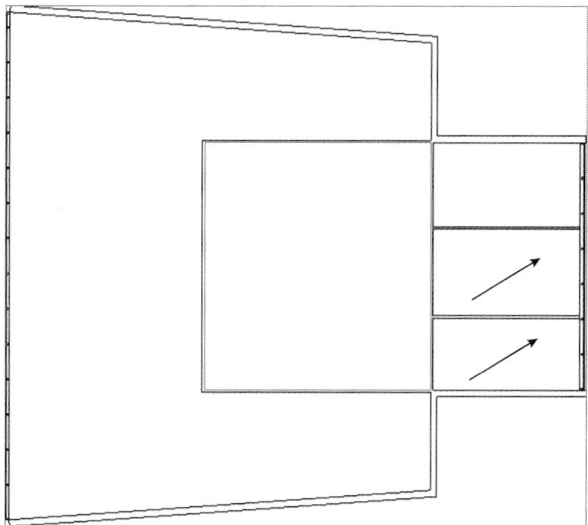

FIGURE 1.23: Add wall segments as shown.

7. From the Annotate tab in the ribbon, locate the Dimension panel and click the Aligned tool. In the Options Bar, notice that the default placement is Wall Centerlines. You can change the default placement any time you use a dimension tool; however, you'll need multiple placement methods in the next step, so leave it as is.

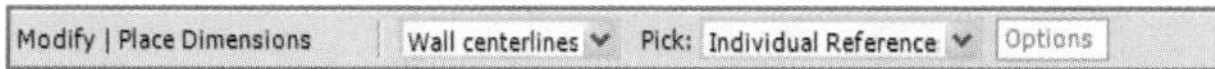

8. In the plan view, click each of the two interior walls you just created. You see one dimension appear between the two walls, but the command is still active. Keep going to the next step.

9. Hover the mouse pointer over one of the two exterior walls, and notice that the centerline of the wall is the default reference. Press the Tab key until you see the inside face of the wall highlight, as shown in Figure 1.24, and then click to add the dimension. Repeat this process for the exterior wall on the other side.

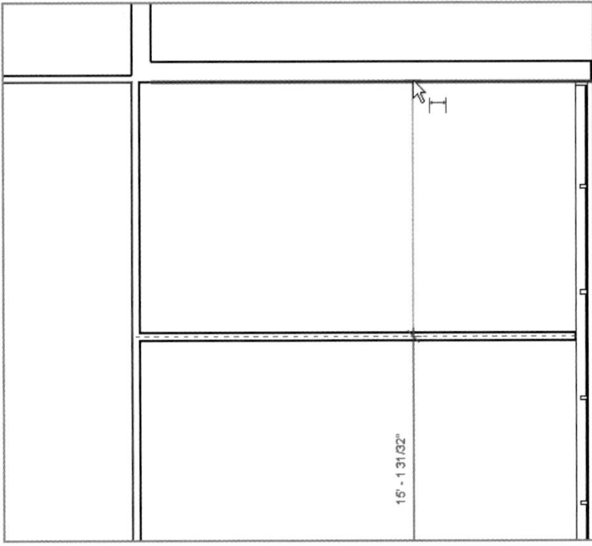

FIGURE 1.24: Use the Tab key to toggle between wall references before you place a dimension.

If you want to see the actual dimension values instead of "EQ" in your dimension strings, right-click the string and select EQ Display to toggle between the two settings.

10. When you've selected all four walls and you want to complete the Dimension command, click in the view window where you'd like the dimension string to be placed. It's important that you don't click another model object or press the Esc key.

11. After the dimension string has been placed, press the Esc key to exit the command and select the dimension you just created. You'll see an EQ symbol with a slash indicating that the dimensions along the string aren't equal. Click this symbol, and the dimensions—along with the wall spacing—become equal.

    Try moving one or both of the exterior walls the dimension string is referencing. You see that the interior walls remain equally spaced as long as the dimension string retains its EQ constraint.

12. Select the dimension string again, and click the EQ symbol to remove the equality constraint.

13. Select one of the two interior walls, and the dimension values to either side turn blue. Click the dimension between the interior wall and the exterior wall, and change the value to 12′-0″ (3.6 m). Repeat this process for the other side.

14. With the dimension string selected, click the lock symbol below each 12′-0″ (3.6 m) dimension to establish a constraint, as shown in Figure 1.25.

    Now try moving each of the exterior walls again. Observe how the constrained dimensions are preserving your intent to keep the outer rooms at their defined dimension.

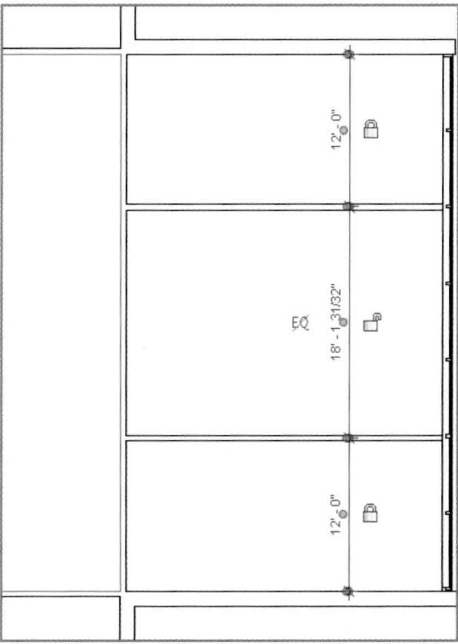

FIGURE 1.25: Lock dimensions along a string to preserve design intent.

Aligning Elements

In the following exercise, you'll use dimensions to precisely place two more walls. You'll then learn how to use the Align tool to preserve a dimensional relationship between two model elements. The Align tool can be used in just about any situation in Revit Architecture and is therefore a valuable addition to your common toolbox.

To begin this exercise, you'll use temporary dimensions to place a wall segment. Elements in Revit Architecture can be initially placed in specific places using temporary dimensions, or you can place them and then modify their positions using temporary or permanent dimensions as you learned in the previous exercise.

Before you begin this exercise, you need to adjust the settings for temporary dimensions. Switch to the Manage tab in the ribbon, and click Additional Settings and then Temporary Dimensions. Change the setting for Walls to Faces and the setting for Doors And Windows to Openings, as shown in Figure 1.26.

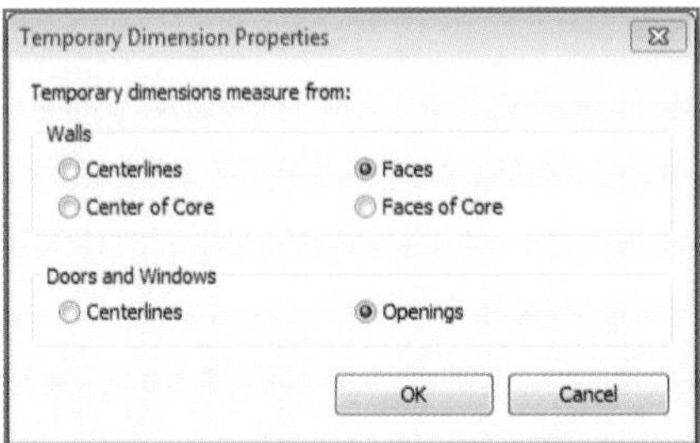

FIGURE 1.26: Modifying the settings for temporary dimensions

Now, follow these steps:

1. Add a wall to the main layout area using Interior - Partition Type A2. Continue to use the Finish Face: Interior location line option; however, use a temporary dimension to place each wall exactly 8′-0″ (2.5 m) from the nearest wall intersection, as shown in Figure 1.27. Repeat this process for the opposite side.

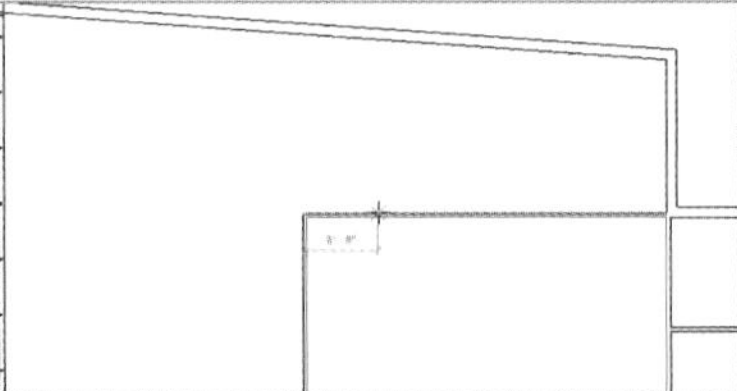

FIGURE 1.27: Place an interior wall using temporary dimensions.

2. Press the Esc key or click the Modify button in the ribbon to exit the Wall command. Select one of the walls you created in step 1. A string of temporary dimensions appears. Drag the grip on the far left of the dimension string so that it aligns with the outside edge of the other wall, as shown in Figure 1.28.

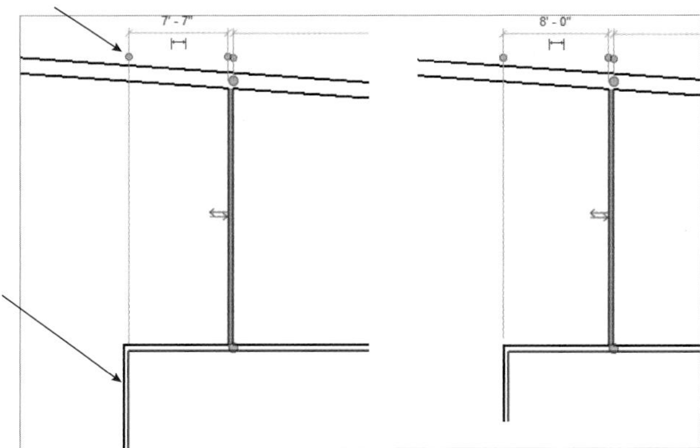

FIGURE 1.28: Adjust references of temporary dimensions by dragging grips.

3. Click the dimension icon just below the length shown in the temporary dimension to convert it into a regular dimension string. Select the dimension string and click the lock symbol to establish a constraint, as shown in Figure 1.29.

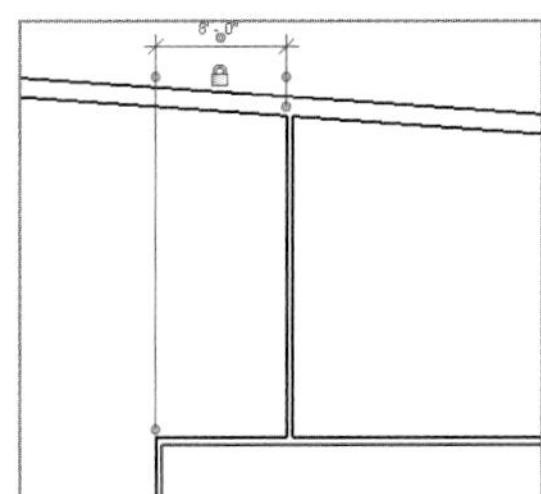

FIGURE 1.29: A temporary dimension has been converted and locked.

4. Zoom out so you can see both new interior wall segments. From the Modify tab in the ribbon, select the Align tool.
5. As illustrated in Figure 1.30, click the face of the wall that has been constrained in step 3 (a), click the corresponding face of the other new wall (b), and then click the lock to constrain the alignment (c).

Once you've completed this exercise, try moving the central interior wall to see how the two flanking walls maintain their dimensional and aligned relationships. Note that the constrained dimension can be deleted while preserving the constraint, as shown in Figure 1.31.

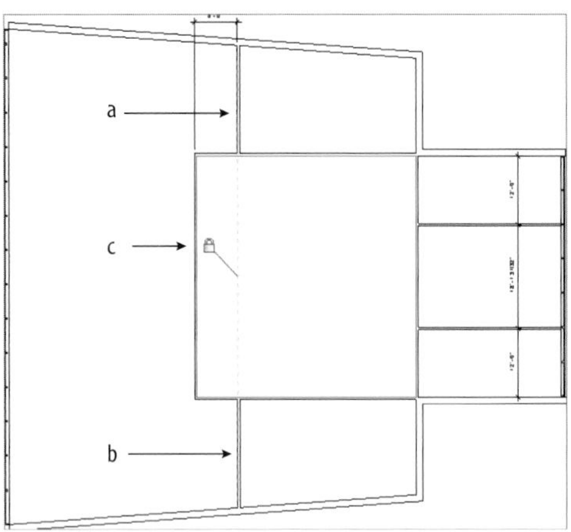

FIGURE 1.30: Use the Align tool to create an alignment and constrain the relationship.

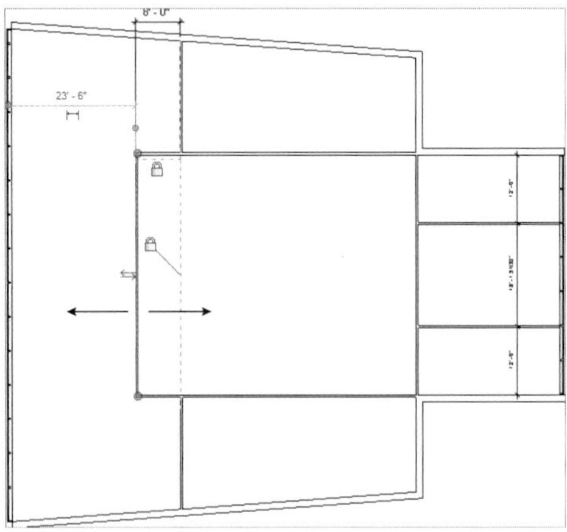

FIGURE 1.31: Try moving the main wall to observe how the flanking walls behave.

Rotating, Grouping, and Arraying

> **Try using temporary dimensions to specify distances between doors and nearby walls before you place them.**
>
> 

Out of all the basic modifying tools we could address in this chapter, the Rotate tool is perhaps the most unique. Rotating elements in Revit Architecture isn't quite the same as in other applications like AutoCAD. For that reason, you'll step through a simple exercise to explore the various ways of rotating content:

1. Activate the Level 1 Furniture floor plan from the Project Browser.
2. From the Architecture tab in the ribbon, click the Door tool. Place a few doors within walls in a variety of places throughout the interior layout. Use the spacebar to flip the rotation of the doors before you place them.

Note that you can disable automatic door tagging by clicking the Tag On Placement button in the contextual tab of the ribbon when the Door command is active.

3. From the Architecture tab in the ribbon, click the Component tool, and select Desk: Type D1 from the Type Selector.
4. In the floor plan, place one desk in the main central space. Press the spacebar once to rotate the desk, and place another desk in one of the spaces in the east wing, as shown in Figure 1.32.
5. Use the Component tool again, and choose Chair-Desk from the Type Selector. Press the spacebar until the chair orients properly with the desk (Figure 1.33).

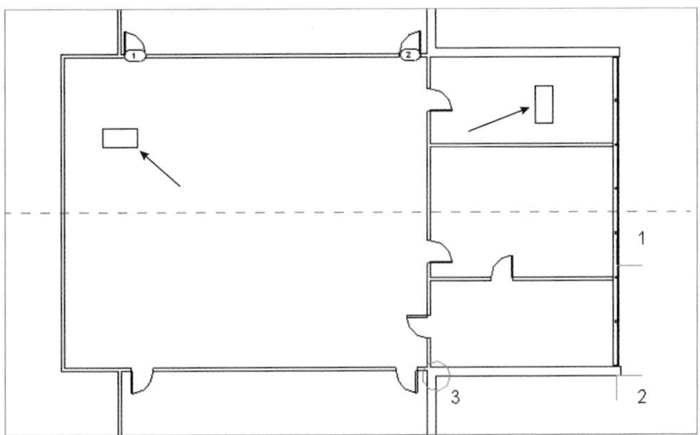

FIGURE 1.32: Place two desks in the layout as shown.

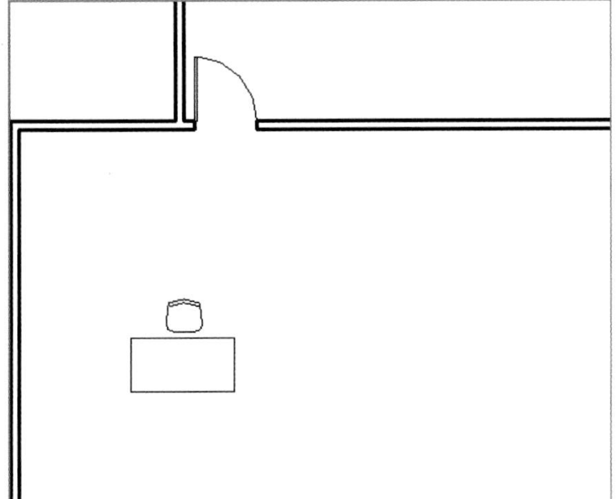

FIGURE 1.33: Place a chair with the desk in the main space.

6. Repeat this process for the desk in the east wing, but add two additional chairs on the opposite side of the desk (Figure 1.34).

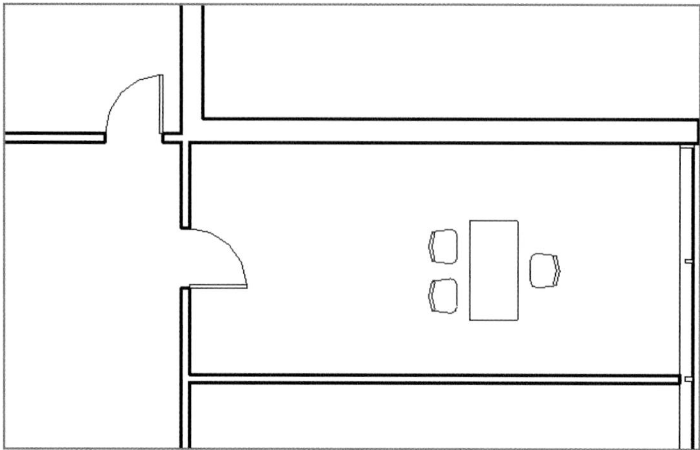

FIGURE 1.34: Place three chairs with the desk in the east wing.

7. Select the desk and chair in the main space, and click the Create Group command in the Create panel of the contextual ribbon. Name the group Desk-Chair-1.
8. Repeat the process for the desk and chairs in the east wing. Name the group Desk-Chair-3.
9. Select the group Desk-Chair-3, and click the Copy command in the ribbon. Set the Constrain and Multiple options in the Options Bar, and place a copy of the group in the three perimeter spaces as shown.

10. With the Copy command still active, uncheck the Constrain option, and place a copy of the group in the space at the north side of the layout. Your copied furniture should look like the image in Figure 1.35.

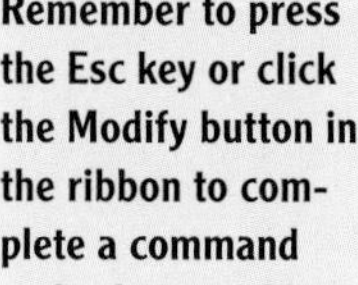

Remember to press the Esc key or click the Modify button in the ribbon to complete a command and select an object.

11. Select the last copied group, and click the Rotate tool in the Modify panel of the ribbon.
12. Drag the rotation center icon to the lower-right corner of the desk.
13. Point the mouse pointer in the east direction, and click. This is the reference angle.
14. Move the mouse pointer in the south direction (Figure 1.36), and click. This is the final rotation.

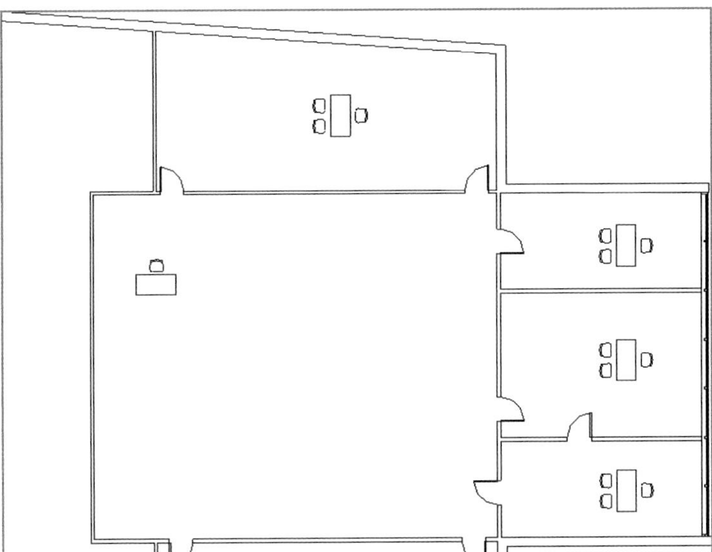

FIGURE 1.35: Create copies of the group with multiple chairs.

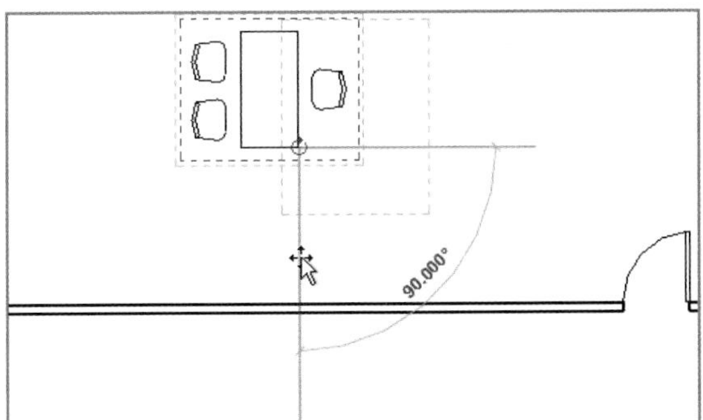

FIGURE 1.36: Use the Rotate tool to modify the last copy of the Desk-Chair-3 group.

15. Select the Desk-Chair-1 group in the main space, and click the Array tool in the Modify panel of the ribbon. In the Options Bar, uncheck the option for Group And Associate, and set Number to 4.

16. In the plan view, click somewhere near the group, point the mouse pointer in the east direction, and then enter 8′-0″ (2.5 m). You see four copies of the group.

17. Use any combination of Copy, Array, and Rotate to complete the layout of the desk-chair groups, as shown in Figure 1.37.

In this exercise, you created a simple group of furniture elements. Groups can be a powerful tool for managing repeatable layouts in a design, but they can cause adverse performance if they're abused. There are far too many opinions and best practices for using groups to list in this chapter; however, you need to be aware of a few important tips. Groups should be kept as simple as possible, and they shouldn't be mirrored. You should also avoid putting hosted elements in groups—but you'll learn more about these types of elements throughout this book.

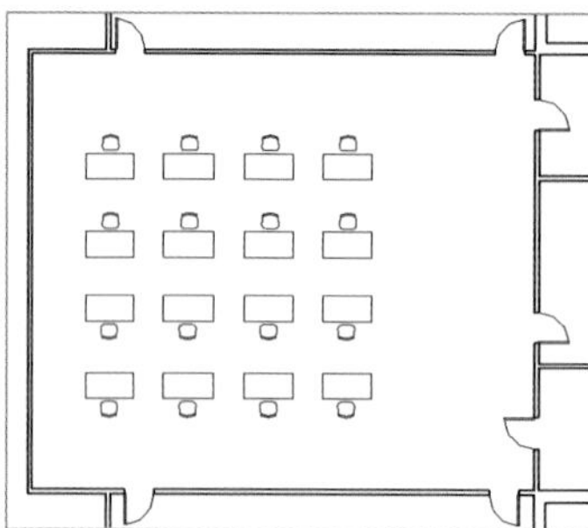

FIGURE 1.37: Complete the finished layout on your own.

Aligned Copying and Group Editing

One powerful and essential tool in Revit Architecture is the copy-to-clipboard command known as Paste Aligned. As you've seen throughout this chapter so far, this is yet another tool that can be used on just about any kind of model or drafting element. In the following exercises, you'll take the interior content you developed in the previous exercises and replicate it on other levels in the building. Here are the steps:

1. Activate the Level 1 Furniture floor plan from the Project Browser.
2. Select all the interior walls, doors, and furniture in the floor plan.
3. In the Clipboard panel of the ribbon, click the Copy To Clipboard tool. You can also press Ctrl+C on your keyboard.
4. Also in the Clipboard panel of the ribbon, click the Paste drop-down button, and select Aligned To Selected Levels. You're prompted with a dialog box to select levels to which the selected content will be copied in exactly the same position (Figure 1.38). Select Level 2 and Level 3 using the Ctrl key to make multiple selections.

   Certification Objective

5. Activate the 3D Cutaway view from the Project Browser to view the results of the aligned copying (Figure 1.39).

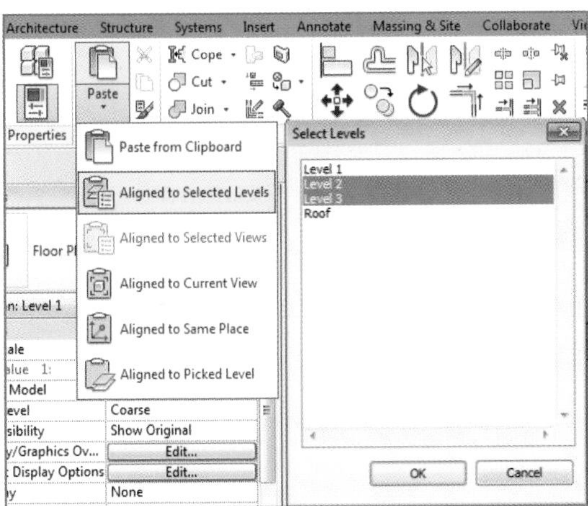

FIGURE 1.38: Use Paste Aligned To Selected Levels to create duplicate floor layouts.

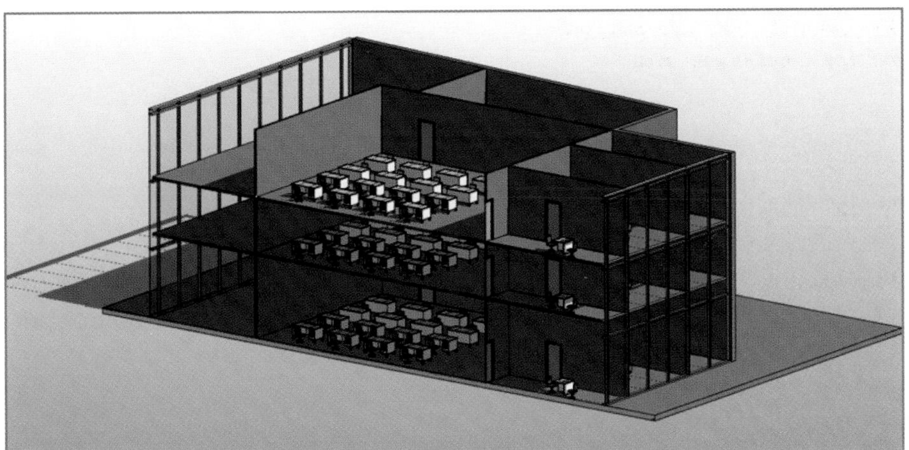

FIGURE 1.39: The 3D Cutaway view uses a section box to display the inside of a building.

Now that you've created many copies of the furniture group on several levels, you can harness the power of the group by making changes to the group and observing how the overall design is updated:

1. Activate the Level 2 floor plan from the Project Browser.
2. Select one of the Desk-Chair-1 furniture groups in the main space. Click the Edit Group button from the contextual ribbon. The view window turns a light shade of yellow, and a temporary toolbar appears at upper left in the view area.

3. Select the chair in the group, and, from the Type Selector, change it to Chair-Executive.
4. Rotate the chair 20 degrees using the Rotate tool (Figure 1.40).

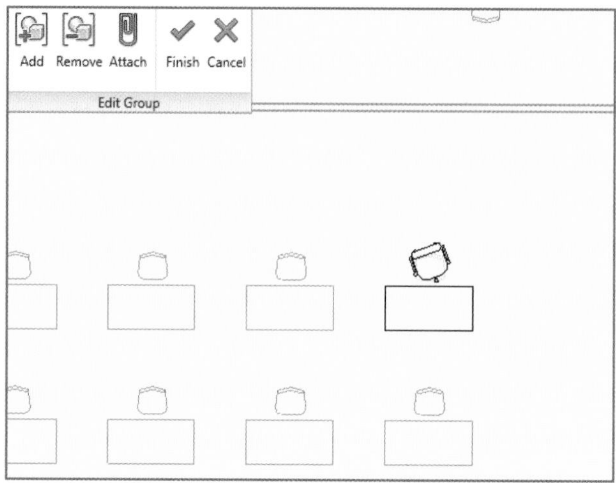

FIGURE 1.40: The view window enters a temporary group-editing mode.

5. Click the Finish button in the Edit Group toolbar, and observe how the changes you made are propagated to all the group instances on all levels. Save your changes, and then activate the Level 1 and Level 3 floor plans to see the extent of the changes.

The Essentials and Beyond

The Revit Architecture interface is organized in a logical manner that enforces repetition and therefore increases predictability. Almost every command can be executed by selecting a view from the Project Browser, choosing a tool from the ribbon, specifying settings in the Options Bar, and then placing an element in the drawing window. Although we covered only the most basic tools in the preceding exercises, you'll be able to apply what you've learned in this chapter to the many exercises exploring other tools in subsequent chapters.

(Continues)

The Essentials and Beyond *(Continued)*

Additional Exercises

- Use the Window and Door tools to place some hosted elements in the walls.
- Create copies of these elements on other levels using the Copy-Paste Aligned tools.
- Experiment with various ways to organize the Revit Architecture interface that support your preferred working method. Try tiling windows and undocking the Properties palette or the Project Browser.
- Try a radial array of furniture by changing the Array tool settings in the Options Bar.

CHAPTER 2

Schematic Design

Design inspiration comes from many sources. Some designers like to sketch by hand, and others use digital tools, but regardless, the design needs to align with the building program. Many modern sketches now happen digitally to make the transition from concept to schematic design easier.

When you begin to migrate your conceptual design from the sketch to the computer, don't start with building elements (walls, floors, and so forth). Instead, start with more primal elements, a process called *massing* in the Autodesk® Revit® Architecture software, to make sure your program is correct. Once you've confirmed that the mass contains the required building program, you'll be able to start placing building elements with far more confidence. Although massing is capable of much more complex form-making than you'll see in this chapter, it's a great starting point for learning Revit Architecture.

In this chapter, you learn the following skills:

- **Working from a sketch**
- **Modeling in-place masses**
- **Creating mass floors**
- **Scheduling mass floors**
- **Updating the massing study**

Working from a Sketch

Sketches can be a great source for starting design massing in Revit Architecture. In certain cases, hand drawings can be scanned from physical pen-and-paper drawings. In some design workflows, sketching directly within a computer application is becoming increasingly common. To support this digital workflow, in 2010 Autodesk released a tool for Apple's iPad called SketchBook Pro (see Figure 2.1) that allows you to sketch directly on an iPad or iPhone using a stylus or even your finger.

The sketch in Figure 2.1 was created on an iPad, but our sample scenario for this chapter will work for any scanned sketch design—even one on tracing paper. In this example, the designer has created sketches of a proposed building form and would like you to import each of the view orientations (plan and elevations) into Revit Architecture and use them as context for a quick massing study. The building program allows a maximum building height of about 800´ (244 m) and requires a gross area of 3.5 million square feet (325,000 square meters).

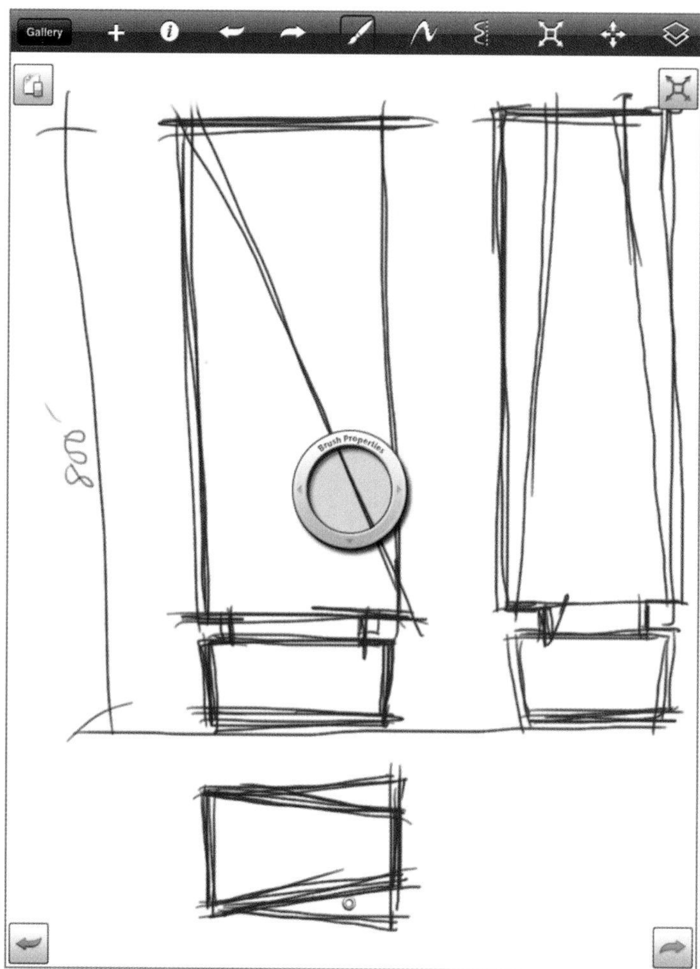

FIGURE 2.1 A hand sketch from Autodesk's SketchBook Pro for the iPad

Importing Background Images

Let's look at how you can combine the design's sketches with the Revit Architecture massing tools to help deliver preliminary feedback about the design. When you open Revit Architecture for the first time, you'll find yourself at the Revit Architecture home screen. This screen keeps a graphic history of the recent projects and families that you've worked on. Now, follow these steps:

1. From the home screen, select Architecture Template to open one of the default Revit Architecture templates. Open the South elevation by double-clicking South in the Project Browser (see Figure 2.2).

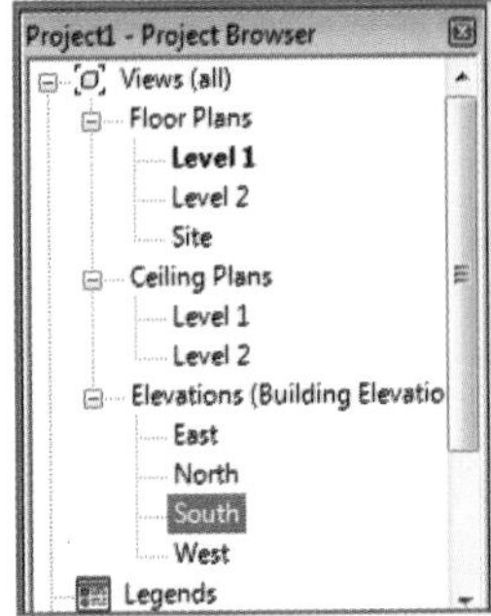

FIGURE 2.2 Open the South elevation.

2. On the Insert tab, select the Import panel and click the Image tool.
3. Select the `c02 Massing Sketch.png` file from the `Chapter 2` folder on this book's web page (`www.sybex.com/go/revit2013essentials`). When you select the image, you're put back in the South elevation view.
4. You see a large, empty-looking box with an X through it. This is the Image Placement tool. Place the image as shown in Figure 2.3 so that the base of the building sketch roughly aligns with Level 1.

As you can tell from Figure 2.3, the scale of the sketch doesn't relate to the real-world units of Revit Architecture. To remedy this, let's quickly scale the imported image.

Accurately Scaling Images

Select the Measure tool from the Quick Access toolbar (QAT) located at the top of the screen. When the tool is active, pick between the two points, as shown in Figure 2.4. As you can see, the real-world distance in the image is about 70´ (52 m). Depending on how you inserted your image, your dimension might vary a bit. That's fine; your next step is to learn how to scale these images.

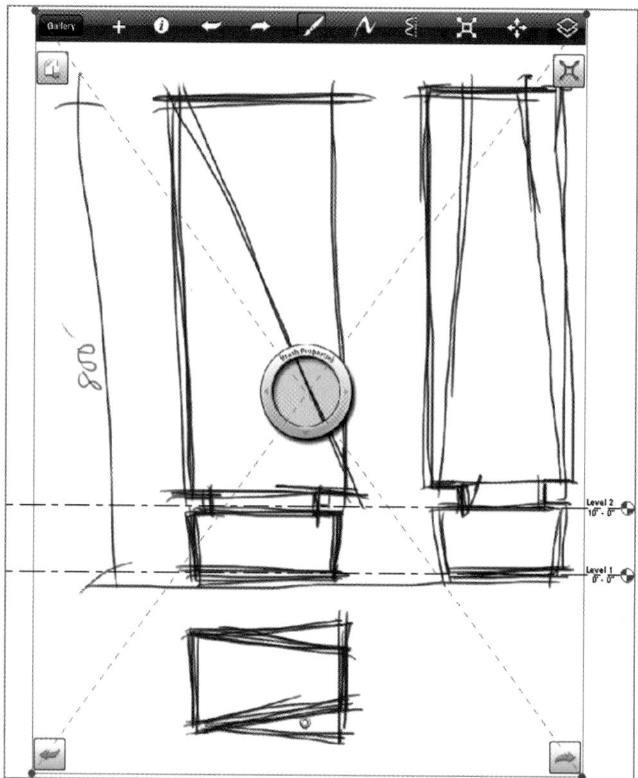

FIGURE 2.3 The placed image. Note the location of the levels relative to the base of the image.

You know the desired distance is 800′ (243 m) between the two points you just measured. One way to change the image size is to select the image and manually enlarge it by dragging the corner grips until the distance is correct—and in many cases this might be close enough. However, we'll show you a more precise method:

1. Select the image, and look at the Properties palette on the left. Notice the current dimension for the Height field is 85′-4″ (26 m) in the example. To modify the image size, you need to increase the Height value with regard to the desired and actual dimensions.
2. To determine this value, use this formula:

   Current Height × (Desired Height / Measured Distance)

   So for this example, you'd use

   85′-4″ × (800′ / 70′) or (26 m × (243 m / 52 m)

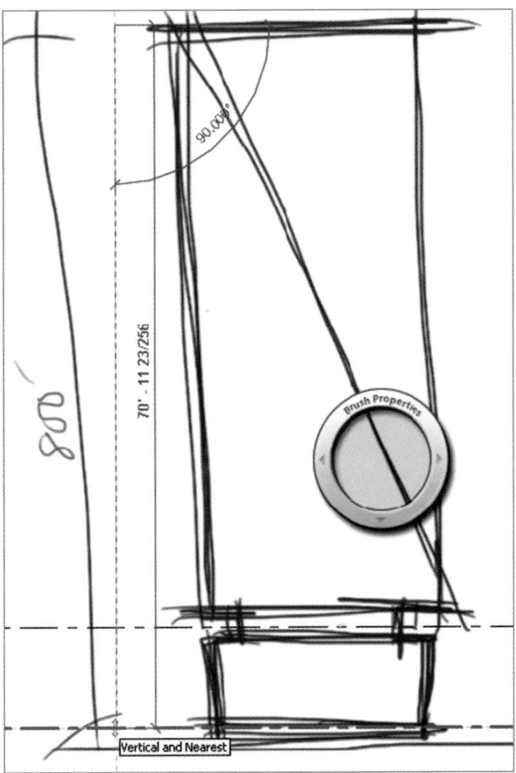

FIGURE 2.4 **Measuring the imported image**

Using built-in database functionality of Revit Architecture, you can do this math right in the Properties palette, as shown in Figure 2.5! Be sure to add the = sign at the beginning of the formula. The height of the image increases significantly (over 975´ [2,735 m]). But now the imported image has proportionally increased the correct amount.

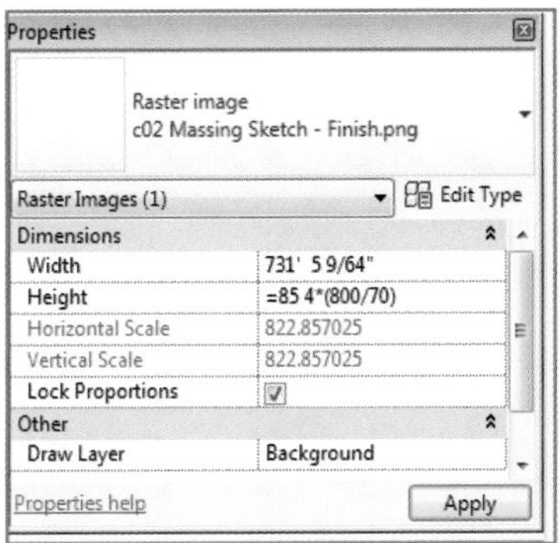

FIGURE 2.5 **A formula for adjusting the image height**

3. Move the lower edge of the sketch to align with Level 1 again. Also, increase the scale of the view to 1″ = 30′-0″ (1:500) so that the level's symbols are more visible (see Figure 2.6).

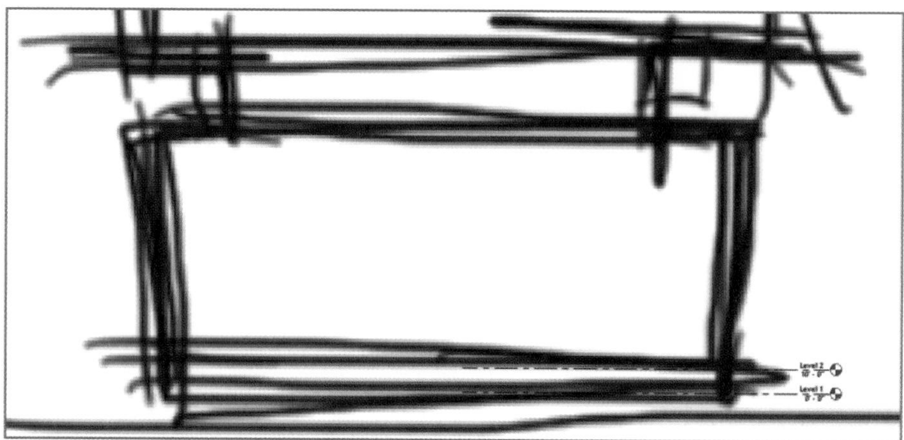

FIGURE 2.6 The resulting image

Reference Planes and Levels

Certification Objective

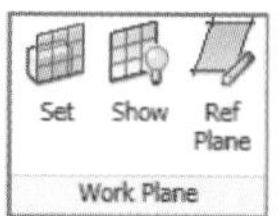

Reference planes are one of the most useful tools in Revit Architecture. The planes are represented in Revit Architecture as green dashed lines, and they display in any view perpendicular to the reference plane. They don't print in your drawing sheets, but they're handy as a tool to align elements that are coplanar. Think of them as levels and grids, except that you don't need to show them on your sheets.

In the example, it's important to use reference planes as guides to help you create the masses in other views, because the image you imported will be visible only in the imported view. Reference planes are like guidelines that can be seen across many views. They will be extremely helpful when you line up the sketch in the South elevation and then in the North elevation or plan view.

To begin, click the Home tab, and on the Work Plane panel, select the Ref Plane tool. Next, create reference lines that correspond with the edges of the sketch by tracing over its vertical boundaries. The dimensions in Figure 2.7 have been added as a reference for you. You don't need to add dimensions—just add the reference planes as shown. We also adjusted the scale of the view so that the level symbols are easy to read.

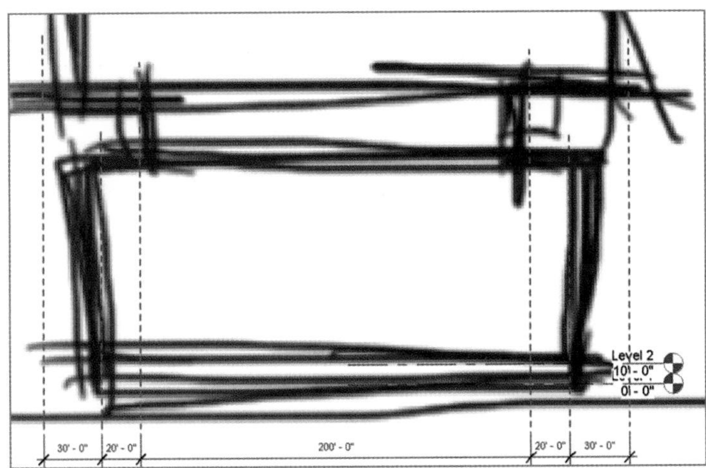

FIGURE 2.7 Dimensioned reference planes

Now let's add some levels to the sketch that will be useful for determining the limit of the three masses you'll add:

1. Move Level 2 to 20′-0″ (6 m) by selecting the 10′-0″ (3 m) value and typing in the new elevation, as shown in Figure 2.8.

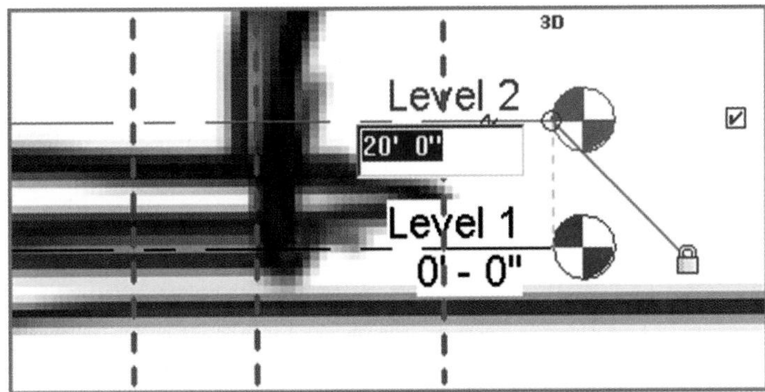

FIGURE 2.8 Enter the new elevation.

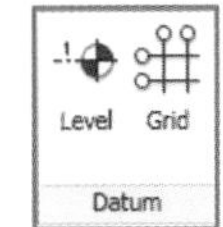
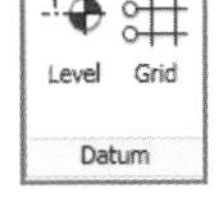

2. To add levels, select the Home tab, and then choose the Level tool from the Datum panel. By clicking and dragging your cursor from left to right, you create a level that also creates a corresponding floor plan. Place Level 3 at 35′-0″ (10 m).

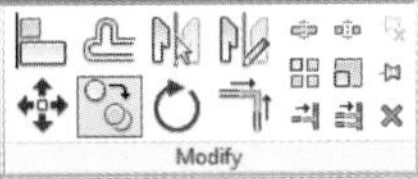

3. You can also create levels by copying an existing level. To try this, use the Copy tool to create Levels 4–10, as shown in Figure 2.9. Start by selecting the level you want to copy, and when the Modify tab appears at the top of the screen, click the Copy tool.

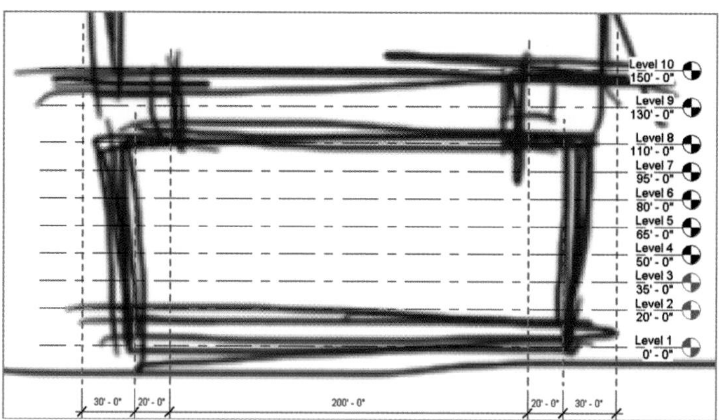

FIGURE 2.9 View vs. reference levels

Levels vs. Reference Levels

Using the Copy tool doesn't create a corresponding floor plan. Rather, it creates what Revit Architecture calls a ***reference level***. Reference levels aren't "hyperlinked," and they show black instead of blue. Levels that have corresponding floor plan views are blue, and when you double-click the blue level marker, they link to those associated views.

In Figure 2.9, Levels 1–3 have corresponding floor plan or level views, whereas Levels 4–10 are reference levels only. Reference levels can be turned into view levels, but during the design process (and later in documentation), you'll find it helpful to create levels that don't necessarily need to be views. Having 100 or more view levels would create a lot of clutter in Revit Architecture and your drawing set.

Now let's create the rest of the levels, as shown in Figure 2.9, by arraying Level 10:

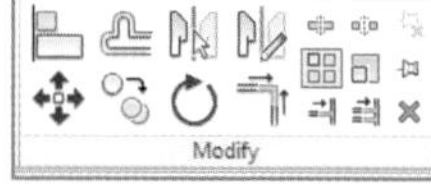

1. Select Level 10. The Modify | Levels menu becomes active. Select the Array tool from the Modify panel.
2. Because Level 10 is at an elevation of 150′-0″ (45 m), you need to create an array with the options shown in Figure 2.10. These options can be adjusted in the Options Bar below the context menu. The Options Bar dynamically changes based on the tools you have selected.
3. Select the second Move To option in the Options Bar, and pick a location that is directly 12′-0″ (3.6 m) above Level 10. Change the value

of the Number field to 55. When you click to place the fifth level, the additional 55 levels at 12′-0″ (3.6 m) are created, and your final level (Level 64) appears at 798-0 (243 m). That's pretty close to your goal of 800′-0″ (243 m).

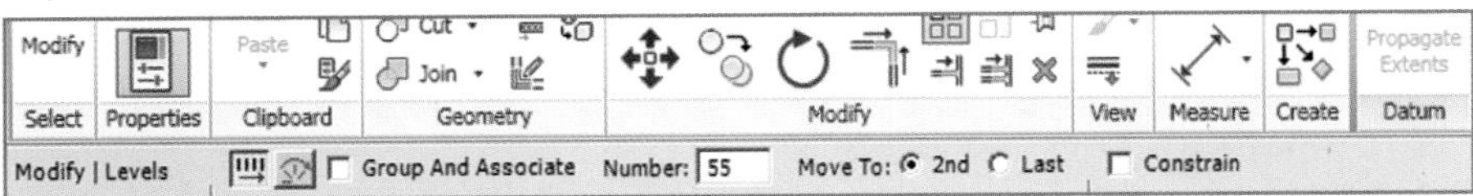

FIGURE 2.10 Array options

The final step before creating the mass is to add the sketched image to the East elevation and Level 1, which you'll do in a moment. Before you add the final elevation, let's discuss a change-management tip. No design work is ever static (it's always changing), so it's important to understand how to keep up with those iterations in Revit Architecture. In this case, you want to be able to manage the ability to update the images in case the designer gives you some new sketches. Keep in mind that if the image changes in size or shape, you'd probably want all the images to change as well. Here is where groups come in handy. A group is similar to what in the Autodesk® AutoCAD® software is called a *block* or in MicroStation, a *cell*. Groups are collections of Revit Architecture elements that you want to move or repeat as a single unit but that you want to have the ability to subdivide or "ungroup" if needed. Let's explore a few uses for groups and then add the final elevation.

Creating and Placing Groups

In this exercise, you'll create a group and explore potential uses for the Group command:

1. Select the image you inserted earlier in the South elevation, and then select the Group tool from the Create panel on the Modify tab.

2. When the Create Detail Group dialog opens, name the group **Massing Sketch 1**, as shown in Figure 2.11, and click OK.

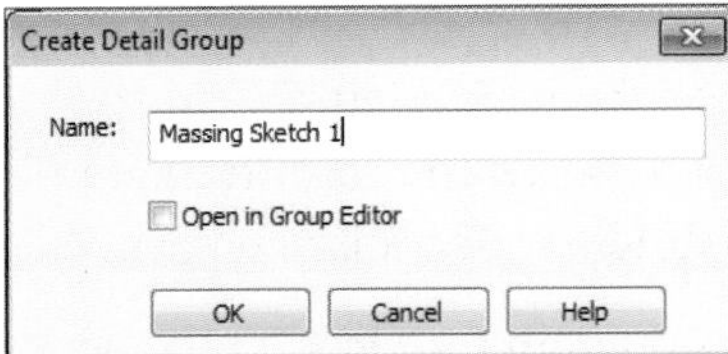

FIGURE 2.11 Create Detail Group dialog

3. In the Project Browser, click Groups and then Detail to see the group that you just created (see Figure 2.12). By clicking and dragging this group into your project window, you can add the detail group to other views in your project.

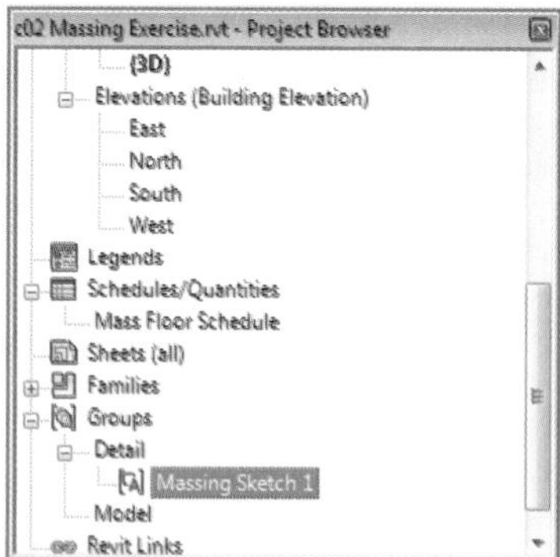

FIGURE 2.12 Finding your new group in the Project Browser

4. Open your East elevation, and drag a copy of the detail group from the Project Browser into the view. Then create some more reference planes, as shown in Figure 2.13, to form guides that will be visible in other views.

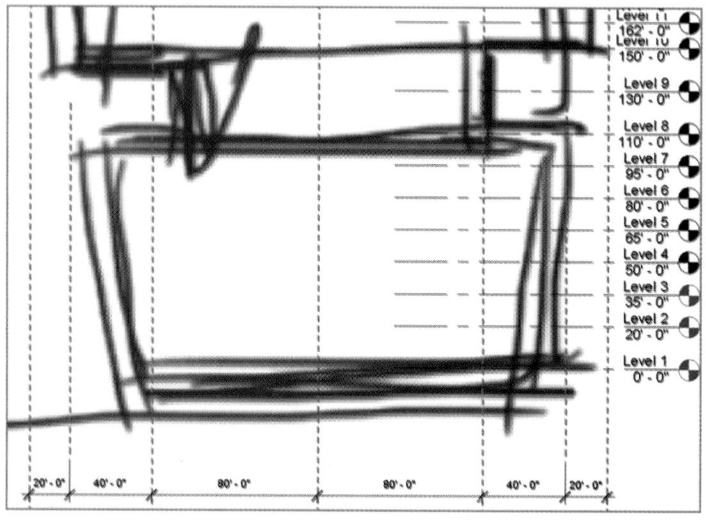

FIGURE 2.13 Creating reference planes in the East elevation

5. Drag a final copy of the detail group into your Level 1 view, and center it in the South and East view reference planes you created, as shown in Figure 2.14. Now you have the three views necessary for massing the building.

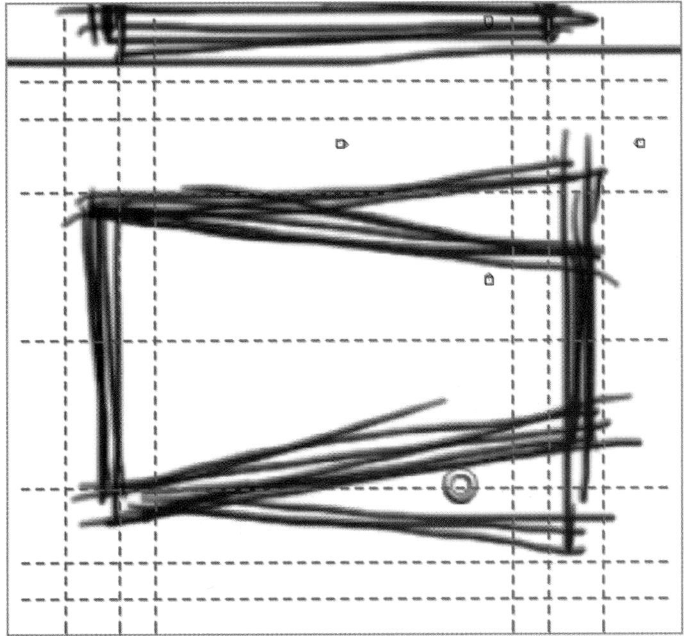

FIGURE 2.14 Reference planes in the Level 1 view

IMAGES AND GROUPS

Each image that you import in Revit Architecture can be seen only in the view in which it's placed. In other words, an image placed in the South elevation view is seen only in that elevation view. In the example, you're trying to assemble a 3D context for modeling geometry, and you'll need to place the image in multiple views.

When you change the scale or proportion of one of the images, you'll likely want to change all of them. Groups are used in Revit Architecture to maintain relationships between collections of elements. When one group changes, all the groups change. This is very helpful for collections of components that are compiled into units, such as furniture layouts, hotel rooms, and apartment types.

Modeling In-Place Masses

Now that you've imported the designer's sketch and drawn the appropriate reference planes for added context, you can start creating the massing elements that will represent the building. You'll do so using a tool called In-Place Mass. Consider masses as families in Revit Architecture that are created directly within the project. This tool allows you to model within the context of the project you're actively working in.

Modeling the Base Mass

To model the base mass, follow these steps:

1. Open your Level 1 floor plan view by double-clicking Level 1 in the Project Browser. New to Revit Architecture 2013 is the ability to turn on and off the tabs within the ribbon.

2. Select the Massing & Site tab on the ribbon, and select the In-Place Mass tool from the Conceptual Mass panel. If you don't see the Massing & Site tab, don't fret. Choose the Application button, and select Options. On the User Interface option, you can check the box to show Massing & Site.
3. Revit Architecture displays a dialog telling you that it has now enabled the Show Mass mode in the current view. Click Close.
4. The Name dialog appears. For this exercise, use the default name, which is Mass 1 (see Figure 2.15). Click OK.

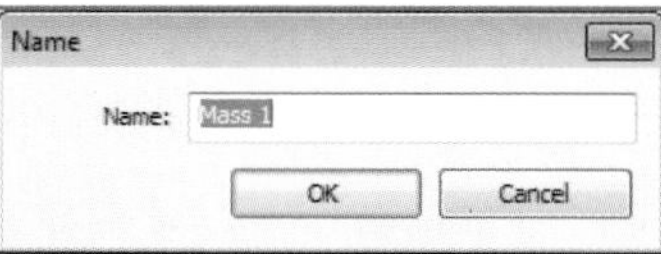

FIGURE 2.15 Use the default mass name.

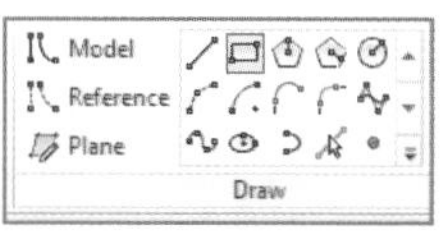

5. Now you're in a special, in-place editor for creating masses in Revit Architecture. Notice that the menu options have changed. Select the Rectangle tool.
6. Using the Rectangle tool, sketch lines as shown in Figure 2.16. These lines should cover the form and be placed along the reference planes you created earlier.

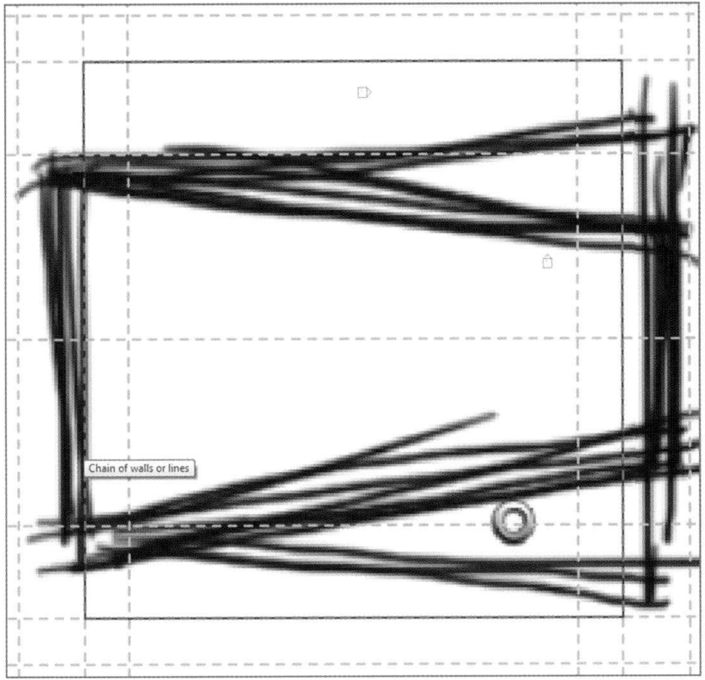

FIGURE 2.16 Sketching a rectangular form

7. Select the lines, and then select the Create Form tool from the Form panel.

The results aren't immediately obvious because you're looking at a solid form in plan. To view the results from another angle, return to the South elevation. Select the top of the form by clicking it, and use the grip arrows, as shown in Figure 2.17, to increase the form's height until it aligns with Level 8. The edge of the forms will "stick" to the level when you're close and snap itself into place.

Sketching Masses

The type of mass you're creating in this exercise is called an ***extrusion***. There are many other configurations of masses, including blends, sweeps, swept blends, and revolves. After you've created the initial mass, it's possible to edit the form dramatically; you can even use voids to carve away at your initial form.

We don't have the space to go into that level of complexity. But modeling more complex masses is something that you'll likely want to learn. Check out `http://au.autodesk.com/?nd=class_listing`.

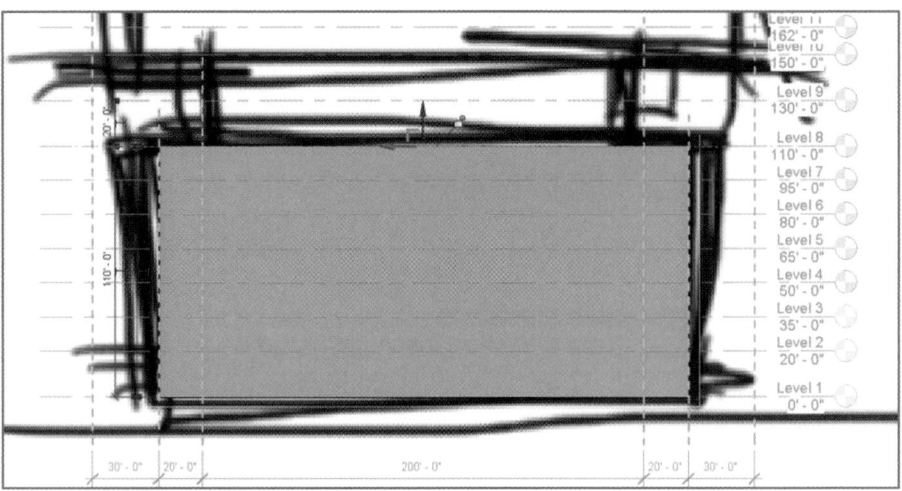

FIGURE 2.17 Increasing the height of the mass

Modeling the Middle Mass

The next step is to model the middle mass form:

1. Return to the Level 1 plan view. Set the view to Wireframe, as shown in Figure 2.18 (so you can see through the mass you've just created). The Wireframe button is located in the View Control Bar at the bottom of the screen.

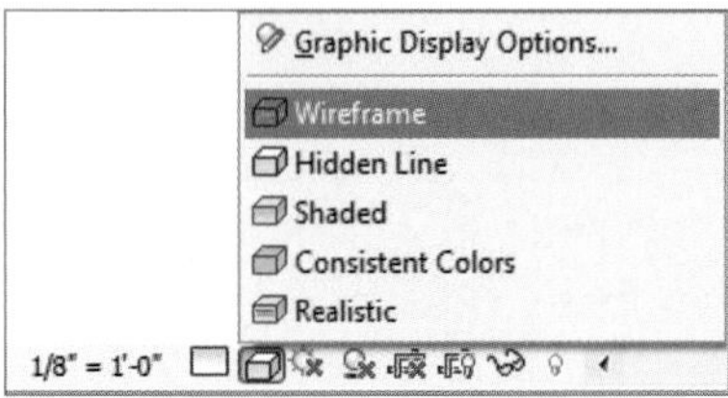

FIGURE 2.18 Setting View to Wireframe

2. Using the same workflow, sketch another rectangle as shown in Figure 2.19. Then select the rectangle and click Create Form, as you did with the previous rectangle.

3. Once again, open the South elevation, and use the grip arrows to move the second mass form so the upper face aligns with Level 10 and the lower face aligns with Level 8, as shown in Figure 2.20. Don't forget that you can set the view display to Wireframe if you need to see through the first mass to the second mass. Changes to one view won't be reflected in every view.

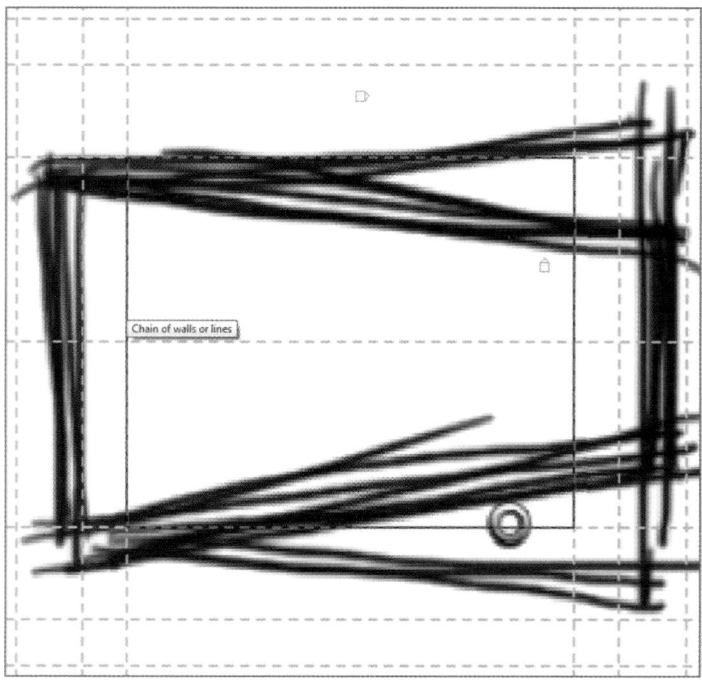

FIGURE 2.19 Sketching the second rectangle

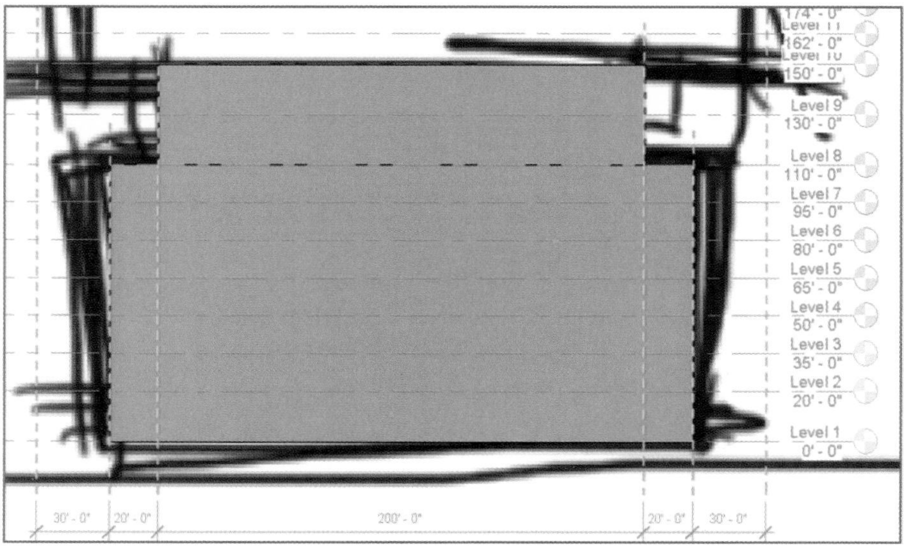

FIGURE 2.20 Second mass in place

Modeling the Upper Mass

The process of creating the third (and uppermost) mass starts the same as for the first two masses:

1. Return to Level 1, and create a rectangular sketch that connects the outermost reference planes, as shown in Figure 2.21. Then select the lines, and click Create Solid. Extend the upper and lower faces to align with Levels 64 and 10, respectively.

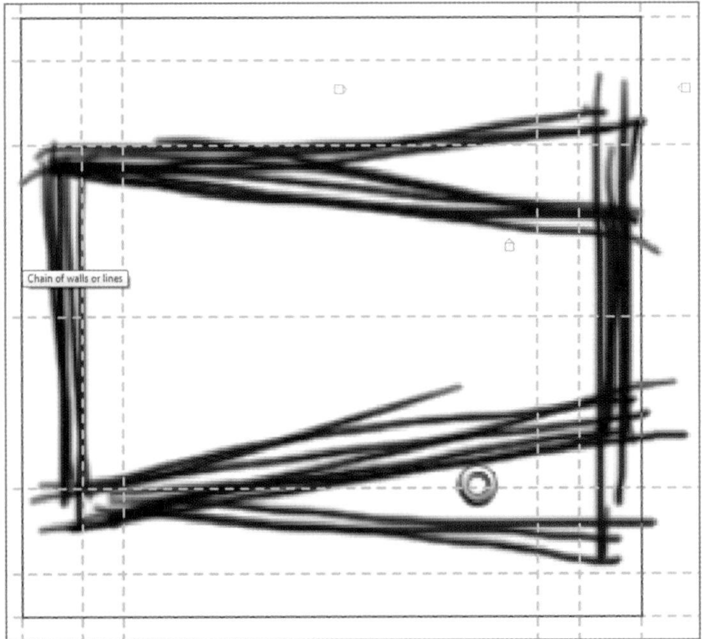

FIGURE 2.21 Creating the third sketch and mass form

2. Return to the South elevation, and use the grip arrows to extend the top and bottom of the form.

You could continue to work in 2D views, but it'll be more helpful if you can see what you're doing in 3D.

Working in 3D

Select the Default 3D View icon from the QAT . Doing so allows you to see the working mass more completely, as shown in Figure 2.22.

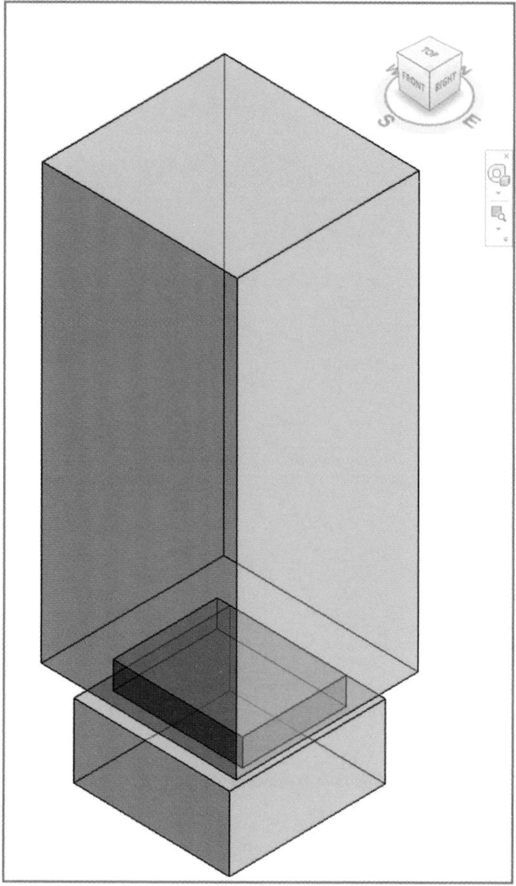

FIGURE 2.22 Default 3D view of the completed mass

You likely noticed from the imported sketches that the East façade of the mass should taper in elevation. The base and the top are different widths. By adding an edge to each face (both North and South), you'll be able to adjust the upper form appropriately:

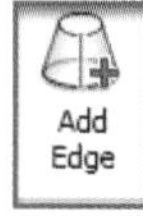

1. Hover over the South face of the upper form, and select the face by clicking it. Doing so activates the Add Edge tool on the Form Element panel.
2. The Add Edge tool divides one plane on the mass by adding another edge that can be adjusted independently of the other edges. Add the edge at the front, lower corner of the upper mass, as shown in Figure 2.23.

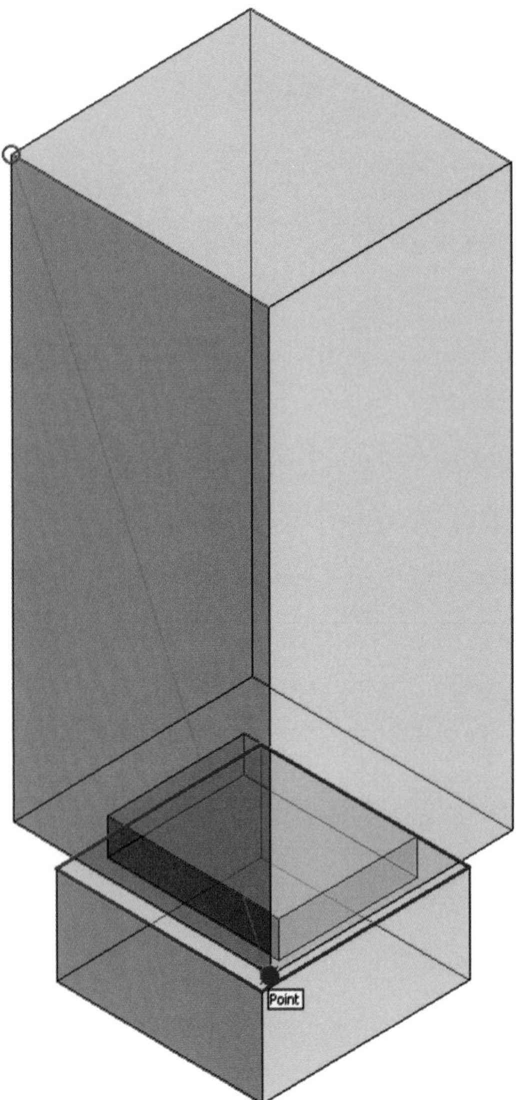

FIGURE 2.23 Adding the South face edge

3. Rotate the model to expose the North face. Do so by selecting the intersection of the ViewCube between the right, back, and top sides. The model will spin around, zoom extents, and center itself.
4. Select the North or Right face to add an edge.

5. Open the East elevation from the Project Browser. Use the grip arrows to adjust this face of the upper mass. As you hover your mouse pointer over the intersection, a vertex control appears as a purple dot at the upper-right corner where you added a face (see Figure 2.24).

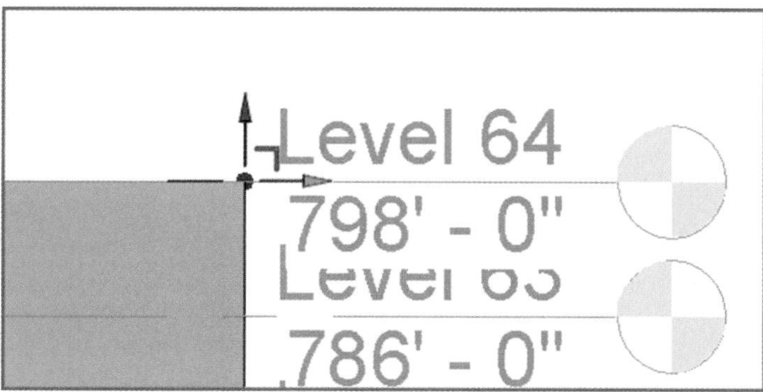

FIGURE 2.24 Selecting the vertex

6. Select this control, and then use the grip arrows to move it to the intersection of the uppermost level and right reference plane. Next, do the same thing to the west side of the mass. The result will resemble Figure 2.25.

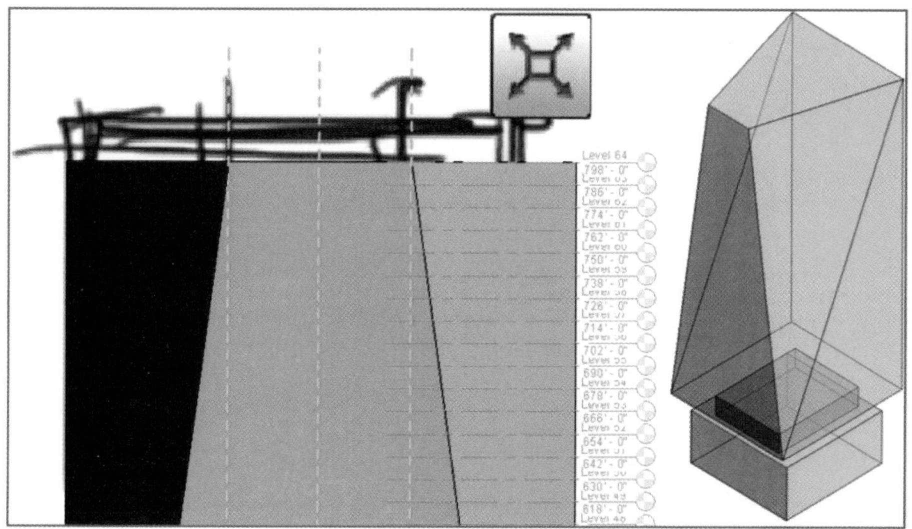

FIGURE 2.25 Resulting South elevation and 3D view

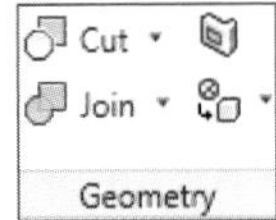

7. Your mass is nearly complete, but first you need to join all the mass geometry together. From the Modify tab, select the Join tool on the Modify panel. Then select the lower and middle forms to join them. Repeat this process for the middle and upper forms.

8. Now that the forms have been joined, select the Finish Mass tool from the In-Place Editor panel. It's the big, green check mark, meaning you're done!

Congratulations! You've just created your first massing study.

Joining Masses

Each mass is an independent object. Masses can even be scheduled independently from each other. You'll find this functionality helpful for creating separate masses for programming purposes (such as convention space or meeting rooms). But be careful if you have overlapping masses.

If overlapping masses aren't properly joined, Revit Architecture will create overlapping mass floors, and your schedules will be incorrect. Furthermore, if you create real floors from the mass floors, the floors will overlap rather than create a single element.

Creating Mass Floors

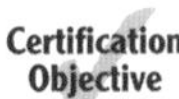

Floor area faces are incredibly useful for getting a sense of the gross area of a building mass at any intersecting level. Furthermore, the results can be quickly and easily scheduled. Any changes to the massing study will update the schedules and all views in real time.

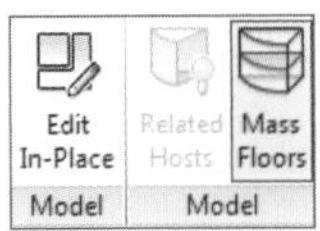

Select the completed mass, and then click the Mass Floors tool in the Model panel. You're given the option to select all the levels in your project. You want to select them all, but rather than select them one at a time, select Level 1, and then scroll down. While pressing Shift, select Level 64. Now all of the levels are selected. Check any box, and all the boxes are automatically checked. Click OK.

Your mass has now been bisected with mass floors (faces with no geometry), as shown in Figure 2.26.

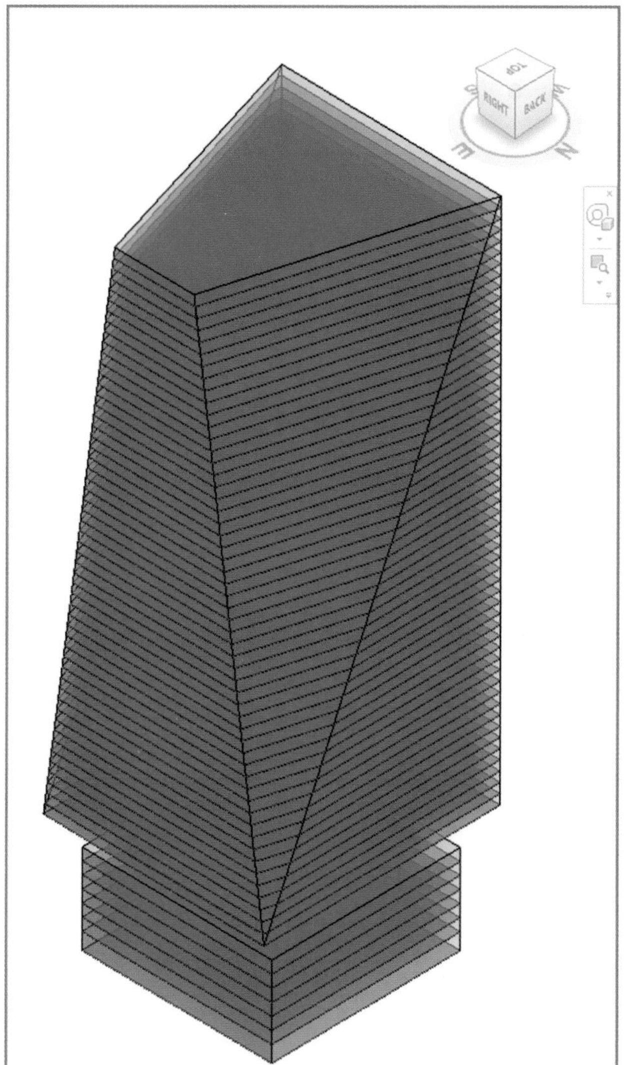

FIGURE 2.26 The mass has been bisected with mass floors.

Scheduling Mass Floors

Creating schedules in Revit Architecture is easy, and schedules can be used across projects (and put in your project template). Doing so allows you to understand the context and impact of your work while you work—rather than at the end of a long design process that can prove to be a waste of time. Schedules can help you not only track elements in Revit Architecture, but also assess how conceptual design work meets your program requirements.

Schedules are just like any other type of view in Revit Architecture—they show you a current, specific look at the model. These views show you this information in a spreadsheet format rather than geometrically, but just like the other view types, schedules dynamically update as changes are made to the model. Follow these steps:

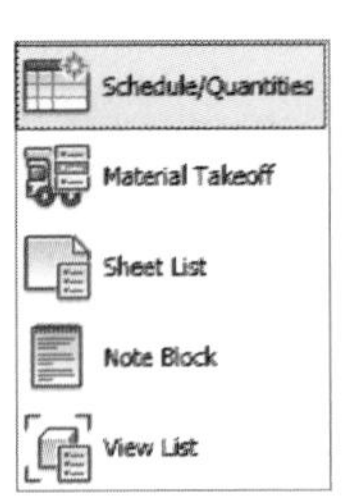

1. To create the mass schedule, select the View tab from the ribbon. Then select the Schedules drop-down in the Create panel. Click Schedules/Quantities.
2. In the New Schedule dialog, select the Mass Floor option from the column on the left, and leave the other fields (Schedule Name and Phase) at their default values. Click OK.
3. The next dialog contains a series of tabs. You'll step through some of these to set up the schedule. On the Fields tab, select the following from the list on the left:

    Level

    Floor Area

    You can double-click these to move them to the box on the right, or highlight them and click the Add button (see Figure 2.27).

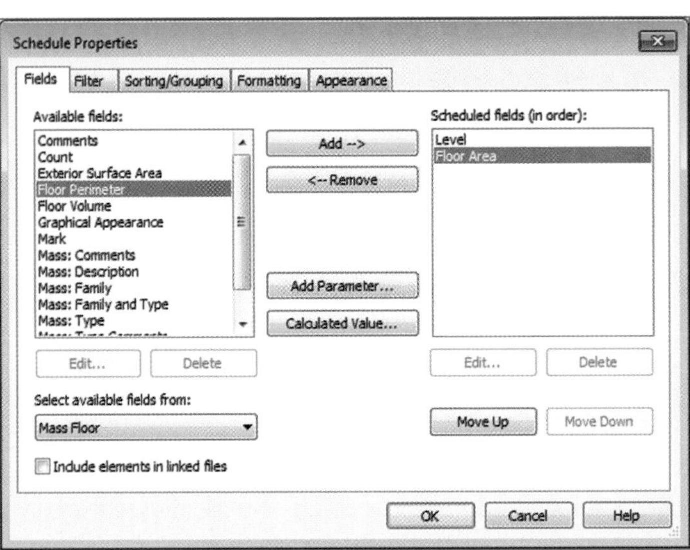

FIGURE 2.27 Selecting the scheduled fields

4. On the Sorting/Grouping tab, change Sort By to Level. Also, check the box at the bottom for Grand Totals, and select Title, Count, And Totals from the drop-down, as shown in Figure 2.28.

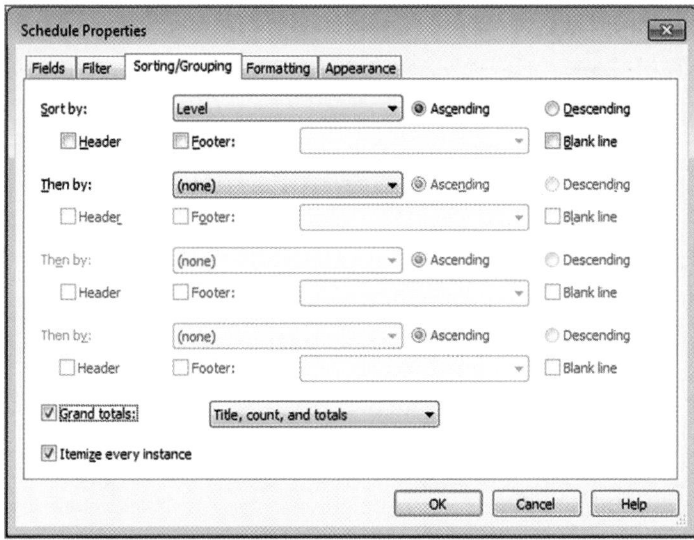

FIGURE 2.28 Selecting the Sorting/Grouping fields

5. On the Formatting tab, select the Floor Area field, and then click the Calculate Totals option (Figure 2.29). Click OK. This creates the schedule.

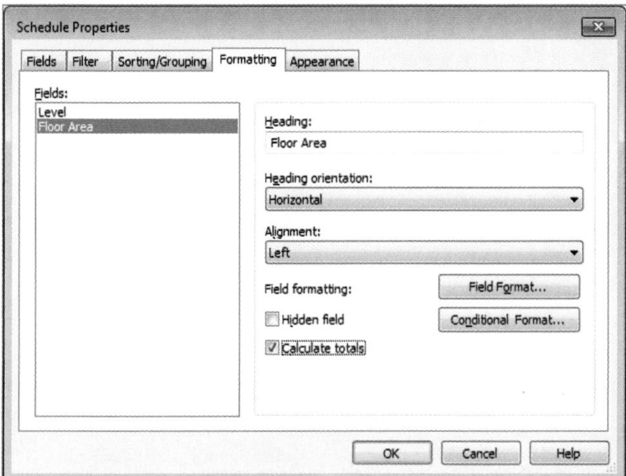

FIGURE 2.29 Calculating totals

Figure 2.30 shows the resulting schedule. With a total of 63 floor levels, Revit Architecture is calculating a gross floor area of just over 4.5 million square feet (418,000 square meters).

Level 59	61769 SF
Level 60	60852 SF
Level 61	59917 SF
Level 62	58963 SF
Level 63	57661 SF
Grand total: 63	4530617 SF

FIGURE 2.30 Gross floor area

Unfortunately, you know from the program (at the beginning of this chapter) that the gross floor area needs to be closer to 3.5 million square feet (325,000 square meters). So, let's get back to that massing study and tweak the form to get it closer to the program goals.

Updating the Massing Study

Begin by selecting the mass in the default 3D view and then clicking the Edit In-Place button on the Model panel. Doing this returns you to In-Place editing mode and allows you to have specific control over mass geometry.

You're going to modify the east and west faces, moving each face 40´-0˝ (12 m) closer to the center. Hover over and select the east face of the upper mass to display a temporary dimension and the shape handles.

Select this dimension and, by clicking the blue text, change the value from 300´-0˝ (91 m) to 260´-0˝ (80 m). Do the same for the middle and lower east faces. Now the gross floor area is closer to 3.25 million square feet (see Figure 2.31), or about 302,000 square meters.

Level 56	47232 SF
Level 57	46601 SF
Level 58	45956 SF
Level 59	45297 SF
Level 60	44625 SF
Level 61	43939 SF
Level 62	43240 SF
Level 63	42327 SF
Grand total: 63	3287039 SF

FIGURE 2.31 Resulting gross floor area

You will need the program to be closer to 3.5 million square feet. A quick discussion with the designer reveals that the base of the building is meant to hold important meeting and conference spaces. So you'll extend the eastern base of the building to 300´ (91 m). Once again, you do so by repeating the previous steps of selecting the mass and returning to In-Place editing mode. Make certain the base element is 300´ deep, and then finish the mass.

When this is finished, the mass looks like Figure 2.32, and the gross floor area is within the required program.

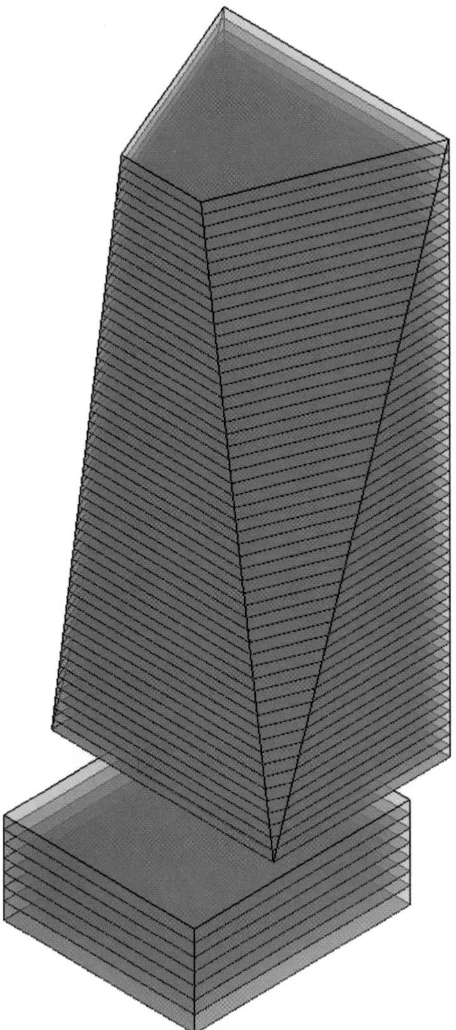

FIGURE 2.32 Final mass

If you would like to download the completed Revit Architecture file, you can find it in the `Chapter 2` folder at the book's web page. The file is called `c02 Massing Exercise.rvt`.

The Essentials and Beyond

Ultimately, masses can be used to host relationships to real building elements that would otherwise be nearly impossible to maintain. Mass floors can be used to control the extents of real floors. Many times, this will allow you to change location of many slab edges at once by changing the mass and then updating the floors within that mass.

Masses can also host walls, curtain walls, and roofs. This allows you to create (and modify) complex design forms that would be nearly impracticable to assemble bit by bit. The idea is that you're working from general to specific: get the big ideas down first (as masses), and then go back and assign real building elements to those faces to build the building.

But keep in mind that it's unlikely you'll be able to use only one mass to host all your building elements. You may need one mass to host floors and control slab edges, another to host roofs, and even another to host walls and curtain wall systems. Don't be afraid to use overlapping masses in these situations to control different host elements. More specific control will often require overlapping masses. But for initial design/programming purposes, using a single mass to resolve gross floor areas is often sufficient.

Additional Exercises

- After you've created your mass and mass floors, use the Floor By Face tool to assign real floors to the mass floors.
- Modify the mass and remake the geometric floors that you created in the previous item.
- Experiment with walls and curtain walls by using the Pick Face tool to assign walls to the face of the mass.
- Modify the mass and remake the walls and curtain walls created in the previous item.
- Explain what you would do if you wanted to control floors and walls with a mass but the floors and the walls didn't always align. For example, what would you do if the floors were set back or deviated from the face of the mass?

CHAPTER 3

Walls and Curtain Walls

Walls in the Autodesk® Revit® Architecture software can range a great deal in complexity. Early in the design process, walls and curtain walls can be more generic, essentially serving as vertical containers for space and function. They can also be associated to masses in order to create incredibly complex shapes. As the design progresses, these generic walls and curtain walls can be swapped out for more specific vertically compound walls that indicate a range of materials as well as geometric sweeps and reveals.

In this chapter, you learn the following skills:

- **Understanding wall types and parameters**
- **Creating generic walls**
- **Creating numerous wall configurations**
- **Modifying walls**
- **Creating curtain walls**
- **Modifying curtain walls**
- **Going beyond the basics**

Understanding Wall Types and Parameters

There are three fundamental types of walls in Revit Architecture: basic, stacked, and curtain walls. In this section, we will take a quick look at some of the important aspects of each. These are not intended to be exhaustive guides to creating and editing each wall system but rather an overview to provide some background knowledge before continuing with the exercises throughout this chapter.

Basic Walls

Many basic walls have no detailed structure. They will be monolithic—and usually named with the prefix "Generic." In other cases, they have highly detailed structures known as *layers*. Each layer is assigned a thickness, material, and function. The function of a wall layer determines how it will join when multiple wall types intersect or when a wall intersects another element such as a floor.

From the Architecture tab in the ribbon, click the Wall tool. In the Type Selector at the top of the Properties palette, select the Generic – 8″ (140 mm) Masonry wall type, and then click Edit Type just below the Type Selector. Click the Preview button at lower left in the Type Properties dialog to see a graphic sample of the wall type. In Figure 3.1, the structural region of this wall is defined by a diagonal crosshatch pattern. This is a basic wall with only one pattern defining the wall's material.

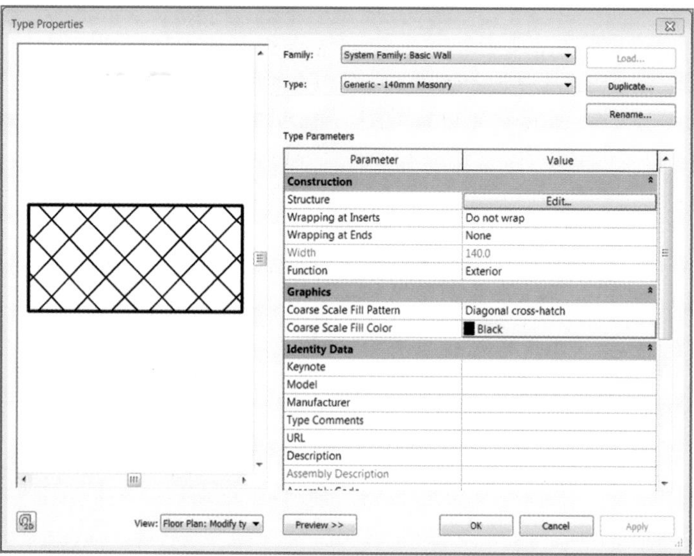

FIGURE 3.1 Masonry structural region of a basic wall

As we previously mentioned, basic walls may contain far more structural detail. With the Type Properties dialog still open, go to the Type drop-down and select the wall type Exterior - Brick on Mtl. Stud, and you'll see the difference (Figure 3.2).

Click the Edit button in the Structure parameter, and notice the numerous values that control the function, material, and thickness for this wall type. These values help you coordinate your project information across views and schedules. If the wall type you select is correct anywhere, it's correct *everywhere*!

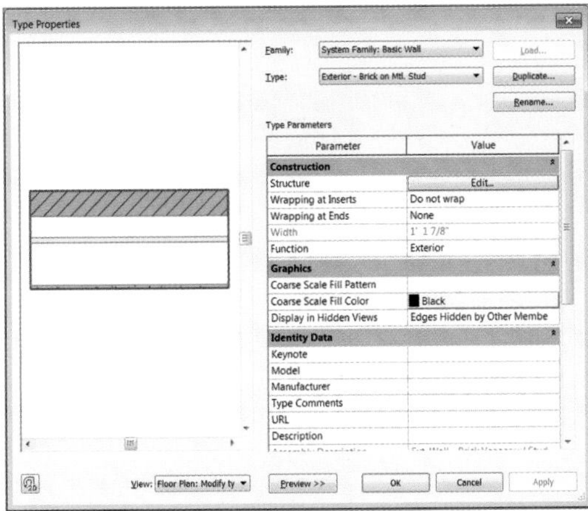

FIGURE 3.2 Compound walls consist of several layers of functional materials.

Basic walls can even have profiles applied to them that are used to add or remove geometry in your walls. If you're still examining the structure of the previous wall, click the Cancel button and select the wall type Exterior - Brick and CMU on MTL. Stud. In the Preview pane, switch the view to Section. If you zoom into the top of the wall sample shown in the preview, you'll see a parapet cap at the top of the wall (Figure 3.3). This is a profile associated to the basic wall type. Although you can manually add profiles to walls in your project on a case-by-case basis, we think you'll find that adding them to the wall definition makes creating and updating wall types easy and quick.

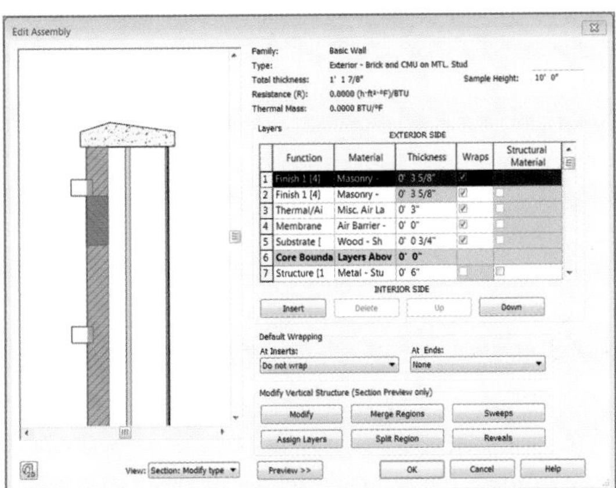

FIGURE 3.3 Wall sweep as part of a wall

Stacked Walls

Stacked walls consist of basic wall types, but combined vertically in a single defined type. Any basic walls can be used to create a stacked wall.

To find the stacked wall types, start the Wall tool, access the Type Selector, and go to the bottom of the list. Select the wall type Exterior - Brick Over CMU w Metal Stud, and click the Edit Type button. As shown in Figure 3.4, this wall type is defined by three different basic walls, but you can add more if necessary. Note that you can't combine stacked walls or add curtain walls to your stacked wall.

One of the stacked-wall segments must be of variable height to accommodate the vertical constraints of the wall instances you place in a project. If all the segments were a fixed height, it would conflict with varying datum geometry in your project. In addition to specifying the height of the segments, you can also adjust the horizontal offset or set a segment to flip its orientation (inside or outside).

Curtain Wall Types

Curtain walls are more complex than basic walls or stacked walls. They consist of a simple wall-segment definition, curtain grids, panels, and mullions. Curtain wall types can be manually constructed, or they can have complete definitions that specify the grid spacing, panels, and mullion types for interior and border conditions (Figure 3.5).

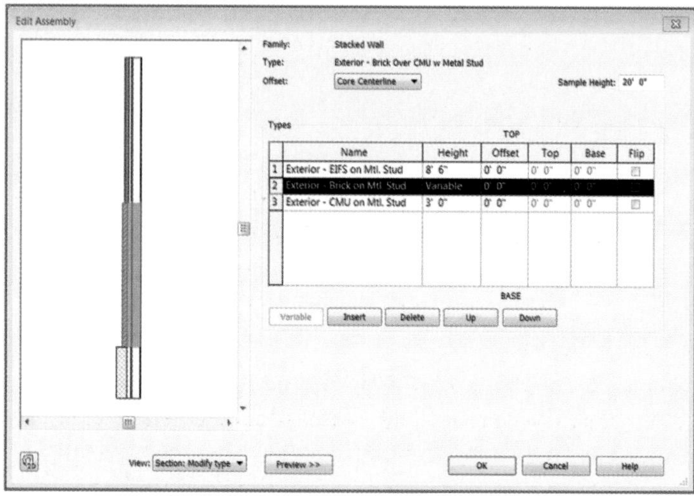

FIGURE 3.4 Type properties of a stacked wall

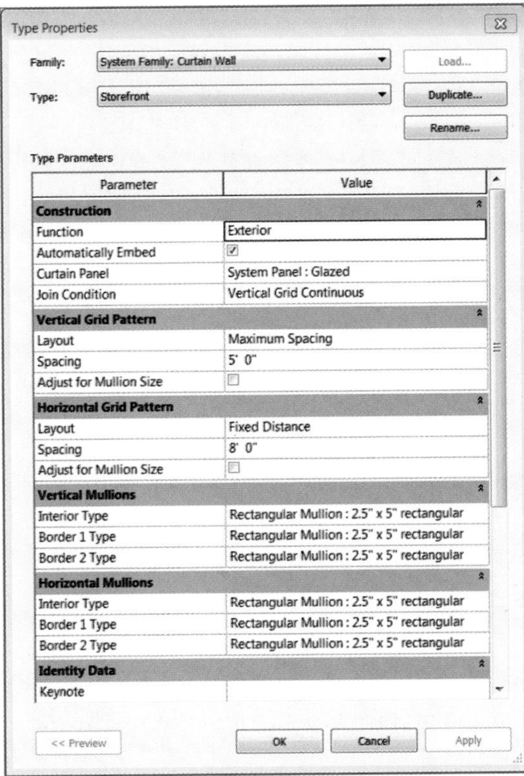

FIGURE 3.5 Curtain wall type definitions

Creating Generic Walls

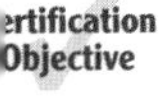

In this section, you will learn how basic walls generally work and how you should modify them. A challenge you may face during the design process is balancing specific model content while you are establishing the basic intent of your designs. Using a program like Revit Architecture can lead to unnecessary confusion if you don't manage this balance carefully.

Revit Architecture uses a system of *generic* walls that in most cases do not consist of specific materials. They are simply meant to illustrate an approximate thickness for the proposed construction type. We recommend using these generic walls during the design process and then swapping them out for more specific geometry later.

By default, the generic walls that have no specific structure are visually identical to walls that contain more detailed structure and finish layers. So, it's a great idea to make your design walls visually unique. This way, you'll know what has to be swapped out for more specificity later. Other techniques, such as giving your walls transparency, will help you quickly and easily visualize your design.

To begin the exercises in this chapter, download the file `c03-Start.rvt` or `c03-Start-Metric.rvt` from the book's companion web page: `www.sybex.com/go/revitessentials2013`.

Let's start by giving your generic walls a material assignment that can be used to distinguish them from more specific wall types:

1. Open the file `c03-Start.rvt`, (`c03-Start-Metric.rvt`) and make sure the Sketching Walls floor plan is activated. Go to the Architecture tab on the ribbon, and select the Wall tool from the Build panel (Figure 3.6).

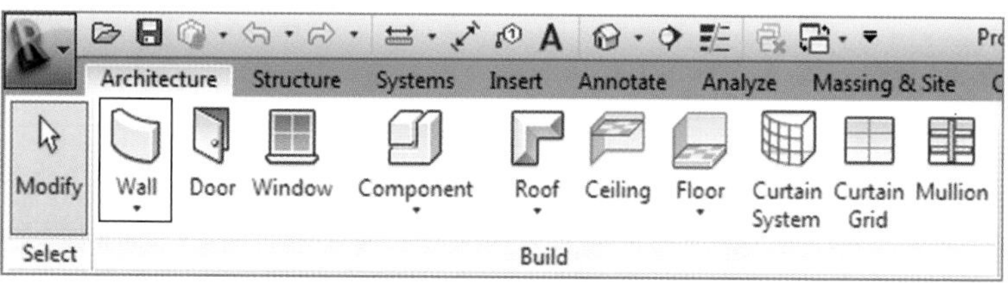

FIGURE 3.6 Choose the Wall tool from the Build panel.

2. Select Basic Wall: Generic – 6″ (Generic 200 mm) from the Type Selector in the Properties palette, and sketch a 20′-0″ (6 m) portion of wall from point 1 to point 2 in the exercise file. Don't worry about any of the other settings for the time being. When you're done, activate the Default 3D View from the Quick Access Toolbar (QAT).

   Select the wall, and look at the instance parameters in the Properties palette. As you can see, many values apply to this particular wall instance. You can change its height, its constraints, and many other values. For now, let's create a unique material to be assigned to the wall's type properties.

Remember that changing the type properties of a wall affects all segments of that wall type.

3. In the Properties palette, click the Edit Type button to open the Type Properties dialog box for the Generic 6″ (Generic 200 mm) wall type. To the right of the Structure label, click the Edit button, and the Edit Assembly dialog box will appear. In the Layers list, find the Material column, and click the ellipsis button in the field currently displaying <By Category>, as shown in Figure 3.7.

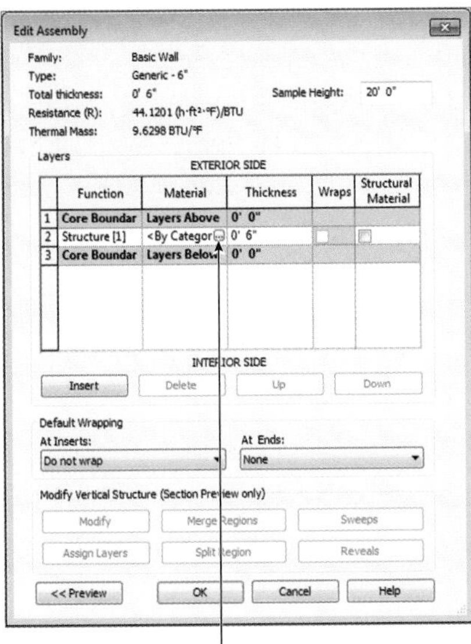

FIGURE 3.7 Select the Material field.

4. Rather than create a material from scratch, let's duplicate one and then modify it. From the In Document Materials list, scroll down to find the Default Wall material. Right-click it, and then select Duplicate, as shown in Figure 3.8. Find the duplicated material in the list named Default Wall (1), right-click it, and select Edit. The Material Editor dialog box opens. Change the name of the material to Generic Design Material.

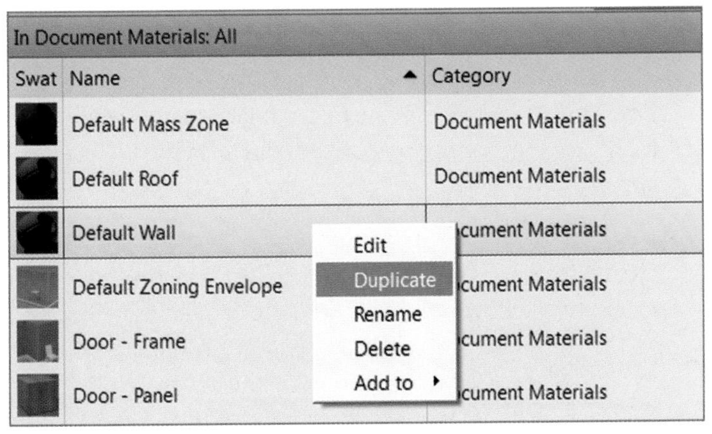

FIGURE 3.8 Duplicating the default wall material

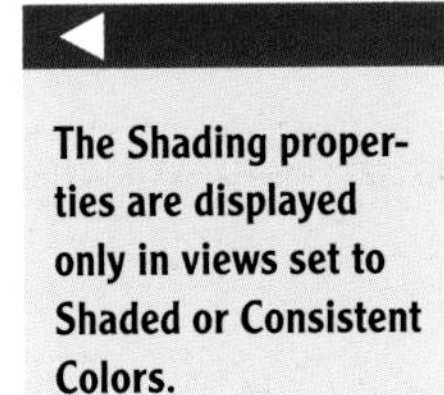

The Shading properties are displayed only in views set to Shaded or Consistent Colors.

Certification Objective

5. In the Properties list, find the Shading values, and click the color sample to open the Color dialog box. Set the Shading value as follows:
    - Red: 170
    - Green: 255
    - Blue: 170

The settings specified in the Appearance tab are displayed only in renderings and views set to Realistic mode.

6. In the Assets list, select the Appearance asset, and click the double-arrow button at the right end of the row (Figure 3.9) to open the Asset Browser.

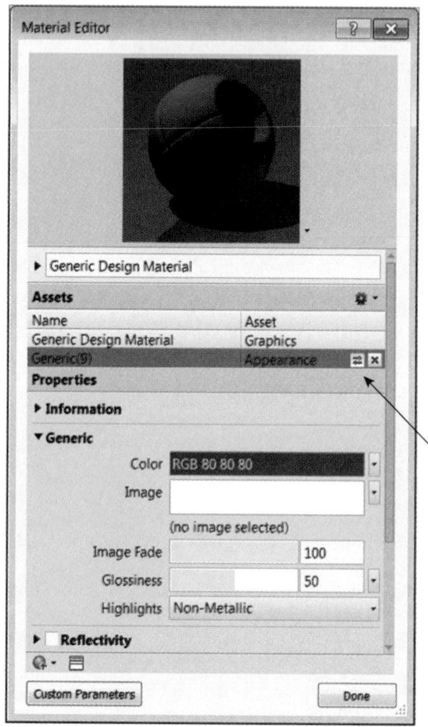

FIGURE 3.9 Editing the Appearance asset

7. In the Asset Browser dialog box, navigate to the Appearance Asset Library. Find the Wall Paint item, expand it, and find Matte. Click Matte, and then select Beige from the list of assets to the right. Click the double-arrow button as shown in Figure 3.10 to assign the Beige appearance asset to the Generic Design Material. This material will be useful for any design elements (floors, ceilings, roofs, and so on) that are used to resolve the design intent when you're not sure of the actual construction or finishes.

8. Close the Asset Browser window, and then click the Done button in the Material Editor dialog box. Click OK to close the Material Browser dialog box and again to close any remaining wall type property dialog boxes.

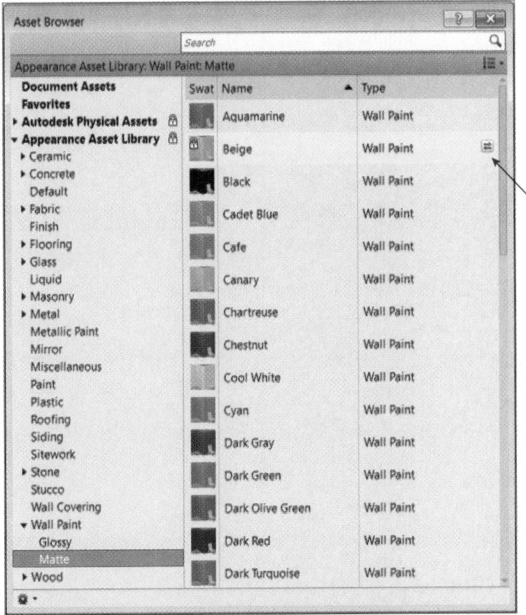

FIGURE 3.10 Assigning an appearance asset to a material

DESIGNING GENERIC ELEMENTS

Generic elements play an important role in your Revit Architecture workflow. When you're creating your design, it's not practical to use lines to represent ideas when you can use content. But if you select something that's too specific, you might become frustrated. A design that is too specific too early has the tendency to be "exactly wrong."

Generic elements and materials help convey the intent of your design with the added benefit of scheduling so that the data about a project can move in the right direction without distracting anyone. They'll help you emphasize "where" something is as well as some of "what" something is without getting into the detail of how it's supposed to be assembled—until the time is right. Most of the frustration in design comes from working specifically to generally, rather than the other way around. Design elements will help you avoid this trap.

> **Remember that you can find other graphic settings for the current view in the Properties palette by clicking the Edit button next to Graphic Display Options.**

The shading and rendering (appearance) values don't need to be the same. And in this case, it's really helpful if they're not. When you use a beige rendered material, you'll get a neutral, matte rendering. But using a light green shading value will help you quickly distinguish between design intent and more specific resolved elements in any working view.

To observe the changes you've made to the generic walls, open the default 3D view. From the View Control Bar at the bottom of the view, click the Visual Style icon (the cube), and set the view to Shaded. Now you can quickly and easily identify your generic design elements from more specific selections.

Creating Numerous Wall Configurations

Now let's return to the Level 1 Floor Plan view and start creating a number of wall configurations. Pick the Wall command, and notice in the ribbon under the Draw panel that a number of configurations are available for creating walls (Figure 3.11). You can see a variety of options for sketching wall segments as well as two icons with arrows that indicate options to pick line segments on which to place walls.

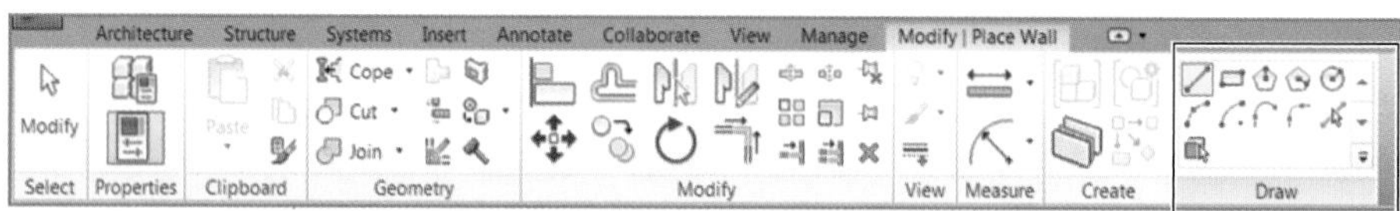

FIGURE 3.11 Geometric configurations for walls

Sketching Walls

You can sketch walls in various configurations by using the options in the Draw panel of the ribbon as shown in Figure 3.11. In the following steps, you will perform some free-form wall sketching exercises to become familiar with the Draw options:

1. Activate the floor plan named Sketching Walls.
2. Start the Wall tool, and practice creating segments of walls using each of the first six configurations in the Draw panel (from Line through Center-Ends Arc). Don't worry about where you create these walls; it's just practice.

3. Be aware of the settings available in the Options Bar when you create more complex configurations such as Inscribed Polygon and Circle. You can apply different settings to the geometry such as the number of polygon sides or the radius of a circle before sketching the wall segment.

Creating Elliptical Walls

Because the need for elliptical walls may occur in your designs, we'll address them now. There are two things you should know. First, elliptical walls can't be sketched using the Draw tools. Second (and more important), they can be created via other workarounds (such as creating an elliptical mass and then picking the face of the mass to create an elliptical wall).

So, what's a better way? Create elliptical wall layouts from a series of tangent arcs. Doing so will give you an approximation that is indistinguishable from an actual ellipse, and you'll be able to guide the walls' construction more accurately in the field.

In the following steps, you will use the Tangent End Arc and Fillet Arc configurations to append wall segments to existing wall elements:

1. Activate the floor plan named Tangent-Fillet Walls. Your goal is to complete the layout of the walls according to the dashed lines shown in the floor plan.
2. In the upper-right corner of the layout, the two perpendicular walls must be joined with a radius wall segment.
3. Select either one of the wall segments, right-click, and select Create Similar from the context menu.
4. From the Draw panel in the ribbon, select the Fillet Arc option.
5. Pick one wall segment and then the other perpendicular segment. After you pick the second wall segment, a curved segment appears.
6. Place the curved segment near the layout line. Before you continue, click the radial dimension value and change it to 6-0 (2000 mm).
7. The Wall command should still be active, so select the two perpendicular walls in the lower-right corner of the layout, and repeat steps 3 through 6.

Notice the difference in using the Fillet Arc option to either close the gap on two wall segments or trim back two walls that are already connected.

8. With the Wall command remaining active, return to the Draw panel in the ribbon, and select the Tangent Arc option.

9. Click the left end of the wall segment at the bottom of the layout, and then click the left end of the wall segment at the top to complete the tangent arc wall. Your results should look like the plan shown in Figure 3.12.

Picking Walls

You can also create walls by picking lines. This approach is helpful if you have a CAD file that needs to be converted to BIM or if a preliminary layout was created in another tool like SketchUp.

In this exercise, a preliminary layout has been drawn with Detail Lines in the sample project. You will use these lines to generate walls:

1. Activate the Picking Walls floor plan, and then start the Wall tool.

2. Choose the Pick Lines option from the Draw panel in the ribbon.

3. In the first set of lines in the sample file, pick each individual line segment to place walls.

4. On the second set of lines, use the chain-select method to place all the wall segments at once. Hover your mouse pointer over one of the line segments, and press the Tab key once. When the chain of lines is highlighted, click the mouse button to place the complete chain of walls. Your results should look like the plan shown in Figure 3.13.

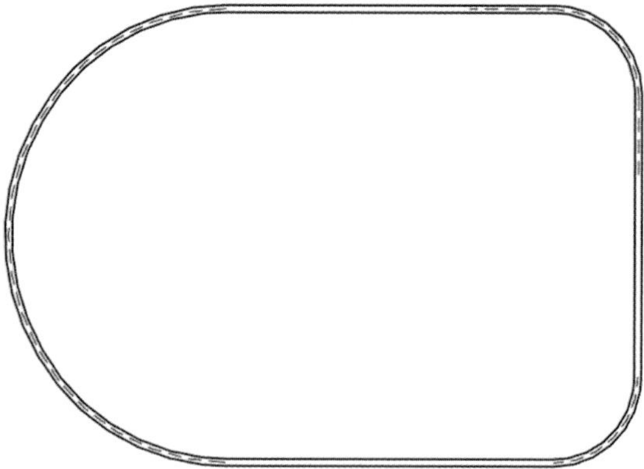

FIGURE 3.12 Results of the Tangent-Fillet Walls exercise

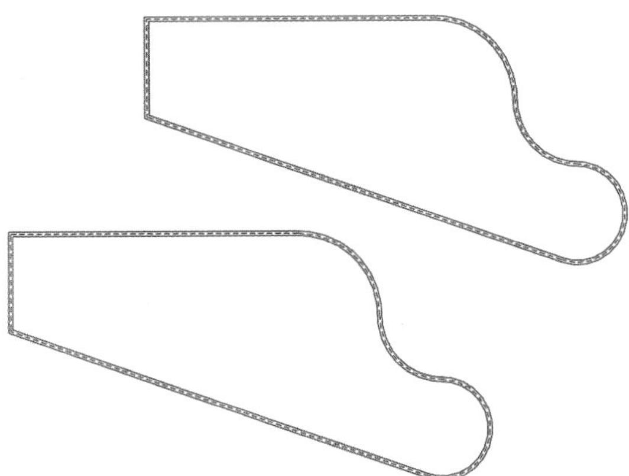

FIGURE 3.13 Results of the Picking Walls exercise

Hosting Elements in Walls

Walls can host other types of elements that are meant to create openings. As long as the walls exist, the elements they are hosting exist as well. Doors and windows are examples of commonly used hosted elements.

Placing a door in a wall is very easy and can be done in plan, elevation, or 3D view. In this exercise, you'll place doors from the Level 1 view. You'll use the very first wall that you created at the beginning of this chapter. From the Architecture tab, select the Door tool from the Build panel.

You may notice that you can only place doors in walls. This is because door families are hosted elements and cannot exist without a host. Because of this relationship, hosted elements are automatically deleted if you delete a host element such as a wall. As you are placing doors in walls, you're shown temporary dimensions that will help you place the door closer to its correct location. Follow these steps:

1. Activate the Sketching Walls floor plan, and place two doors as shown in Figure 3.14.

Remember that you can disable the Tag On Placement setting in the Modify | Place Door contextual tab in the ribbon.

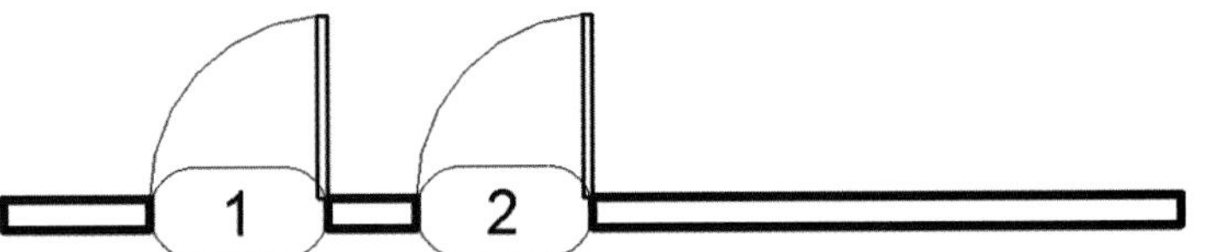

FIGURE 3.14 Hosting doors in a wall

2. Select the Window tool from the Build panel in the Architecture tab. Hover over the same wall, and place a window as shown in Figure 3.15. As with any hosted element, you can place it only within a host.

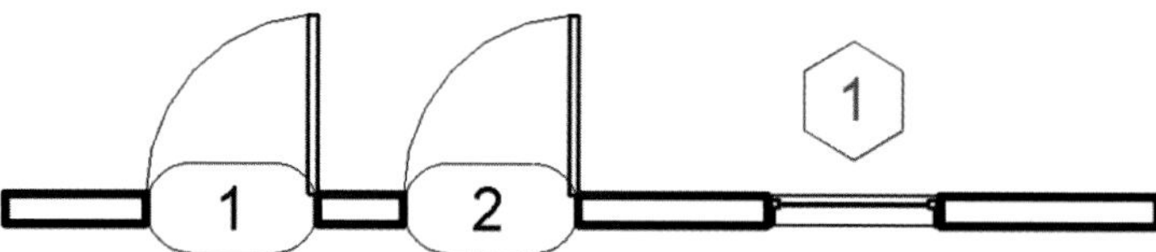

FIGURE 3.15 Hosted window

Modifying Walls

Now that you've created a few wall configurations, it's important to understand how you can modify them. Sometimes this is done simply by selecting the wall and dragging a wall end or a shape handle to a new position. In other cases, you want to be more exact and assign a specific value.

Your approach depends on where you are in the design process. Just remember that you can update design decisions, and all your views, schedules, tagging, and so forth will update—don't get concerned with being too exact early in your design. Let's work through a quick exercise for modifying walls:

1. Create a new project using the default project template. Sketch a straight segment of a wall, but this time as you draw the wall, type **40** (or **12 m**). Depending on the default units, typing **40** creates a 40′ segment.

   Notice that you didn't have to indicate the units as feet. If you wanted to indicate inches, you'd only have to put a space between the first and second values. Thus, 40′-6″ can easily be entered as **40**(space)**6**.

2. Press the Esc key twice or click the Modify button in the ribbon. Select the segment of wall you just created.

3. There are two options to modify the length, as shown in (Figure 3.16). You can type in a new value by selecting the temporary dimension, or you can simply drag either wall end to a new location.

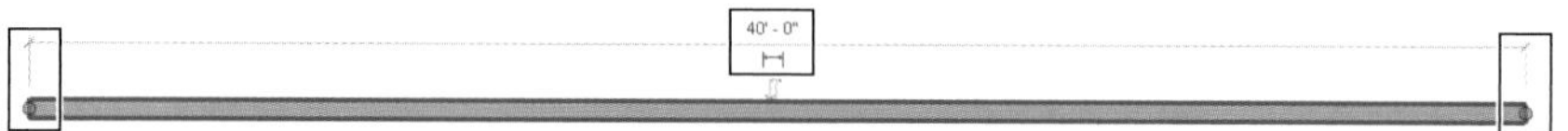

FIGURE 3.16 Modifying the wall length

4. Go to the default 3D view, and look at some other options. The highlighted areas of Figure 3.17 are called *shape handles*. You can click and drag them to adjust the top and bottom locations of a wall. As you drag the shape handle, the new location is shown, whereas the existing location is "ghosted" until you release the shape handle.

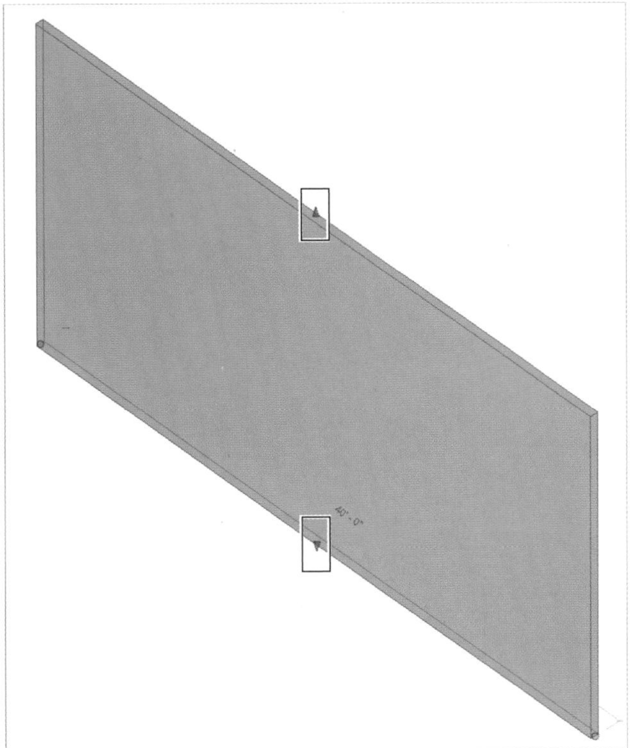

FIGURE 3.17 Wall shape handles

Instance Parameters

In many cases, you'll want to enter more exact values or have more specific control over a particular wall instance. You can do this by adjusting the instance parameters in the Properties palette (Figure 3.18). Select the wall, and look at the properties:

Location Line The location line is the origin of the wall. If you swap one wall for another, the location line will be maintained. In other words, if you create an exterior wall and the location line is the inside face, then when you change the properties or select a thicker wall, it will grow to the outside—away from the location line.

Base Constraint The base constraint is the bottom of the wall. Be careful! Deleting a datum (in this case, Level 1) to which an object is constrained also deletes what is associated to the constraint!

Base Offset / Top Offset The Base or Top Offset is the value above or below the respective constraint. If you wanted the bottom of a wall associated to Level 1 but 3′-0″ (1 m) below, the value for Base Offset would be -3′-0″.

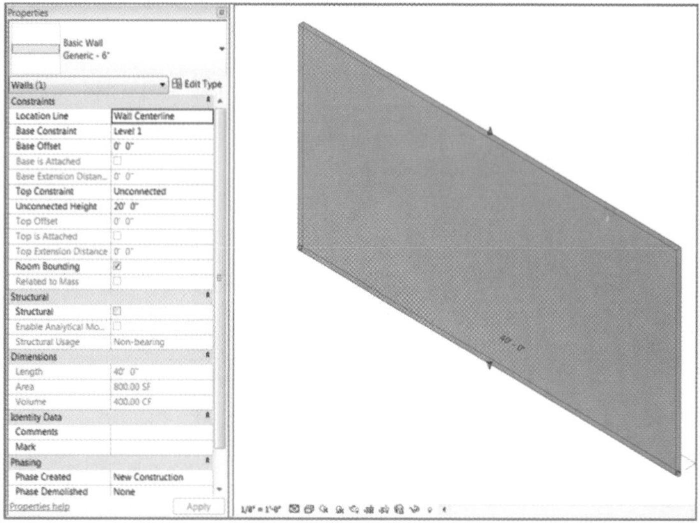

FIGURE 3.18 Instance parameters displayed in the Properties palette

Base Is Attached / Top Is Attached The Base or Top Is Attached value indicates whether the bottom or top of a wall is attached to another wall, floor, or roof.

Top Constraint / Unconnected Height Top Constraint is the method by which you determine the height of a wall instance. The Unconnected Height value is the height of the wall when you do not use a specific datum for Top Constraint. If you try to change the Top Constraint value to Up To Level: Level 2, the Unconnected Height parameter becomes inactive.

Room Bounding The last value you should be aware of is the Room Bounding option. Walls often are meant to contain space and remain space aware; however, if you have a situation where you don't want walls to define a space, you can deselect this option, and the Room object will ignore the wall.

Editing Profiles

Of course, not all walls are rectilinear in elevation. For these situations, you can edit the profile of a wall. Note that you'll only be able to edit the profile of a straight wall, not a curved wall.

When you edit a wall's profile, the wall is temporarily converted to an outline sketch in elevation. Because the sketch is not plan-based, you can edit a profile only in a section, an elevation, or an orthogonal 3D view. You can draw as many closed-loop sketches as you like within the wall's profile, but each loop must be closed.

Follow these steps:

1. Continuing with the wall you created in the previous exercise, select the 40´ (12 m) wall, and click Edit Profile from the Modify | Walls tab.
2. From the South Elevation view, create the sketch as shown in the top illustration in Figure 3.17. (Don't worry about following the exact dimensions in this illustration—we're just showing them for reference.) Delete the top line, and trim the two side sketch lines. Note that the reference lines indicating the extents of the original wall remain, as shown in the bottom illustration in Figure 3.19.

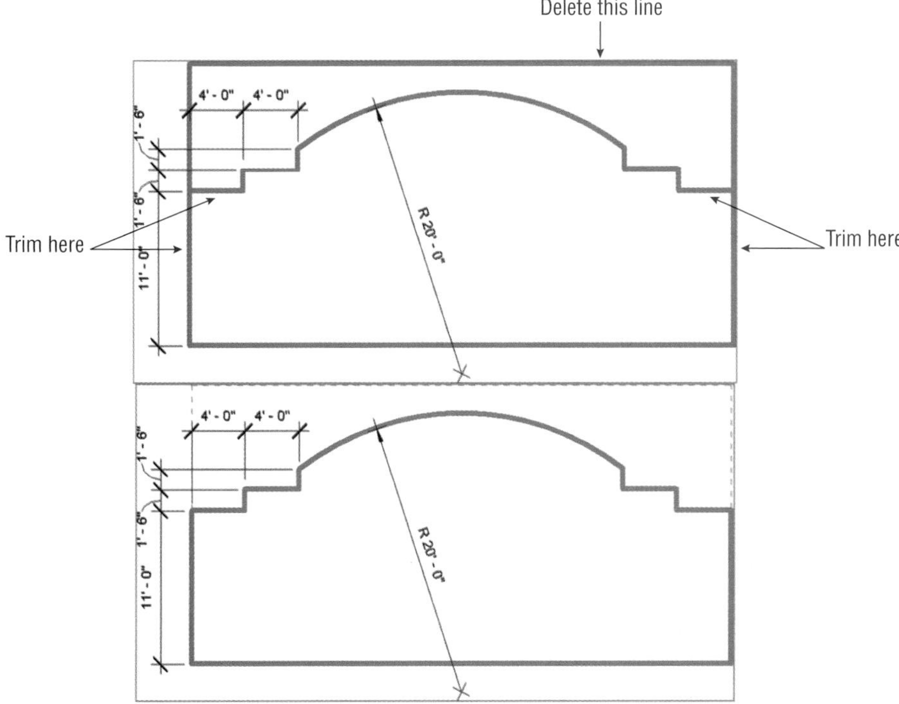

FIGURE 3.19 Adding new sketch lines

Use the Trim tools as necessary to clean up the sketch so that it remains as one closed loop. If you have crossing lines or open segments, you will receive an error when you attempt to finish the sketch in the next step.

3. When you are done, click Finish Sketch Mode.

Attaching and Detaching the Top and Base

We've previously discussed the ability to use a project datum as the base constraint or top constraint of a wall, but walls can also be attached to the top or bottom of other objects—even other walls. Let's do this with a copy of the wall from the "Editing Profiles" exercise:

> **You can also use Windows clipboard commands to copy elements. Just remember to paste them to the new location.**

1. Select the wall, and then use the Copy tool in the ribbon to create a copy off to the side.
2. Select the copied wall, and click Edit Profile. Modify the exterior sketch as shown in Figure 3.20. Don't forget to trim and delete unnecessary sketch lines. Then finish the sketch.

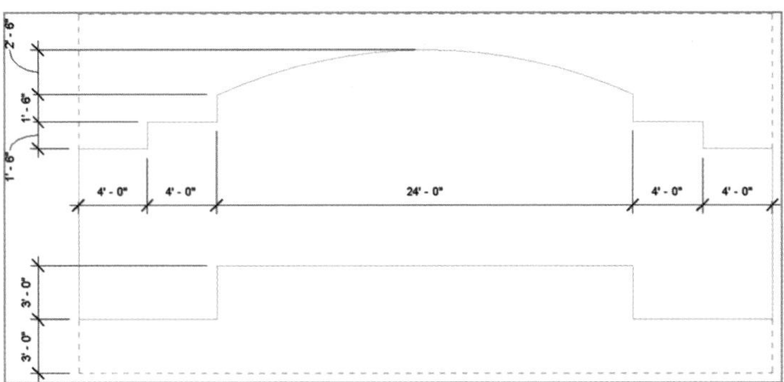

FIGURE 3.20 Edited wall profile

3. Return to your Level 1 floor plan, and sketch another wall right on top of the same location as the wall you just edited. In this case, use a Generic 12″ (300 mm) wall, and set the height in the Options Bar to 3-0 (1000 mm). The walls may overlap, but that's okay.
4. Open the default 3D view to complete this step. Select the thicker wall, and then click Attach Top/Base (Figure 3.21). Now select the wall with the profile that you just edited. (Note that this may be a little tricky because the thinner, edited wall is likely completely inside

the thicker wall.) This attaches the top of the thicker wall to the underside of the upper wall, as shown on the right side of the figure.

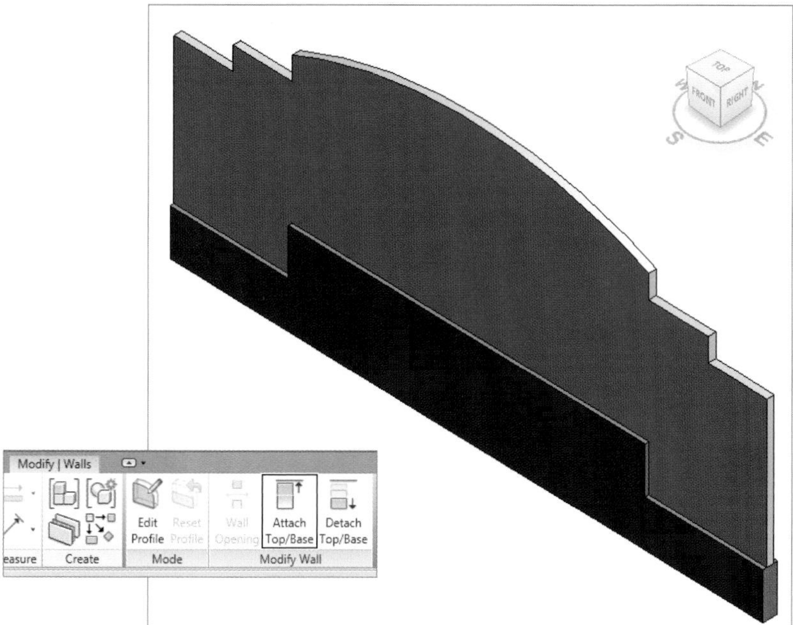

FIGURE 3.21 Attach Top/Base

The great thing about this technique is that relationships between the two walls are maintained if you edit the elevation profile of the upper wall. Performing these steps is a lot faster than having to edit the elevation profile of both walls! And remember, the most common use of this technique is to attach walls to sloped elements such as the underside of roofs.

Resetting Profiles

If you need to remove the edited condition of a wall, don't re-enter Edit Profile mode and manually remove the sketches. Select the wall, and click Reset Profile in the Mode panel on the Modify | Walls tab. Doing so will reset the extents of the wall and remove any interior sketches.

Cutting Openings

Openings can be cut in both straight and curved walls. The command tends to be used in curved walls because you already have the option to edit the elevation profile in straight walls. And when you cut an opening, you cannot sketch beyond the extents of the wall boundary or create shapes that are not rectilinear. Here are the steps to create a rectilinear opening in a curved wall:

1. Create a curved wall segment, and then go to your default 3D view and select the wall.
2. The Wall Opening option appears on the Modify | Walls tab, as shown in Figure 3.20 on the left. Select this command, and then hover over the wall; you are prompted to create a rectilinear opening, as shown on Figure 3.22 on the right.

   To delete an opening, hover over the opening, select it, and then press the Delete key.

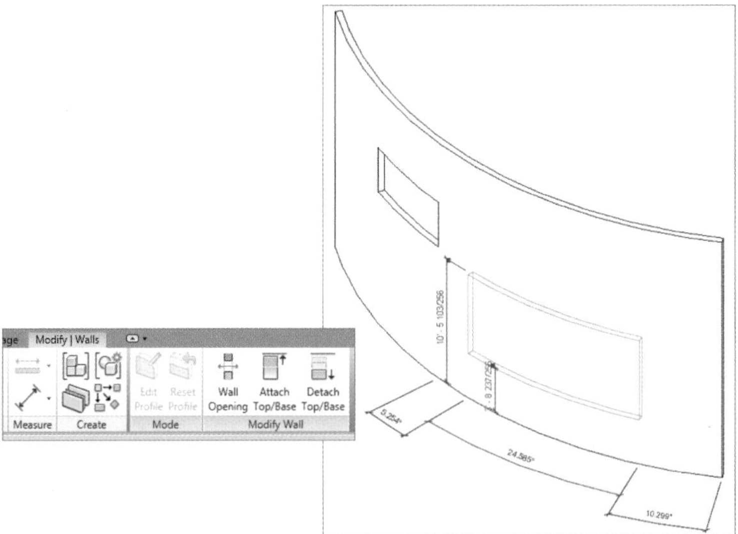

FIGURE 3.22 Creating wall openings

Splitting Walls

Sometimes, after you've created walls, you realize that you don't need an inner segment—or you need to change a segment to another wall type. The process of deleting and re-creating walls would be tedious work; however, Revit Architecture offers a Split tool that allows you to divide walls, effectively breaking them into smaller pieces. This can be done along both horizontal and vertical edges of either curved or straight walls.

Let's experiment with this technique by creating a plan configuration of walls, as shown in Figure 3.23. The dimensions are shown for reference.

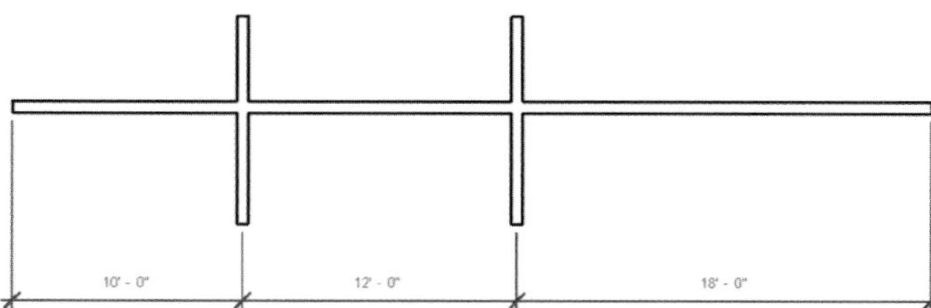

FIGURE 3.23 Configuration of walls

In this case the section of wall between the two parallel walls is not needed. But rather than delete the wall and create three new walls, let's split the wall twice and delete the inner wall:

1. Select the Split Element command from the Modify tab.
2. Hover over the location of the wall that you intend to split. You are prompted with a reference line that helps indicate which wall you're splitting. Split the wall twice, once at each intersection.
3. Delete the inner segment. Your wall layout now resembles Figure 3.24.

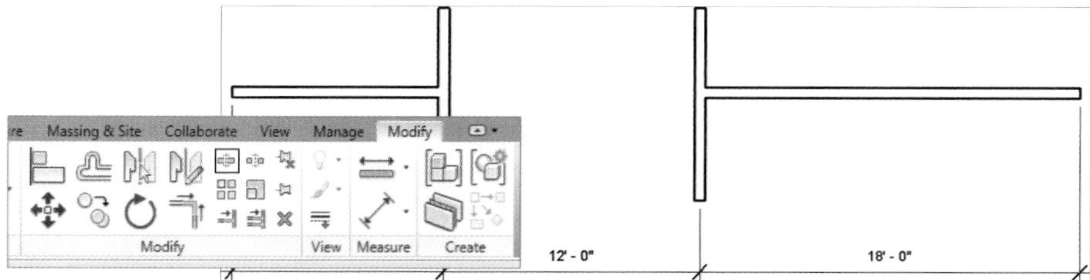

FIGURE 3.24 Using the Split Element command

Swapping Walls

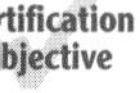

Swapping walls for different types prevents the rework of deleting them and creating new ones. Doing so is as easy as selecting a wall and then selecting the new type from the Properties palette:

1. Use the wall from the section "Attaching and Detaching the Top and Base." Select the lower wall, and then go to the Type Selector at the top of the Properties palette.
2. Change the lower wall to Generic – 12″ (300 mm) Masonry. Once you select the new wall type, the result resembles the wall in Figure 3.25.

Note that the patterns of the individual CMU courses are shown on the wall's surface in accordance with the new wall type's material properties.

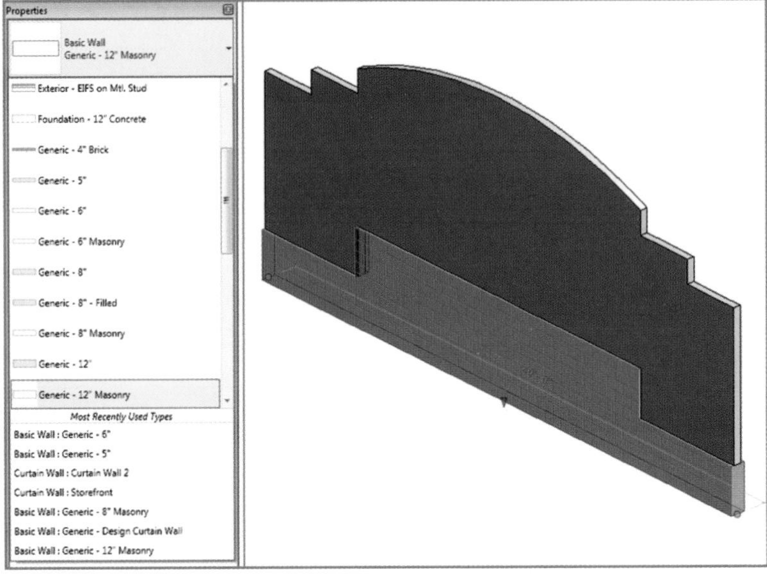

FIGURE 3.25 Selecting a new wall type

Creating Curtain Walls

Certification Objective

Curtain walls are created in much the same way as regular walls: by selecting the type of curtain wall and then sketching the desired shape. Despite this similarity, the available parameters for curtain walls are rather different. In this section you will create a curtain wall using manual techniques for adding curtain grids and mullions to give the wall a more detailed definition. You can continue to use the project file created for the "Modifying Walls" exercise, or you can create a new project using the default template.

Begin the exercise by creating a 40´-0˝ (12 m) segment, using Curtain Wall 1 as the wall type from the Type Selector. Most of the following exercise steps are easier to accomplish in the default 3D view: activate it from the QAT or by double-clicking the 3D view named {3D} in the Project Browser. You'll continue in the following sections.

Curtain Grids

Before adding mullions, you need to add curtain grids to the wall. These grids will subdivide the wall into smaller panels and allow mullions to be added. Follow these steps:

1. Select the Curtain Grid tool from the Build panel in the Architecture tab of the ribbon.
2. As you hover over the edge of the curtain panel, you are prompted with a dashed line that indicates the grid location. Also notice that the grid location becomes somewhat "sticky" at the midpoint and at one-third lengths along the edge.
3. Place two evenly spaced curtain grids along the horizontal and vertical edges. When you're finished, the curtain panel looks like Figure 3.26.

Adding Mullions

Now that you've added curtain grids, you can add mullions to the curtain panel:

1. Select the Mullion tool from the Build panel. You're given three different options to place the mullions: continuously along a grid line, on a segment of a grid line, or on all empty grids including the boundary. Select the third option (Figure 3.27).

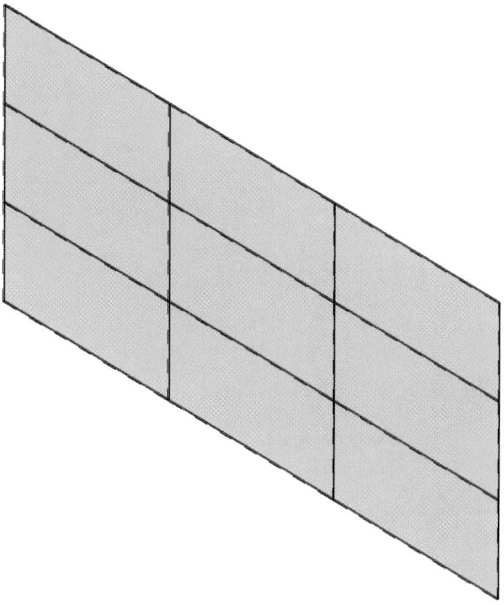

FIGURE 3.26 Completed curtain grids

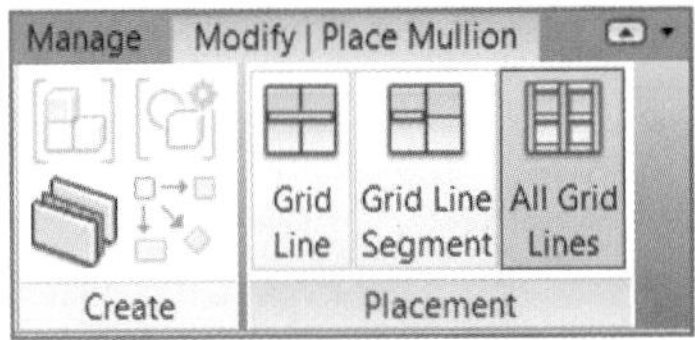

FIGURE 3.27 Selecting the Mullion tool's All Grid Lines option

The default mullion is fine for this exercise, but note that there are several mullions in the default template. You can even create mullions with user-defined profiles.

2. Hover over the curtain wall, and left-click. The mullion is assigned to all empty grids.

3. To modify any element in the curtain-wall segment, hover over the location and press and release the Tab key (don't just hold down the Tab key). Doing so sequentially selects the mullion, the grid line, the nearest panel, or the entire curtain wall.

4. Selecting the grid line and temporary dimensions allows you to enter exact values (or even click and drag to move the grid), as shown in Figure 3.28.

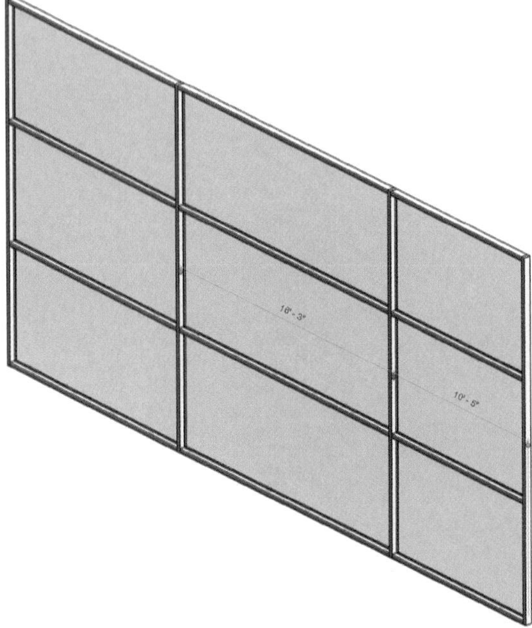

FIGURE 3.28 Moving the grid line

Curved Curtain Panels

Curved curtain-wall segments that you create will appear flat until you add the vertical grid lines. But specifying exact grid locations during the design process is often tedious—and difficult to correct. To help, you can create a design panel from a specially created wall that is very thin and transparent. Use this wall to figure out the design, and then swap it out for a curtain wall later. The wall can even have a pattern file associated to it that visually helps it to read as a curtain panel. You can find an example of this type of wall in `c03-Curtain Walls.rvt`, which is available with this chapter's exercise files.

Embedding Curtain Walls

Curtain walls can also be embedded in walls. Follow these steps:

1. Create a 40´-0˝ segment (12 m) of a generic wall.
2. Using the Storefront curtain-wall type, sketch a 30´-0˝ (9 m) segment directly in line with the generic wall segment (Figure 3.29). Note that this curtain wall type has grid spacing and mullions defined in the type properties.

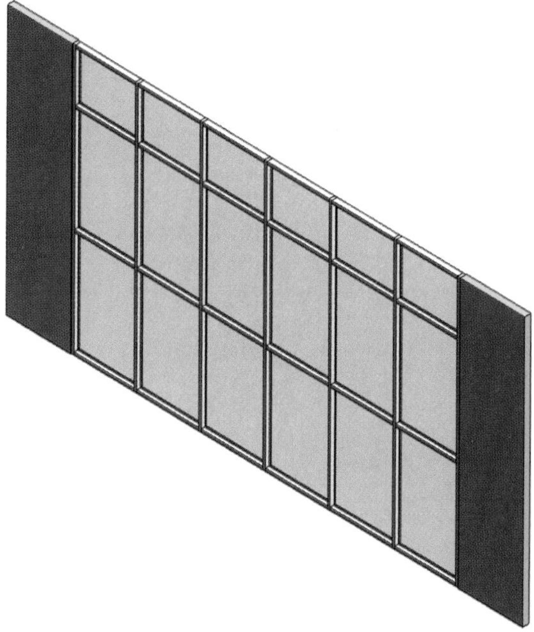

FIGURE 3.29 Embedding curtain walls

As you can see, the curtain wall automatically embeds itself in the generic wall. This behavior is controlled by a parameter (Automatically Embed) in the curtain wall's type properties.

Modifying Curtain Walls

It's very seldom that your design ends up exactly where you started. So, let's experiment with modifying the embedded curtain wall. This is a very important step not only in grasping how certain functionality works in but also in understanding the flexibility in your workflow and how Revit Architecture will accommodate it.

Editing the Elevation Profile

In this exercise, you will continue to use the project file you started in the "Creating Curtain Walls" exercise. The commands and tools you will use are similar to those you learned in the "Editing Profiles" exercise. Complete the following steps to modify the elevation profile of a curtain wall—even one embedded in another wall:

1. Select the entire embedded curtain-wall segment by hovering over the outer edge of the curtain panel and selecting it. Make sure you have the whole curtain wall segment selected and not just a panel, mullion, or grid segment.
2. In the ribbon, click Edit Profile, and modify the sketch of the curtain wall as shown in Figure 3.30. Remember, you need to switch to an elevation or 3D view to edit the sketch of a wall.

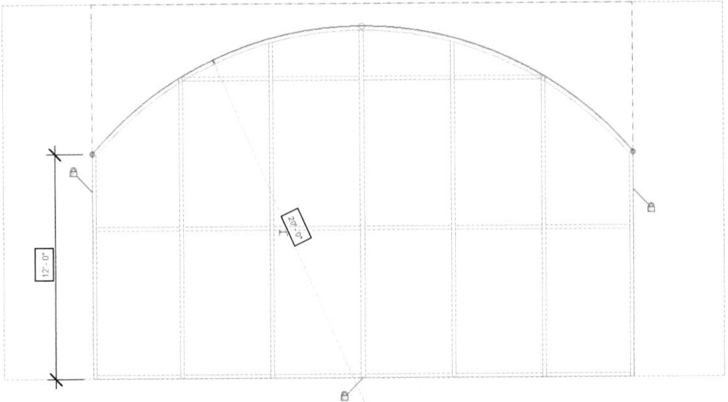

FIGURE 3.30 Modifying the sketch lines

3. Trim the side sketch lines and delete the top sketch line before finishing the sketch. Then click OK.

4. When you attempt to finish the sketch, Revit Architecture warns you that some of the mullions in the original system can't be maintained. This is fine, because some of the mullions are outside the sketch area. Click Delete Elements to continue.

The outer generic wall has already been healed to match the new boundary condition.

Adding and Modifying Grids and Mullions

Certification Objective

Continuing the "Modifying Curtain Walls" exercises, you will now add some additional grids that are not part of this defined system:

1. From the Architecture tab in the ribbon, select the Curtain Grid tool. Hover over the curtain-wall segment, as shown in Figure 3.31.

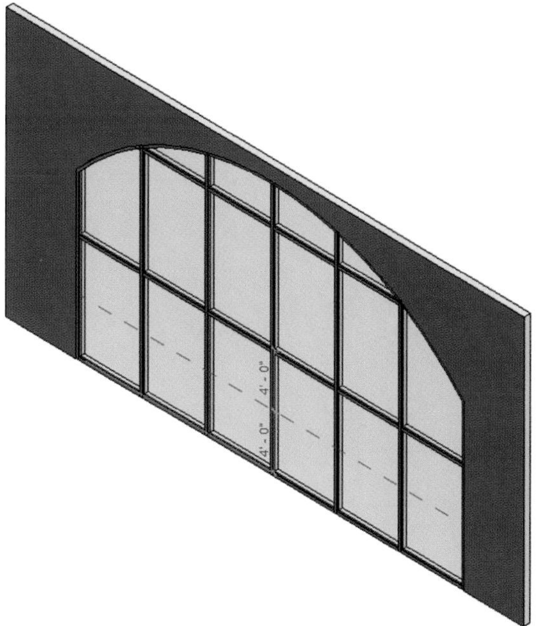

FIGURE 3.31 Adding a new grid and mullion

2. When the grid line is evenly spaced between the first and second horizontal mullions, place the new grid line. Because this curtain wall type already has a defined mullion type, the mullions are automatically added when you place the grid line.

Unpinning and Toggling Mullions

When a curtain-wall type contains defined spacing and mullions, you can still modify an individual segment of curtain wall to meet the needs of your design. As you continue this exercise, you will need to *unpin* some the elements before you can modify them. The *unpinning* action means you are removing a system constraint so that an element can be customized.

In the following steps, you will remove two mullion segments and swap two of the curtain panels for door panels:

1. Zoom into the curtain-wall segment, and hover over one of the mullions you created in the previous exercise. You may need to press the Tab key momentarily to cycle through the choice of elements at the mouse pointer. When it highlights, select the mullion.
2. Notice the pin icon just above the mullion in Figure 3.32. Click the pin icon to unpin the mullion.

FIGURE 3.32 Unpinning the mullion

3. Repeat step 2 for the mullion directly below the one you just deleted (at the base of the wall). This clears the way for you to place the curtain-wall door.

Modifying Curtain-Grid Segments

Before you swap out the glazing panel for a door, you need to "weld" these two panels into a single panel. To do this, one segment of the curtain grid must be removed. Follow these steps:

1. Click the Modify button in the ribbon, hover the mouse pointer over the curtain grid that is bisecting the two panels, and select the line shown in Figure 3.33.

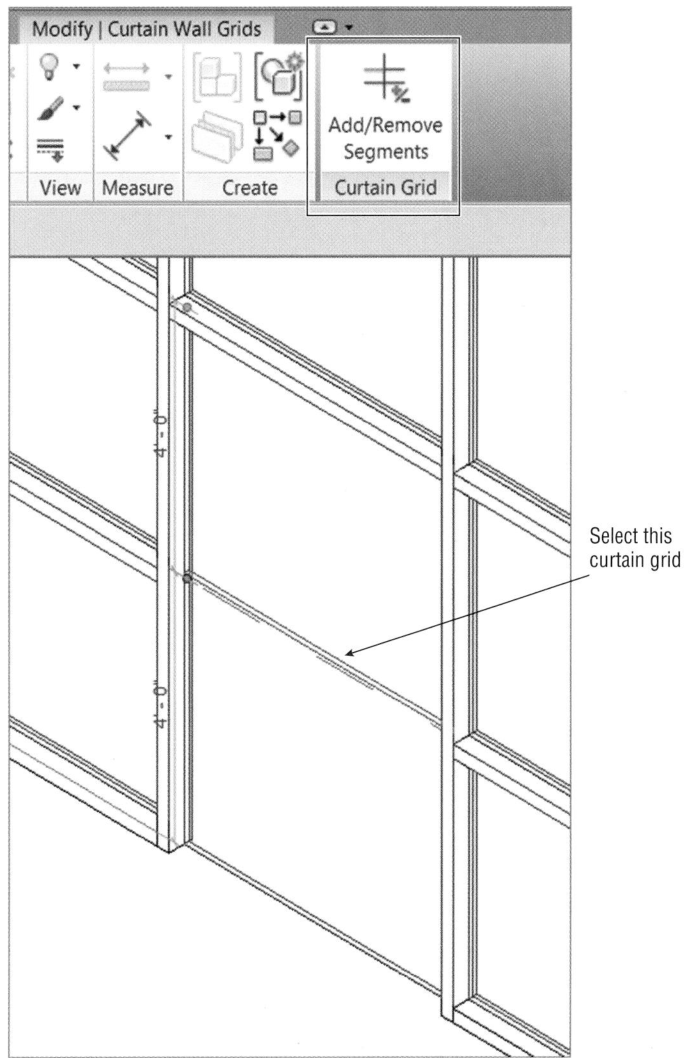

FIGURE 3.33 Preparing to use Add/Remove Segments

2. In the ribbon, click Add/Remove Segments, and then select the grid line that separates the two curtain panels. Now you have a single panel rather than two panels, because the two panels have been welded together.

After you remove the curtain-grid segment that was splitting the panel in two, notice that the curtain grid looks like it is still there. The curtain grid is expressed across the entire length of a curtain-wall segment, but you can add or remove segments of the grid to customize your design. To add a segment back to an existing grid line, do *not* use the Curtain Grid tool. Instead, use the Add/Remove Segments tool, and follow the same steps you learned in this exercise.

Modifying Curtain Panels

In the final exercise of this section, you will place a door in the curtain wall. This process is different than placing a door in a basic wall because the curtain-wall door must be built and placed as a curtain panel. You will change one of the defined panels in the curtain wall segment into a door, but you won't use the Door tool.

Note that you can only place curtain-wall doors in curtain walls. Any other type of door won't work.

Before you swap out the glazed panel for curtain-wall doors, you need to load the appropriate family into the project. There's little point in getting ready to exchange the panel if you don't have the new panel ready to go:

1. From the Insert tab, select the Load Family option on the Load From Library palette. From the `Doors` folder, select the Curtain Wall Dbl Glass family. The family is now loaded into your project and you can exchange it for the default curtain panel.
2. Select the panel that you want to replace. Right away, you can see that the panel is pinned because it's being defined by the type properties for the curtain-wall system—just like the mullions. As you'll recall, pinned elements can't be exchanged until they're unpinned. The same holds true for this panel.
3. Select the panel, and click the pin icon. Now you can select a new panel type from the Type Selector palette. Choose Curtain Wall Dbl Glass, and the panel appears in the wall segment as shown in Figure 3.34.

The curtain-wall doors panel automatically expands to fill the space of the entire panel that preceded it. These are special doors that are really a curtain panel category. If you want a real door, you can swap out the curtain panel for a wall (even a wall made only of glass) and then place the door in the wall.

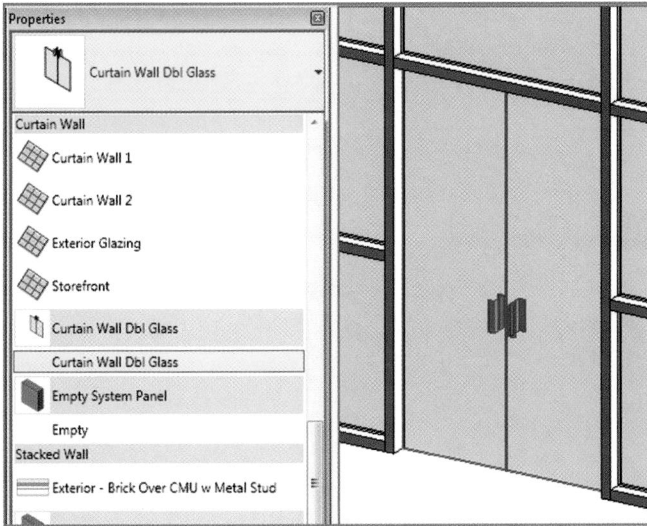

FIGURE 3.34 Exchanging the panel for a door

Going Beyond the Basics

Walls and curtain walls can be far more complex than the examples you've created in this chapter. If you want to examine all the types, go to the Chapter 3 folder at this book's web page at `www.sybex.com/go/revit2013essentials` and download `c03-Walls-and-Curtain-Walls.rvt`.

First, there's the option to create walls by picking a face (Figure 3.33). Essentially, you create a mass and then assign walls to the face of the mass. If the mass is modified, you can reassign walls to the modified faces. As you can see in Figure 3.35, the results can be complex.

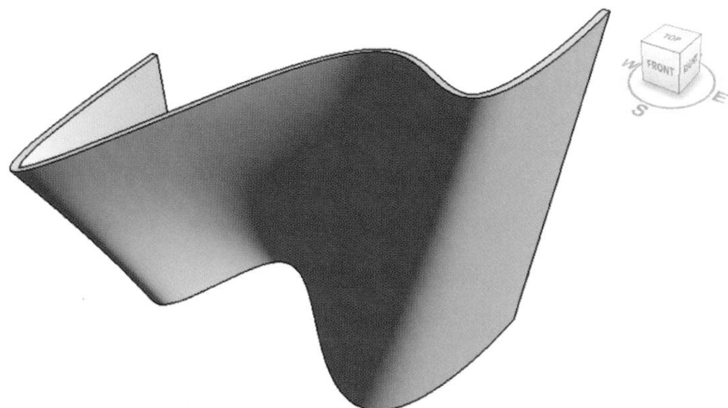

FIGURE 3.35 Walls created by picking a face

Not only can you create walls in this manner, but you can also create complex curtain systems. These mass-based curtain types can contain *very* complex panel configurations. In some cases, the results may not even resemble a typical glazed system (Figure 3.36).

FIGURE 3.36 Curtain panel system

Once again, the important thing is to understand the basics. Resolve your design intent. Don't get hung up on modeling when you can sketch. Get feedback from someone who's a Revit Architecture expert and is willing to share.

THE ESSENTIALS AND BEYOND

Creating complex wall conditions is possible but takes time and patience. In more complex conditions, walls can also be embedded into other walls. But for an essential understanding of Revit Architecture, this is a great start; you've created walls of many types, added hosted elements—and even edited their profiles.

Additional Exercises

Create the following curtain wall condition. Note that the mullions are angled. You'll need to modify the Type, Instance, and Grid Layout properties to come up with the most flexible solution.

(Continues)

THE ESSENTIALS AND BEYOND *(Continued)*

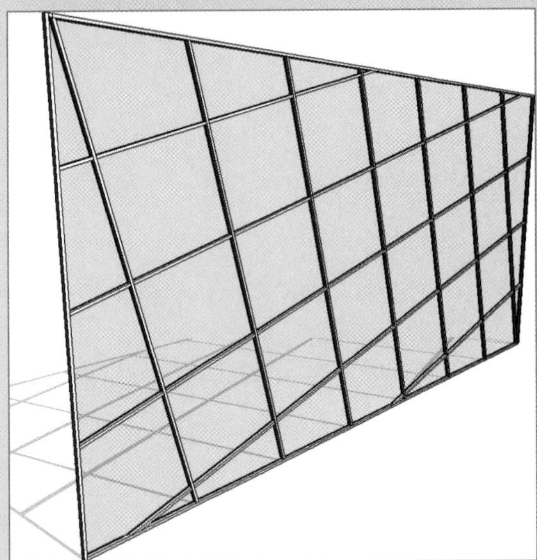

The curved wall in the next graphic has a complex star-shaped opening that is being filled by another curved wall that is star shaped (and fits exactly inside that opening). You can't create non-rectilinear openings in curved walls with the Wall Opening tool. You'll need to use an in-place family.

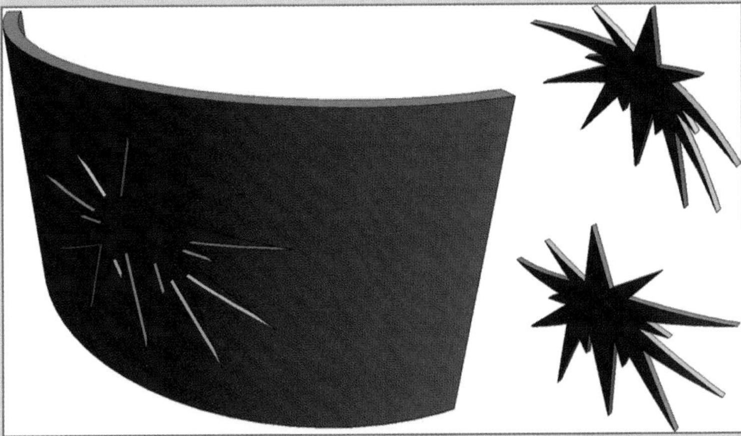

If you get stuck, both of these walls are in this chapter's sample project (`c03-Walls-and-Curtain-Walls.rvt`) at the book's web page.

CHAPTER 4

Floors, Roofs, and Ceilings

We've approached this chapter by grouping together horizontal host elements that make up your building. Although the initial creation of a floor, roof, or ceiling is somewhat different, the tools used to edit the initial design element have a lot of overlap and similarity.

In this chapter, you learn the following skills:

- **Creating floors**
- **Laying out roofs**
- **Adding ceilings**

Creating Floors

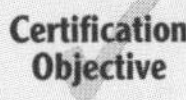

There are quite a few ways to create floors in the Autodesk® Revit® Architecture software. But we honestly don't have the space to dig deep into all these variations! Quite frankly, they're not important for early design iteration.

What's important is that you understand what the various approaches to a single floor type will do and what kind of relationships they'll make. So, let's get started! Begin by downloading the file `c04_Floors_Roofs_and_Ceilings-start.rvt` from this book's companion web page: `www.sybex.com/go/revit2013essentials`.

Sketching

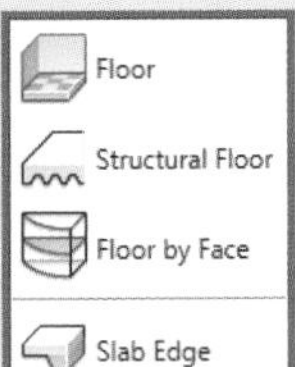

First, let's create floors by sketching the desired shape in the Level 1 floor plan view. The floor type you'll be using is Generic – 12″. Follow these steps:

1. Select the Floor tool on the Build panel of the Architecture tab.
2. Enter Sketch mode, which will allow you to create a sketch that will eventually be used to define the boundary of your floor.

3. Create a simple sketch for the floor, 15´ × 30´ (4.5 m × 9 m). The dimensions are for reference only; even though this is a simple shape, what's more important is how you can manipulate the shape.

4. Finish the sketch, and select your default 3D view. Select the Floor tool, and your floor resembles the one shown in Figure 4.1.

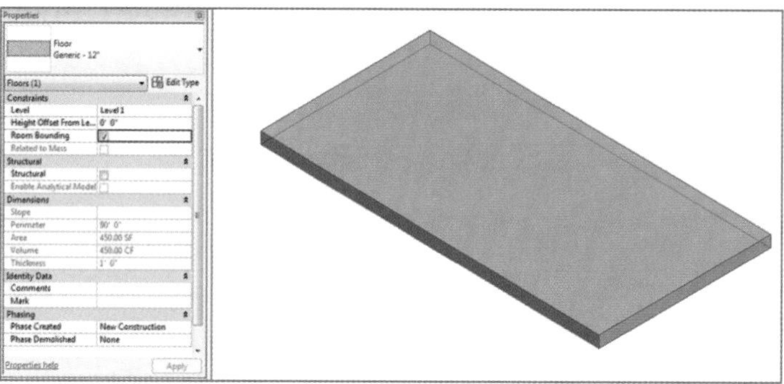

FIGURE 4.1 The finished floor

Editing the Boundary

You can see a couple of things right away in the instant properties: metadata about the floor (location, area, volume, and so on) as well as the ability to revise the geometry via sketching or spot elevations. Continue the example with these steps:

1. While the floor is still selected (reselect the floor if necessary), select Edit Boundary from the Modify Floors tab, and return to the Level 1 floor plan.

2. Add additional sketch lines to generate the shape at the lower right in Figure 4.2. Don't forget to trim back any intersecting lines.

3. Finish the sketch by clicking the green check button. Select the floor, and notice that the options and metadata have already updated, as shown in Figure 4.3.

4. Create another floor of the same type and same initial dimensions, 15´ × 30´ (4.5 m × 9 m), just above the first floor. Leave some space between the two floors.

5. Offset the floor 1´-0˝ (300 mm) above Level 1 by entering this distance into the Properties palette.

6. Finish the sketch to complete the floor (Figure 4.4).

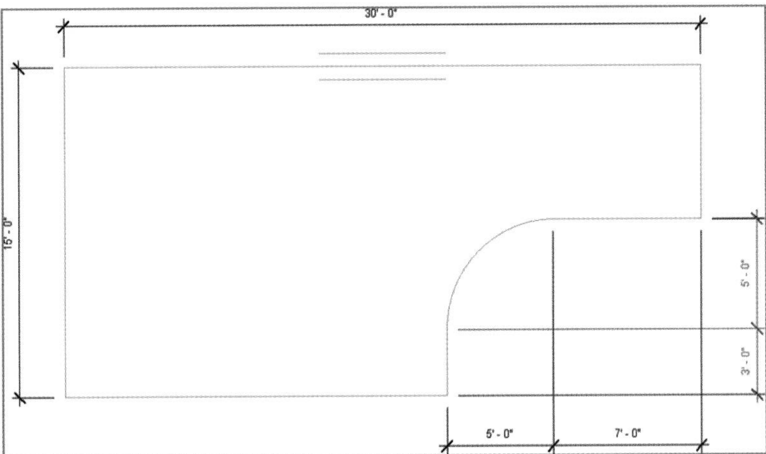

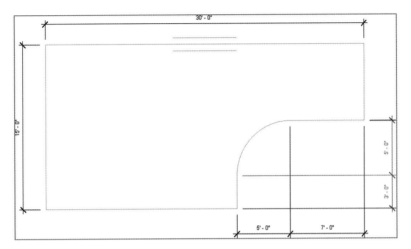

FIGURE 4.2 Modifying the floor sketch

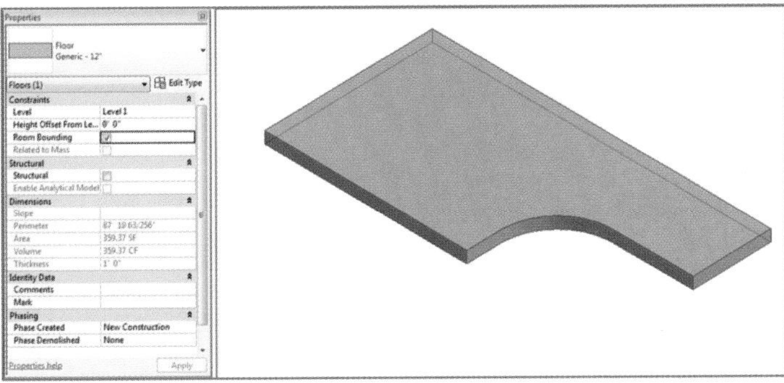

FIGURE 4.3 The modified floor

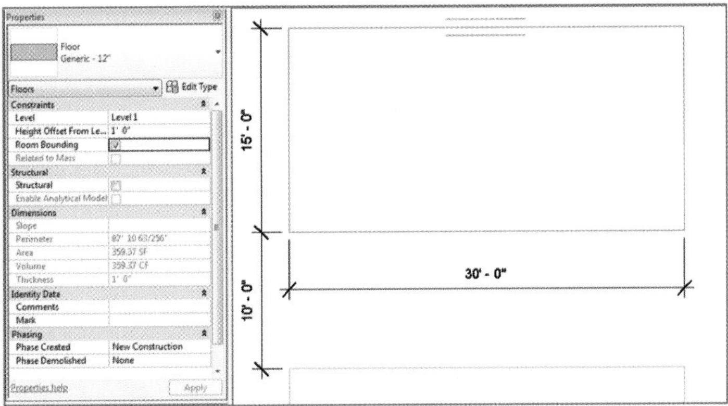

FIGURE 4.4 New floor 1´-0˝ above Level 1

Sloped Arrows and Floors

Not all floors are flat, and many have large openings. Let's investigate both options. You'll begin by bridging another sloped floor between the first two from the previous section:

1. Sketch another floor between the two previous floors, filling the gap between the two (Figure 4.5).

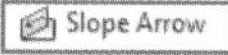

2. If you were to finish the sketch like this, the floor wouldn't connect the upper and lower sections. You need to add a slope arrow. Do so by selecting the Slope Arrow tool on the Draw panel.

   Sketch the arrow as shown in Figure 4.6. The first location that you pick is the tail of the arrow; the second location is the head.

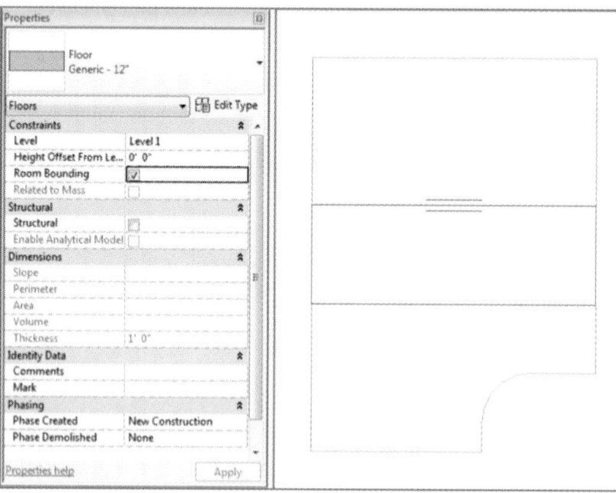

FIGURE 4.5 New floor at Level 1

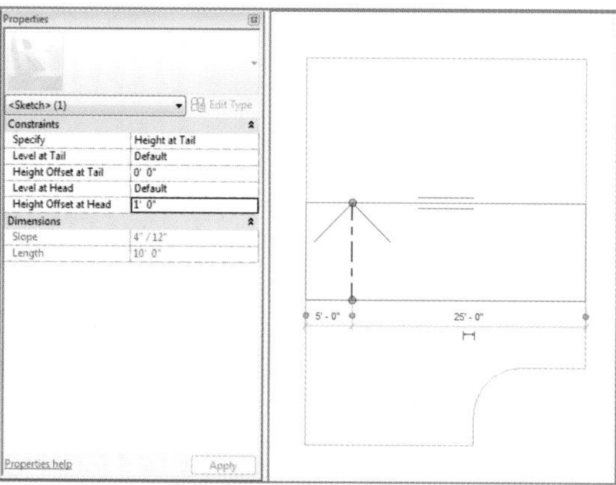

FIGURE 4.6 Slope arrow constraints

3. Select the slope arrow, and modify the parameters as shown in Figure 4.6 so they match the location of the upper and lower floors. Be sure to specify the heights of the tail and head.

4. Finish the sketch, and return to your default 3D view (Figure 4.7), which shows the finished condition. Now the sloped floor connects the lower and upper floors.

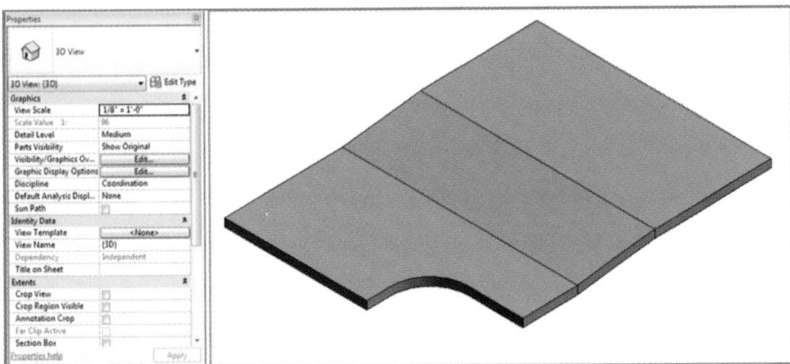

FIGURE 4.7 Completed sloped floor

Sloped Floors via Shape Editing

Slightly sloped floors and depressions could be created with slope arrows and separate floors—but this approach would probably be too complex because you'd have to create a lot of separate pieces of geometry. For these kinds of conditions, you have the Shape Editing tools.

Continue the example with these steps:

1. Return to Level 1, and select the upper floor. Now you can see the Shape Editing tools in the Shape Editing panel on the Modify Floors tab.

2. Let's suppose that this entire floor is at the correct level, except for one small portion that needs to be slightly depressed in order to accommodate a loading area.

   Define the upper and lower boundaries of this depressed area by selecting the Add Split Line option from the Shape Editing panel. Add the lines as shown in Figure 4.8. Dimensions are shown for reference.

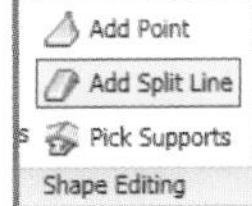

3. Now that you've added the proper locations to break the slope, you need to modify the points at the ends of the lines to change the slope of the floor. Start by returning to your default 3D view. As you hover over the endpoint of the line, Revit Architecture highlights the shape handles. Press the Tab key to highlight a specific handle, and then select it (Figure 4.9).

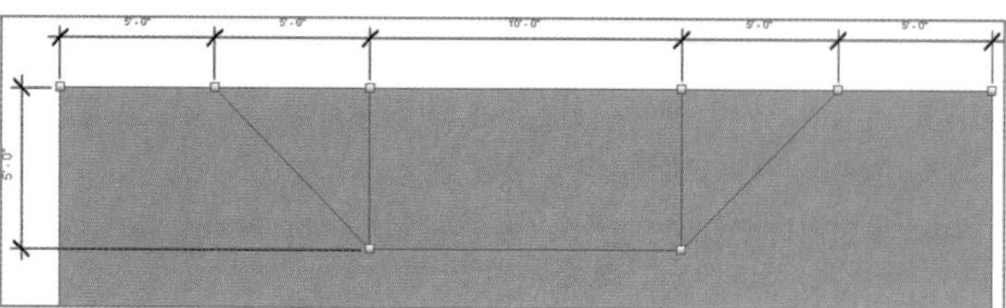

FIGURE 4.8 Adding split lines

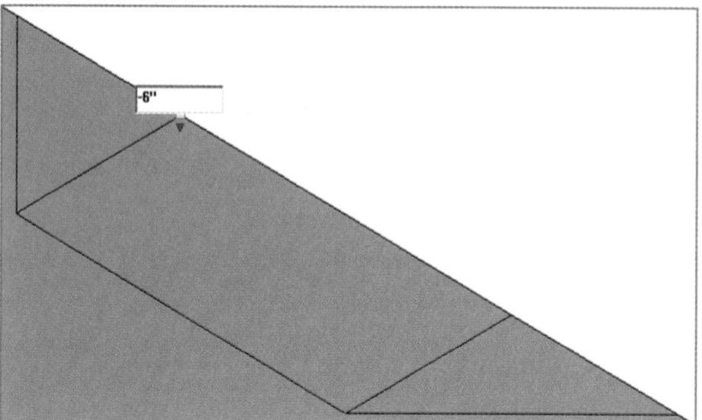

FIGURE 4.9 Editing the shape handle

4. Adjust the elevation of the shape handle as shown in Figure 4.9. In this case, you're depressing the floor, so the value must be negative. But you could also increase the elevation in a small area by using a positive value.

5. Do the same for the shape handle to the right. When you're done, the depressed area resembles Figure 4.10.

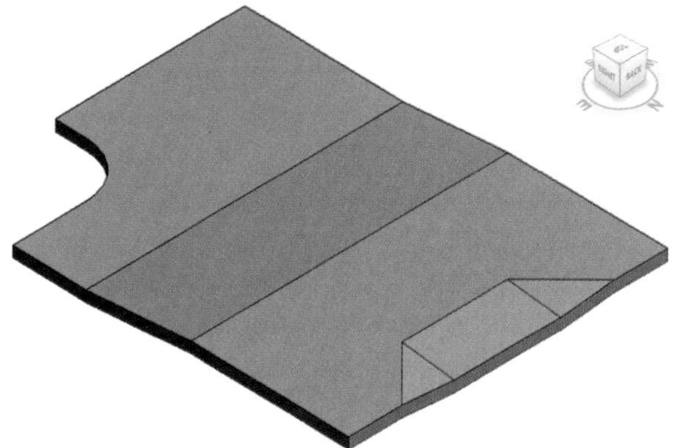

FIGURE 4.10 The finished depression

Creating Openings by Sketching

For the occasional or irregular opening in a floor, it's easy to add a secondary opening using the Opening tool. Using the same example file, follow these steps:

1. From the Architecture tab on the ribbon, select the By Face tool from the Opening panel. Select an edge of the sloped floor slab you created to enter Sketch mode.

2. Sketch an opening 10´ × 3´ (3 m × 1 m) in the center floor panel. The result resembles Figure 4.11.

   There's no limit to the number of interior sketches you can create. You can also edit previously created sketches by using the same method.

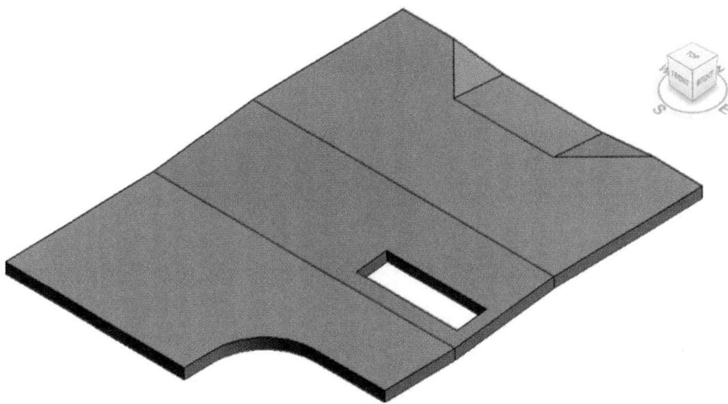

FIGURE 4.11 The finished opening

   An opening of this type remains perpendicular to the slope of the floor, roof, or ceiling. On the other hand, a vertical opening remains perpendicular to the level on which it was created.

3. Select the Vertical tool from the Opening panel, and sketch a new opening of the same size and dimensions above the first one. The result resembles Figure 4.12.

The differences are subtle but very important. By creating a section through both openings, you can see the difference in an opening that remains perpendicular to the floor compared to one that remains perpendicular to the level (Figure 4.13).

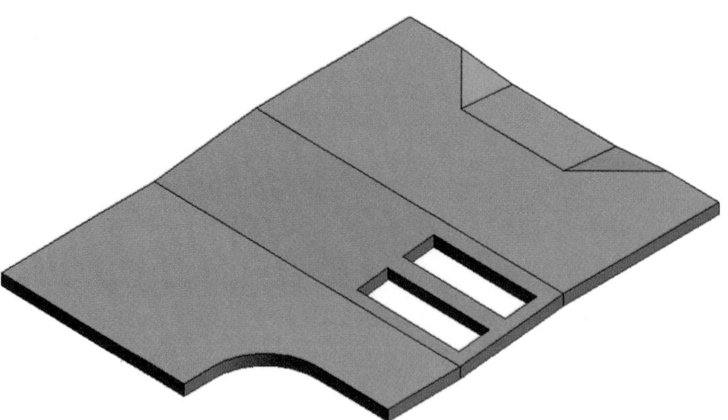

FIGURE 4.12 Sketch a new opening of the same size and dimensions.

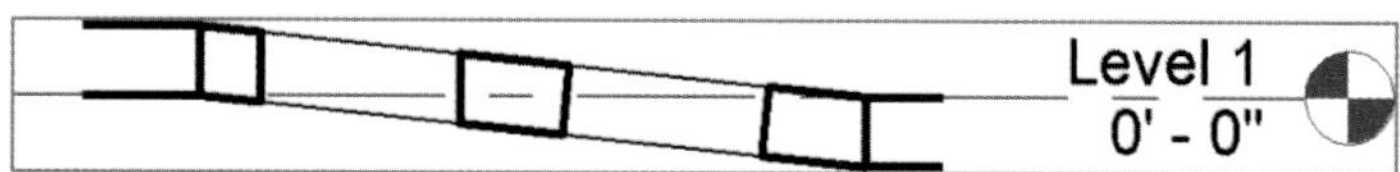

FIGURE 4.13 Finished parallel and perpendicular openings

Keep in mind that from a project-management standpoint, if you have a number of openings that are predictably shaped (circular, rectilinear, and so on), *highly* repetitive, and scattered throughout your project, you're better off creating a host- or face-based opening (with parameters for options) as a family component and then loading it for use in your project.

Creating Openings with Shafts

For openings that occur from level to level and are vertically repetitive (like a shaft or an elevator core), you can use the Shaft tool. This tool allows you to create openings in numerous floors, roofs, and ceilings quickly and easily. Continue the example as follows:

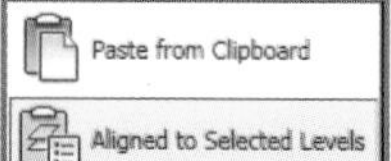

1. Add a few more levels to your project so you have 10 levels that are evenly spaced.

2. Select all three floors on Level 1, and copy them by pressing Ctrl+C. Now the geometry is ready to be pasted to each of the levels. The best way to do this is by using the Paste tool, which allows you to select all the levels to which you intend to paste the floors.

3. Select Paste from the Clipboard palette, and then select Aligned To Selected Levels. You're given the option to select all the levels: select Levels 2–10 (Figure 4.14). The resulting floors are shown in the same figure.

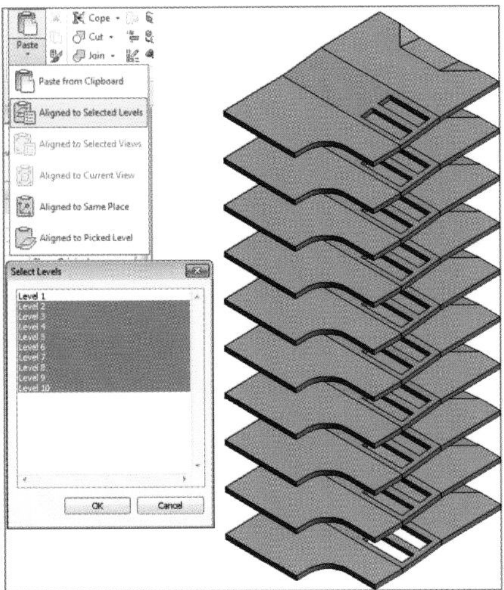

FIGURE 4.14 Pasted geometry

4. Return to the Level 1 view, and select the Shaft tool from the Opening panel. Once again, you enter Sketch mode. Create a new 20′ × 3′ (6 m × 1 m) rectangle perpendicular to the last two you drew. Be sure to modify the top constraint so the shaft goes up to Level 10. Also be certain to assign a Top Offset value, because the upper floor is slightly above the level (Figure 4.15).

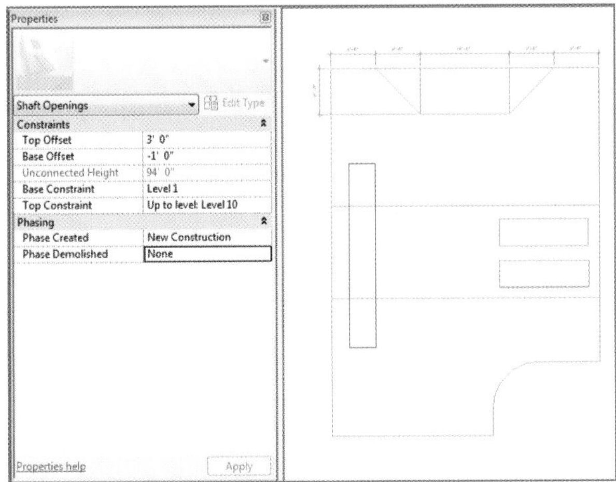

FIGURE 4.15 Creating a multistory shaft

Figure 4.16 shows the resulting shaft in 3D. All the floors were cut automatically. Any ceilings, roofs, and additional floors that may be added in the future will be cut automatically as well.

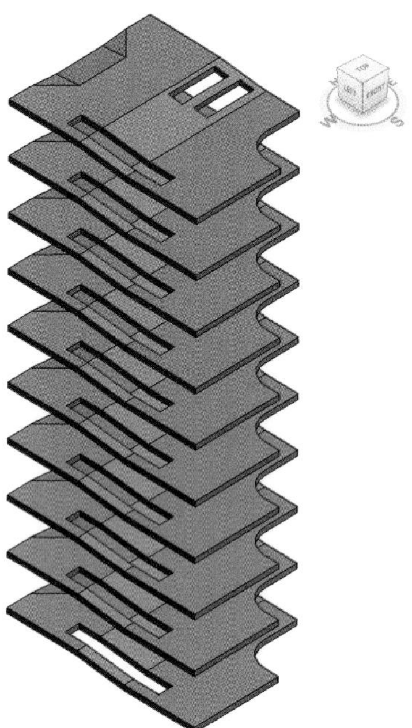

FIGURE 4.16 The finished multistory shaft

Picking Walls

Pan a bit toward the right of the floors in the previous exercise. Start the next exercise by creating a series of walls on Level 1 that resembles Figure 4.17. Then, continue with these steps:

1. Select the Floor tool on the Build panel of the Architecture tab to enter Sketch mode. This time, you don't want to sketch the boundary of the floor manually. There's an easier way: select the Pick Wall tool from the Draw palette. Doing so allows you to select an individual wall or an entire chain of walls.

2. Hover over one of the wall edges, and then press and release the Tab key. Your selection cycles from one wall to the series of walls. When all of the walls highlight, select them with one pick.

   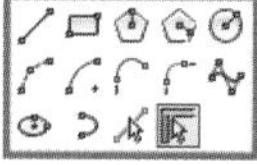

   Note that the edge of the new floor is constructed where your mouse clicks when you pick the wall in reference to the interior or exterior of the wall. The floor goes to the outside of the wall; in order to do that, you have to pick the outside edge of the wall—otherwise, the floor aligns with the interior. The entire chain of lines is created that correspond to all the walls.

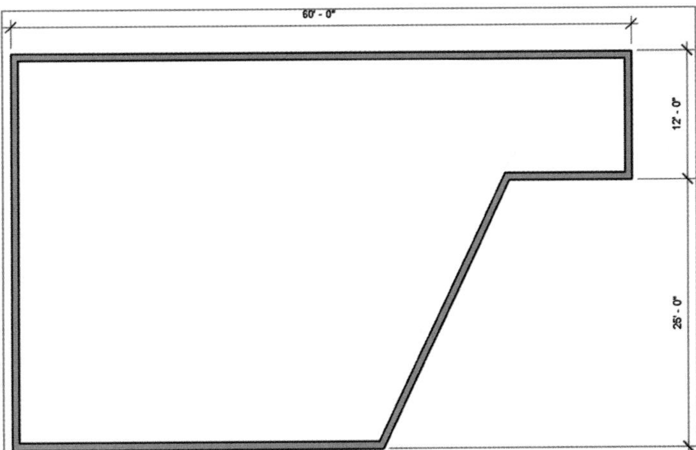

FIGURE 4.17 Creating a chain of walls

If you move the walls that were used to determine the floor sketch, the boundary of the floor will automatically update. This is incredibly powerful for a multistory building, where updating one floor at a time would be nearly impossible. As soon as one update was complete, the design would likely have changed, requiring you to start over.

Laying Out Roofs

You create roofs much like you do floors: from a sketch resulting from either drawn lines or picked walls. And as with floors, if you pick the exterior walls as a reference, then moving the walls will move the corresponding edges of the roof. Roofs can also be created in elevation (which we'll get to in a bit).

Roofs tend to slope, for a lot of good reasons. Let's create some roofs and investigate a few slope options.

Picking Walls

Let's start by adding a roof to the same walls you used in the previous floor exercise. Follow these steps:

1. Return to your Level 1 plan view. Select the Roof tool on the Architecture tab, and choose Roof By Footprint. At this point, Revit Architecture automatically asks you to select the level with which this roof is associated; select Level 3.

2. Again, you don't have to pick all the walls individually or sketch all the roof boundary lines. Select the Pick Walls option on the Draw panel of the Modify Create Roof Footprint tab. Then hover over one of the exterior walls, and press the Tab key to select the entire chain. All the roof boundary lines are created.

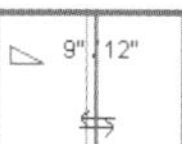

   Note the icon with double arrows on the sketch lines for the roof: clicking it flips the boundary lines to the inside or outside of the wall face. Click this icon to move all the boundary lines to the inside of the wall's faces.

3. Because this will be a sloped roof, you can make the slope perpendicular to the left edge by deselecting the Defines Slope check box located below the Modify panel for all the other lines.

4. Define the slope from the Sketch Line for the roof of the left edge with a 1/12 rise over run (about 8 percent).

5. Finish the sketch, and look at the project in 3D. Although the roof begins at Level 3 and has the proper slope, it's immediately obvious that the walls don't extend beyond the roof.

   Revit Architecture excels at helping your team during the design process with issues like this one. You can identify conflicts earlier rather than later so you can resolve them before other design issues create circular conflicts.

Slope Arrow

6. Select all the walls (using the Tab key to select the entire chain), and set Top Constraint to Level 4 in the Properties palette. The results resemble Figure 4.18.

FIGURE 4.18 Adjusting the wall height

Sloped Arrows

You can determine the slope of a roof using slope arrows. Slope arrows let you specify a slope, and they also allow you to specify the levels of the arrow at both the head and tail. Continue the example with these steps:

1. Select the roof, and reenter Sketch mode.
2. The tail of the slope arrow must reside on the boundary of the sketch, but the head of the slope arrow may point in practically any direction. Select the Slope Arrow tool on the Draw panel, and add a slope arrow as shown in Figure 4.19. Note that the Height Offset At Head value is set to 6´ (2m). Make sure you uncheck the Define Slope option ▷ for the edges of the roof to see the full effect of using the slope arrow.

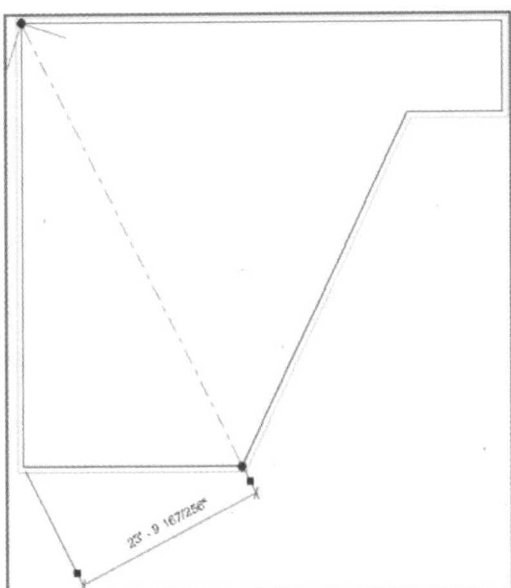

FIGURE 4.19 Sloping the roof

3. Finish the sketch. Notice that a single slope proceeds across the roof. A single slope in this direction would be nearly impossible to specify without slope arrows.

You can also create roof slopes using multiple slope arrows. This technique is incredibly helpful when you want to create sloped conditions where two perpendicular slopes must meet at exactly the same location. Again, this is something that's difficult to do without slope arrows.

Let's explore this topic by reentering Sketch mode with the previously created roof:

1. Delete the existing slope arrow by editing the sketch.
2. Sketch two new slope arrows so that the heads of the arrows meet at the upper-left corner of the roof. The slope arrow should have the following properties:

   Head Offset At Tail: 0″

   Head Offset At Head: 6′ (2 m)

   Make sure Height Offset is the same for both Tails and Heads.
3. Finish the sketch. The results resemble the roof in Figure 4.20.

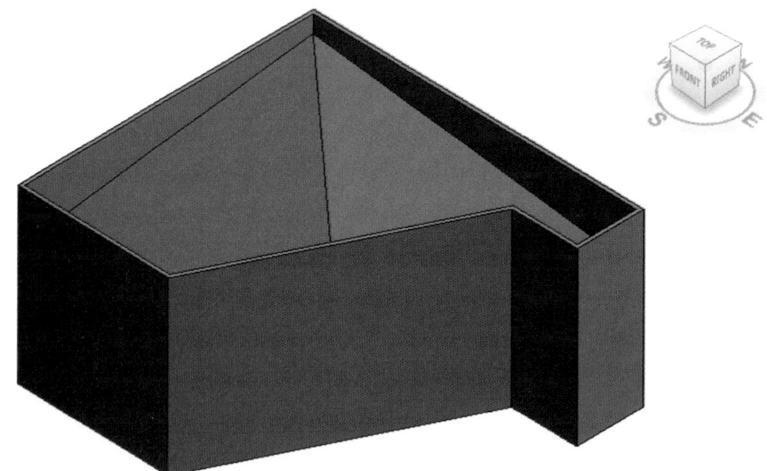

FIGURE 4.20 Roof created from two slope arrows

Another common condition in residential-styled roofs is multiple slopes that are perpendicular to their many edges. To create this condition in the example, follow these steps:

1. Reenter Sketch mode for the previously created roof, and delete both slope arrows.
2. Select all the lines that represent the roof sketch. You can do this by holding down Ctrl and selecting the lines individually or by clicking one line and pressing Tab to highlight the rest of the lines.
3. With the lines selected, in the Options Bar, enter 3′ (1 m) for the overhang.

4. Select the Defines Slope option for all the boundary edges from the Properties palette. Also modify the Slope property for a slope of 9/12. The roof should look like Figure 4.21.

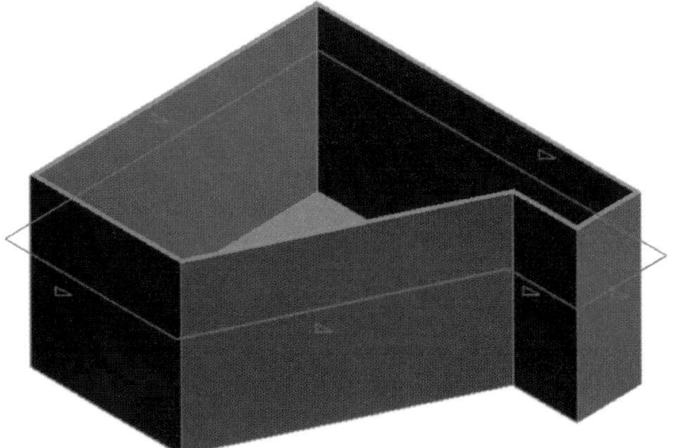

FIGURE 4.21 Offsetting the roof sketch, and defining slopes

5. Finish the sketch. Initially, the edges of the wall extend beyond the overhang of the roof. Select all the exterior walls (use the Tab key), and then select the Attach Top/Base option on the Modify | Wall tab. The result resembles Figure 4.22.

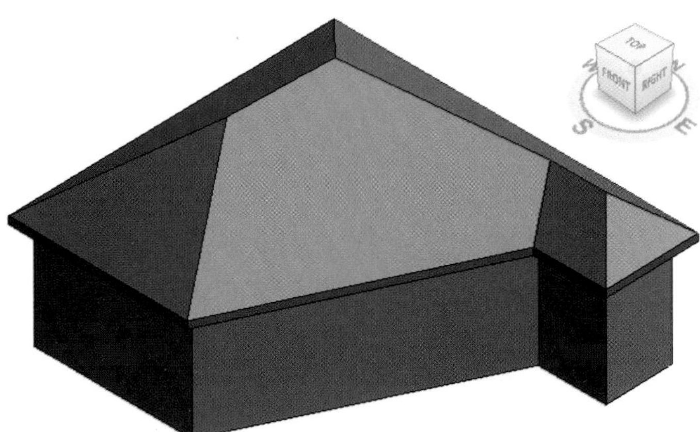

FIGURE 4.22 Attaching the walls to the roof

6. The great thing about attaching walls is that if the roof's angle or slopes change, the walls will automatically react to the new condition. To test this, reenter Sketch mode and remove the Defines Slope option for one of the edges.

7. Finish the sketch, and the results resemble Figure 4.23. Because the walls were previously told to attach to the roof, the gable condition is already updated.

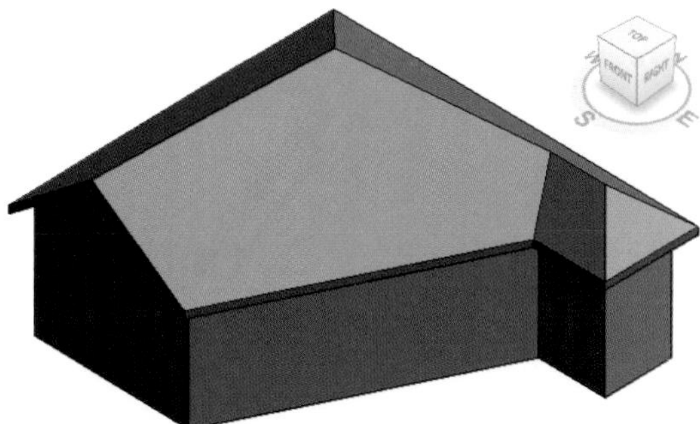

FIGURE 4.23 Removing a defined slope

Extruded Roofs

Slope Arrow

In addition to being able to create roofs in a plan or footprint orientation, you can extrude roofs from vertically planer surfaces. To do so, follow these steps:

1. Select the Roof By Extrusion command from the Roof flyout on the Architecture tab. You're immediately prompted to select the plane from which the extruded roof will spring. Select the roof face highlighted in Figure 4.24.

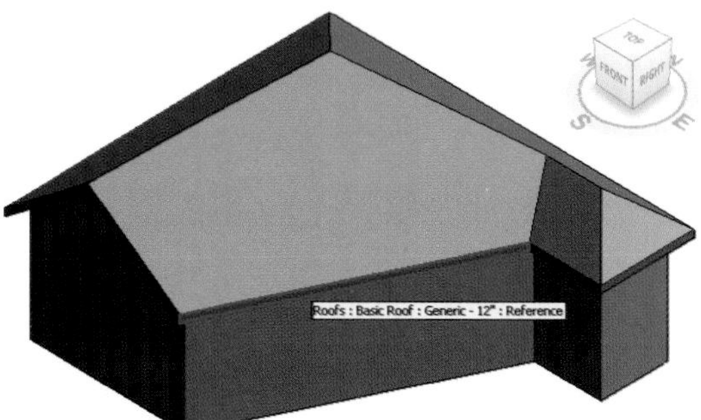

FIGURE 4.24 Selecting the roof face

2. You're prompted to associate the roof to the appropriate level. This step is important for scheduling purposes; you can modify the value later. For now, select Level 3 because it's closest to the base of the extruded roof.

   Next you'll create the sketch for the extruded roof. The sketch line isn't a closed loop: it's just a line (or series of connected lines) that defines the top of the extruded roof. For this example, you'll create an arc.

3. Select the Arc tool from the Draw panel.
4. Create the arc approximately as shown in Figure 4.25. The important detail is that you set Extrusion End in the Properties palette to 20′-0″ (6 m).

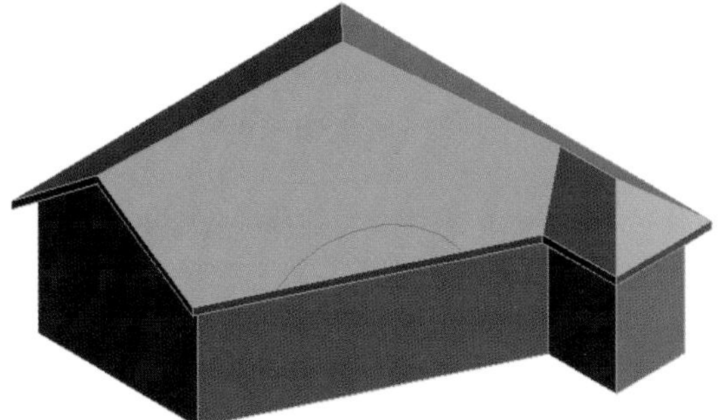

FIGURE 4.25 Creating the arc

5. Finish the sketch. The roof springs from the arc you created, but it's not reaching back and connecting to the roof face. This issue is easy to resolve.
6. Select the roof, and then select the Join/Unjoin Roof option on the Geometry panel.
7. Hover over the rear edge of the extruded roof, as shown in the left image of Figure 4.26.
8. Select the face of the previously created roof that you want to connect to the extruded roof. The extruded roof now extends back to meet the face of the other roof (Figure 4.27). If either roof is modified, Revit Architecture will do its best to maintain this connected relationship.

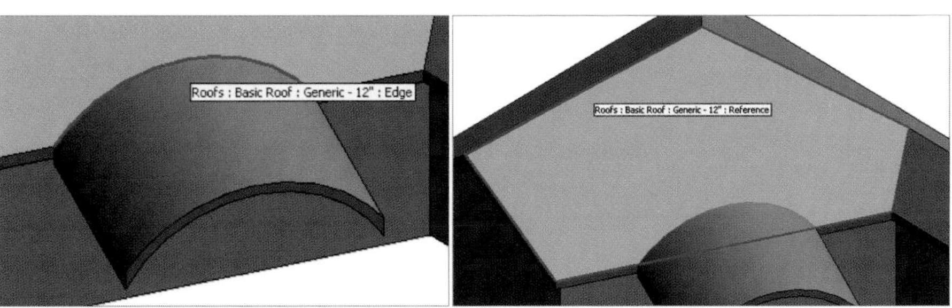

FIGURE 4.26 Attaching the roof

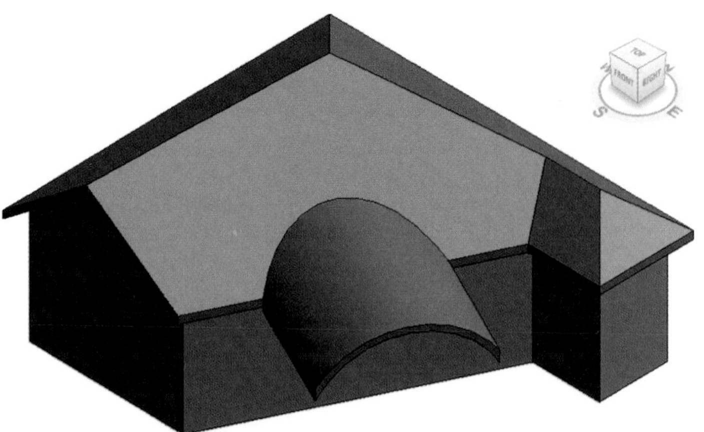

FIGURE 4.27 Joined roofs

We could talk about many other complex areas with regard to roofs, from point elevations to more instance and type parameters. But once again, this is beyond the space limitations for an introduction to Revit Architecture. Learning how to use Revit Architecture organically is a better approach: begin with the basics of design iteration and then build on these concepts as the need arises.

Adding Ceilings

Ceilings in Revit Architecture are easy to place as well as modify. As you move the walls, the ceiling associated to those walls will stretch to fit the new conditions.

The example in this section returns to the Level 1 floor plan of the previous exercise. Add 10´-0˝ (3 m) high walls and doors to create individual, shared, and open spaces (Figure 4.28). You'll continue in the sections that follow.

Automatic Ceilings

The Ceiling tool is found on the Build palette of the Architecture tab. When you select the tool, the default condition is Automatic Ceiling. This means that as you hover over a space, Revit Architecture will attempt to find the boundary of walls. Follow these steps:

1. Let's do this for the space at the bottom of the image (Figure 4.29). As you hover over the space, Revit Architecture indicates the boundary with a broad, red line.
2. As you can see from the Properties dialog, Revit Architecture offers four default ceiling types: one basic type and three compound types. Select the 2´ × 2´ (600 mm × 600 mm) system.

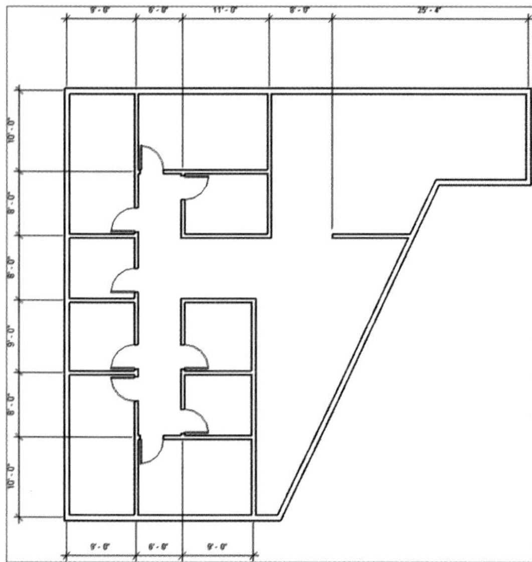

FIGURE 4.28 Level 1 with walls

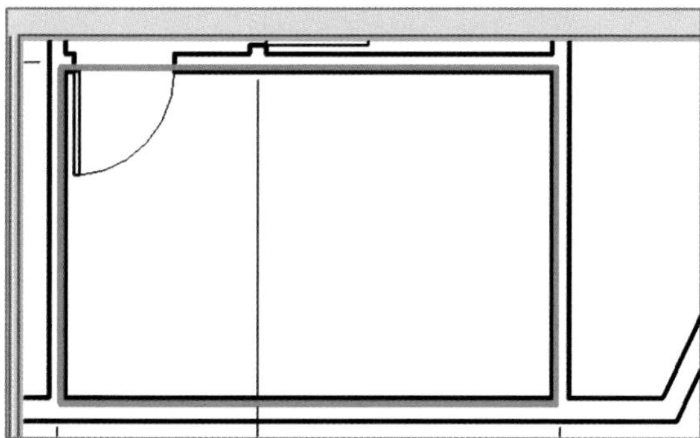

FIGURE 4.29 Revit Architecture outlines the boundary.

3. As you place the first ceiling in the Floor plan view, you get a warning. This happens frequently and for good reason: you've placed the ceiling, but you can't see it. As a rule, you shouldn't ignore warnings. We've seen people click and click only to find that they've repeatedly placed ceilings in the same space.

Go to the proper view in the Project Browser to see the ceiling—in this case, the ceiling plan for Level 1. Now you can plainly see the ceiling you've created.

4. Select the Ceiling tool from the Architecture tab and pick inside the rooms to automatically place the remaining ceilings as shown in Figure 4.30. Notice that Revit Architecture centers the grid based on the space you've selected.

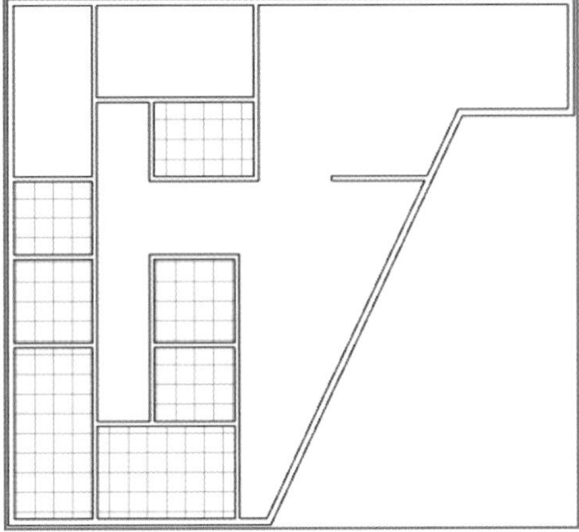

FIGURE 4.30 Resulting ceiling

Sketching Ceilings

Next you'll place ceilings in the upper-left corner of the ceiling plan for Level 1, but this time you'll share the ceiling between the two spaces. This practice is common in interior projects. The partitions extend only to the underside of the ceiling (rather than connect to the structure above). Follow these steps:

1. Selecting Sketch Ceiling on the Ceiling panel of the Modify Place Ceiling tab. Add sketch lines as shown in the first image in Figure 4.31. The result is shown in the second image.

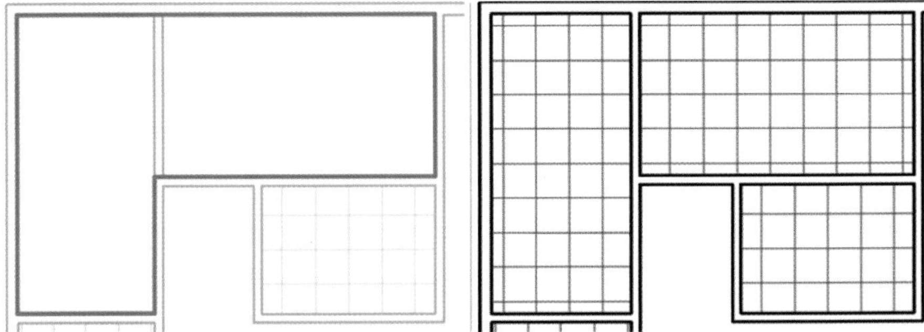

FIGURE 4.31 Sketching the ceiling

2. Place a ceiling at upper right in the plan, but this time sketch a 2´ × 4´ (1.2m × 600mm) system (Figure 4.32). Choose this new system from the Type Selector before you finish the sketch of the ceiling.

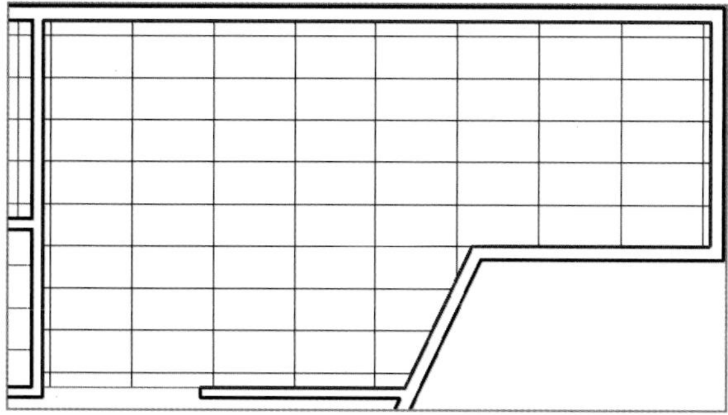

FIGURE 4.32 2´ 4´ (1.2m × 600mm) ceiling

3. Create a GWB on Mtl. Stud Ceiling for the area shown in Figure 4.33.

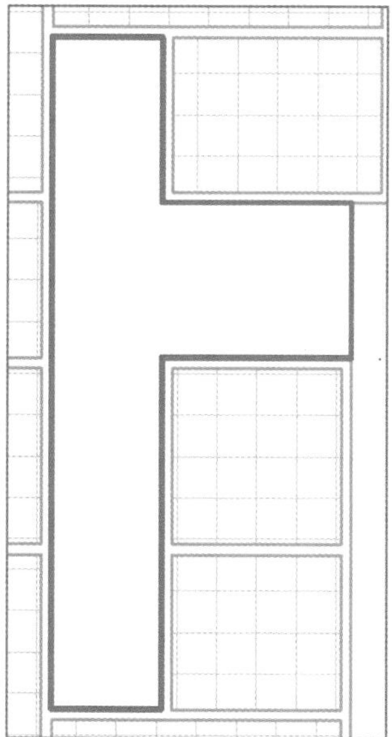

FIGURE 4.33 Creating a GWB on Mtl. Stud Ceiling

By default, the GWB material doesn't have a surface pattern. Although this material would be too graphically busy for walls, it's fine for ceilings. So, let's create a new material for GWB associated to ceilings and give it a pattern.

4. Select an edge of the ceiling, and click Edit Type from the Properties palette.

5. Click the Structure button from the Type Properties dialog to open the Edit Assembly window.

6. Select the Gypsum Wall Board material option, and duplicate the existing material. Name the new material **Gypsum Ceiling Board.**

7. Associate the surface pattern called Sand to the material.

8. Click OK until you close all the dialog boxes and return to the Ceiling plan view. The result is shown in Figure 4.34. You can now distinguish the ceiling from the open areas that have no ceiling.

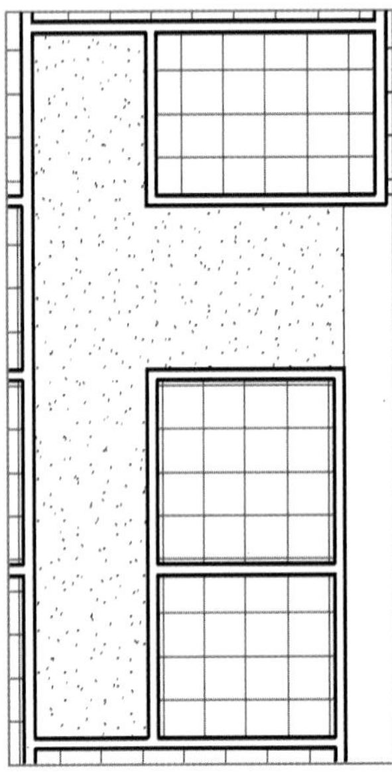

FIGURE 4.34 Assigning materials to a ceiling

Bulkhead Conditions

Creating a bulkhead to separate two ceilings is straightforward.

1. Place the walls that will act as the bulkhead, as shown in Figure 4.35. Be sure to set the Height Offset From Level value in the Properties palette of the walls to 7´-9˝ (2.3 m) and the Unconnected Height value to 2´-3˝ (700 cm). This creates two walls above head height.

2. It requires a bit of finesse to delete or edit a placed ceiling. Most beginners simply select the grid. But you actually need to select the *edge* of the ceiling to edit it. Hover over the edge of the ceiling, and use the Tab key to cycle through options until the edge of the ceiling is highlighted. Then select it, and choose Edit Boundary from the Mode panel on the Modify Ceilings tab. Modify the ceiling as shown in the first image in Figure 4.36.

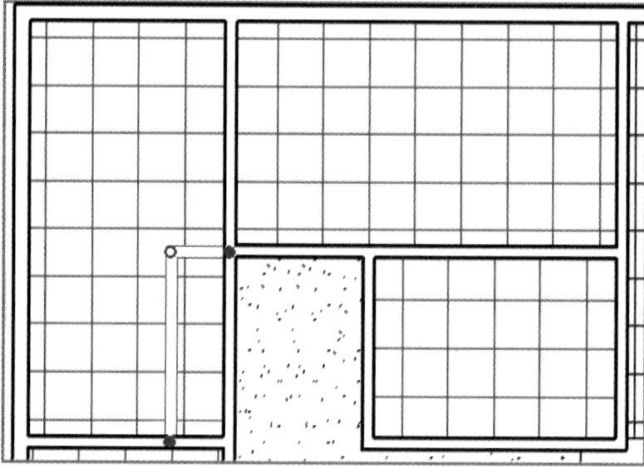

FIGURE 4.35 Creating a bulkhead

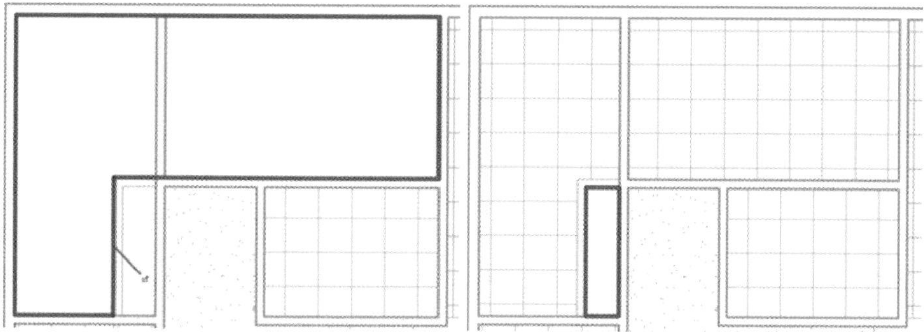

FIGURE 4.36 Editing the boundary

3. Sketch a new GWB ceiling that is 9′-0″ (2.7 m), and finish the sketch. The second image in Figure 4.36 shows the finished ceiling.

4. To get a better idea of the finished configuration in 3D, go to a 3D view and orient a section box of the Level 1 plan view. Right-click the ViewCube, and from the Floor Plans flyout of the context menu, select Level 1. Use the grip arrows to pull the boundaries of the section box to resemble Figure 4.37. You'll find that working this way is

helpful because having both 2D and 3D views aids in communicating any design issues.

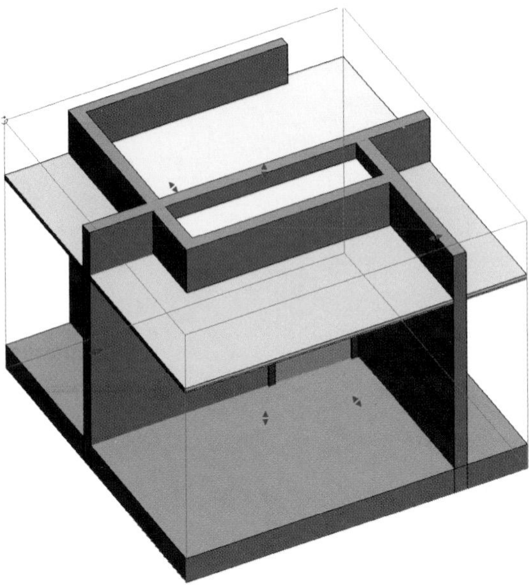

FIGURE 4.37 Orienting the section box to the 3D view

Adding Lights and Rotating the Grid

Adding lights is easy; and because they're hosted by the ceiling, lights will often create openings for you. Let's begin the next example by loading one of the lighting families using the file from the previous example:

1. From the Insert tab, select Load Family from the Load From Library panel. Open the `Lighting Fixtures` folder, and double-click the family `Ceiling Light - Linear Box.rfa`.
2. You're prompted to place the first family type of the family in your ceiling, but be sure to select the 2′ × 4′ type from the Type Selector. You'll place lighting fixtures into the 2′ × 4′ ceiling in the upper-right ceiling plan.
3. The insertion point for the light is the center of the light. Place the first light, and then use the Align tool to move it into the right spot.
4. Use the Copy tool on the Modify panel to copy the first light based on the intersection of the ceiling grid. All the lights are shown in Figure 4.38 on the left.

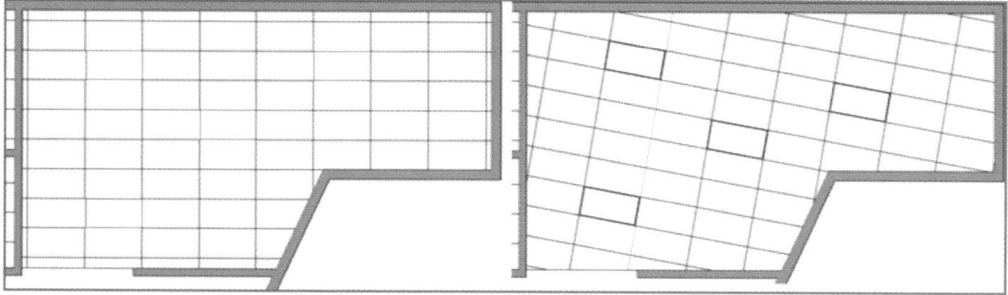

FIGURE 4.38 Placing lights and rotating the grid

5. To rotate the grid, select any grid line, and use the Rotate tool on the Modify panel to rotate it. In this case, specify a 10-degree angle. Notice that the lights rotate as well.
6. Click and drag the ceiling grid lines to better center the lights in the overall space. Again, the lights move with the grid.

   This technique is incredibly helpful for maintaining design coordination. The finished condition is shown on the right in Figure 4.38.

Changing the Ceiling

Ceiling types often change during the design process. Again, most beginners struggle because they mistakenly select the ceiling grid (which means they actually select the material). Instead, you need to select the geometry of the ceiling, which you do by selecting the *edge* of the ceiling. Continue the previous example with these steps:

1. Select the edge of the ceiling.
2. Pull down the Properties menu on the Properties palette, and select the GWB option for this ceiling (Figure 4.39. The result is shown in the left image in Figure 4.39.

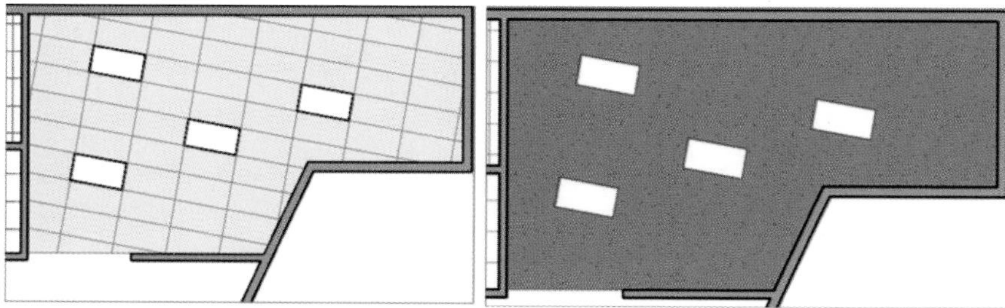

FIGURE 4.39 Selecting ceiling geometry

Sloping the Ceiling

You can even slope the ceiling by placing a slope arrow while editing the boundary of the ceiling. This is basically the same process as sloping a floor or a roof:

1. Select the edge of the ceiling, and choose Edit Boundary from the Mode panel on the Modify Ceilings tab.
2. Place a slope arrow as shown at left in Figure 4.40. Set the Height Offsets for the Tail and Head to 0 and 3´ (1 m), respectively.
3. Finish the sketch. The result (on the right in Figure 4.40) is shown in 3D using a section box. The lights even follow the revised ceiling slope!

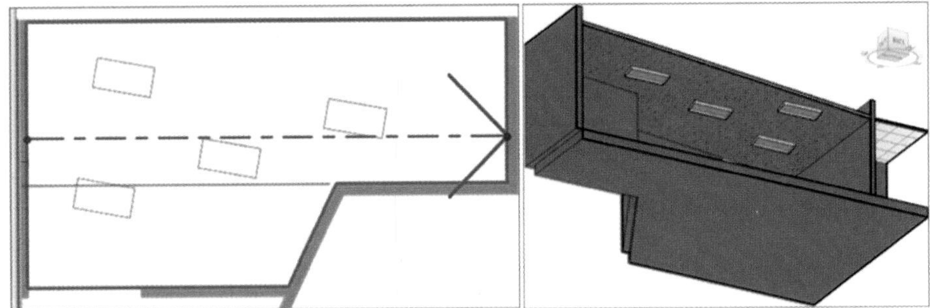

FIGURE 4.40 Adding a slope arrow to the ceiling

The Essentials and Beyond

In this chapter, you learned to create floors, lay out roofs, and add ceilings.

Additional Exercises

- Create a mass and intersecting levels, and then create mass floors from those levels. Use the mass floors to create floors using the Floor By Face.
- Modify the mass from the previous exercise, and update the floors created with the Floor By Face tool.
- Create a shaft opening, and intersect it with all the floors created by the Floor By Face tool from the previous exercise.
- Create a roof or floor, and then use the Shape Editing tools to model slopes for drainage.

CHAPTER 5

Stairs, Ramps, and Railings

The Autodesk® Revit® Architecture software is capable of creating wonderfully complex and elegant railings, stairs, and ramps. In Revit Architecture, these elements are created and controlled with separate tools, but they can be just as easily combined to form elegant design solutions.

In this chapter, you learn the following skills:

- **Creating stair configurations**
- **Designing ramps**
- **Building railings for level and sloped conditions**
- **From basics to creative art**

Creating Stair Configurations

Stairs contain many, many parameters, but not all of the parameter controls are equally important during the design process. Design is often about the intent of what something is as well as where it is meant to go. Once the intent is resolved, it's necessary to go back and revise the specifics of how something will be carefully assembled.

Revit Architecture 2013 includes a new stair tool. This tool allows you to divide your stair into *assemblies* to better define and break down the various elements that create the stair. This tool is a big departure from the original stair tool in Revit Architecture. Fortunately, if you're working with experienced teams, Revit Architecture includes both the new and the old stair tools to provide maximum flexibility for your design process. We'll walk through using both tools to create a set of stairs.

Because the tools for railings, stairs, and ramps are somewhat separate, let's begin the stair by first creating a simplified railing. This way, when you create a series of stair configurations, you'll have a new, default railing to apply to each of them.

Creating the Generic Railing

Begin by opening the default architectural template and expanding the Family tree in the Project Browser. Let's start by creating a railing that is useful from a design standpoint. Too much specificity too soon can cause a lot of confusion, so you'll simplify the geometry. You'll do this by duplicating a railing definition that's close to what you need and then modifying it to suit your purposes.

Here are the steps for duplicating and creating your own custom handrail that you'll use for designing stairs:

1. Open the default 3D view by selecting the small house icon from the Quick Access toolbar (QAT). Select the Architecture tab, and choose the Railing flyout from the Circulation panel. Select the Sketch Path option to enter sketch mode.
2. Before you draw a railing, let's create a new type. Select Edit Type from the Properties palette, and click Duplicate in the Type Properties dialog box. Name the new railing **Handrail – Design**, and click OK to exit all the dialog boxes.
3. Draw a line approximately 30′ (10m) long. This line will define your railing.
4. Click the green check in the Mode panel to finish the sketch and create the railing. This is Revit Architecture's default rail (Figure 5.1).

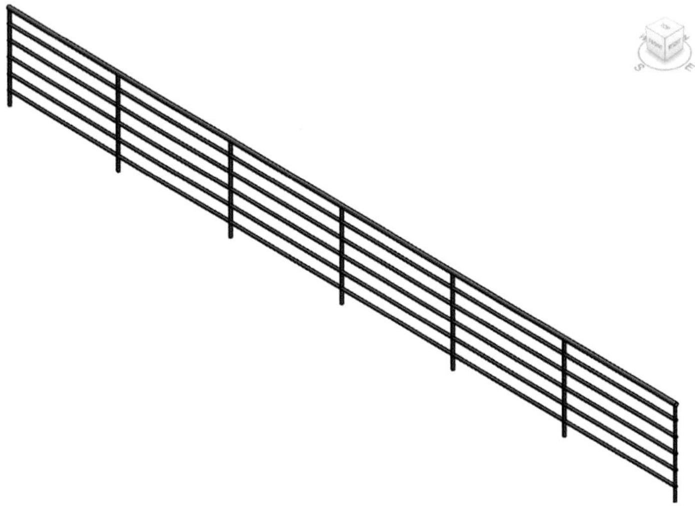

FIGURE 5.1 Default railing : Railing Handrail - Rectangular

Because railings (like walls and floors) are system families, you have to modify the ones that Revit Architecture gives you rather than creating your own in the Family Editor. To create your railing, you're going to modify the one you just created:

1. Select the railing, and choose Edit Type from the Type Selector to open the Type Properties dialog shown in Figure 5.2.

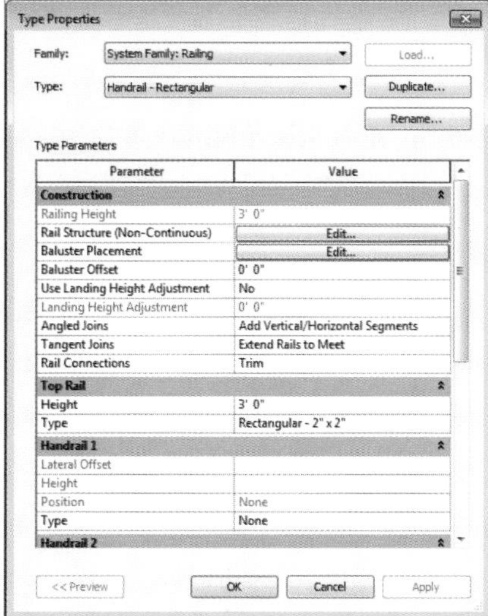

FIGURE 5.2 Railing type properties

2. Click Edit for the Rail Structure (Non-Continuous) parameter. In the resulting dialog box shown in Figure 5.3, delete Rail 1 through Rail 5 by selecting each line (such as Rail 2) and clicking the Delete button. Doing so eliminates all the horizontal rails under the top rail. Close the dialog box by clicking OK. New to Revit Architecture 2013, the top rail is controlled by its own parameter in the main Type Properties dialog box.

Next you need to edit the balusters:

1. In the Type Properties dialog box, click the Edit button for the Baluster Placement parameter.

2. In the resulting dialog box, find the Main Pattern panel, select the second line (Regular Baluster), and set its Baluster Family value to None.

3. In the Posts panel, set the Baluster Family value for the Start Post, Corner Post, and End Post to None (as you see us doing in Figure 5.4). This effectively eliminates any balusters from your railings.

4. Click OK to close the Edit Baluster Placement dialog box, and click OK again to close the Type Properties dialog box.

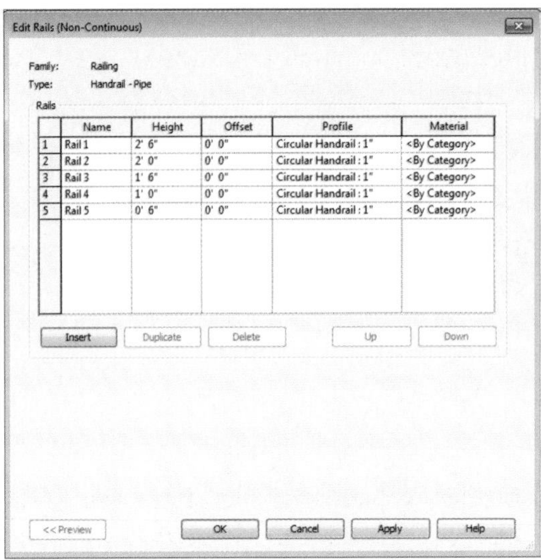

FIGURE 5.3 Deleting railing types

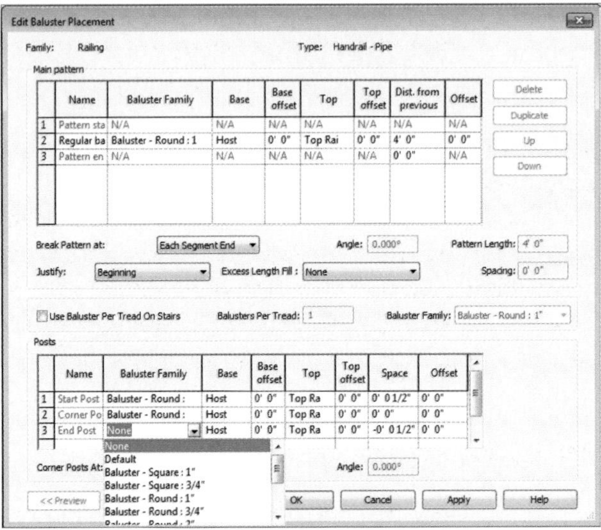

FIGURE 5.4 Edit Baluster Placement settings

Now let's begin creating the "design" stair.

Creating Your Design Stair

As we mentioned earlier in this chapter, there are now two stair tools in Revit Architecture. The tools are located on the Architecture tab on the Circulation panel.

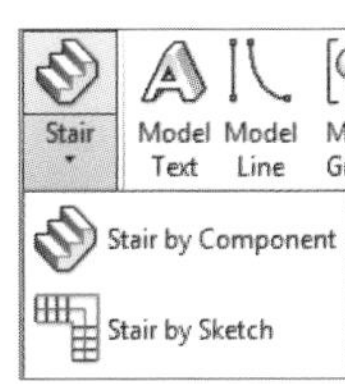

The new stair tool is called Stair by Component. As the name suggests, this tool will help you create stairs that can be broken down into their individual components for quicker detailing. The original stair tool, Stair by Sketch, still exists as well.

It's important to note that the Stair by Component tool is new and does not provide the breadth of design options that the original stair tool does. Because of this limitation, we're going to walk you through creating a stair using both tools. Depending on your project, you'll need to choose the right stair tool for the job.

Straight Run

Let's begin with the classic Stair by Sketch tool. Select this tool, and you'll enter sketch mode, similar to what you saw with the railing. Before you draw a stair, rename the default stair: click Edit Type in the Type Selector, click the Duplicate button in the Type Properties dialog box, and name the new stair **Stair-Design**. This is the stair you'll use to create numerous configurations.

Swapping Out Family Types Is Easy

Note that stairs, railings, and ramps, like other system families, can be changed dynamically using the Type Selector. This process works the same for Revit Architecture component families as well. Suppose your design changed, and a wood stair is now a steel stair. If you already have that stair type created, you only need to swap out one family type for another—your stair as well as all your views will update accordingly. This makes a very good case for creating a file of common stair types for your office's library.

Let's start by creating a straight-run stair:

1. From the Level 1 plan view, pick a point to the left and then move your cursor to the right. As you do, Revit Architecture tells you how many treads remain to complete a stair that starts on Level 1 and goes through Level 2 (Figure 5.5).

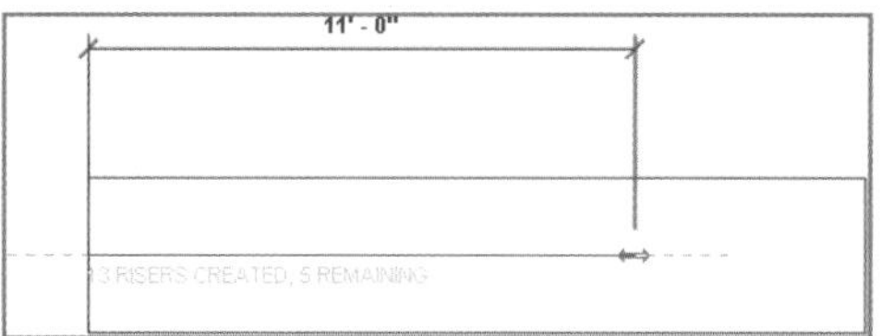

FIGURE 5.5 Sketching the straight-run stair

2. Select the Railings Type option in the Tools palette. Specify the Handrail – Design type that you created earlier (Figure 5.6), and click OK. Revit Architecture will use this default handrail whenever you create this stair, until you specify another type.

3. Close sketch mode by clicking the green check in the Mode panel. The resulting stair is shown in the default 3D view in Figure 5.7.

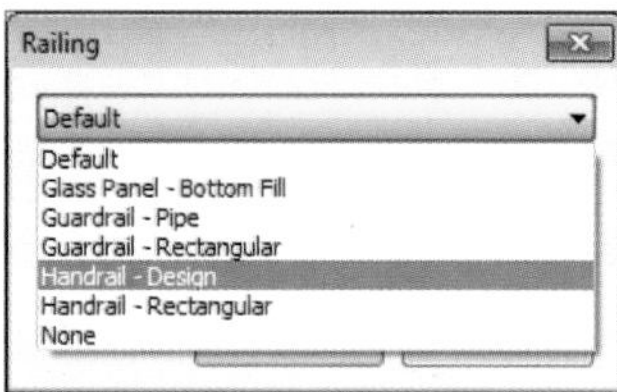

FIGURE 5.6 Specifying the railing type

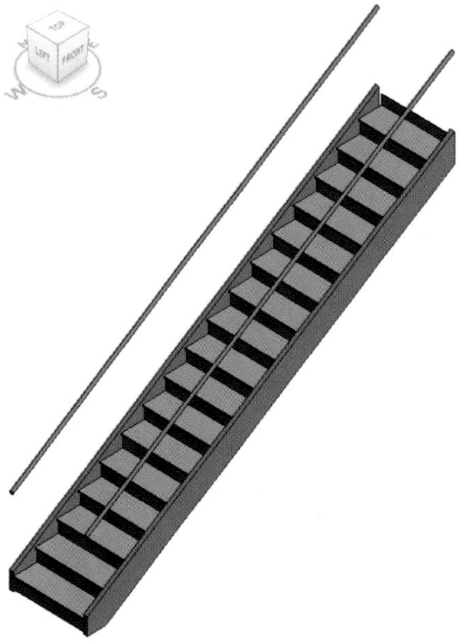

FIGURE 5.7 The resulting stair

With the stair created, let's create the same stair with the new stair tool. Begin by selecting the Stair by Component tool from the Circulation panel. Then continue as follows:

1. From the Level 1 plan view, pick a point to the left and then move your cursor to the right as you did in the previous exercise. The tool behaves just like the Stair by Sketch tool, telling you how many treads remain to complete the stair.

2. Finish the sketch. The stair looks slightly different than the one created with the previous tool. Revit Architecture gives you the start stair count and the end stair count (Figure 5.8).

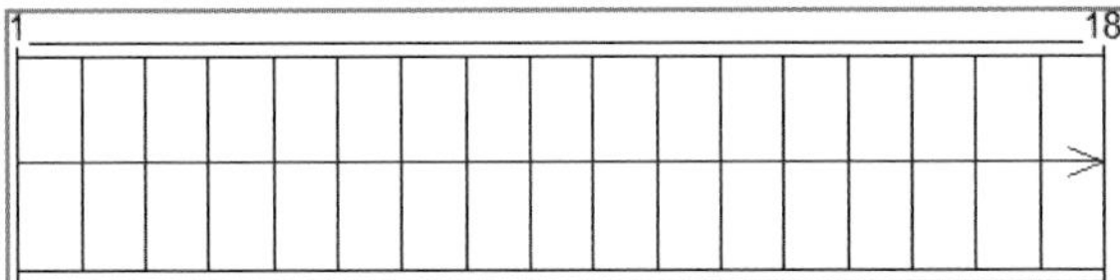

FIGURE 5.8 Sketching the straight-run stair with the Stair by Component tool

One of the nice features about this new tool is the ability to dynamically change the stair. Select the stair, and you see the familiar blue arrows ► used to drag objects. Select the bottom one, and drag it down to change the width of the stair (Figure 5.9).

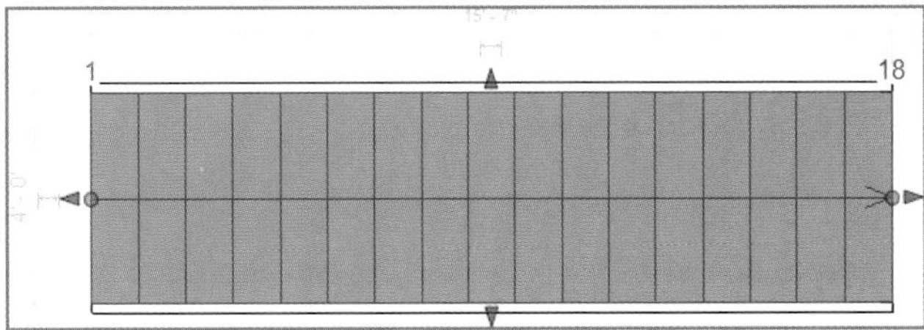

FIGURE 5.9 Dragging the stair to change the width

3. Click the green check to finish the stair and open the default 3D view. You see your two stairs side by side.

Select the stair to see one of the other differences: you can select the classic Revit Architecture stair only all as one element. The stair created with the new stair tool allows you to select the stringers separately from the treads by tabbing to them during selection. This type of stair allows you to change the properties and style of the stringers as part of their own family type (Figure 5.10).

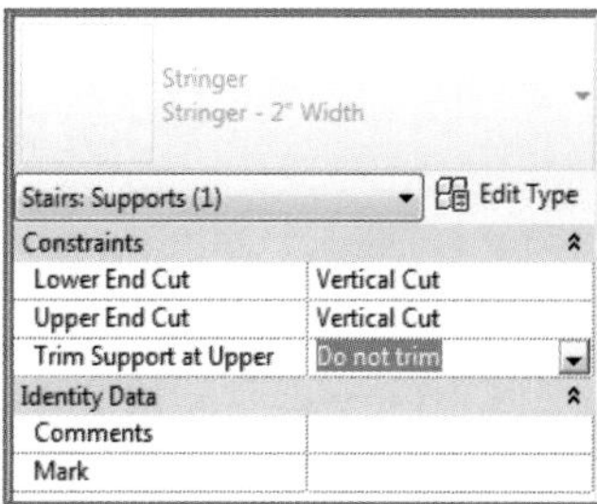

FIGURE 5.10 Modifying the stair stringer

Straight Run with Landing

You just created the most basic type of stair: a straight run with a pair of railings. However, it's important to understand how to create a variety of stair types, including stairs with landings:

1. Let's start the sketch using the classic stair tool. In the Level 1 plan view, select the Stair by Sketch tool. Draw a straight run, but stop nine risers in—about halfway through the run.

2. Start the second run of stairs, as shown in Figure 5.11. When you finish the second run of stairs, Revit Architecture creates the landing between the two runs automatically.

3. Let's modify the width of these stairs. The green boundary line that runs perpendicular to the risers represents the stringer location and can be modified to change the width or shape of the stair. In this stair, assume that the lower run is a different shape than the upper run.

   Select the lower green boundary line. You see round, blue grips. Choose the one at the base of the stair, and drag it downward to create a triangle-shaped run. As you drag, notice that the black lines (which represent the treads and risers) lengthen with the boundary edge. If any of these lines does not connect to another line, your stair can't be created. In Figure 5.12, each of the boundary lines is stretched except the first one.

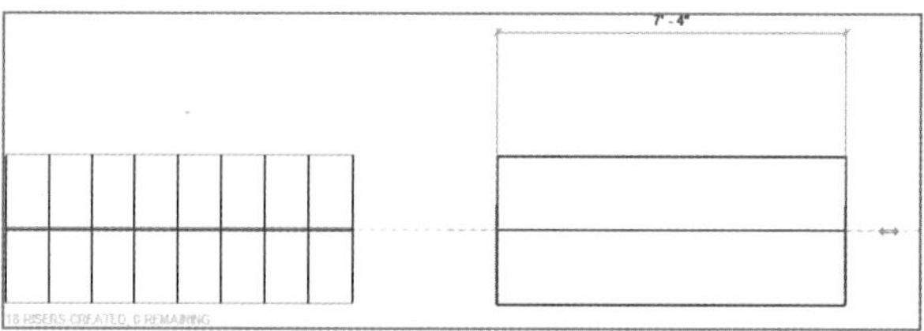

FIGURE 5.11 A second run of stairs and landing

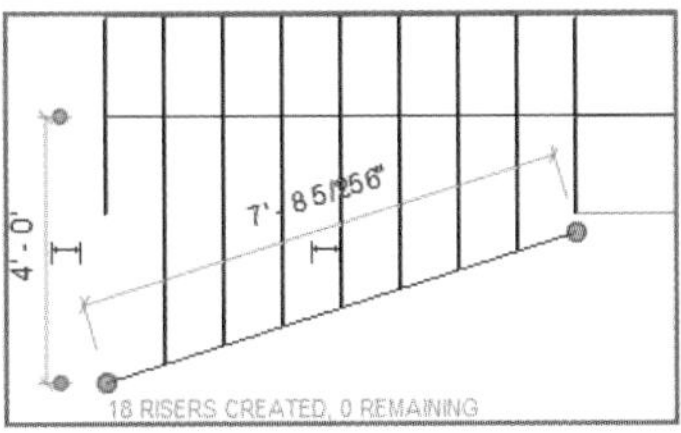

FIGURE 5.12 Modifying the stair boundary

4. Resolve this gap by choosing the Trim tool from the Modify panel and selecting the boundary line and the black riser line. Doing so closes the stair. Click the green check to finish the stair.
5. Finish the sketch. The stair resembles Figure 5.13 in the default 3D view.

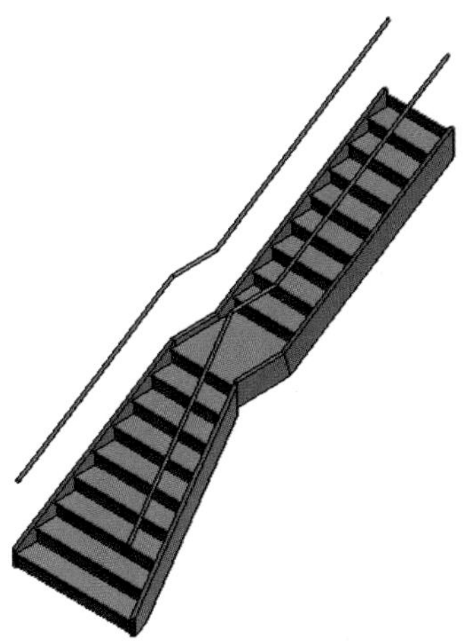

FIGURE 5.13 Complete stairs with a middle landing

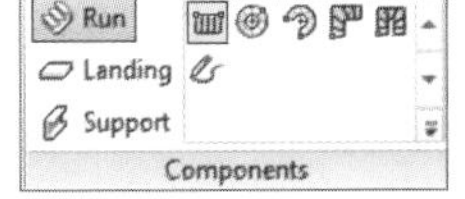

Creating this same stair with the Stair by Component tool uses a slightly different approach. Open the Level 1 plan view again, and select the Stair by Component tool. The Components panel offers a toolkit that differs from that used for the classic stair. You have tools to create a straight run (default) but also circular, curved, dog-legged, and U-shaped stairs. Follow these steps:

1. Because the stair you're creating is a straight run with a landing, leave the default selected. Start the stair similar to the last run by clicking and then moving the mouse to the right until you've placed nine risers. Click again to end that run.

2. By moving the mouse further right, you can define the landing. Click to begin the second run of stairs, and click again to end it after you've placed all the risers. The full stair in sketch mode looks like Figure 5.14. Note that when you use this tool, Revit Architecture supplies you with a tread count.

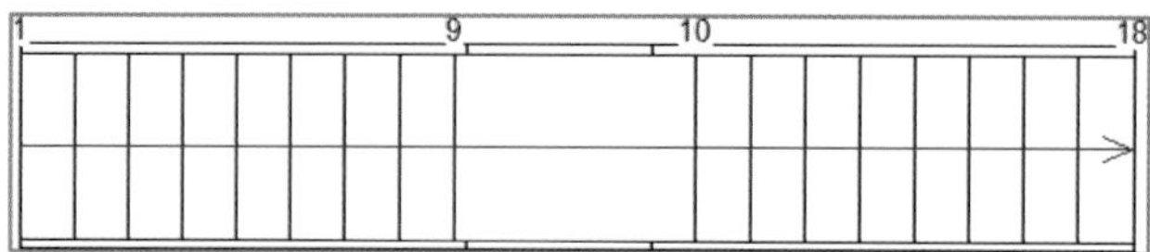

FIGURE 5.14 A second run of stairs and landing

3. Click the green check to finish the stair.

Multistory Runs

For multistory runs, Revit Architecture is able to take a stair that goes between two levels and repeat it continuously. This will work only if all the level-to-level heights are identical. Let's create a multistory stair:

1. You need to create some additional levels. As shown in Figure 5.15, open the South elevation and click the Level tool on the Datum panel of the Architecture tab. Click the elevation and drag the mouse from left to right to place the level, taking care that the heights are equally spaced.

   As discussed earlier, you can change the level heights by clicking the blue elevation text. For this example, repeat the levels at 10′-0″ (3 m) increments—up to 40′-0″ (15 m). Figure 5.15 shows several stair types, including the ones you've created.

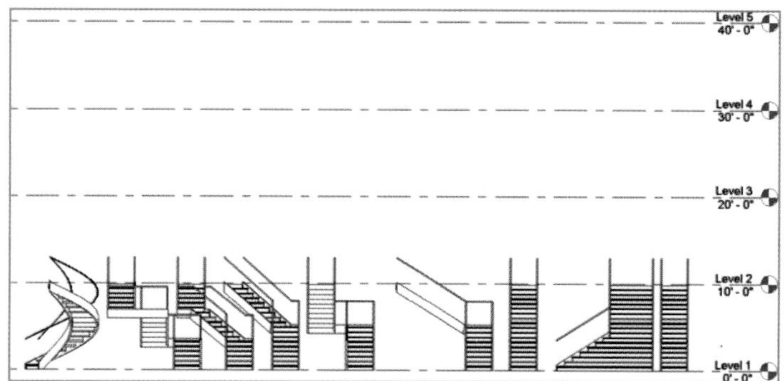

FIGURE 5.15 Adding additional levels to the model

2. Creating a multistory stair works the same for each of the stair tools. Select one of the tools, and create a U-shaped stair. Select a start point for the stair, and mouse to the right. Click to select the top of this run. Now, move the mouse down, and create a run from right to left, parallel to the first run (Figure 5.16).

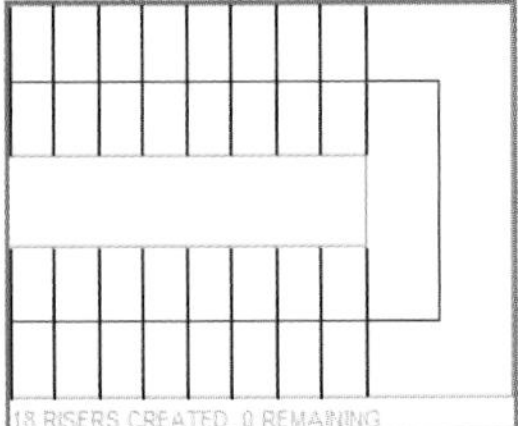

FIGURE 5.16 Creating the stair run

3. Before you complete the stair, you need to change the stair properties. In the Properties palette, each stair has a Base Level and a Top Level. Below those settings is the Multistory Top Level parameter. Because your stairs run from Level 1 to Level 2 and then repeat for the floors above, you need to change the Multistory Top Level parameter to Level 4—or whatever your highest level is (Figure 5.17).

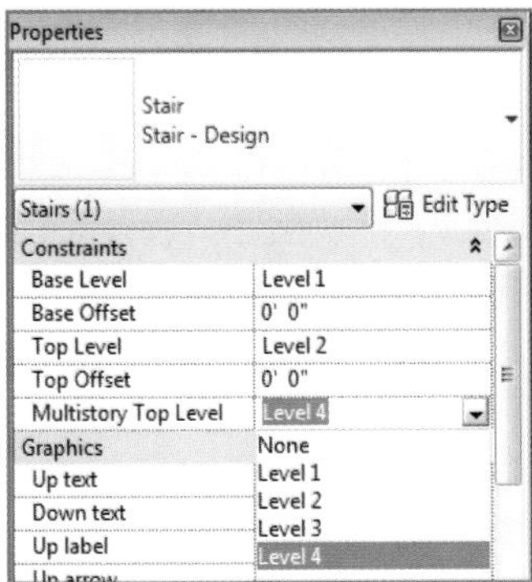

FIGURE 5.17 Changing the property to a multistory stair

4. Once you complete the multistory stair, the stair quickly propagates across all levels (Figure 5.18). If you edit the stair or railings associated to the multistory stair, the entire multistory configuration changes as well.

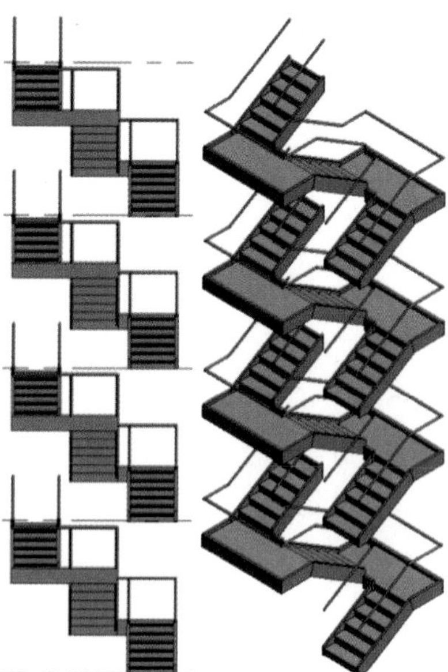

FIGURE 5.18 The completed multistory stair

Setting the Host Function for Railings

By now you've noticed that railings have special relationships to stairs. By default, Revit Architecture creates railings at the same location as the boundary sketch of the stair. You can then select the railing and modify its sketch to suit a particular condition. It's important to understand that railings are hosted by stairs, and this relationship allows railings to follow the path of the stair.

So, let's create another stair that's wider than the stairs you've created thus far, to work with the railings a bit more. Also, remember to use the Pick New Host tool to host the railing to the stair. Here are the steps:

1. Create the stair shown in Figure 5.19 using either stair tool. Notice the landing as well as the extra width that will easily allow traffic in both directions. Finish the sketch by clicking the green check on the Modify tab of the ribbon.

2. Add two separate railing sketches using the Sketch Path tool: one for the lower run and another for the upper run. Choose the Handrail – Design railing you created earlier in this chapter. Each of these railings is created out of three separate line segments: the railing and the railing extension at either end.

In Figure 5.20, each dimension represents a different line segment. Because railings must be created as continuous lines, each set of lines must be created separately. Once you've created the set on the left run, finish the sketch and create the right side.

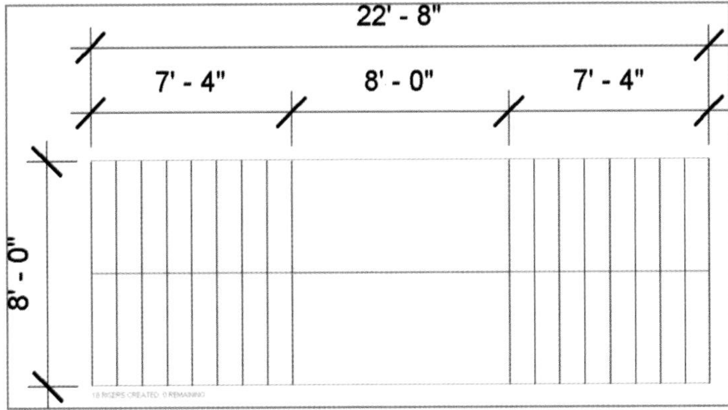

FIGURE 5.19 Stair sketch for hosting the center railing

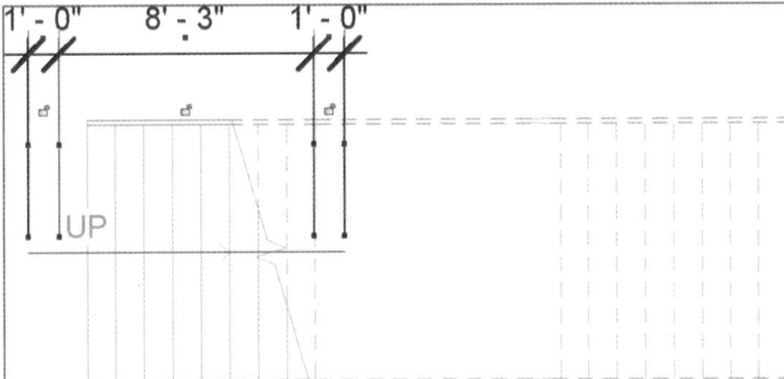

FIGURE 5.20 Lower railing sketch

3. Once you've created the railing and completed the sketch, you need to host the rail to the stair. Select either rail, and click the Pick New Host icon on the Tools palette; then select the stair. It highlights when you hover over it.

4. In Figure 5.21, notice the blue highlighted railing under the stair. This is the unhosted railing. The railing running down the center of the stair is the first railing you've hosted to the stair. Select the upper rail and, using the Pick New Host tool, host it to the stair as well.

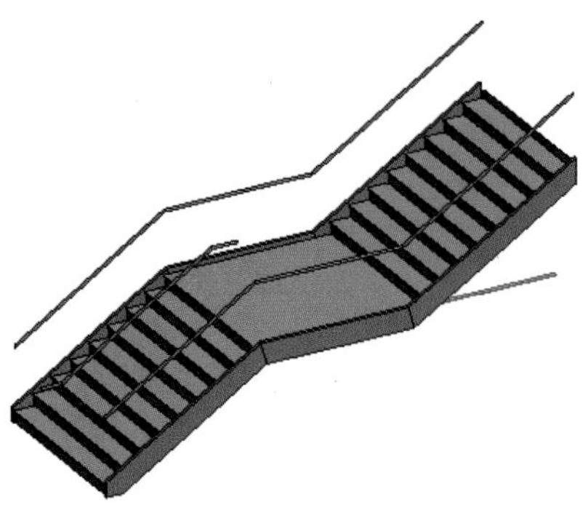

FIGURE 5.21 Adding the handrail to the stairs

One final note: not only is hosting important for railings and stairs, but it's also something you'll deal with when creating ramps and sloped floors.

Designing Ramps

Now that you're familiar with designing a number of stair configurations, ramps will come easily. It's the same basic process of sketching a desired shape and then completing the sketch, with one major difference: far more frequent landings and a shallower slope.

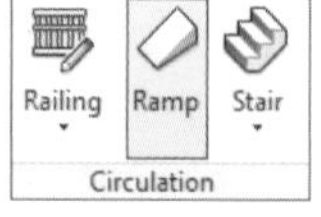

You access the Ramp tool from the Circulation panel on the Architecture tab. Keep in mind that ramps have different constraints than stairs based on slope and length. Understand that the maximum length of a ramp in one section is 30′-0″ (9 m) with a 1:12 slope (8 percent). These parameters can be changed, but by default they correlate to common code requirements.

Straight Runs

Let's start by creating a ramp in a straight run. Because you're traversing Level 1 to Level 2 (and they are 10′ [3 m] apart), this will require a ramp length of 120′ (36.5 m) at a maximum 1:12 slope, not including landings. You'll be limited to runs of 30′ (9 m) in length. So, you know that four runs will be required, with three landings:

1. Sketch the straight runs as shown in Figure 5.22. To get all the landings and ramps into the right location, you can select them as if they were linework and move them using the Move tool from the Modify panel.

Note that the run lines that indicate slope versus landings are different. Blue lines indicate slope, whereas black lines indicate level landings.

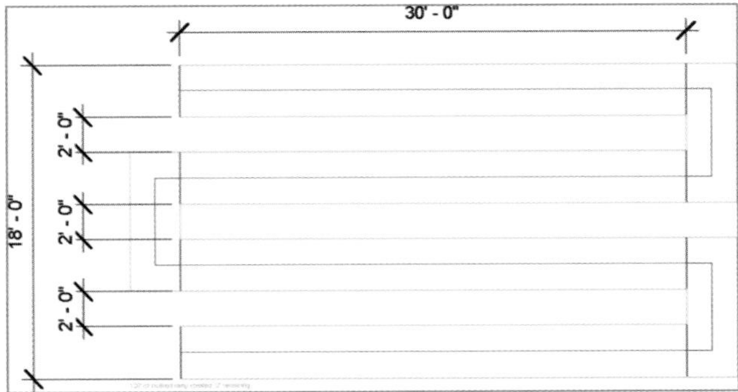

FIGURE 5.22 Straight runs of ramps

2. Apply the Design – Handrail railings using the Railing tool, and then finish the sketch. You see something like Figure 5.23, which displays the results in 3D.

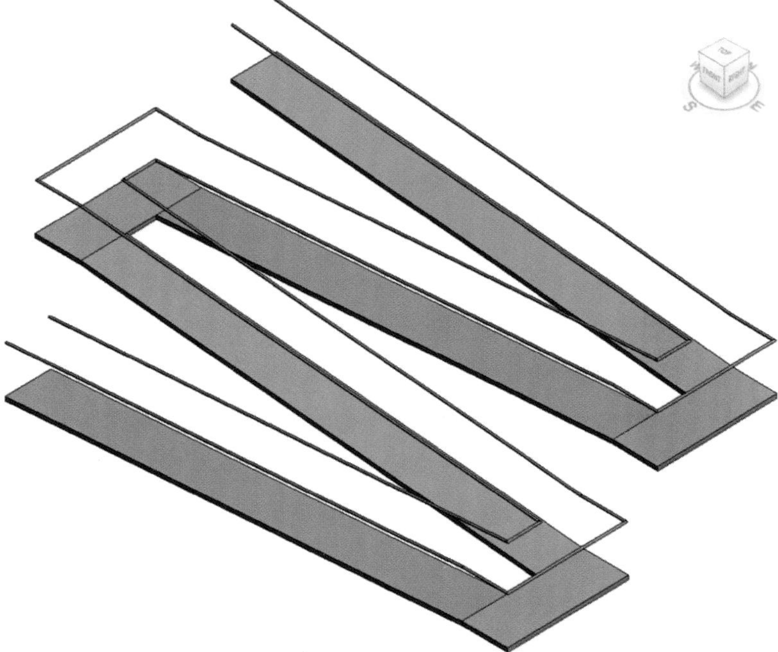

FIGURE 5.23 Ramp runs with associated railings

The process is the same as that for all the other stair configurations you've created. Multistory rules are permitted, and you must use the Set Host function when creating additional railings.

Editing Boundary Conditions

Editing boundary conditions of both stairs and ramps typically modifies the railings associated with those elements. Let's test this now with the ramp you just created:

1. Return to Level 1, select the ramp, and enter sketch mode by selecting the Edit Sketch button from the Modify context tab.
2. Delete the three green boundary lines that represent the outside edge of the landings, as shown in Figure 5.24.

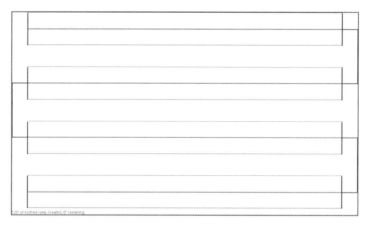

FIGURE 5.24 The modified ramp in plan with removed exterior boundary edges

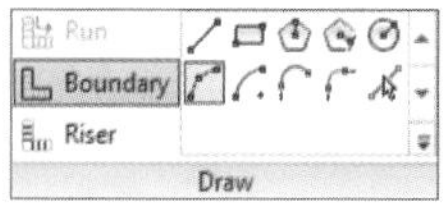

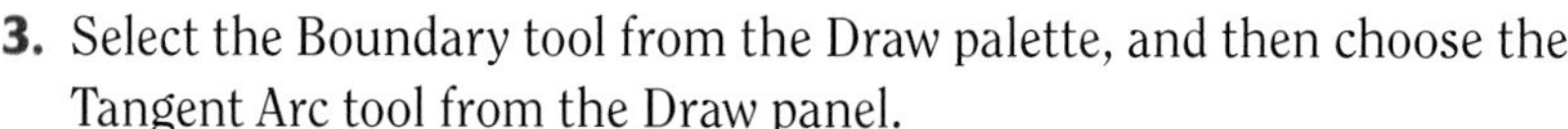

3. Select the Boundary tool from the Draw palette, and then choose the Tangent Arc tool from the Draw panel.

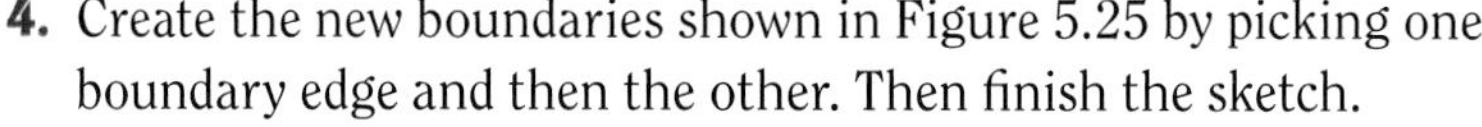

4. Create the new boundaries shown in Figure 5.25 by picking one boundary edge and then the other. Then finish the sketch.

The finished ramp is shown in 3D on the right in Figure 5.25. Revit Architecture has already modified the railings to accommodate the new boundary.

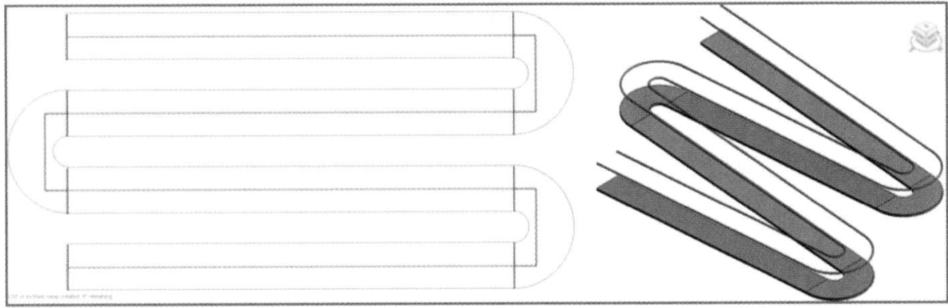

FIGURE 5.25 Modified ramp with curved boundary

Building Railings for Level and Sloped Conditions

Sketches for railings must consist of a series of connected lines—sketches with gaps or overlapping lines aren't permitted. Sketches that cross or fail to intersect properly will also produce an error message. Both sketches shown in Figure 5.26 will generate errors and will not be completed.

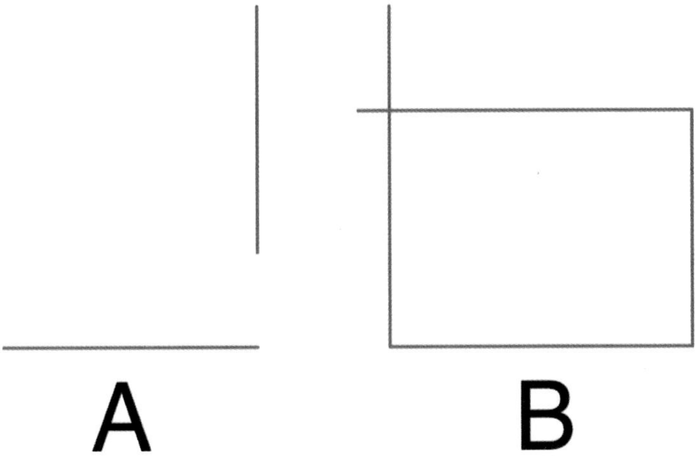

FIGURE 5.26 A doesn't join; B crosses itself.

If you attempt to complete railings like either of the ones in Figure 5.26, you'll get the warning shown in Figure 5.27.

FIGURE 5.27 Error for railings that can't complete

Like ramps, floors can also be sloped, so let's create this condition as well.

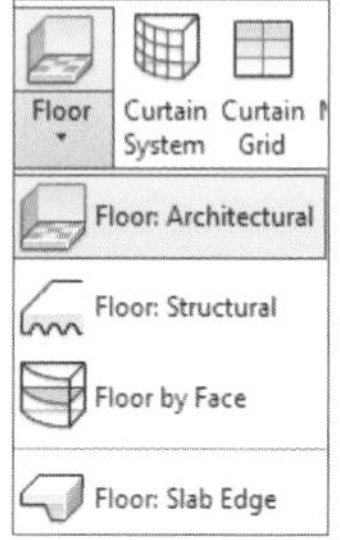

1. Open the floor plan, Level 2, and create a floor using the Floor: Architectural tool from the Build panel of the Architecture tab. Create the floor boundaries shown in Figure 5.28. If you need to review how to create floors, please refer to Chapter 4, "Floors, Roofs, and Ceilings." Don't complete the sketch just yet.

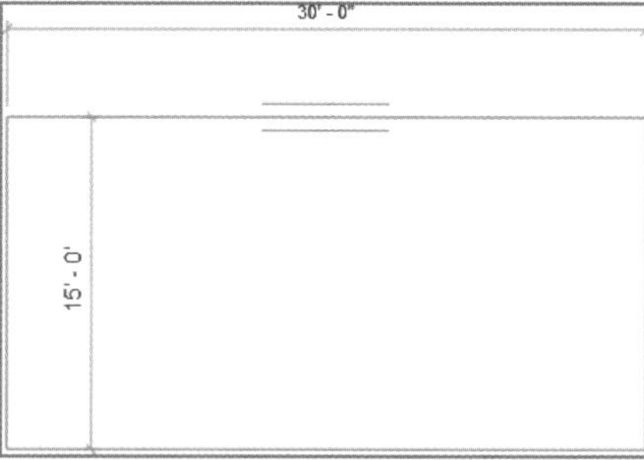

FIGURE 5.28 Creating a floor

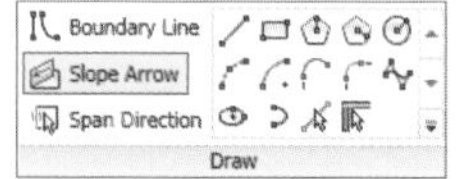

2. Select the Slope Arrow tool from the Draw panel, and then pick two points: first to the left and then the right in the center of the floor sketch.
3. In the Properties palette, set the Height Offset At Tail value to 0′-0″.
4. Set the Height Offset At Head value to 3′-0″ (1 m). Your floor should resemble the one shown in Figure 5.29 with the associated slope arrow.
5. Finish the sketch by clicking the green check in the Mode panel. This creates a floor with a 3′ (1 m) slope.

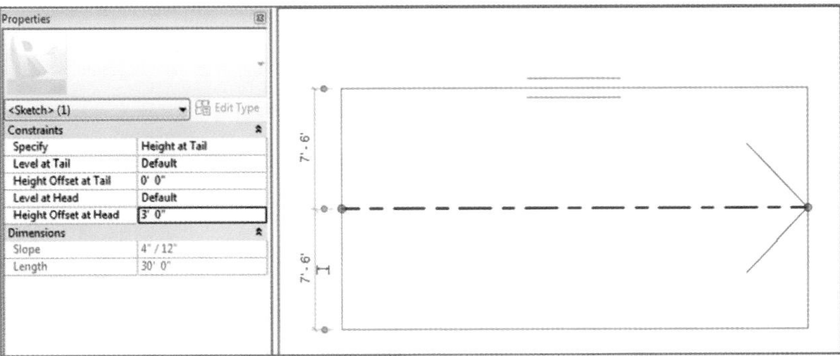

FIGURE 5.29 Adding the slope arrow

Set Host Function

Next, let's add a curved railing that follows the slope of the floor:

1. Select the Railing ➢ Sketch Path tool from the Architecture tab, which places you in sketch mode.
2. Select Pick New Host from the Modify tab, and then select the floor you just created. You'll need to select the edge of the floor to pick it.
3. Create a curved sketch for the railing, as shown in Figure 5.30. Then finish the sketch by clicking the green check.

   That's all there is to it! The railing now follows the path of the floor, even if you change the configuration of the railing sketch or the floor's slope direction. You can also swap out different railing types using the Type Selector; Figure 5.30 shows one of the other default railing types in Revit Architecture.

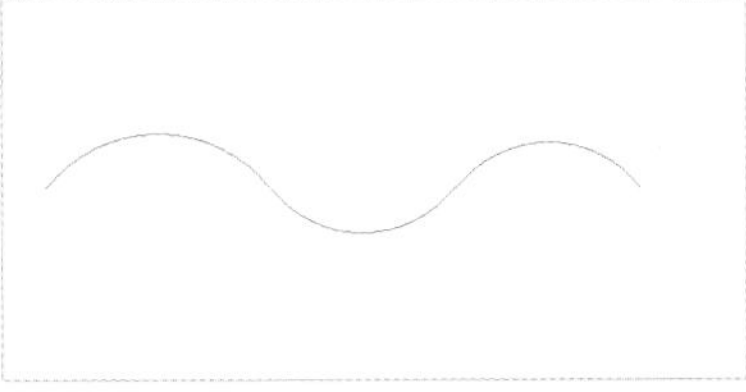

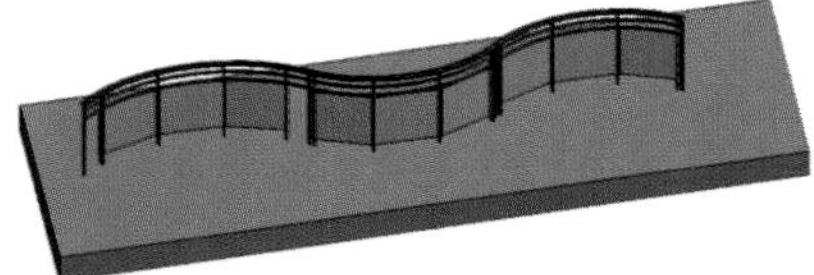

FIGURE 5.30 Curved railing sketch in elevation view

If you would like to download the completed Revit Architecture file that was created during this chapter, it's available from the book's companion web page. The file is named c05_Stairs_Ramps_Railings.rvt.

From Basics to Creative Art

Keep in mind that what you start with can be quickly and easily swapped out with more complex configurations and designs later. The important thing during design is that you resolve *what* something is and *where* it is. Then, after the initial design is approved, you can return to your intent and begin to specifically resolve the details and how it will be assembled.

Revit Architecture can be used to create incredibly complex and compelling stairs and railings! Creating these types of system families is discussed in depth in *Mastering Autodesk Revit Architecture* (Sybex 2012).

Again, don't get ahead of yourself. Concentrate on the basics. Once you have those down, you'll be able to create far more detailed stairs, ramps, and railings.

Stairs and railings can be architectural works of art, and Revit Architecture gives you the tools to be really creative with them. The following is an example of what you can create if you stretch the limits of the stairs tools. Your stairs can be elegant and versatile. The image at bottom left is a very creative use of the stair tool—an elevated railing system! The bollards hold up the track (which is the railing).

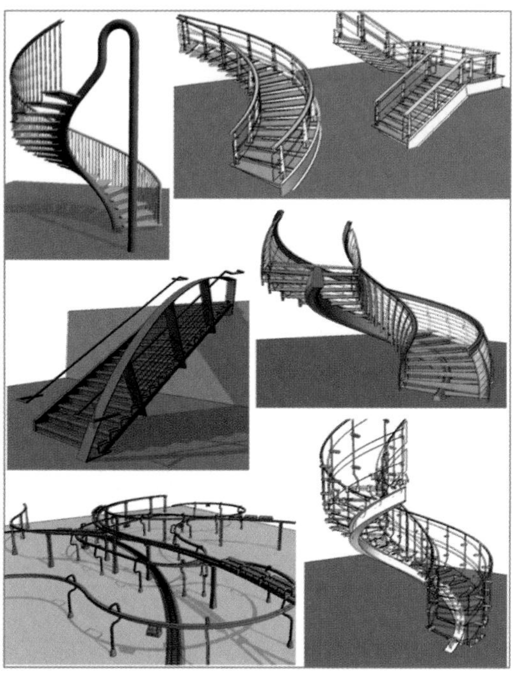

The Essentials and Beyond

You can use the default stairs, railing, and ramp tools to create the vast majority of standard conditions during your early design processes. Because this is book is about "getting started," we don't want to get too far ahead of ourselves. One day at a time!

Additional Exercises

- Try to create any of the stair configurations shown in the following graphics. Everything you need is in the default file; you won't have to load any external content. Just create and modify new stair types.
- The stair in the first graphic is actually two separate stairs that share half a landing, but they appear to be a single stair that splits at the landing. They're a combination of straight and curved sections. In some cases, you'll need to sketch boundary and riser locations manually as well as reconfigure railing sketches.

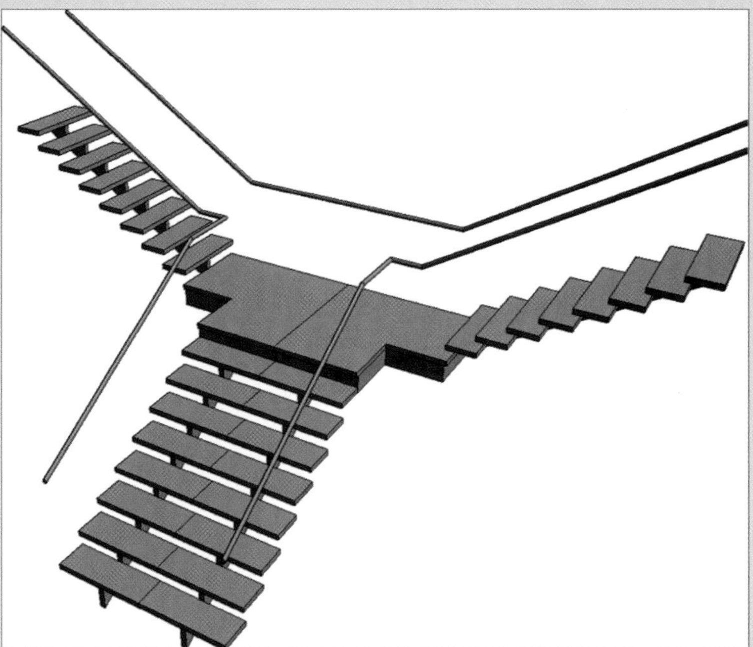

(Continues)

The Essentials and Beyond *(Continued)*

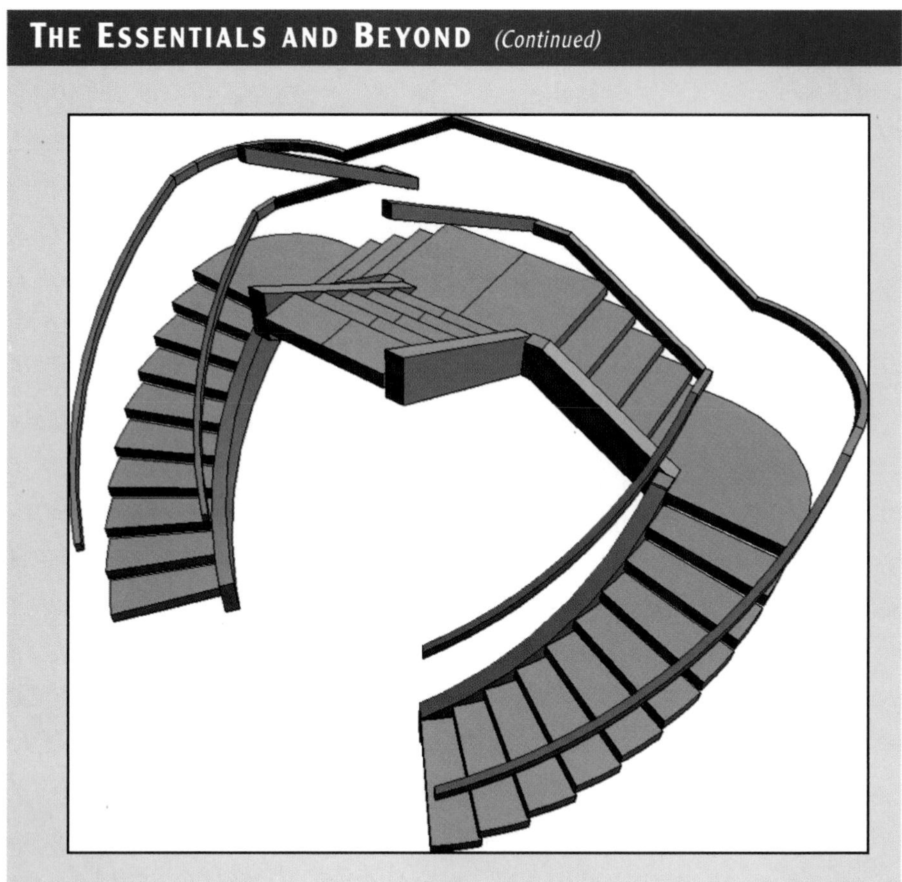

CHAPTER 6

Adding Families

What is a family in the Autodesk® Revit® Architecture software? In the simplest terms, a family can be thought of as repeatable geometry for use in a project. We will now take a step back from the modeling exercises in the previous chapters and help you develop a better understanding of the basic building blocks that make up a Revit Architecture project.

In this chapter, you learn the following skills:

- **Understanding the model hierarchy**
- **Working with system families**
- **Working with component families**

Understanding the Model Hierarchy

In Chapters 3 ("Walls and Curtain Walls"), 4 ("Floors, Roofs, and Ceilings"), and 5 ("Stairs, Ramps, and Railings"), you learned about some basic model elements such as walls, floors, and roofs. These types of objects are known as *system families* in Revit Architecture software. To better explain what a family is and how it relates to your workflow, let's explore how data is organized in the Revit Architecture platform.

One of the unique characteristics of the program is its inherent model hierarchy. In a simple description, this hierarchy can be expressed as (from broad to specific) *project*, *category*, *family*, *type*, and *instance*:

Project The overall container for the model geometry and information.

Category The structure of the content that will be placed in the project. This is how Revit s Architecture oftware ensures consistency and manages behavior of elements such as how a door interacts with a wall. You also use categories to manage graphic display and visibility of elements.

Family Similar to blocks in AutoCAD, families are the basis of geometry you create in a Revit Architecture project. An example might be a six-panel door family (you can find this family in the default Imperial Library in the `Doors` folder as `Single-Panel 4.rfa`).

Type A repeatable variation within a family. For example, the types in the six-panel door family may be size or material variations.

Instance An actual element you place in the project model. For example, door number 607 may be the twenty-fifth instance you've placed in the project of the *36× 80 Wood* type of the six-panel door family.

Let's take a quick look at this hierarchy by examining a sample Revit Architecture project file. First download and open the file `c06-Model-Hierarchy.rvt` from this book's web page at `www.sybex.com/go/revit2013essentials`. In the following exercise, you will modify some display properties throughout the entire project using the Object Styles dialog box and then change the settings of one view using the Visibility/Graphics dialog:

1. Go to Manage tab ➢ Settings panel ➢ Object Styles. The categories you see in the Object Styles dialog box (Figure 6.1) are those that are established by the software and cannot be changed. You can use these categories to modify the display characteristics of elements, but you cannot edit the names of categories.
2. Find the Walls category, and click in the Line Color field to open the Color dialog box. Set the line color to Red, and click OK.

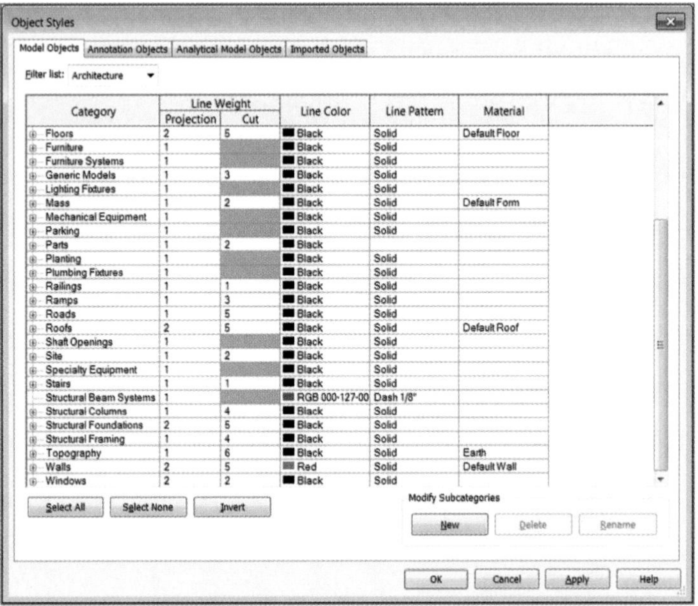

FIGURE 6.1: Categories are listed in the Object Styles dialog box.

3. Click OK to close the Object Styles dialog box. All walls in the project (even in the Level 2 floor plan) are now displayed with red lines instead of black.

4. Activate the Level 1 floor plan, and press **VG** on your keyboard (this is the keyboard shortcut for the Visibility/Graphics command, located in the View tab of the ribbon).

5. In the Visibility/Graphics dialog box, find the Doors category, and deselect it in the Visibility column.

6. Click OK to close the dialog box. Doors are no longer displayed in the Level 1 floor plan, yet they are still visible in other views.

In the preceding exercise, you used categories to make project-wide and view-specific modifications to entire groups of objects; however, these settings did not affect one particular family over another. In other words, the changes were at the category level (Walls and Doors).

Assigning Families to Categories

So, how do families get assigned to specific categories? A family's category is determined when it is created. To explore this without an actual lesson on creating families, let's walk through the first few steps to gain an understanding of the fundamental concepts:

1. From the Application button, click New ➢ Family. The New Family - Select Template File dialog box opens (Figure 6.2).

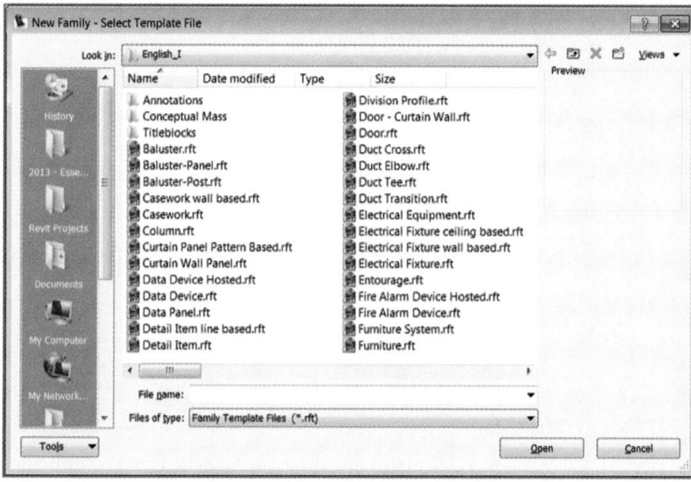

FIGURE 6.2: Selecting a family template

The list of family templates is consistent with the list of categories you saw in the project environment (Object Styles, Visibility/Graphics). Each of the available family templates is preconfigured for a specific category in terms of properties, basic materials, and reference planes.

2. Select Plumbing Fixture.rft, and click Open. The Revit Architecture user interface changes slightly to what is known as the Family Editor. Although some training materials may use this term, we must clarify that the family-editing mode is still within the main Revit Architecture application.

3. Go to Create tab ➢ Properties panel ➢ Family Category And Parameters button. The Family Category And Parameters dialog box opens (Figure 6.3); it shows the category to which the family is assigned (Plumbing Fixtures).

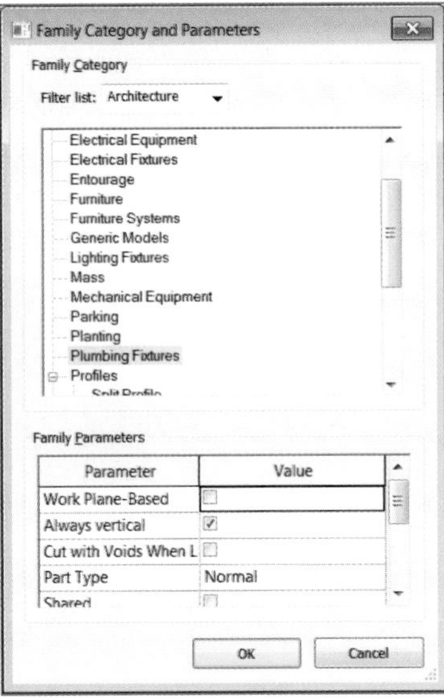

FIGURE 6.3: Editing the family category and parameters

Note that you have the option to change the category of a family before loading it into a project; however, we do not recommend frequent manipulation of a family's category. Such changes may have adverse effects on both the family and the projects into which it may be loaded. For example, it wouldn't make much sense to change a plumbing fixture family to the Doors category, because the template geometry and parameters are quite different and you may disrupt style and visibility settings in the project environment.

Revit Architecture uses two main types of families: *system* and *component*. System families exist only in the project file, whereas component families are created and stored as RFA files outside the project environment. A third type of family, known as an *in-place family*, should be used only for unique, one-of-a-kind objects for which you require nearby geometry as a reference to design. There are both 2D and 3D types of system and component families; in the following sections, we will explore these family types in greater detail.

Working with System Families

The best way to characterize system families is to consider them the *hosts* for other types of geometry. 3D elements such as walls, floors, ceilings, and roofs allow other elements such as doors and windows to exist on them or in them. Other 3D elements, such as stairs and railings, are also system families.

System families are unique in that they create geometry by using a set of rules applied to guiding geometry. If you think about a simple wall, for example, its thickness is defined by a series of structural layers (framing, sheathing, and finishes), its length is expressed by a linear path, and its height is established by some set of horizontal boundaries (either a datum or another element like a roof). As another example, a floor's thickness is defined by a series of structural layers, its vertical location is determined by a datum (level), and its boundary extents are defined by a series of lines.

Some system families are 2D. These types of system families include text, dimensions, and fill regions. Although the 2D variety are still considered system families, we think they are better referred to as *project settings* to avoid confusing them with the more common understanding of families.

Loading System Families

Because system families exist only in the project environment, there are only a few ways you can load them between projects. The first method is to use the Transfer Project Standards command. This method transfers all the families and types in a selected category between projects.

A more informal method of transferring system families is to use the Windows clipboard functions and copy/paste content between projects. This method is useful if you want to load a limited number of specific families into your active project.

Although it isn't an active loading method, the final technique to manage system families is to include them in your project templates. After you establish a level of comfort with working in Revit Architecture, you will begin to customize your own templates, thus minimizing the amount of loading required throughout the design and production process.

Let's explore the Transfer Project Standards command with the following exercise. You should already have the file `c06-Model-Hierarchy.rvt` open. If not, download it from the book's website. Then follow these steps:

1. Keep the `c06-Model-Hierarchy` model open, and create a new project using the default architectural template.
2. In the new project, go to the Manage tab ➢ Settings panel ➢ Transfer Project Standards.
3. In the Select Items To Copy dialog box, click the Check None button, and then select Text Types and Wall Types from the list, as shown in Figure 6.4. Make sure `c06-Model-Hierarchy.rvt` is shown in the Copy From drop-down in this dialog box. It is important to verify this if you have more than two project files open.

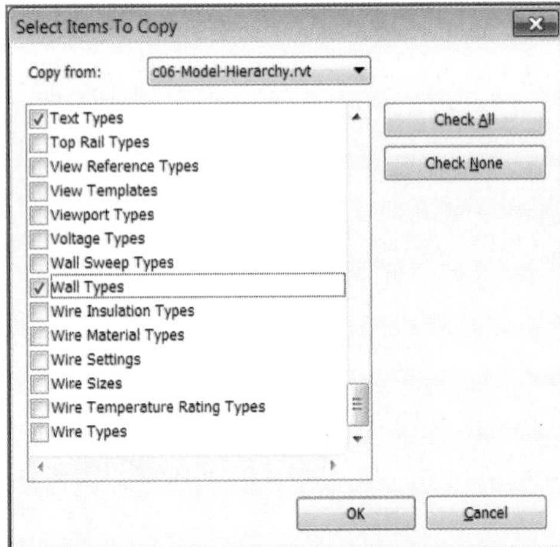

FIGURE 6.4: Selecting system families to transfer between projects

4. Click OK to close the dialog box and complete the transfer.
5. Start the Wall tool from the Home tab in the new project, and locate the transferred wall types that begin with `c06`. Create some wall segments with these types.

Placing System Families

Whether you are working with system or component families, we must clarify that you don't ever place a *family*. You always work with *types*, whether you are choosing an element in the Type Selector or using any other method. System families really don't lend themselves to being placed. Instead, they are the result of using unique commands such as Wall, Floor, and Ceiling. That said, there is an alternative method for placing any kind of family—system or component.

Follow these steps to explore placing a system family:

1. In the Project Browser, toward the bottom of the list, expand the Families heading.
2. Expand the Walls category, and you see three values: Basic Wall, Curtain Wall, and Stacked Wall. These are the three families of walls contained within a project.
3. Expand the Basic Wall list, and you see all the wall types in the Basic Wall family. Using the mouse pointer, click and drag the wall type named Exterior - Brick on CMU from the Project Browser into the view window.
4. The Wall command has been activated using the selected wall type. Draw some wall segments, and then press the Esc key to exit the command.

Working with Component Families

The second type of family you need to understand is the *component* family. These types of families live outside the project environment in RFA files and consist of everything from doors and windows to furniture and equipment. You might think of component families as anything that would be manufactured away from the job site and delivered for installation. This is in contrast to the aforementioned system families, which can be thought of as anything that is assembled at the job site.

Similar to system families, there are also 2D versions of component families including tags, detail components, and profiles:

Tags These component families are scale-dependent annotations that contain what are known as *labels* (the equivalent of block attributes in AutoCAD). Labels are special text elements that report information from model elements.

Remember, the information (number, name, keynote, and so on) is stored in the component—not in the tag.

Detail Components Used in drafting views or to embellish model views, detail components can be used as a more intelligent alternative to simple drafting lines. These components can be tagged or keynoted as if they were model components. You will find much more information on detailing in Chapter 11, "Details and Annotations."

Profiles Profile families consist of a simple outline of a shape. They are used only in conjunction with other system families such as railings, wall sweeps, and curtain-wall mullions. After you create a profile family, it must be loaded into a project and then associated with a respective system family. A profile's function must be defined in the family parameters (Figure 6.5).

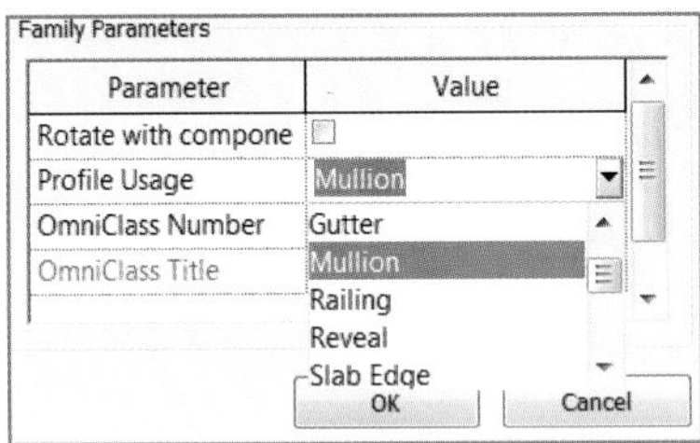

FIGURE 6.5: Defining a profile's function

Loading Component Families

You can use a few different techniques to load component families into a project. The first method is to launch the Load Family command from the ribbon. When you activate any component-based command such as Door, Window, or even the Component command itself, the Load Family command will be available toward the right end of the ribbon. You can also find the Load Family command in the ribbon's Insert tab. Remember, you can select multiple files in the Load Family dialog box (Figure 6.6) by using the Ctrl key when selecting files. If you choose to load multiple files during a component command, you may need to select a family and type from the Type Selector before placing the content in your project.

Another method to load families is dragging and dropping from any folder on your computer into the Revit Architecture window. For example, download the `c06_Face-Based_Box.rfa` file to your computer, and then drag and drop it into the `c06-Model-Hierarchy` project. (This family will be used in the next exercise.)

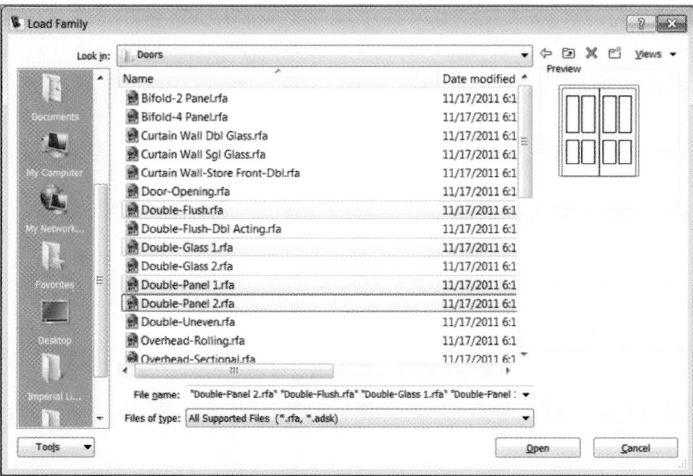

FIGURE 6.6: Selecting multiple files when loading families

Finally, you can load component families into your project templates the same way you loaded system families. Once families are loaded into a project, you can place them by starting one of the component commands or simply by dragging them out of the Project Browser and into a view window.

Using Hosted Families

For 3D component families, one key distinction you should understand is whether a family is *hosted*. How do you know if a family is hosted or unhosted? A simple way to find out is to observe the mouse pointer when a component command is activated. Let's explore this with a quick exercise:

1. Open the `c06-Model-Hierarchy.rvt` file, and activate the Level 1 floor plan.
2. From the Architecture tab, select the Door tool, and select any door from the Type Selector.
3. Hover the mouse pointer anywhere in the view window, but not near a wall. The mouse pointer displays this icon ⃠, indicating that you cannot place a door without an appropriate host: a wall.
4. Go back to the Architecture tab, and select the Component tool. From the Type Selector, choose Chair-Stacking.
5. Move the mouse pointer to any location in the Level 1 floor plan. The Chair-Stacking family can be placed anywhere because it is unhosted.

The main limitation to a hosted family is that it cannot exist without its host. Certain component families, such as doors and windows, must be hosted because their behavior dictates that they cut their host geometry when placed.

You can easily move selected components from one level to another by changing the Level parameter in the Properties palette.

Other components, such as furniture, plumbing, and light fixtures, may not need to be modeled as hosted components. These types of objects are placed in a model and almost always maintain a reference to the level on which they were placed. Notice in Figure 6.7 that the selected chair has a Level property designated as Level 1.

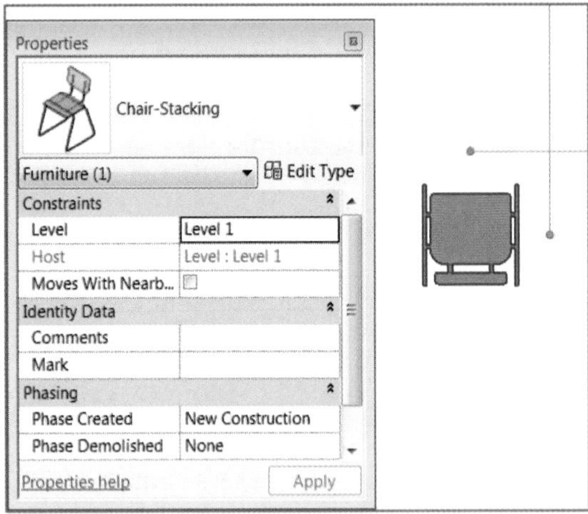

FIGURE 6.7: Examining an object's Level assignment

In the following exercise, you will observe the consequences of using hosted components and an unhosted alternative:

1. Open the `c06-Model-Hierarchy.rvt` file, and activate the Level 2 floor plan. Also download the files `c06-WC-Hosted.rfa` and `c06-WC-Unhosted.rfa`.

2. From the Architecture tab, select the Component tool, and then click Load Family in the ribbon. Navigate to the location of the downloaded family files, and load the `c06-WC-Hosted.rfa` file.

3. In the room at upper right in the layout, place two of the `c06-WC-Hosted` families on the wall at the left side of the room (Figure 6.8). Notice that you can only place these components on a wall.

4. Click the Modify button on the ribbon or press the Esc key to exit the command, and then move the host wall to the left and right. Observe how the components move with the wall.

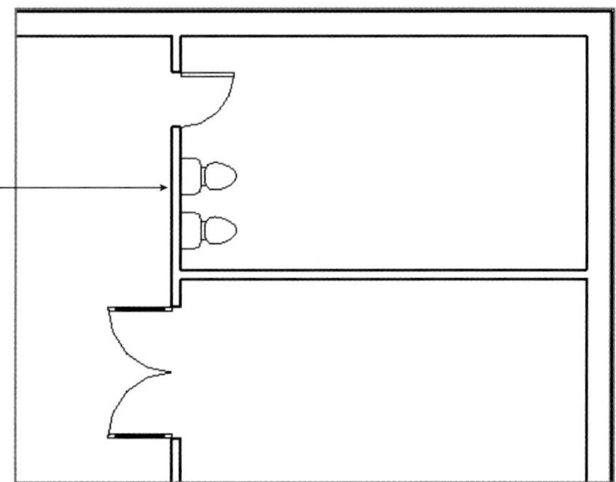

FIGURE 6.8: Placing hosted components in a model

5. Delete the wall segment where you placed the components in step 3 (indicated in Figure 6.8).

   The hosted plumbing fixtures are automatically deleted when the wall segment is deleted. Let's continue the exercise, but you'll use an unhosted version this time.

6. Start the Component command again, and click the Load Family button. Navigate to the `c06-WC-Unhosted.rfa` file, and load it into your project.

7. Place two `c06-WC-Unhosted` families along the southern wall of the same room, as shown in Figure 6.9.

Use the spacebar to rotate components while you're placing them.

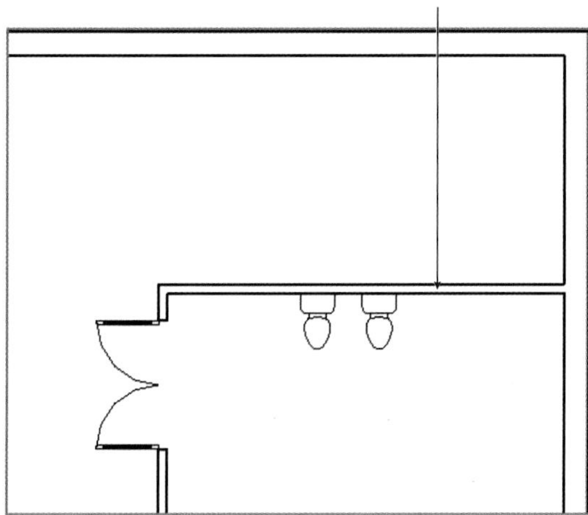

FIGURE 6.9: Placing unhosted components in a model

8. Click the Modify button on the ribbon, select the two fixtures, and then move them 3″ (75 mm) away from the wall.
9. With the two fixtures still selected, go to the Options Bar and select the Moves With Nearby Elements setting.
10. Move the host wall in the north-south direction, and observe that the fixtures display the same behavior as the hosted versions.
11. Delete the wall segment where you placed the components in step 7 (indicated in Figure 6.9). The fixtures remain.

We realize that you may not fully understand how to convert a hosted family into an unhosted family; however, with this introductory knowledge we hope you will continue to model effectively and efficiently as you develop your skills. There are more detailed skill-building exercises related to families in *Mastering Revit Architecture 2013* (Sybex, 2012).

Using Face-Based Families

A slightly different version of a hosted family is known as a *face-based family*. These types of families can be placed on virtually any surface or work plane, but they don't suffer the same limitations as hosted families. Face-based families can exist without a host element even after a host is deleted.

Let's experiment with face-based families. Continue to use the `c06-Model-Hierarchy.rvt` file from the previous exercise:

1. Activate the default 3D view, and you see the extents of the sample project, including a sloping roof. From the Architecture tab in the ribbon, select the Component tool.
2. The `c06_Face-Based_Box` family should already be loaded in your project from a previous exercise. If you can't find it in the Type Selector, click Load Family and load it into the project.
3. Place a few instances of the face-based box family around the project—on the roof and on vertical wall faces. Notice in the ribbon that the default placement method is Place On Face. If you try to place an instance on the ground plane (Level 1), you are not allowed to do so.
4. In the ribbon, change the placement method to Place On Work Plane, and then try placing some instances outside the building envelope (Figure 6.10).

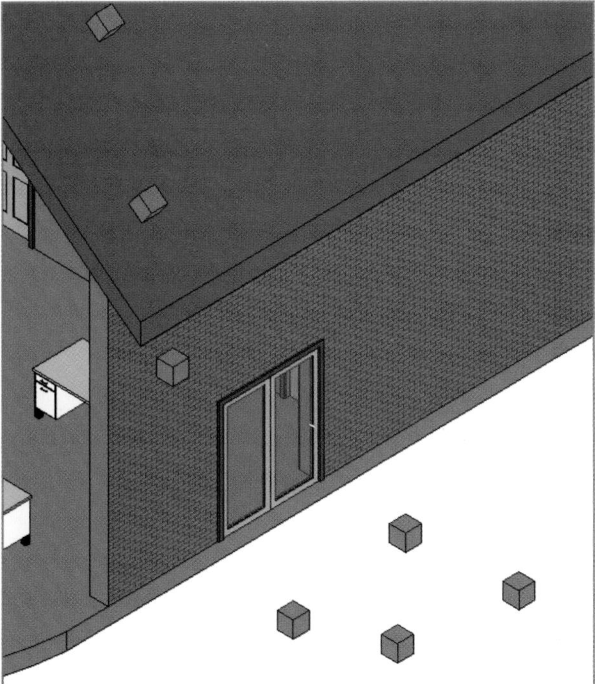

FIGURE 6.10: Placement of face-based families

Finding Content

Now that we have reviewed the fundamentals of Revit Architecture families, let's discuss one of the most important issues you may face as you start designing: the discovery of suitable content. The best place to begin is the content installed with Revit Architecture. These default families are created with relatively simple geometry and should be sufficient as a basis for the most common building types. If you installed Revit Architecture with the default settings, you will be able to access the default library whenever you use the Load Family command.

From the Insert tab, click the Load Family tool. In the Load Family dialog box (Figure 6.11), the default libraries are shown as shortcuts on the left side.

In addition to the default Revit Architecture families, various online resources provide content either free or for a fee. We have created a listing of the latest content websites on our blog, with descriptions of the content you might find on each site: `www.architecture-tech.com/2011/12/bim-content-for-revit.html`.

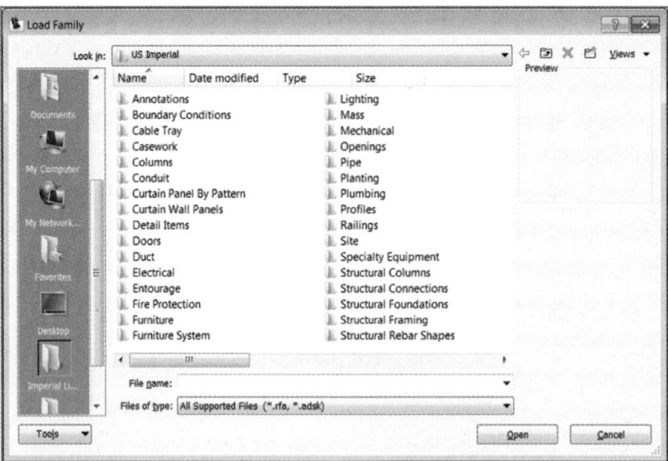

FIGURE 6.11: The Load Family dialog box

Autodesk has created an online resource called Autodesk Seek to provide content for its design software (`http://seek.autodesk.com`). You can search for families on Autodesk Seek directly from Revit Architecture. Let's explore this option:

1. Go to the Insert tab ➢ Autodesk Seek panel.
2. In the search bar, type **chairs**, and press the Enter key.
3. Your default web browser opens to the Autodesk Seek website. The results displayed match the search criteria of "chairs" and are filtered to show only content that offers Revit Architecture families (Figure 6.12).

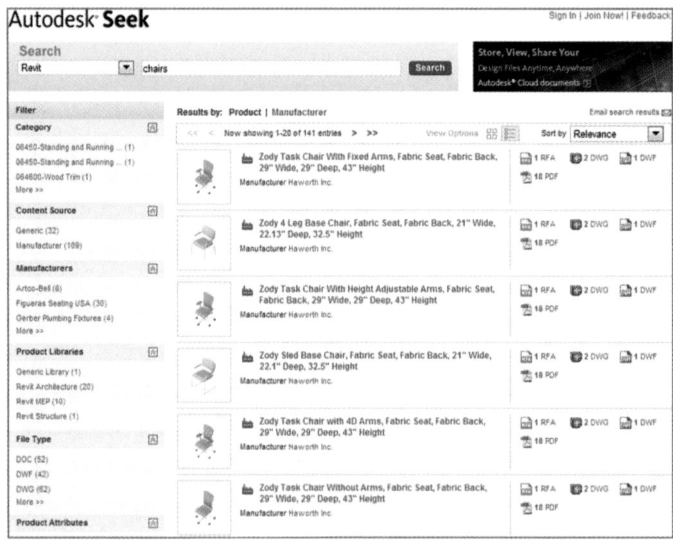

FIGURE 6.12: Content search results in Autodesk Seek

You will note on Autodesk Seek that you can choose from generic or manufacturers' content. The generic content is similar to that found in the installed library. Other content should be used with a level of care. Although an exhaustive review of such criteria is outside the scope of this book, here are some aspects you should understand about component families:

Avoid Imported Geometry Component families should not be created by simply opening an RFA file and importing 3D geometry from other modeling software. Content with imported geometry may also adversely affect functions such as rendering. For example, a light-fixture family using an imported CAD model might not have the correct material transparency to allow a light source to render properly.

Watch for Over-Modeling Families should contain only geometry necessary to document the component. That said, this level of modeling will be slightly different depending on whether you want to create a photorealistic rendering or a construction document. Excessive modeling such as fasteners, switches, knobs, dials, and so on, should be avoided.

Use Appropriate Repetition A Revit Architecture family should have a moderate level of repetition built into it. The repetition should not be too complex (all possible variations in one family), nor should it be too simple (a separate family for each variation). Reasonable content will offer a family for each set of common geometry (for example, one model line of a light fixture) with types for subtle variations (the various lamping and size options of that light fixture model).

The Essentials and Beyond

Adding families to your project is easily done either by using the default family library that is provided with Revit Architecture or by creating your own. Now that you have a better understanding of how families work and the different family types, you can create a host of new elements for any project.

Additional Exercises

- Open a Generic model template. Modify the family category. What are some of the categories to which you cannot change the Generic model?
- Try loading other types of content, such as different window and door types. Tag these objects, and observe the difference in behavior.
- Locate all the instances of a particular family type by using Select All Instances.
- Try using copy/paste to transfer system families and component families between projects. Observe the differences in behavior.

CHAPTER 7

Modifying Families

Now that you have added a number of families to your project and the design has progressed, you'll often find it necessary to modify the families. Sometimes swapping out a generic family component for one that is more specific is the best solution. In other cases, it's simply a matter of opening the component family that you started with and tweaking the geometry to better fit your design. Either solution is viable—which you choose depends on the result that is better for your design process.

In this chapter, you learn the following skills:

- **Editing view display and detail level**
- **Changing the family category**
- **Modifying family geometry**

Editing View Display and Detail Level

As you learned in Chapter 6, "Adding Families," finding and placing content is pretty straightforward, but learning to modify it will take a bit more time. One of the first things you want to consider when loading a family into your project is the level of detail the family displays at different orientations and scales. It's not likely that every part of a component family needs to display at all scales. It's more likely that too much detail will be confusing (particularly at smaller scales). Just a decade or so ago, when we used pencils, knowing when to stop drawing detail was pretty easy. But high-resolution computer displays that give you the ability to zoom in and out, as well as modern printing technologies, have allowed us to create far more detail than is necessary or meaningful. So, how do you display just the right level of detail in Autodesk® Revit® Architecture? In this chapter, we'll explore some fundamental techniques you can use to modify families to meet your needs.

To complete the exercises in this chapter, download the file `c07_Modifying_Families_Start.rvt` from the book's web page. To download other content you will create during this chapter, go to `www.sybex.com/go/revit2013essentials`. From there, you can download the family files `c07_Three_Light_Fixed.rfa` and `c07_L_Shaped_Handrail.rfa`.

First, go to the South elevation in the exercise project. Create a copy of the desk to the right of the first one. You can zoom to fit by right-clicking in the view and selecting Zoom To Fit. But this only shows you everything in your view—it doesn't give you a sense of what is going to legibly print (Figure 7.1).

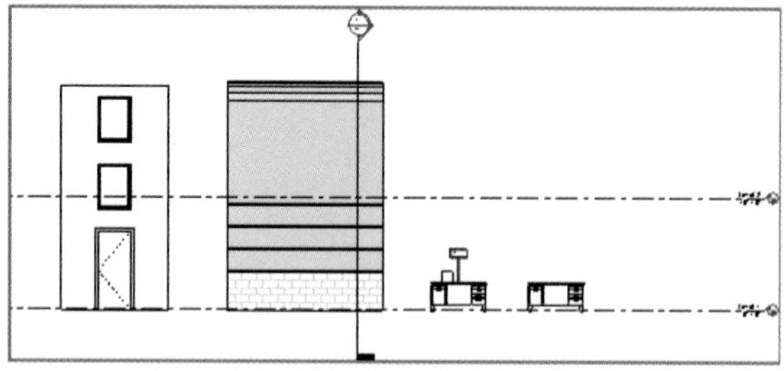

FIGURE 7.1 Zoom To Fit

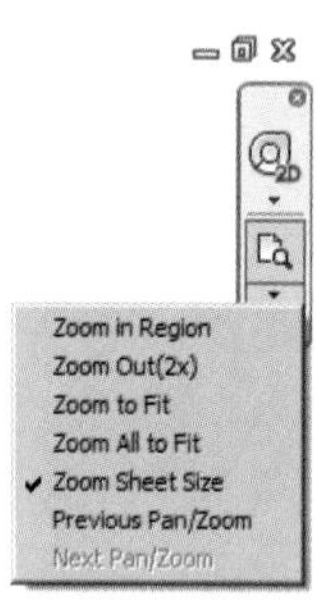

A great way to tell what will be graphically legible when you print is to select the Zoom Sheet Size option from the Navigation bar on the right side of the view. Doing so will take the scale of the view into account when zooming in (or out). The difference is shown in Figure 7.2. If you need to see what's important in a view (and you don't want to get carried away with details that don't yet matter), this is a great tool.

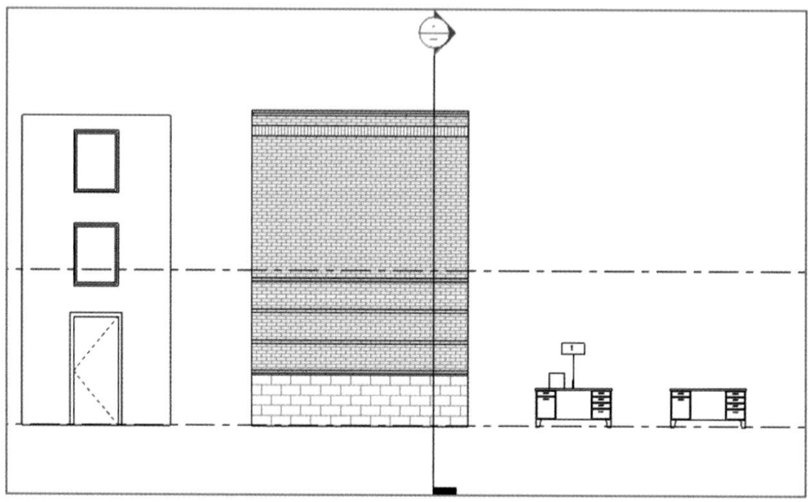

FIGURE 7.2 Zoom Sheet Size

Try changing the scale in the View Control Bar to 1/2″ = 1′ -0″ (1:20), and then click the Zoom Sheet Size button again. You will see a more visible difference in what is displayed on the screen relative to the scale of the view.

Notice in both the previous figures that the hardware on the desk is completely visible in both views—which is reasonable to expect. But let's see what happens when the view scale changes. Figure 7.3 illustrates the same desk in elevation at dramatically different scales (1′ = 50′ [1:50], 1′ = 20′ [1:20], and 1′ = 10′ [1:10], respectively).

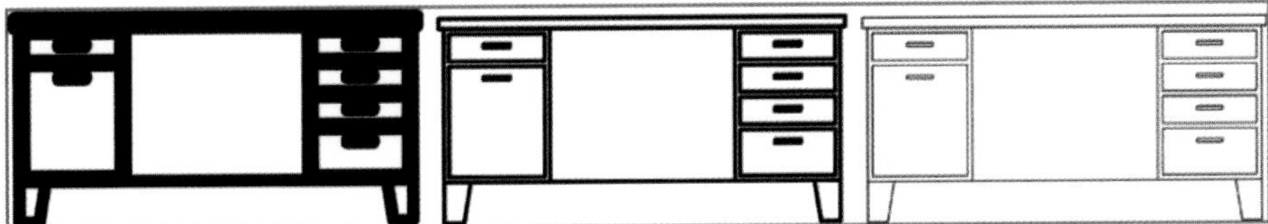

FIGURE 7.3 Elevation at different scales

View Scale and Detail Level

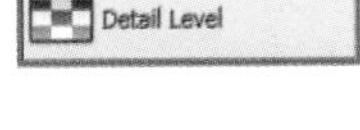

As you can see, all the geometry of the desk—drawers and hardware—is visible at all view scales. But it doesn't have to be this way. Our rule of thumb is that if two lines are overlapping to the point that they'll print like a single line, they probably don't need to be seen. Nor do you want your computer to expend processing power displaying, printing, and exporting information that isn't important. There are built-in settings for displaying information at different scales. You can find them in the Manage tab under Additional Settings ➢ Detail Level, as shown in Figure 7.4.

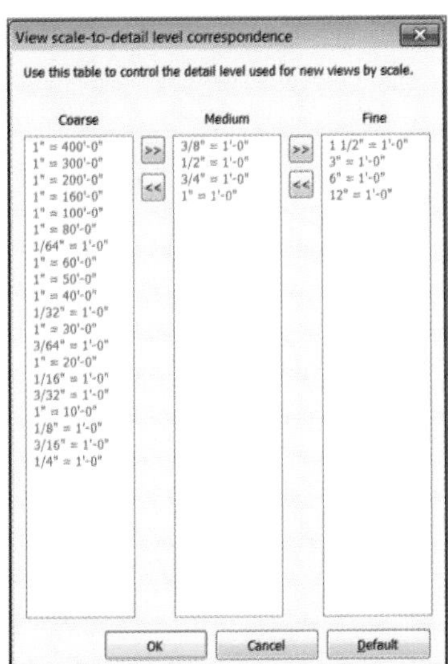

FIGURE 7.4 View Scale-To-Detail Level Correspondence settings

In the Detail View settings, you can choose which view scales use one of three detail levels: coarse, medium, or fine. Based on the scale of the view when a view is first created, some elements will automatically display or hide. But to take advantage of this power, you must make sure the content in your project has the appropriate view scale–to–detail level correspondence. You should also know that the Detail Level and View Scale parameters are separate properties of project views. As such, if you change the scale of a view, the detail level does not automatically change. The settings shown in Figure 7.4 are automatically applied only when a view is first created.

Let's look at another common example. Create a default stair run, as shown in Figure 7.5. Then look at the stair in the South elevation at a couple of different scales (Figure 7.6).

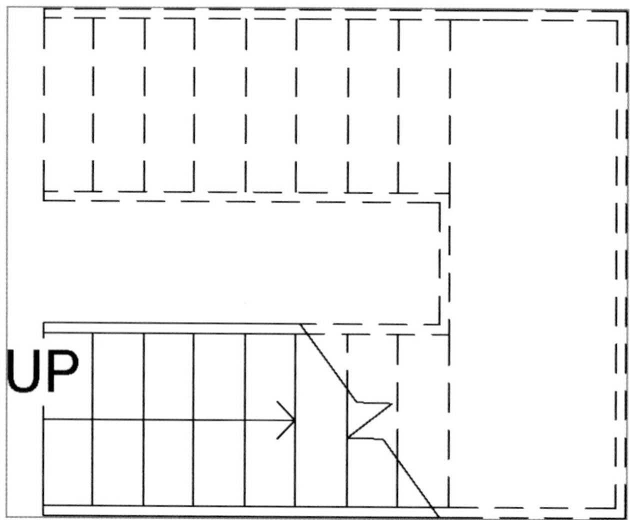

FIGURE 7.5 Default stair run (plan)

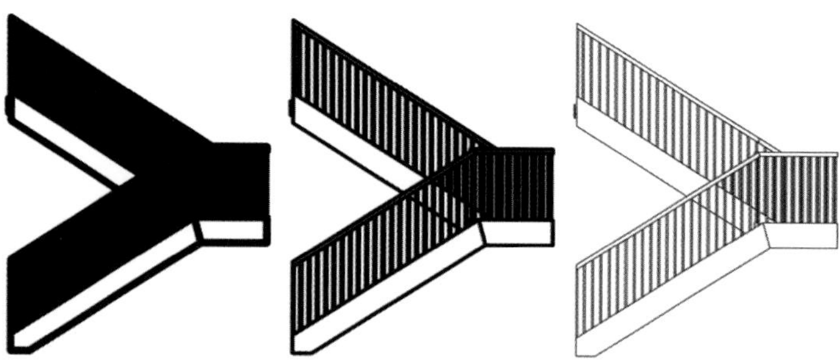

FIGURE 7.6 Default stair run (elevation)

Figure 7.6 illustrates three scales (1′ = 100′ [1:100], 1′ = 50′ [1:50], and 1′ = 10′ [1:10]). As you can see, the balusters show up at every level of detail—even to the point that they're displaying as a solid black blob! This isn't the kind of graphic communication you want from your project.

The scale for each of the views illustrated is correct, but why isn't the model geometry automatically hiding at the coarser scales? You must first ensure that the content is assigned to the appropriate detail levels in the Family Editor. Some library and template content will be configured correctly, but some families will require modification.

Level of Detail

In this section, you will modify the detail level settings for the desk and stair examples and then reload them into the sample project. Let's start with the desk:

1. Select the desk, and choose Edit Family from the Modify menu, or right-click and choose Edit Family from the context menu.

   When you open a family or use the Edit Family command from within a project, the user interface (UI) changes to offer you various tools and commands for developing families. This mode is known as the Family Editor.

2. Make sure the default 3D view is active, and select the hardware (the drawer pulls) on the front of the desk. You will need to press the Ctrl key to select both sets. Click the Visibility Settings button on the Modify tab of the ribbon to open the Family Element Visibility Settings dialog box.

   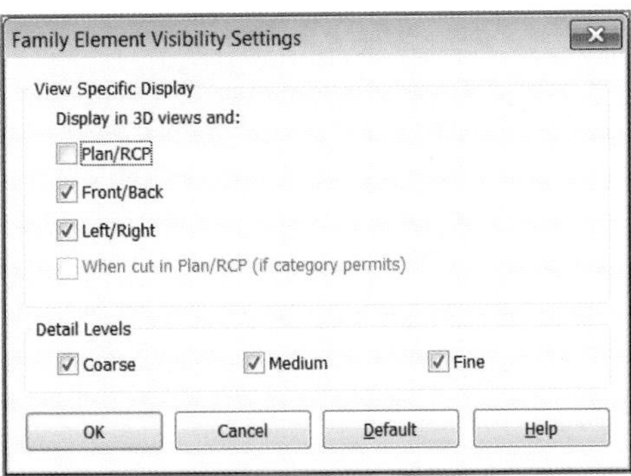

   This dialog box allows you to determine the visibility for both the orientation and level of detail for the hardware. As you can see, the hardware is already set to not display in plain view.

3. The hardware shows up at all levels of detail (Coarse, Medium, and Fine). Change the settings so that it *only* shows up at a Fine level of detail. Do the same for the hardware on the other side of the desk (Figure 7.7).

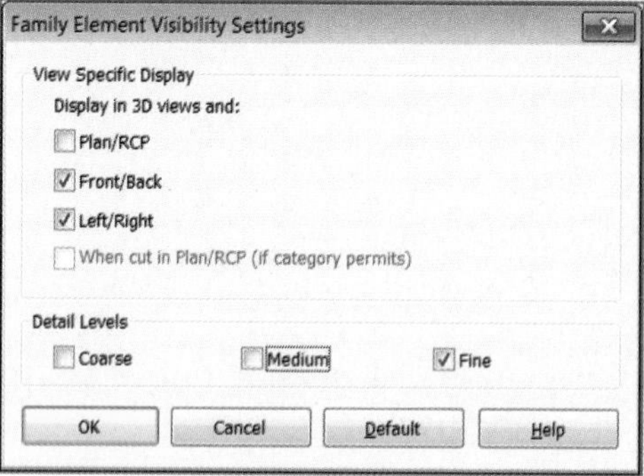

FIGURE 7.7 Editing levels of detail for hardware

4. Select the faces of the drawers. Change the visibility settings so they show up at the Medium *and* Fine levels of detail (but not Coarse).

5. On the Modify tab of the ribbon, click the Load Into Project button to reload the desk family into the project. The results are shown at the same detail levels as before (Figure 7.8), but legibility has been increased.

FIGURE 7.8 The level of detail corresponds to scale.

Next you'll repeat the same procedure for the stairs. The trick is that the balusters are not editable by selecting the railings. Railings are a system family, so you have to select the family from the Project Browser.

6. In the Project Browser, expand the Families tree and then Railings. Right-click Baluster-Square, and choose Edit to open the family in the Family Editor.
7. Select the element on the screen, and click Visibility Settings in the Modify tab of the ribbon. Uncheck the Coarse detail level. Note that the Plan/RCP views are already unchecked, meaning the baluster will not display by default in those views.
8. Click Load Into Project in the Modify tab of the ribbon to reload the family into the project, and the balusters display only at the Medium and Fine levels of detail. You now see results in a much cleaner graphic display.

Changing the Family Category

Certification Objective

Family components schedule according to their category, which is determined when you start to model a new family component. When you create a new family component, you must first select the appropriate template.

But in many cases, you will realize afterward that you need to change this category to another. You may have to do this for a family component that you created as well as ones you've downloaded. Changing categories is easy to do.

Editing the Family Category

For this exercise, select the face-based box that we provided in the previous chapter. It's placed on top of the desk in this chapter's sample project file. Follow these steps:

1. Right-click the face-based box, and choose Edit Family from the context menu.

   When the family opens, the box is resting on a large platform. Don't worry about this—it's the context for the "face" of the face-based family (Figure 7.9). Face-based and hosted families already have geometric context (along with critical parameters and reference planes) in their templates so you can model in context and test parametric behavior.

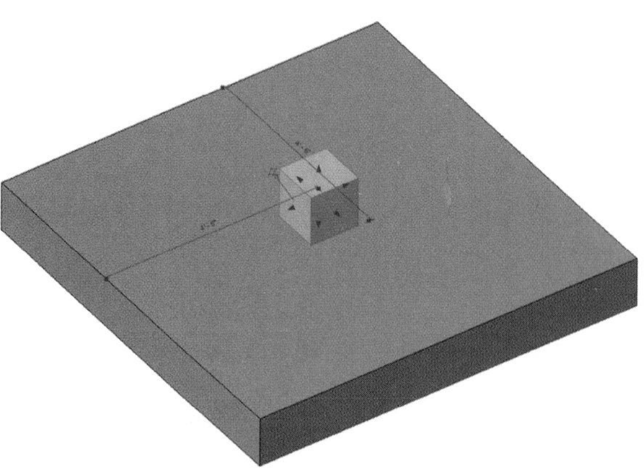

FIGURE 7.9 Editing the face-based family

When you modeled this component, you didn't know what the category would be, so you left it as a Generic Model. But now the design has progressed and the component needs to schedule as Specialty Equipment. You will now take the steps necessary to change the family's category.

2. Select Home tab ➢ Properties panel ➢ Family Category And Parameters.

3. When the Family Category And Parameters dialog box appears, the current category is selected. Select Specialty Equipment from the list (Figure 7.10), and click OK.

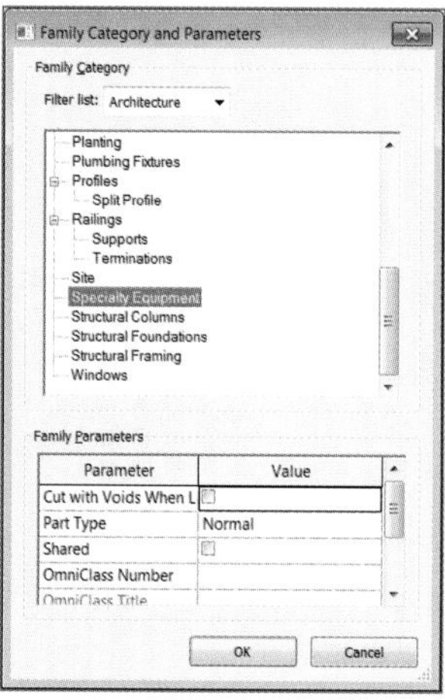

FIGURE 7.10 Changing the family category

4. Click Load Into Project from the Modify tab on the ribbon to reload the family into the project environment; select the option to override the existing version. In a CAD environment, this step would be just like reloading a block—you're simply updating the element with the new information. The family doesn't appear to have changed, but it now schedules according to its new category.

Editing the Insertion Point

Another adjustment you may need to make is to change the insertion point of a family. This issue arises for one of two reasons. First, a family will flex about its insertion point; therefore, the insertion point is maintained when the family's dimensions change. Second, if you need to replace one family with another of the same category, they should swap at the same insertion point. If you have a family with an insertion point that is at a corner and swap it with another family whose insertion point is at the center, all the instances of that family throughout your project will shift. To solve this, you'll have to edit the insertion point:

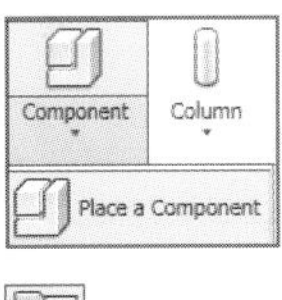

1. For this example, go to the Level 1 plan view. Go to the Architecture tab ➢ the Component flyout ➢ Place A Component.

2. From the Modify | Place Component contextual menu, click the Load Family button; under the `Furniture` folder, choose the `Chair-Executive.rfa` family. Place it as shown in the left image in Figure 7.11, making sure the chair is centered under the desk's opening.

FIGURE 7.11 Loading and placing the chair in the project

3. Select the desk. In the Type Selector, choose the 72″ × 36″ (180cm × 90cm) type. The changes in the desk dimensions are applied from the upper-right corner; therefore, the chair is no longer centered and will have to be moved. If there were many chairs and desks in this situation (such as an office layout), this task would be very tedious! Let's change the insertion point of the desk to avoid this situation in future design iterations.

4. Select the desk, and click Edit Family in the ribbon to open the desk in the Family Editor. Open the Ground Floor, floor plan view.

   The insertion point of a family is determined by any two reference planes that have the Defines Origin property. In the next step, you will change the reference planes with this parameter.

5. For each of the two reference planes indicated with arrows in Figure 7.12, select the plane and select the check box for the Defines Origin parameter in the Properties palette. You may need to press the Tab key several times while hovering the mouse cursor over the horizontal reference plane because of its close proximity to other geometry.

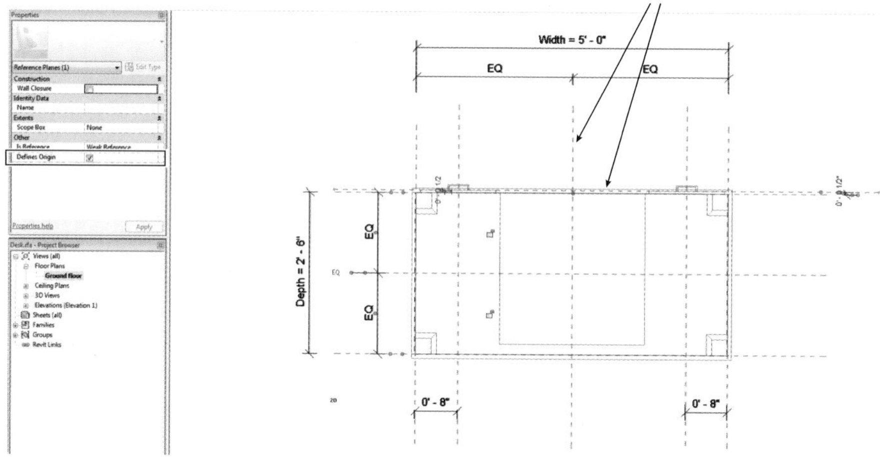

FIGURE 7.12 Editing the origin of a family

6. Click Load Into Project from the ribbon to reload the family into the project, and select Overwrite The Existing Version from the Family Already Exists warning dialog that will automatically pop up in your view. The family initially moves to align the old insertion point with the new insertion point, effectively relocating the desk. Select the desk, and move it back relative to the chair.

   Test different desk sizes. The family flexes with respect to the location of the chair (Figure 7.13).

FIGURE 7.13 Different-sized desks

Modifying Family Geometry

Now comes the tricky part. Even though you're just starting out and you won't be expected to create new content from scratch, it's likely that you'll be expected to modify existing content that will become part of your project.

As the design progresses, generic elements that have been used as meaningful placeholders will in many cases need to be modified to include more detail. In other cases, existing context will be exchanged for components that are already detailed. So, let's start editing components of different categories.

Editing the Family

Let's begin by modifying a 2D element already placed in the sample project. Suppose that according to your firm's graphic standards, the Furniture tag should have rounded sides. Go to the South elevation to see the Furniture tag (Figure 7.14). The chair you placed in the previous exercise has been temporarily hidden in the image for clarity.

Rather than create another Furniture tag for the project, let's modify the one already loaded and used in this chapter's sample file:

1. In the Project Browser, expand the Families category and then Annotation Symbols. Find the Furniture Tag family, right-click it, and then select Edit from the context menu.

2. In the Family Editor, add arc lines to either side of the tag and delete the vertical lines, as shown in the middle image in Figure 7.14. Then click Load Into Project from the ribbon to reload the tag into the project and overwrite the existing tag.

   It's really that easy. Every tag throughout the entire project is updated (see the right image in Figure 7.14).

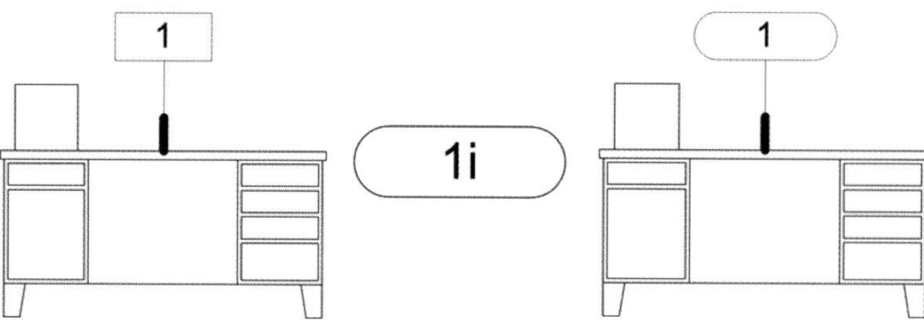

FIGURE 7.14 Editing the Furniture tag

You have just seen one reason you don't need to configure all your standards and settings in order to begin your first project. It's easy to update your entire project as it develops!

Editing Profiles

Now let's revisit the default handrail profile you used when you created a default stair. Profiles are also located in the Project Browser under Families. Here are the steps:

1. In the Project Browser under Families, click to expand Profiles, and then right-click Rectangular Handrail. Choose Edit from the context menu; Rectangular Handrail opens in the Family Editor.

   Because you want to keep your existing handrail profile intact, from the Application button choose Save As, and name the new profile **L Shaped Handrail**.

2. There are some parameters that you want to maintain in this family. To make them visible, go to the Visibility/Graphic Overrides dialog box (press VG on your keyboard), and select the Annotation Categories tab. Select all the options, as shown in Figure 7.15, and click OK to close the dialog box.

   The profile view resembles the image in Figure 7.16.

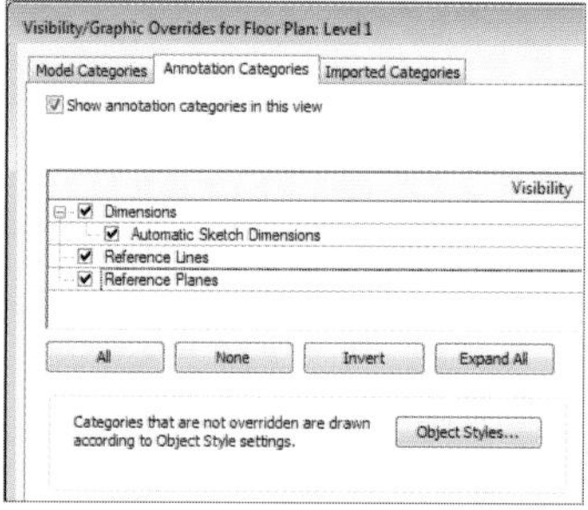

FIGURE 7.15 Adjusting the Visibility/Graphic Overrides of the profile

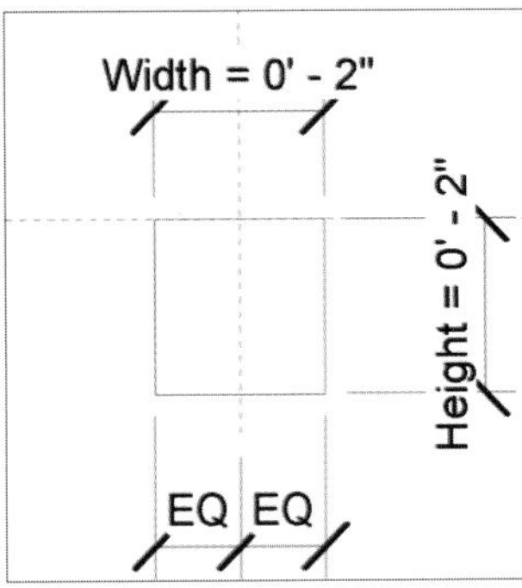

FIGURE 7.16 The modified baluster

3. From the Create tab in the ribbon, click the Line tool, and add new profile lines to resemble Figure 7.17. Note that the parameters for Width and EQ have been retained. Load the profile into your project; the L Shaped Handrail profile family is now listed in your Project Browser along with the other profile families.

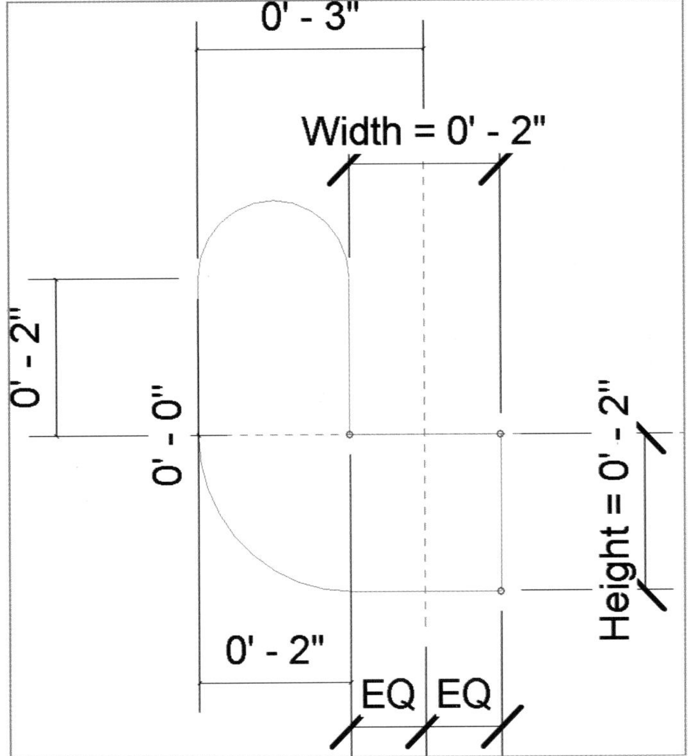

FIGURE 7.17 New handrail profile

Now you will create a new railing type and associate the railing to the existing stair. The default railing type in the sample project is named Handrail - Rectangular.

4. In the Project Browser, go to Families ➢ Railings ➢ Railing, and right-click Handrail - Rectangular. Select Duplicate from the context menu. The copy is named Handrail - Rectangular 2: right-click it, and select Rename from the context menu. Change the name to **L Shaped Handrail.**

5. You need to modify the properties of the railing to include the new handrail profile. To do so, right-click the L Shaped Handrail type in the Project Browser, and select Type Properties; or just double-click it.

6. In the Type Properties dialog box, select Edit from the Rail Structure option. Doing so opens the Edit Rails dialog box (Figure 7.18). Pull down the profile menu, and select the L Shaped Handrail profile, as shown in Figure 7.18.

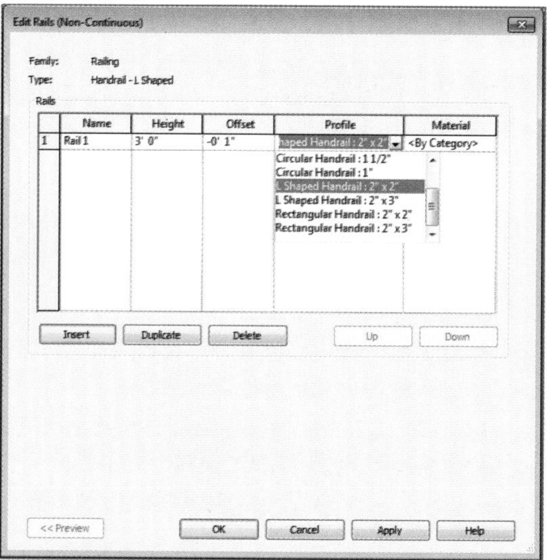

FIGURE 7.18 Editing the type properties of the railing

7. The new profile has been associated to the duplicate railing. All you need to do is swap out the default stair railing for the new one! Select the handrails assigned to the stair, and then choose the L Shaped Handrail from the Type Selector in the Properties palette (Figure 7.19).

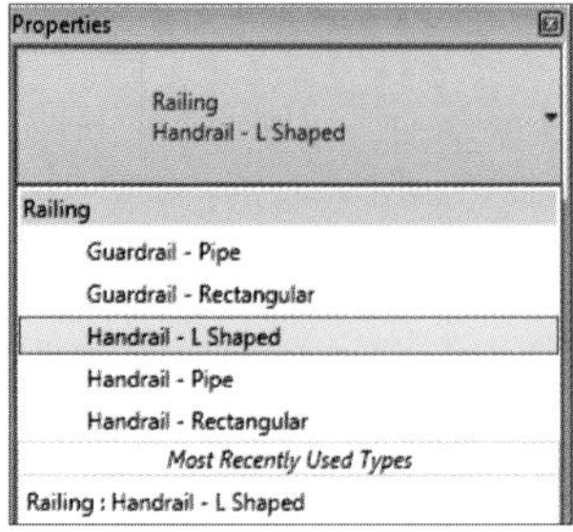

FIGURE 7.19 Selecting the new railing

Detail Components

Imagine the following scenario: You're working to integrate your office standards into your project template, and the break line in the default library doesn't match the graphic standards of your office. To get the match-line detail component consistent with your standards, begin by opening the break-line family in the Family Editor. Here's how to make the changes:

1. In the sample project for this chapter, activate the South elevation. Double-click the head of the wall section. In the wall section, double-click the head of the callout at the top of the wall.
2. In the detail callout view is a default break line that you need to modify. Select the break line, and click Edit Family from the ribbon to open the family in the Family Editor.
3. Select the break line in the Family Editor, and then click Edit Boundary from the ribbon.

   This element is not a line (see Figure 7.20). It's actually a masking region (kind of like a white solid hatch) that is used to obscure geometry in your project. Some of the boundary line styles are Medium Lines, and some are Invisible Lines.

Reference planes and dimensions are usually turned off in families so the thumbnail preview image of the family will be more legible.

4. Before you begin to modify the masking region, you should be aware of any constraints established in the family. Press VV on the keyboard or click the Edit button next to Visibility/Graphics Overrides in the Properties palette. Switch to the Annotation Categories tab, and check both the Dimensions and Reference Planes options. Click OK to close the dialog box.

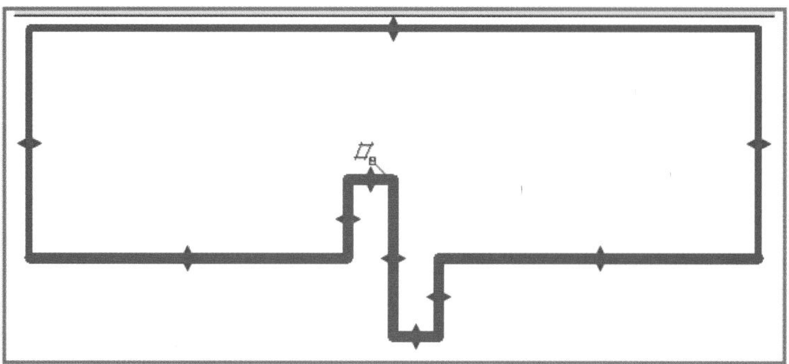

FIGURE 7.20 Editing the detail component break line

5. In the View Control Bar, change the scale of the view to 1 1/2″ = 1′-0″ (1:10) so the dimensions are more legible. Use Zoom To Fit to see the extents of the constraints (Figure 7.21).

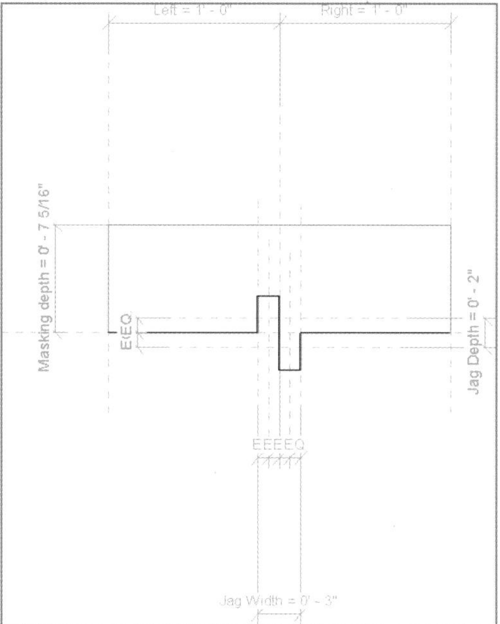

FIGURE 7.21 The masking region with all constraints displayed

6. Delete the squared jag lines, as shown in Figure 7.22. Notice that the original boundary of the masking region remains displayed in the background for reference.

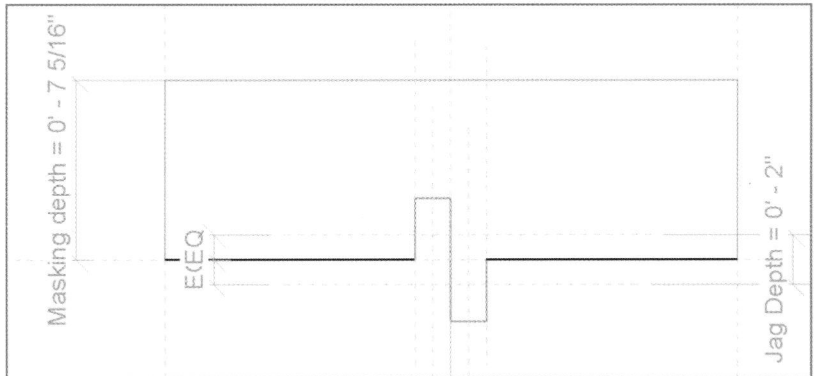

FIGURE 7.22 Delete the existing jag lines in the masking region.

7. From the Create tab in the ribbon, click the Line tool, and make sure Subcategory is set to Medium Lines at the right end of the ribbon. Draw new jag lines, as shown in Figure 7.23. Make sure the lines you draw snap to the midpoints of the previous jag lines and the end points of the remaining straight lines.

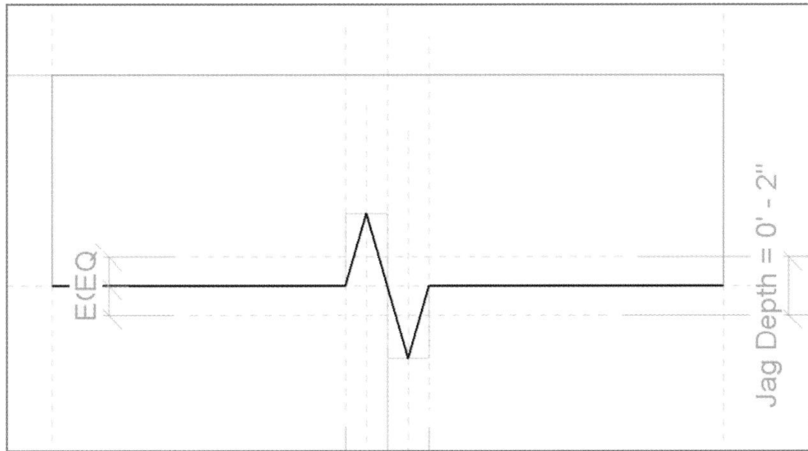

FIGURE 7.23 Sketch new jag lines in the masking region boundary.

8. Click the green check button in the Mode panel of the ribbon to finish the sketch.

9. Go to the Modify tab ➢ Properties panel ➢ Family Types button. Change the Jag Depth value to 0′ 6″, as shown in Figure 7.24, and then click Apply. The size of the jag in the masking region should change. Try a few different values for Jag Depth to make sure the masking region flexes correctly. Click OK to close the dialog box.

It is important to flex families with parametric dimensions before you load them into projects.

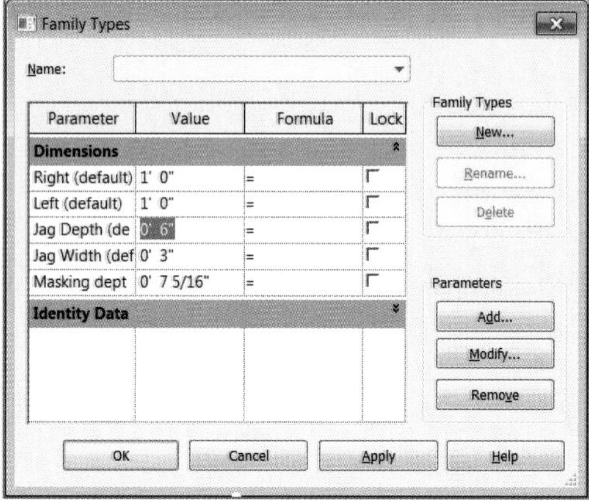

FIGURE 7.24 Change the Jag Depth value to flex the masking region.

10. Click Load Into Project from the ribbon to reload the break line into your project. It updates in all views, as shown here:

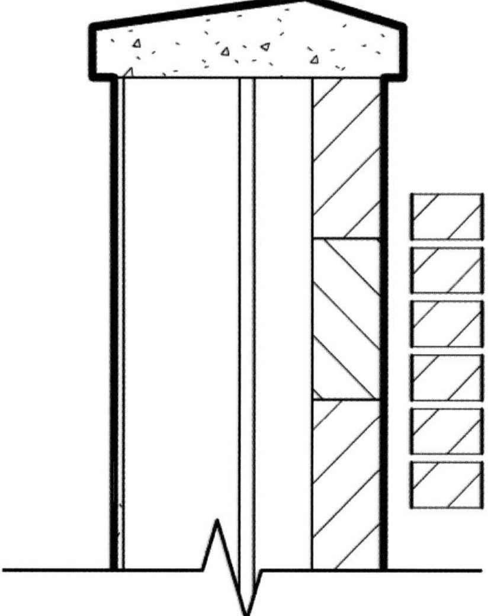

Repeating Details

Repeating details are based on component families that are given rules to repeat, based on a defined spacing and rotation. As an example, elements like brick or concrete masonry units (CMU) in a wall section are elements that repeat on a regular interval. Rather than use an array each time you need to draw these elements in a detail, the repeating detail component allows you to create persistent rules for these components. You can then draw a repeating detail with the ease of drawing a simple line.

In this chapter's sample project, activate the section view named Callout of Section 1. Notice the segment of a brick repeating detail to the right of the wall section. Select it, and then click Edit Type in the Properties palette. As shown in Figure 7.25, you will see that the repeating detail uses the Brick Standard detail family. The type used is named Running Section, and thus the family:type convention is displayed as Brick Standard:Running Section. You will also notice other settings for layout, spacing, and rotation; however, you won't be concerned with those parameters for this exercise.

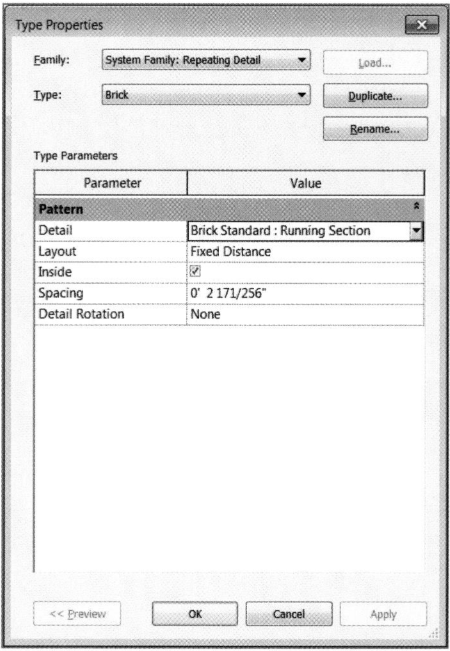

FIGURE 7.25 The Type Properties of a repeating detail family

Click OK to close the Type Properties dialog box. Observing the brick detail component, what's missing is a mortar joint between courses. This joint will help obscure the hatch pattern of the wall. Follow these steps to add it:

1. In the Project Browser, under Families, expand Detail Items. Right-click Brick Standard, and choose Edit from the context menu. The detail component opens in the Family Editor (Figure 7.26).

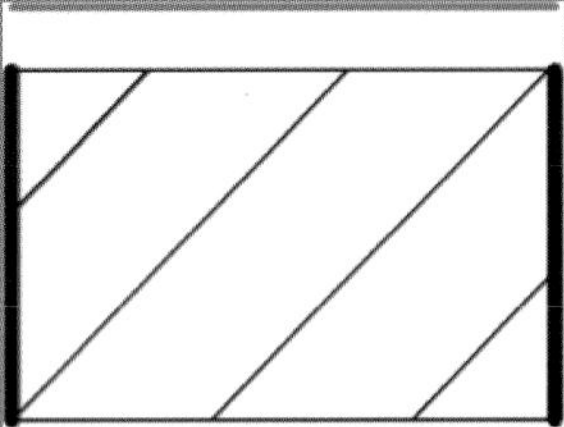

FIGURE 7.26 The default component

Because you will be creating a new filled region in this detail component, you need to load a new filled region type into the family. There are three ways to accomplish this: using Transfer Project Standards to transfer all filled region types, creating a new filled region type from scratch, or using the clipboard to copy and paste a single filled region into the family. Let's use the Transfer Project Standards option for fill patterns.

2. Go to the Manage tab ➢ Settings panel ➢ Transfer Project Standards. Make sure the sample project file is shown in the Copy From drop-down at the top of the dialog box. In the Select Items To Copy dialog box, click the Check None button and then select Fill Patterns (Figure 7.27). Click OK to complete the command. In the Duplicate Types warning dialog box, click New Only.

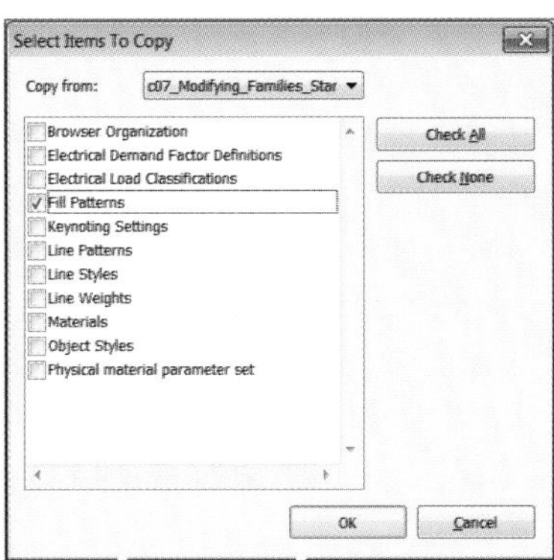

FIGURE 7.27 Using the Transfer Project Standards command

Now that you have loaded the fill patterns from the sample project, you need to create a new filled region type to represent the mortar joint.

3. From the Create tab in the ribbon, click the Filled Region tool. From the Properties palette, click Edit Type. In the Type Properties dialog box, click the Duplicate button and name the new type **Mortar**.

4. In the Fill Pattern parameter, click the ellipsis button to open the Fill Patterns dialog box. Select Sand - Dense, and click OK to return to the Type Properties dialog box. Make sure the Background parameter is set to Opaque, and then click OK to continue (Figure 7.28).

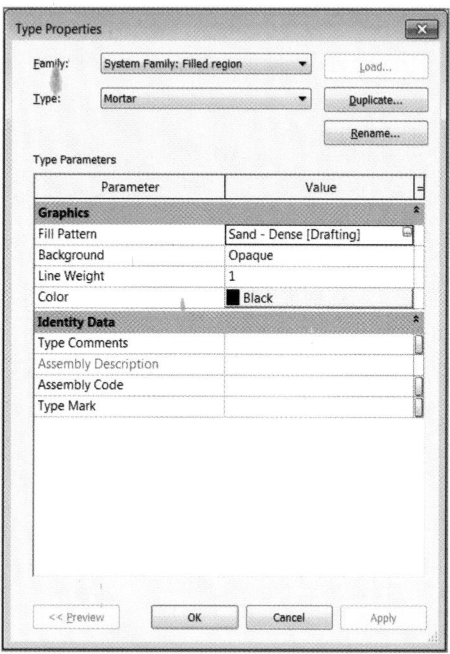

FIGURE 7.28 Define the type properties for a new filled region.

5. The Mortar filled region type should be active in the Type Selector. Draw the boundary as shown in Figure 7.29 using the Detail Items subcategory in the ribbon.

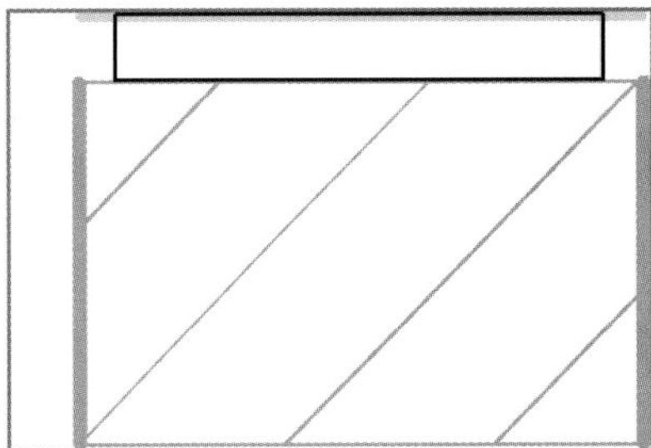

FIGURE 7.29 Sketching the filled region

6. Click the green check in the ribbon to finish the sketch.
7. Click the Load Into Project button to load the modified family into your project. Overwrite the existing version in your project when prompted.

Now that the family has been modified, the repeating detail associated with the same family has been modified as well (Figure 7.30). You can complete the section by adding individual detail components or adding repeating details.

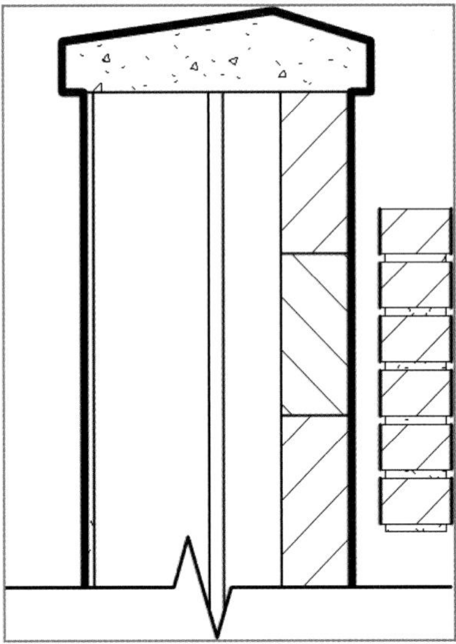

FIGURE 7.30 The repeating detail associated with the same family has been modified.

Now let's investigate editing other 2D annotations by modifying the default title block family.

Title Blocks

Title blocks are also 2D elements, similar to tags and detail components. For pilot projects, it may be fine to start with the default title block and then modify it later. Grids are also helpful when you're organizing views on title blocks, but as you've noticed by now, the default title block doesn't have a grid. You will add a grid to a default title block in the following exercise:

1. In this chapter's sample project, activate the sheet A101 from the Project Browser. Select the title block, and then choose Edit Family from the ribbon.

   Before going any further, you need to create a new line type to use for the grid. It will have a slight color so you can easily distinguish it from the rest of the graphics on the title block as well as any project views.

2. Go to the Manage tab ➢ Settings panel ➢ Object Styles. When the Object Styles dialog box opens, click New under Modify Subcategories. Use the New Subcategory dialog box to create a new line called **Grid Lines**, as shown in Figure 7.31. From the Subcategory Of drop-down, select Title Blocks. Then click OK.

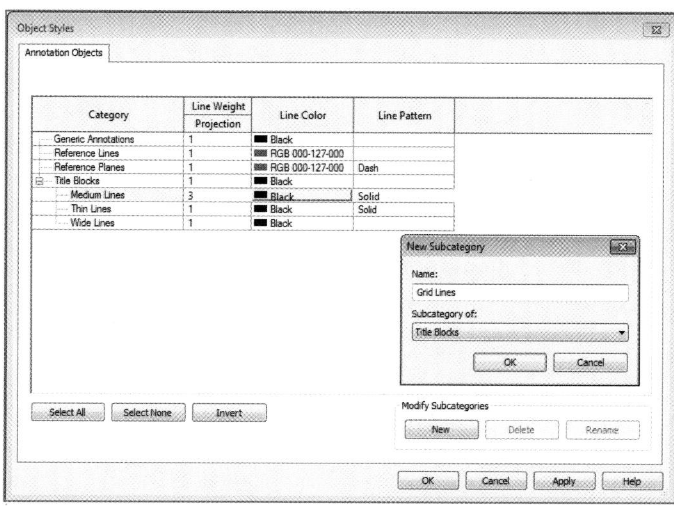

FIGURE 7.31 Adding a new subcategory

3. Select the Line Color option, and modify the color to a light blue. Click OK to close the Object Styles dialog box.
4. You're ready to draw the grid lines. Go to the Create tab ➢ Detail panel ➢ Line tool. Select the Grid Lines subcategory at the right end of the ribbon.
5. Draw five vertical lines and four horizontal lines (Figure 7.32). Dimension them with a continuous dimension (the dimensions will not show up in the project environment). Select the EQ option, and all the lines become equally spaced.

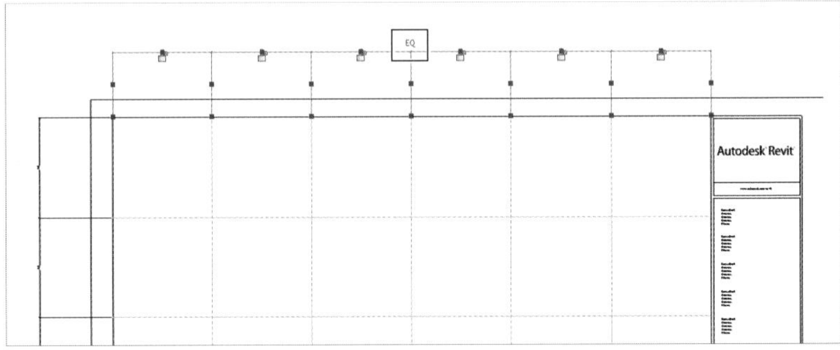

FIGURE 7.32 Adding and dimensioning grid lines

If you were to reload this sheet in the project, you'd be able to control the visibility of the grid like any other object: via Visibility/Graphic Overrides. But it's useful to be able to turn the visibility of the grid on and off throughout the project—not just one sheet at a time. You can do this by associating a type parameter to the grid lines that you've just created. Then when you're done using the grid line to set up your project views, you can turn it off with one click!

6. Select all the grid lines you just created. In the Properties palette, click the small button to the right of the Visible check box to open the Associate Family Parameter dialog box.
7. Click Add Parameter to open the Parameter Properties dialog box. In the Name field, type **Grid Visibility**. Click the Type radio button, and set Group Parameter Under to Graphics, as shown in Figure 7.33.
8. When you're finished, click OK to close both dialog boxes. Notice that the Visible property is now inactive because it is being controlled by the new Grid Visibility parameter. This is how you expose properties of individual family elements in the project environment.

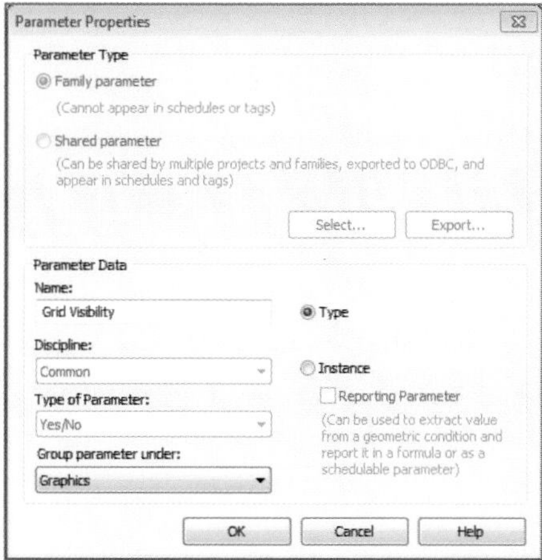

FIGURE 7.33 Creating a visibility parameter

9. Click Load Into Project to reload the title block into your project, overwriting the parameters of the existing title block.
10. Select the title block in the project, and click Edit Type in the Properties palette to open the Type Properties dialog box (Figure 7.34). If you uncheck the Grid Visibility parameter, it turns off the grid throughout your project (rather than just one view at a time).

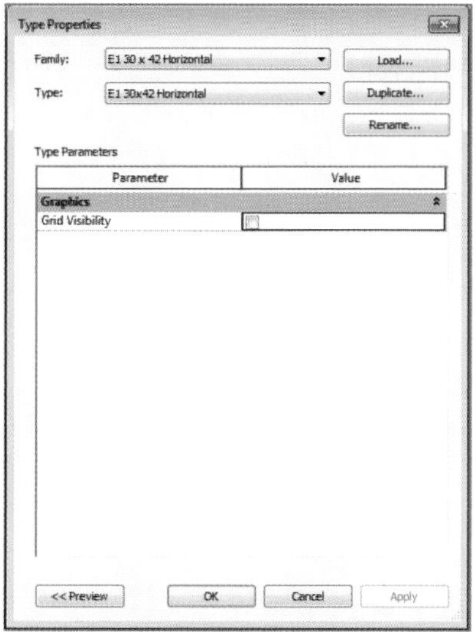

FIGURE 7.34 The Grid Visibility parameter in the Type Properties dialog box

11. Deselect the parameter. When you click OK, the grid is no longer visible in the title block.

Now that you've modified 2D family components, let's experiment with editing 3D elements. You've already modified the geometry of a non-hosted element (the desk in the Level of Detail exercise). Next you will modify a hosted component.

Hosted Components

A hosted family has a required relationship to a specific host category, such as Floors, Walls, Roofs, or Ceilings. Without the host, the hosted family can't be placed. For example, a wall-hosted family can only be placed in a wall, and so on.

For this exercise, you'll modify the generic fixed window that is part of the default library:

1. In this chapter's sample project, go to the Project Browser and expand Families and then Windows. Right-click Fixed, and select Edit from the context menu to open the family in the Family Editor (Figure 7.35).

   You want to keep the existing type, so begin by renaming the family via Save As.

FIGURE 7.35 Window opened in the Family Editor

2. Press VV on the keyboard to access Visibility/Graphic Overrides (the left image in Figure 7.36). Make sure the Walls category is checked as shown. The 3D view now resembles the image on the right in Figure 7.36. Use Zoom To Fit to adjust your view.

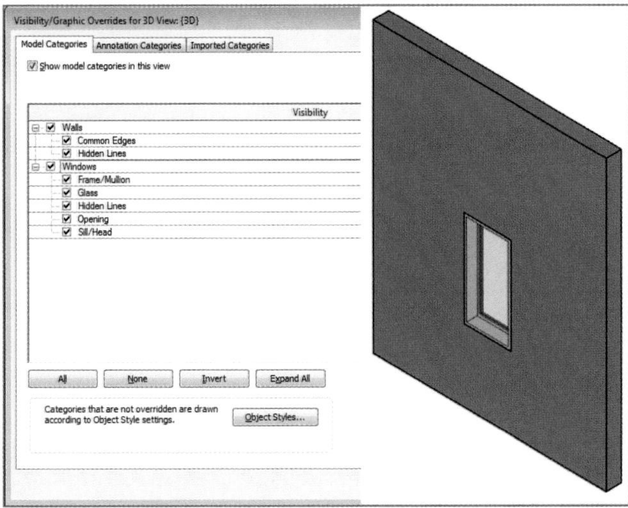

FIGURE 7.36 Visibility/Graphic Overrides for the host wall

3. Activate the Exterior elevation view from the Project Browser window by double-clicking the Exterior elevation view (Figure 7.37).

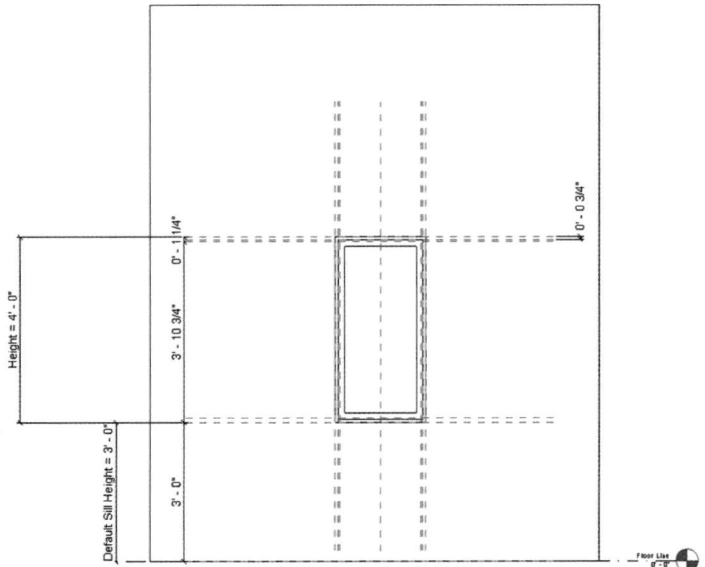

FIGURE 7.37 Reference planes and dimension parameters

Reference planes (displayed as green dashed lines) serve as guides that allow the geometry to flex. As you can see, the window geometry has not been directly assigned to dimension parameters. Instead, the parameters are associated to the reference planes. The window geometry is then associated to the planes. This is the preferred method for constructing family geometry.

4. Go to the Create tab ➢ Datum panel ➢ Reference Plane tool. Draw a horizontal plane around the midpoint of the window.

5. Go to the Modify tab ➢ Measure panel ➢ Aligned Dimension tool. Create a continuous dimension between the two outermost horizontal reference planes and the new plane you created in step 4. Click the temporary EQ icon that is active when you select the dimension just created to establish an equality constraint (Figure 7.38). In other words, no matter how the window height changes, the new reference plane will remain centered.

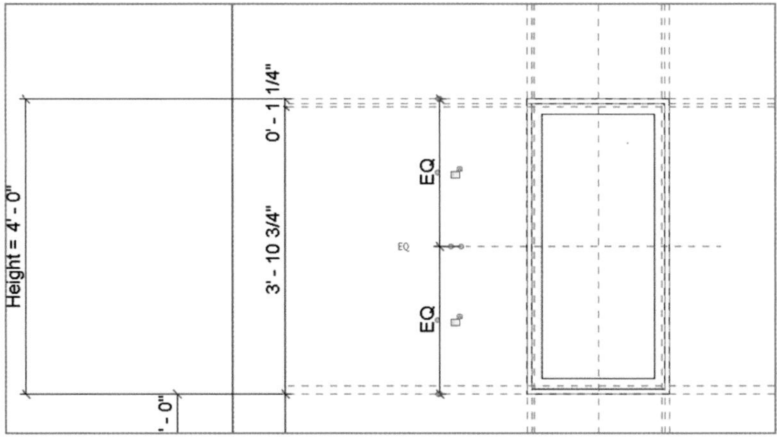

FIGURE 7.38 Adding a new reference plane and keeping it equally spaced

This process is an important part of modifying existing content. This window family is full of dimension parameters that control different types. These parameters are extremely useful, so you do not want to delete them!

You do not need to create new geometry from scratch; you can modify what is already in the family. This approach may seem like cheating, but this is usually how content is modified. In addition to this process being efficient, the geometry that you modify will likely continue to "remember" existing relationships to reference planes and other parameters.

6. Select the Frame/Mullion Extrusion, and click Edit Extrusion from the ribbon. Sketch new internal lines, as shown in Figure 7.39, to split the window into three panels. Before you finish the sketch, delete the sketch segments between the new lines, as indicated in Figure 7.39, using the Split tool with the Delete Inner Segment option checked located on the lower panel of the ribbon.

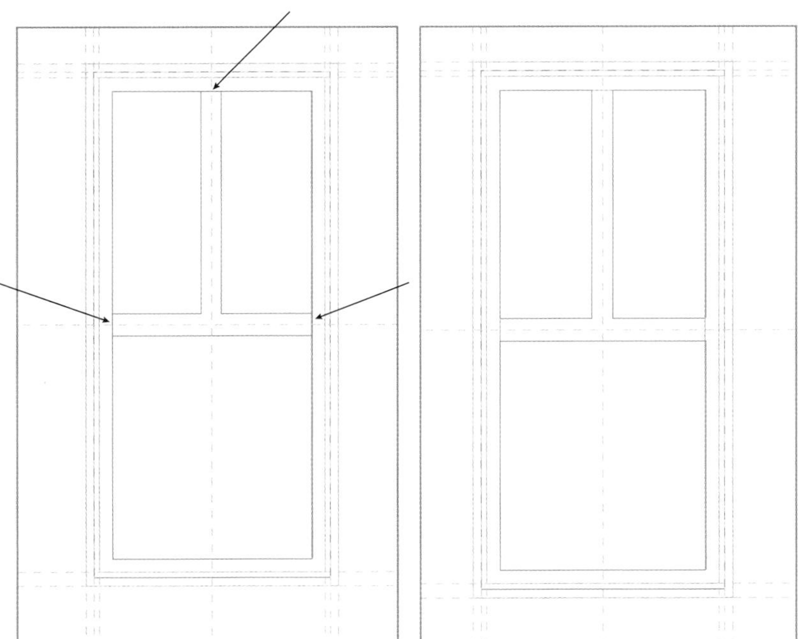

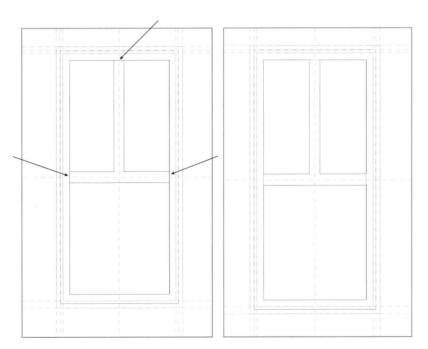

FIGURE 7.39 Editing the existing window frame

7. Click the green check in the ribbon to finish the sketch. After the sketch is finished, it's important to flex the family to make sure the different sizes will behave before you load the family into the project.

Certification Objective

8. Click the Family Types button to view all the various family types. Select a few different types from the drop-down at the top of the dialog box, and click Apply after each type is specified.

9. Click OK to close the dialog box, and look at the window in 3D. The window geometry is flexing, but the window pane is still one piece of glazing.

10. Select the glazing, and then click the Edit Extrusion button from the Mode panel in the contextual Modify | Frame Mullion tab. Return to the exterior elevation, and add sketch lines aligned with your previously modified window trim as shown in Figure 7.40. You can even use the Pick Lines option in the Draw panel to make this process even easier. Remember to remove the segments of outer line using the Split tool, as you did in step 6.

FIGURE 7.40 Modifying the window glazing

Finish the sketch, and then repeat the previous process of testing a few different family-type parameters in order to make sure the window glazing will flex with the different sizes.

Now that the window has been modified, load it into your project. Select one of the existing windows, and then use the Properties palette to swap out the existing window with the component you've just created. Because the insertion points are the same, the window location will remain consistent.

The Essentials and Beyond

Rather than starting from scratch, it's often faster to find a family or element close to what you need and modify it. You learned how to edit view display and detail level, as well as change the family category and modify family geometry.

Additional Exercises

- Select another family, and modify its level of detail so the appropriate geometry is displayed at the right scale and detail level in the project environment.
- Explain how you would modify a family from face-based or hosted to one that is not.
- Explain how you would modify a family that is not face-based or hosted to one that is.
- Nest a family into another family, and select the Shared option. Verify that this nested family schedules when placed in the project.
- Add a new subcategory to a family, and assign geometry to the category. From the project environment, compare the visibility options under the main category (Doors, Furniture, Specialty Equipment, and so forth) of this family before and after the family is loaded into a project.

CHAPTER 8

Groups and Phasing

Overall project management is a large part of the design development process. Much of the time, managing design is a process of managing change. Projects often develop as moving targets; communicating the program results in needing to answer questions that no one anticipated.

The more the program develops, the more change management is required—sometimes in an exponential fashion. Although managing this kind of change becomes practically untenable in CAD, the Autodesk® Revit® Architecture software allows you to manage multiple, simultaneous relationships faster than in any other application.

Groups and phasing help you quickly and easily manage change in your project. Modifying one family component will update throughout a project. But groups can contain multiple host and family components. Phasing applies to views (filtered to show only a slice of a project's timeline) as well as geometry.

Will design get any easier in the process? It depends on your perspective. You'll be able to make design decisions faster and from nearly anywhere in the project. You'll also be able to find conflicts and poor design decisions far earlier in the process.

In this chapter, you learn the following skills:

- **Using groups**
- **Using phasing**

Using Groups

A Revit Architecture project includes many kinds of elements. With regard to geometry, there are *host families* (which are created directly in the project environment) and *component families* (which are created in the Family Editor).

We like to describe a building as fundamentally assembled from *repetitive relationships,* or things that are connected. Pieces become parts, parts become assemblages, and assemblages become architectural constructs. The ability to edit the properties of either type of object (host or family) is incredibly elegant, because doing so will in turn have an immediate effect on your entire project.

This is where groups come into play by allowing the editing of a single component to propagate through the entire project. Groups are created in the project environment and contain collections of component families, host families, or perhaps a combination of both. As a matter of fact, collections of groups can become other groups. There are predominantly two types of groups: model and detail. Model groups are collections of 3D geometries, whereas detail groups are strictly 2D collections.

We can't cover every possible bit of obscure functionality in groups. But we do want to make sure you gain the confidence to use groups in the way they're most often used.

Creating Groups

Start by opening the file `c08_Groups_and_Phasing_Start.rvt`. It's available for download at this book's web page, `www.sybex.com/go/revit2013essentials`. This project file has been preloaded with content for this scenario. As you can see in Figure 8.1, we've gone ahead and loaded into the project all the furniture you'll use for this chapter's exercises.

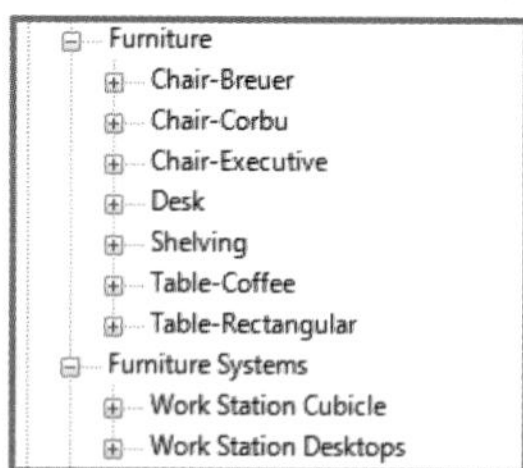

FIGURE 8.1 Groups and phasing file

Let's start by adding a collection of furniture to one of the offices:

1. Open the Level 1 floor plan view, and add the components shown in Figure 8.2. To add components, go to the Architecture tab ➢ Component button ➢ Type Selector, and choose the following:
    - Executive Chair (1)
    - Breuer Chair (2)
    - Shelf (1)
    - Desk (1)

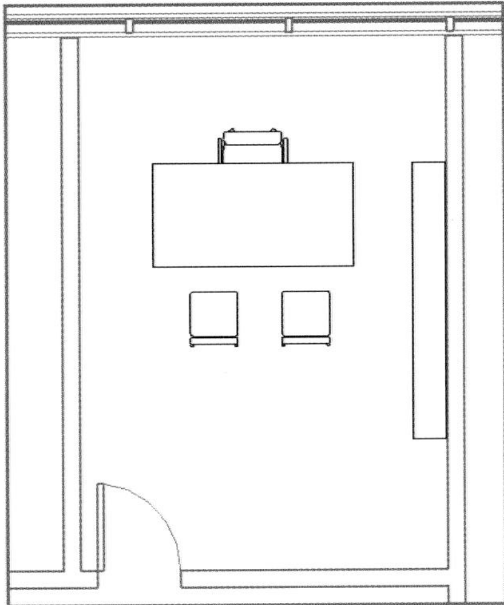

FIGURE 8.2 Adding furniture to the office

Now imagine that you need to copy this configuration throughout a few offices. You can accomplish this easily by copying, but what if you needed to change one of the elements in all the offices after you finished copying? You'd have to manually locate all the components that had to be modified and then change them one by one. To avoid these manual changes, you can create a group and use it to place a specific configuration of elements (in this case, office furniture). Then, if you need to make a change to the configuration, you simply change the group, and all the groups are dynamically updated.

2. To create a group of the elements you just added, select all the furniture and then choose the Create Group tool from the Create palette on the Modify context menu.

3. Revit Architecture prompts you to name the group. To avoid a project full of confusing default names, name the group **Office Furniture 1** (see Figure 8.3). Leave the Open In Group Editor check box deselected, and click OK.

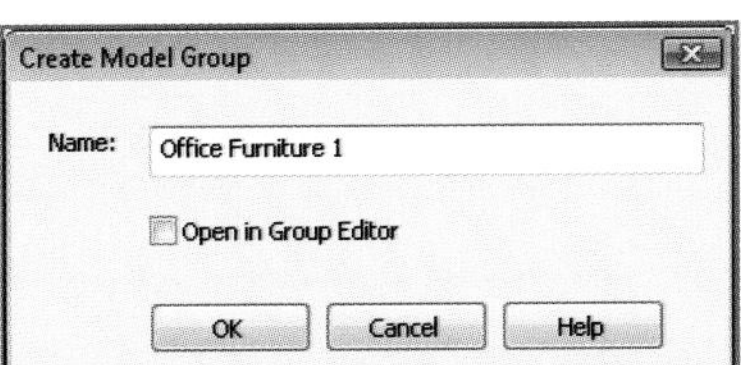

FIGURE 8.3 Naming the group

When the group is finished, you see its elements surrounded by a dashed line as well as an insertion point for the group (Figure 8.4). The insertion point is the location that the group will maintain when you exchange one group for another.

4. Move the insertion point to the upper-right corner of the shelves by dragging the center of the insertion to its new location (Figure 8.5). Then, rotate the insertion point by dragging either end node, as shown in Figure 8.5.

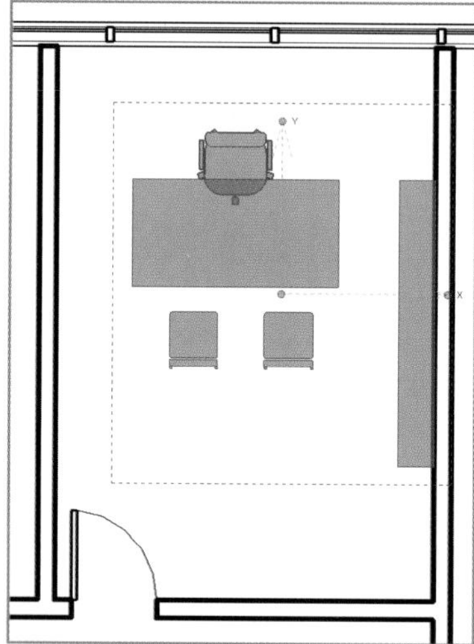

FIGURE 8.4 Group with the default insertion point

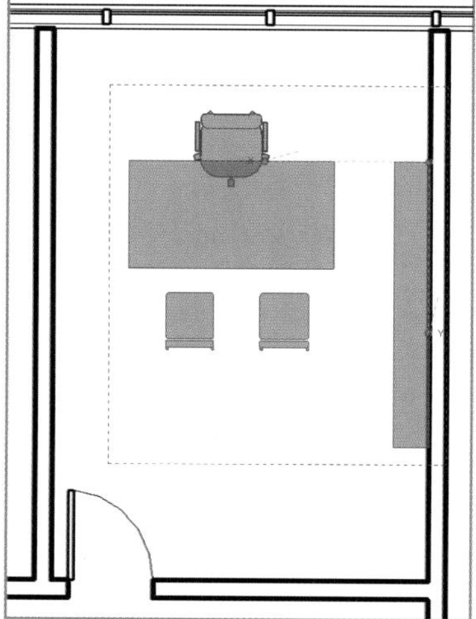

FIGURE 8.5 Relocating and rotating the insertion point

Copying Groups

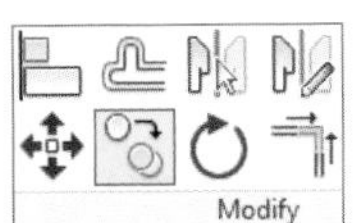

Next, let's copy this group to a few new locations. You have a couple of good options to choose from for this workflow. If there's already an instance of the group in the view that you're working in, select the group and then click the Copy tool from the Modify tab.

Another option is to use the Create Similar command on the Create panel. Either will help you create a duplicate of your group.

Continue the exercise as follows:

1. Choose whichever group-copy option you like, and insert the group furniture configuration in the individual offices by clicking where you want the new group located (Figure 8.6).
2. Rotate the copies in order to orient them properly. The default rotation point is the new origin you just established.

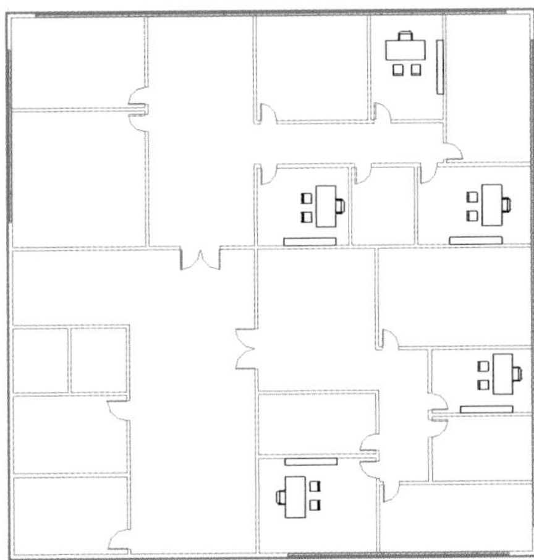

FIGURE 8.6 Creating copies of groups

Duplicating Groups

In many cases, you'll start with one group and then create permutations of that group as the design progresses. The first step in creating these variations is duplicating a group you've already created. One way is to duplicate any of the groups in the Project Browser. (In the Project Browser, choose Edit Type and then Duplicate.)

Let's duplicate a group:

1. Select one of the instances of the Office Furniture 1 group; then click Edit Type from the Properties palette. This opens the Type Properties dialog box.
2. Click the Duplicate button to duplicate the group. Name the new group **Office Furniture 2** (Figure 8.7).

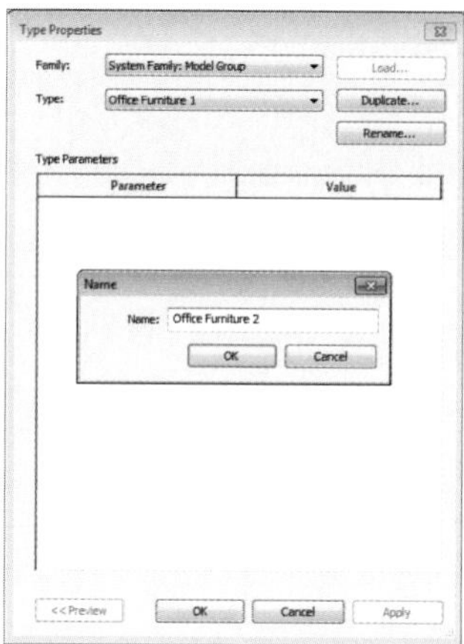

FIGURE 8.7 Duplicating the group

3. Click OK twice to exit all the dialog boxes.

Now let's edit this new group.

Editing Groups

Continue with the following steps:

1. Select the Office Furniture 2 group that you just created. On the Group panel of the contextual Modify|Model Groups tab, select the Edit Group option to enter Edit Group mode.

   Everything in the group you're editing is now shown as usual, whereas everything not in the group is given a temporary sepia tone (Figure 8.8).
2. Reconfigure the seating and add a coffee table, as shown in Figure 8.9. To add the coffee table, click the Component button from the Architecture tab.
3. Finish the group by clicking Finish.

4. Copy another instance of the group in your project, as shown in Figure 8.10. To do this, highlight the group at lower right, and use the Copy tool from the Modify tab to create a copy in the empty office space highlighted at the top. Keep in mind that every time you copy a group, all your other project views and schedules update in real time!

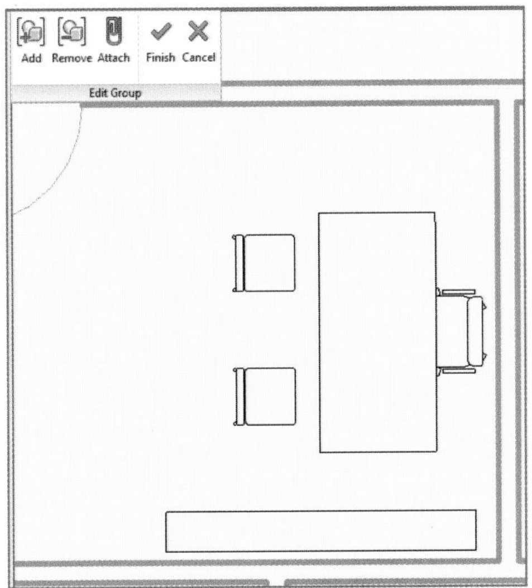

FIGURE 8.8 In Edit Group mode, everything not in the group is given a temporary sepia tone.

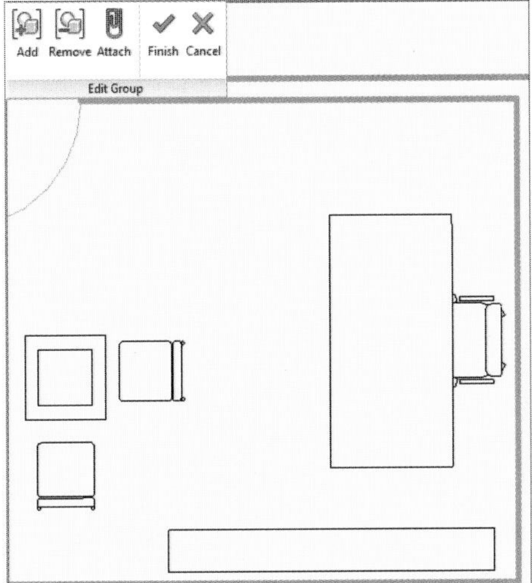

FIGURE 8.9 Modifying the group

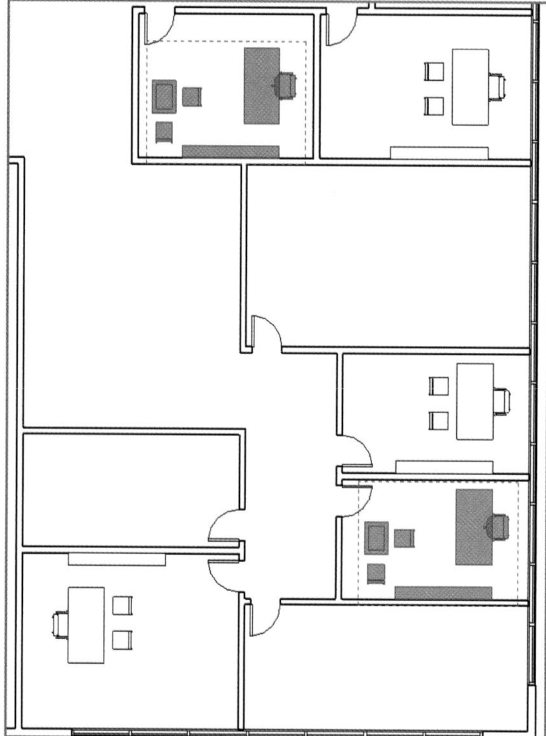

FIGURE 8.10 Copying the group

Exchanging Groups

Any group can be exchanged for any other group, the same way different families can be swapped out for another one. Before you exchange one group for another, you may want to check that the insertion points of the two groups are properly located in order to keep the replaced group from shifting its location.

Follow these steps:

1. Select the group you want to replace, and then click the Type Selector pull-down menu in the Properties palette. You see all the other groups in the same category. In this case, there are two: Office Furniture 1 and Office Furniture 2.
2. Exchange the group Office Furniture 1 for Office Furniture 2 by selecting the other group from the Type Selector (Figure 8.11).

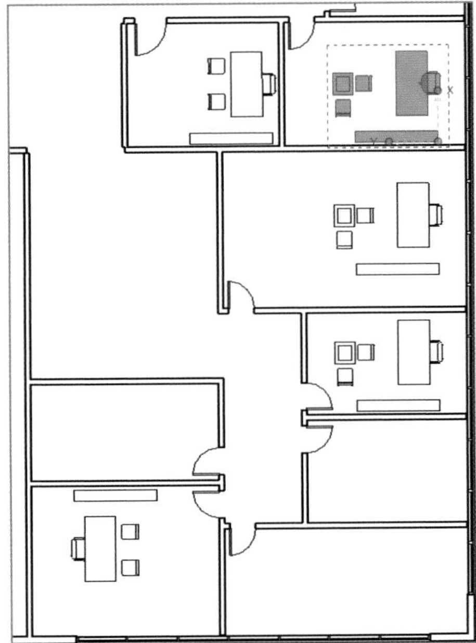

FIGURE 8.11 Exchanging groups

Saving Groups

You may find it helpful to work on very large or complex groups outside the project environment and then reload them into your project when the edits are complete. To do this, Revit Architecture allows you to save any of your groups to separate Revit Architecture project (RVT) files. Let's try it:

1. Select the Office Furniture 2 group name from the Project Browser, right-click, and choose Save Group from the context menu, as shown in Figure 8.12.

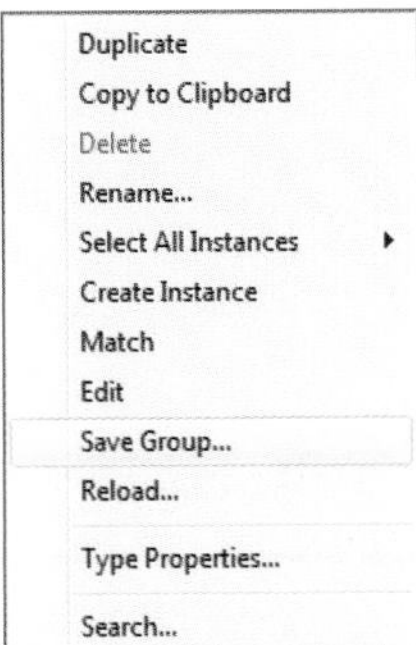

FIGURE 8.12 Saving the group

By default, you're prompted to save the group with the same name as the group (Figure 8.13); notice that Same As Group Name appears in the File Name box. You can change this to anything you want, but keeping it similar to the group name allows for external editing and reimporting. By default, the file is saved as a Revit Architecture project (`*.rvt`).

2. Click Save. You can now open the RVT file and modify it as required.

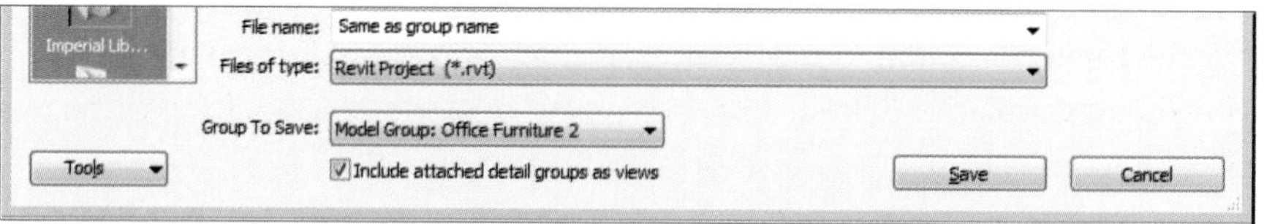

FIGURE 8.13 Saving the group as a project file (`.rvt` extension)

Loading Groups

When you're finished editing the group, you can easily reload it by selecting the group name, right-clicking, and choosing Reload from the context menu (Figure 8.14).

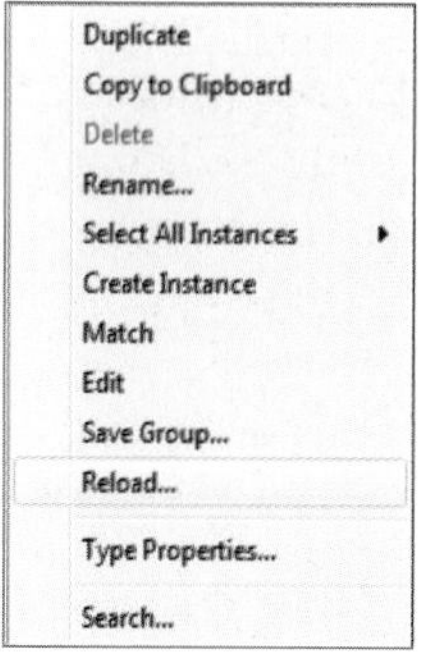

FIGURE 8.14
Reloading the group

In other cases, you'll want to load groups without replacing anything. Such groups are resolved assemblages that can help speed the design process. Bathroom and utility cores, office furniture, and meeting rooms (even unit types, as in hotels) can be saved from other successful projects and reused.

To load a group without replacing anything, go to the Insert tab ➢ Load From Library panel, and select Load As Group.

Some Best Practices

It's easy to want to overuse groups because they're effective for maintaining lots of relationships in your projects. On the other hand, you can quickly confuse new team members with an overabundance of groups that bring only diminishing returns. To get the most out of groups, follow these best practices for working with them:

Don't Put Datums (Levels and Grids) into Groups You don't want to copy datums around your project every time you place a new instance of the group. To avoid this, either create your groups from views that don't have datums shown (such as a plan or 3D view) or use the Filter function to make sure there are no levels or grids in your selection.

Avoid Nesting Groups Within Groups Nesting groups may seem like a good idea, but you'll probably want to avoid it. It can lead to an overabundance of groups, which in turn will lead to confusion as your project develops.

Keep the Host and Hosted Together When you're creating groups that contain hosted families, it's a good idea to keep the host and hosted together. Otherwise, you have to remember to create the host on which one of the grouped elements depends. Deleting the host (outside the group) that has a relationship to elements in the group can lead to project errors.

Avoid Attached Relationships with Walls If, for example, a wall is attached to a top level and then added to a group, everything will be fine as long as all the levels are equally spaced. But if one of the levels moves, all the other walls in the group will try to update accordingly, potentially changing the geometry or relationship inside your group. Because the levels they're associated to have not moved, you'll get errors and strange wall overlaps.

Create Left and Right Options When Necessary Although mirroring CAD files (or even 3D components) seems fine in principle, a lot of content isn't manufactured in left and right options. Unfortunately, content in Revit Architecture doesn't have an option to disallow mirroring, so if someone mirrors a component, it may look fine in the plan. But in reality, they're indicating to another team member (such as an engineer) that a piece of equipment will be serviced on a side that doesn't exist. For example, mirroring can put the hot water on the right and the cold on the left. So, we suggest you create left and right options. Yes, updating two options will take a bit more time—but doing so will help you avoid expensive field changes that result from someone unknowingly mirroring fixtures, furniture, and equipment.

Using Phasing

Phasing allows your project to express the component of time. All project geometry has a phase component (such as when items are built or demolished). And all views have a component in them that allows you to filter within a specific range of time. Let's continue the previous exercise, where you established some office spaces using groups, and create a phasing exercise.

Geometry Phases

Let's look at the phasing properties for some of the walls in the project file. Select the wall in the upper-right quadrant of the view. Note that there are Phase Created and Phase Demolished properties for the wall in the Properties palette (Figure 8.15). Each of these phasing options has multiple settings. Phase Created can be set to Existing, Demolished, or New Construction (shown in Figure 8.15). Phase Demolished outlines when (or if) an element is to be demolished. In the figure, it's set to None, but other options are Existing and Proposed.

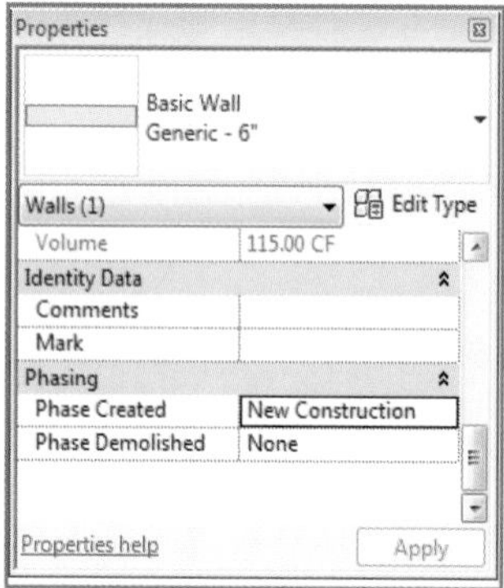

FIGURE 8.15 Geometry phases

When you began this chapter, all the elements in the `c08_Groups_and_Phasing_Start.rvt` file (all the walls, doors, curtain walls, and so) were created on the *Existing phase*. All the furniture and groups that were created in this chapter were placed on the *Proposed phase*. Imagine a scenario where you have an existing tenant space that is empty and needs to be configured for a new use, and you'll get the idea of where this section's exercise is headed.

At the moment, there are only two phases in the project (Existing and Proposed), and these properties can be assigned to any geometry. Don't worry about having a distinct Demolition phase, because demolition occurs during either Existing or Proposed.

View Phases

All views have phases as well. These phases allow you to filter views so you can isolate geometry based on when it's created, demolished, or proposed. Figure 8.16 shows the present view phase of the Phase filter.

First, it's important to note that the phase of the view is the same phase that will be assigned to the geometry you create in that view. So if the view's Phase property is set to Existing, the geometry will be considered existing; if it's set to Proposed, the geometry will be given the Proposed phase. But don't worry if you get this wrong or need to change a Phase property later—this property is easily modified.

Second, several phase filters are defined in a Revit Architecture template (Figure 8.17). We don't need to cover them all now, but we do want to point out what the various phases do.

At the moment, Phase is set to Proposed and Phase Filter is set to Show All, so both existing and proposed elements are being shown. Let's see how you can easily isolate the geometry from either phase.

Figure 8.18 shows what is visible if you set Phase Filter to Show Previous Phase. Because the phase of the current view is Proposed, the previous phase shows existing elements.

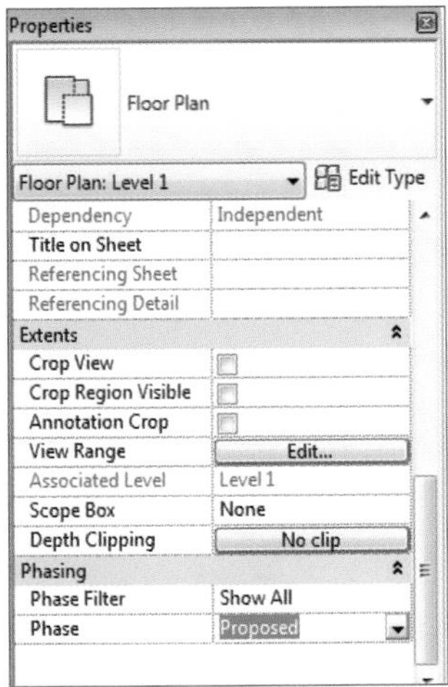

FIGURE 8.16 View phases

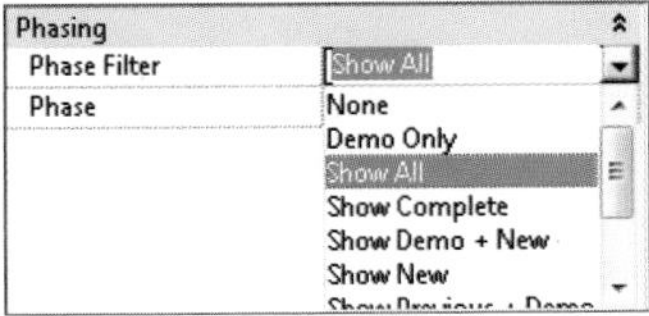

FIGURE 8.17 Phase filters

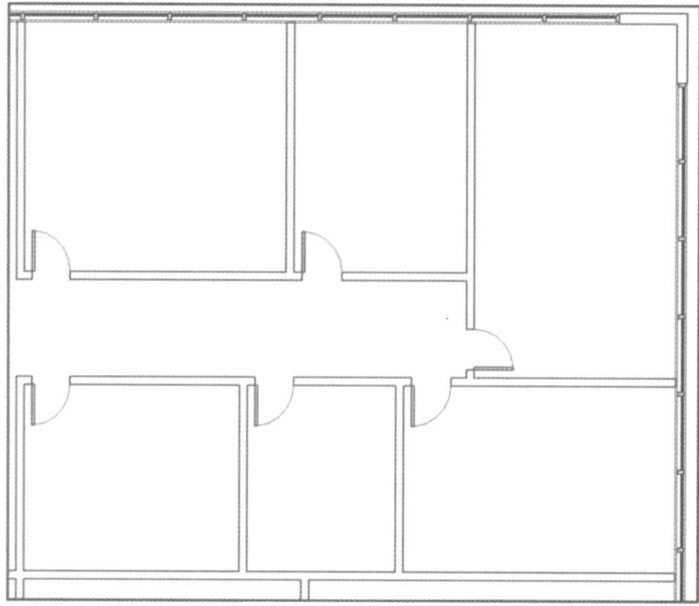

FIGURE 8.18 You see this if Phase Filter is set to Show Previous Phase.

Select Show New. Now only the new, or proposed, elements are shown, as you can see in Figure 8.19.

If you choose Show Previous + New, the existing and proposed elements are shown (Figure 8.20).

Set the view back to Show All for the remaining exercises.

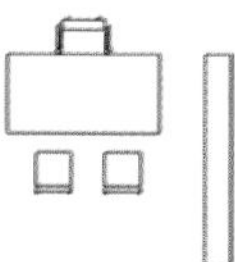

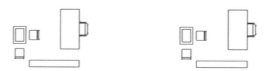

FIGURE 8.19 Phase Filter set to Show New

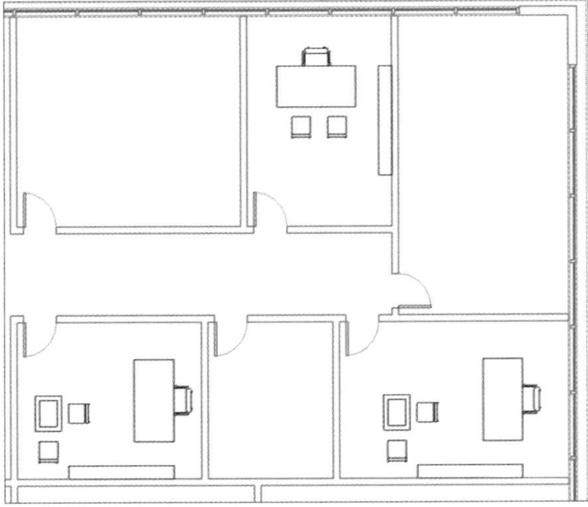

FIGURE 8.20 Geometry phases

Demolition and Proposed Elements

As part of this scenario, you're going to turn the two separate tenant spaces into a single space. You'll do so by demolishing a few elements and adding proposed elements. Follow these steps:

1. Select the Modify tab, and click the Demolish tool in the Geometry panel.

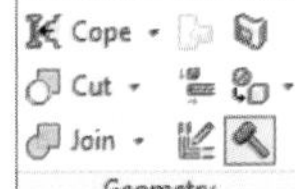

2. Select the two doors and the wall shown in Figure 8.21. Notice that as you select the elements for demolition, they're given a dashed representation in the plan view (a common graphic convention to indicate demolition).

FIGURE 8.21 Demolished elements

If you switch to the default 3D view (the house button in the Quick Access toolbar (QAT) ![house button], the demolished walls are indicated by red. And if you look closely, you'll notice that Revit Architecture has replaced the demolished door with a new wall (Figure 8.22).

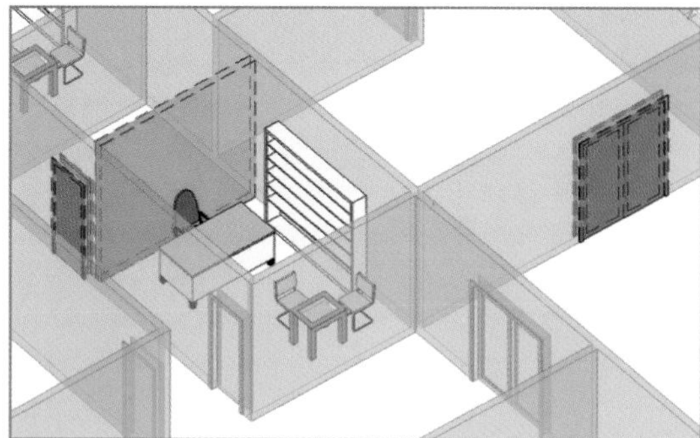

FIGURE 8.22 Demolished view in 3D

3. You need to reconfigure this office to accommodate passage to the other space. Move the furniture group to the right, and add a new wall and door to complete the revised office space (Figure 8.23). Be sure the new walls have a height of 10′ to match the existing walls.

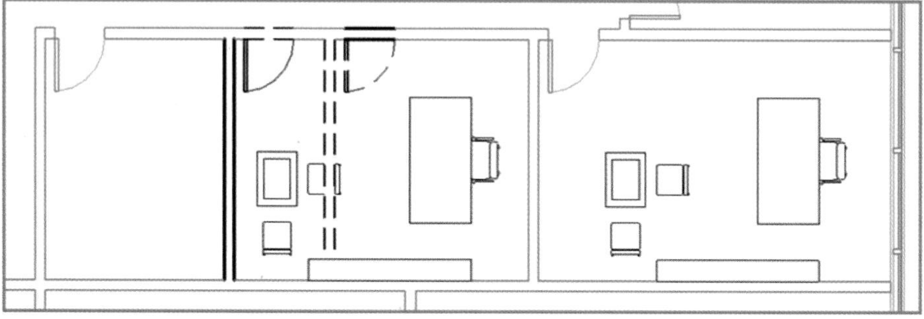

FIGURE 8.23 Proposed elements in 2D

Notice that Revit Architecture has automatically demolished the portion of the existing wall that needs to accommodate the proposed door (Figure 8.24).

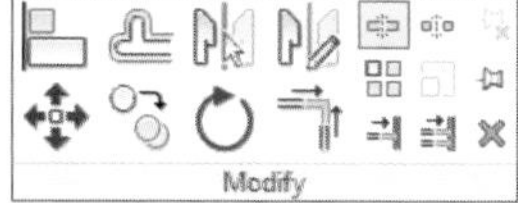

4. Use the Split Element tool to split the upper wall at the intersection of the new wall (at the location shown in Figure 8.25) so you can demolish only a portion of the existing wall.

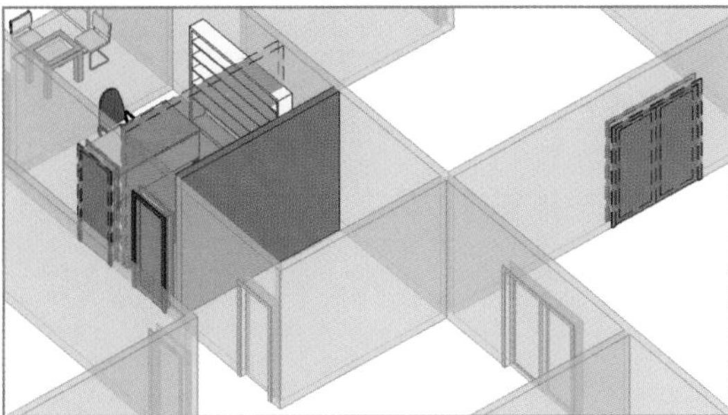

FIGURE 8.24 Proposed elements in 3D

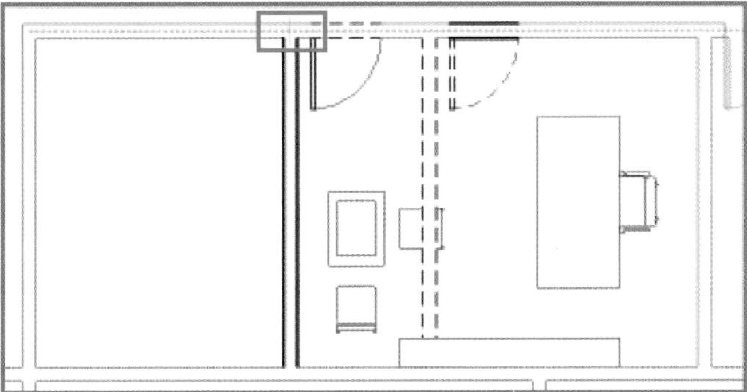

FIGURE 8.25 Splitting the wall

5. Demolish the two left walls, as shown in Figure 8.26. Note that the door (a hosted element) has been automatically demolished as well. This makes sense because the door wouldn't be able to exist without the wall.
6. Split the lower wall as shown in Figure 8.27.

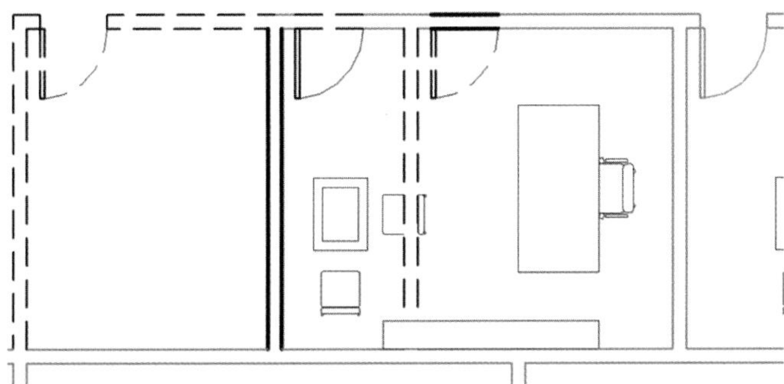

FIGURE 8.26 Demolishing the walls

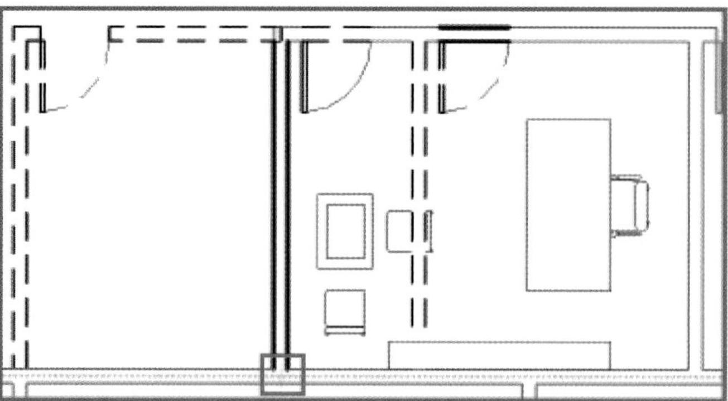

FIGURE 8.27 Splitting the lower wall

7. When using the phasing tools, you'll often have to clean up wall conditions between the intersection of existing walls that remain and their demolished walls. Select the demolished wall (the wall on the far left in Figure 8.27): blue nodes indicate each endpoint. By default, the wall attempts to automatically join the other walls.

8. To modify this condition, you need to exit the Demolish tool. Any time you want to exit a tool, either press the Esc key twice or click the Modify arrow in the upper-left corner available on all the tabs. Then, right-click the blue node, and select Disallow Join from the context menu (Figure 8.28).

9. Drag the wall away from the undesirable joined condition. Once you do this, the remaining walls join properly.

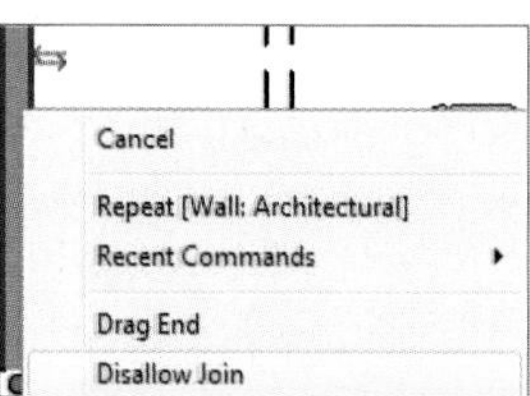

FIGURE 8.28 Splitting the wall

10. Repeat the process for all the intersections marked in Figure 8.29.

It's a good idea to resolve wall joins periodically as you work, rather than put them off to do at the last minute.

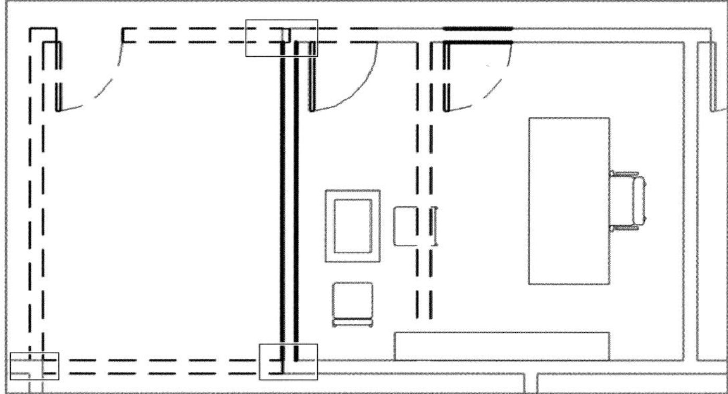

FIGURE 8.29 Cleaning wall joins

Completed Views

Go back to your 3D view, and let's look at the different stages of the Existing phase that you need to complete. Follow these steps:

1. Set Phase to Existing and Phase Filter to Show New. That way, you see only the existing elements (before any demolition or proposed furniture), as shown in Figure 8.30.

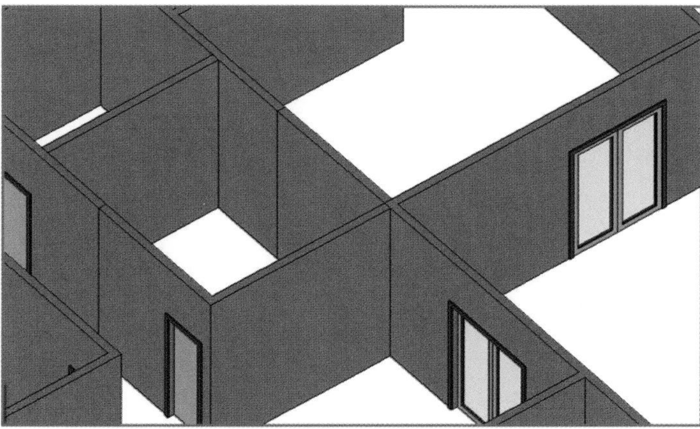

FIGURE 8.30 Existing phase

2. Set Phase to Proposed and Phase Filter to Show Previous + Demo. None of the proposed elements are shown, but the existing elements are displayed along with the elements that will be demolished (Figure 8.31).
3. Set Phase Filter to Show Complete. The existing walls remain, along with the newly proposed elements (Figure 8.32).

   Figure 8.33 shows the same view in 2D.

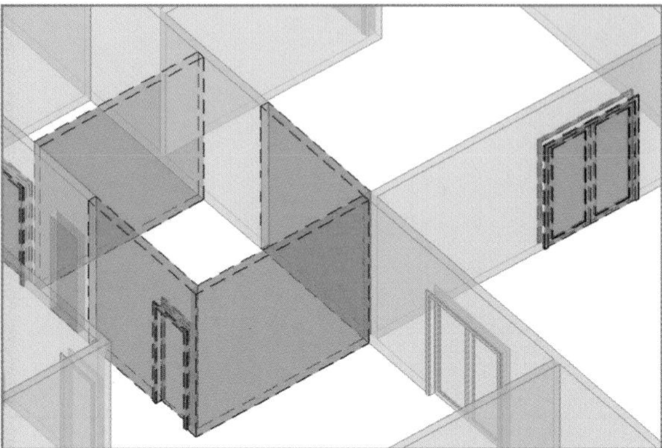

FIGURE 8.31 Existing and demolition shown

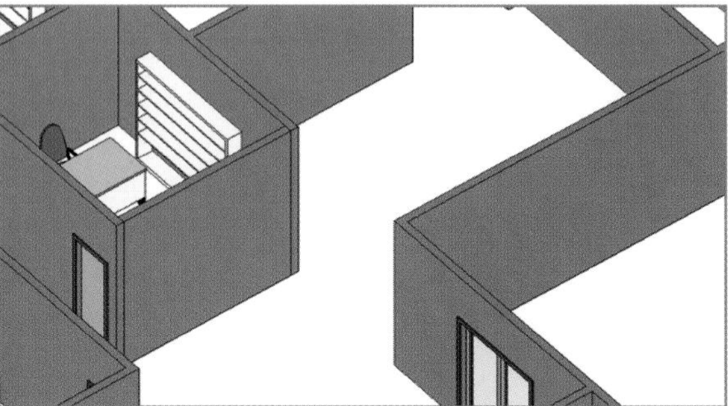

FIGURE 8.32 Show Complete filter

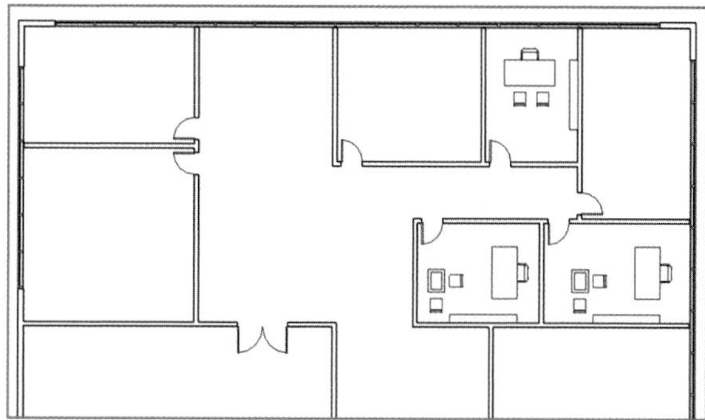

FIGURE 8.33 Show Complete filter in 2D

The Essentials and Beyond

If this were a real project, you'd simply duplicate your project views and give them different Phase and Phase Filter settings. Then you'd take the multiple views (2D, 3D, and even schedules) and assemble them on multiple sheets for documentation. The great thing about Revit Architecture is that, as a phased project evolves and you need to demolish, propose, and even "undemolish" project elements, all of the project views and documentation remain fully coordinated.

If you'd like to review the completed file, go to `www.sybex.com/go/revit2013essentials` and download `c08_Groups_and_Phasing_Finish.rvt`.

Additional Exercises

- Revit Architecture files may be linked and later bound. The bound link becomes a group in the project. Link and bind another RVT file into your project. What are the advantages? Disadvantages?
- Create a group, and copy a few instances. Exclude elements from one of the groups. What are some of the advantages of doing this in a real project?
- How might you indicate a Future phase to show a present condition in context with the finished version?
- Create groups of frequently used assemblages, and put them in a central location (like family components) so other design teams have access to them.

CHAPTER 9

Rooms and Color-Fill Plans

In the previous chapters of this book, we have discussed the creation of physical elements such as walls, floors, roofs, stairs, and railings; however, one of the most important elements in architecture is the spaces bounded by those elements. In the Autodesk® Revit® Architecture software, you have the ability to create and manage rooms as unique elements with extended data properties. Keeping room names and areas coordinated has the potential to free hours of manual effort for more productive and meaningful design-related tasks. Once rooms are tagged, you'll be able to create coordinated color-fill plans that automatically reflect any data about the rooms in your project. Any changes to the rooms are immediately reflected throughout the entire project.

In this chapter, you learn the following skills:

- **Defining rooms in spaces**
- **Creating a key schedule**
- **Generating color-fill room plans**

Defining Rooms in Spaces

Rooms are special types of objects because they do not have a clear physical representation like other model elements such as furniture and doors. Their horizontal extents are automatically determined by bounding objects in the form of walls, columns, or boundary lines that you can customize. These planar boundaries will determine the area of each room. As an additional option, you can allow Revit Architecture to calculate room volumes. The volumetric or vertical extents of rooms are determined by floors, ceilings, and roofs.

To access these calculation options, find the Room and Area panel on the Architecture tab (or the Home tab if you are using the Revit Architecture stand-alone software). Click the panel title to expose the special commands, and select Area and Volume Computations (Figure 9.1).

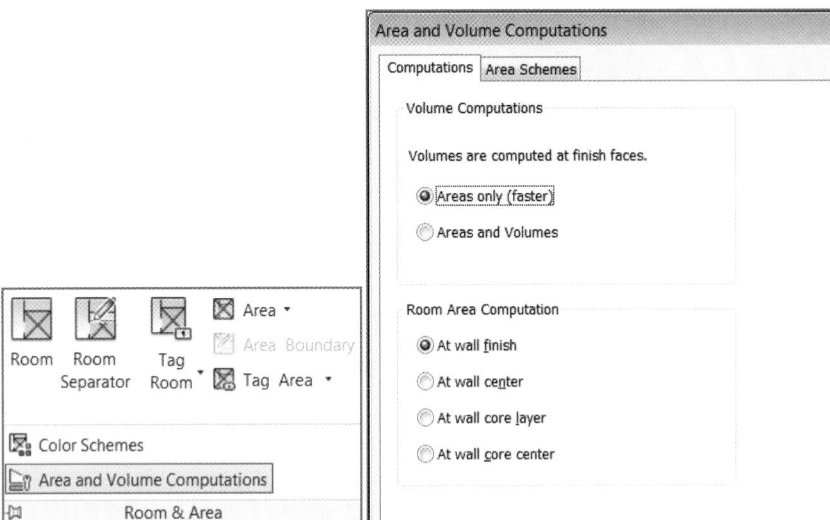

FIGURE 9.1: Customizing area and volume computations

The area and volume settings are shown at the right of Figure 9.1. In addition to setting the volume computation option, you have the ability to customize the area computation as it relates to walls. This is important to understand because it will affect the area values displayed in room tags. In this section you will place rooms and room tags in a floor plan of a project in progress.

Start by opening the project file you completed at the end of Chapter 8, "Groups and Phasing." If you haven't yet completed the chapter, you can go to the book's web page at `www.sybex.com/go/revit2013essentials` and download the project file `c09_Rooms_and_Color_Fills_Start.rvt`. Make sure the Level 1 floor plan is activated and set the scale to 1/4″ = 1′-0″ (1:50).

When you've finished the exercises in this chapter, you can inspect the file in its finished state on the book's web page. Download the file titled `c09_Rooms_and_Color_Fills_Finish.rvt`.

Room Tags

Before you start placing room objects, you should understand the distinction between rooms and room tags. The *room* is the spatial object that contains all the metadata about the space. The *tag* merely reports those values. In many cases, you can change the values in the room tag, and the room properties will update (and vice versa). But whereas deleting the room will delete the tag, the opposite is not true. You can delete a room tag, and the room will remain. This makes sense, because the room may not be tagged in all views.

To add a room to your project, follow these steps:

1. Go to the Architecture tab ➢ Room & Area panel, and select the Room tool.

   The context menu that lets you modify and place rooms becomes available. As you hover over enclosed spaces, the room boundary highlights, indicating the space in which you're about to place a room object (Figure 9.2). You don't have to tag rooms as you place them, but by default this option is selected.

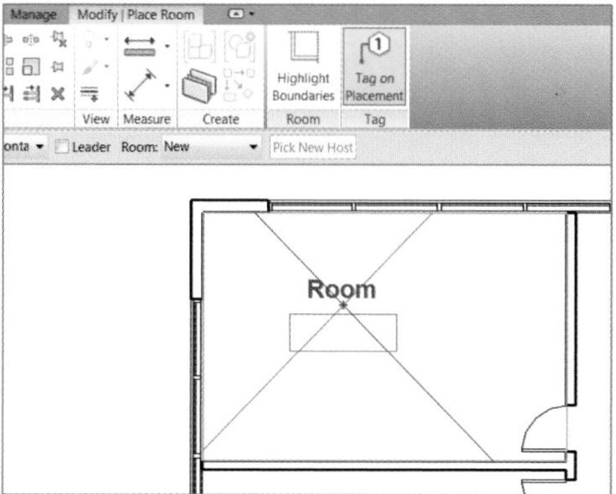

FIGURE 9.2: Adding a room and room tag

2. Place a room in the upper left space on the Level 1 floor plan. Notice that the default room tag indicates only the room name and number (Figure 9.3), but more options are available.
3. Click the Modify button or press the Esc key to exit the Room command, and then select one of the room tags.

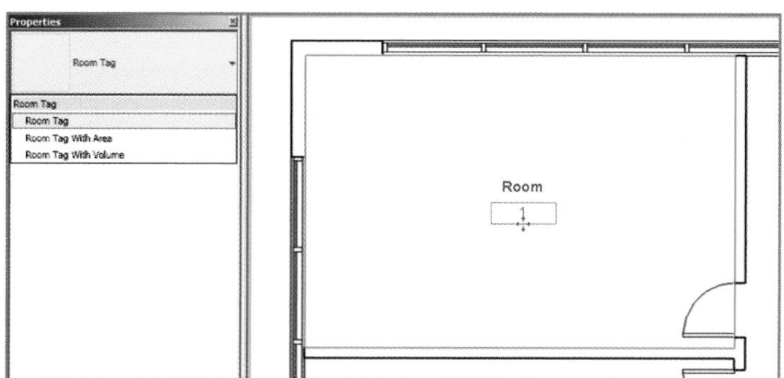

FIGURE 9.3: Room tag

4. From the Type Selector, choose the Room Tag With Area option. The room tag shows the area based on your project units (Figure 9.4). In this case, the room is 274 square feet. This feature is incredibly helpful if you want to create rooms as your design develops; you can constantly confirm that your spatial program requirements are being maintained.

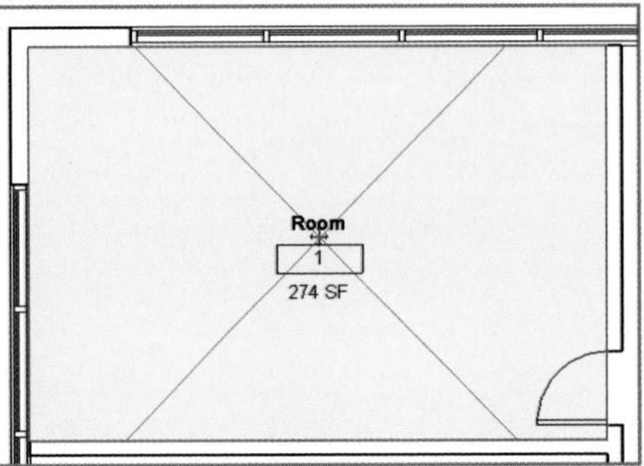

FIGURE 9.4: Room tag with area

5. Select the first room you created, and examine its properties in the Properties palette. You can modify the room name and number here or by directly editing the values in the room tag. It doesn't matter where you modify the data, because it is all stored in the room object. This makes it easy to create various plan diagrams to suit your needs.

> **You can change the automatic numbering of rooms by editing the room number of the first one placed and then continue placing others.**

6. Change the name of the room to **Small Meeting**, and change the number to **101**. Place some other rooms, and observe how the numbering scheme has changed.

Because rooms do not represent physical objects, they have two unique properties to help you visualize and select them. One is a reference—a pair of invisible, crossing vectors that are usually near the middle of the space. You can find these by moving your mouse pointer around in a space. The reference will highlight when your mouse pointer is over one. The second unique property of a room is an interior fill. You can make these properties visible in the Visibility/Graphics Settings for any view (Figure 9.5).

Room Boundaries

Rooms will automatically fill an enclosed area and will always recalculate their area when bounding objects are adjusted. Elements such as walls, floors, columns, and ceilings have a Room Bounding property that let you customize this behavior to suit your designs. You can find this property in the Properties palette when you select one of the aforementioned model elements.

Now let's see what happens if you move a wall that defines this space. Select the wall at the right, as shown in Figure 9.6, and move it 2′-0″ (600 mm) to the left. The moment you release the wall, the room updates with the new area information, which is immediately reported by the room tag (Figure 9.7).

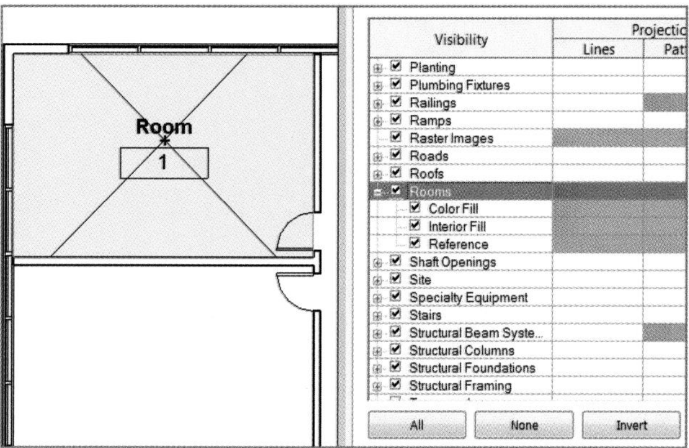

FIGURE 9.5: Room references and interior fill in the Visibility/Graphics settings

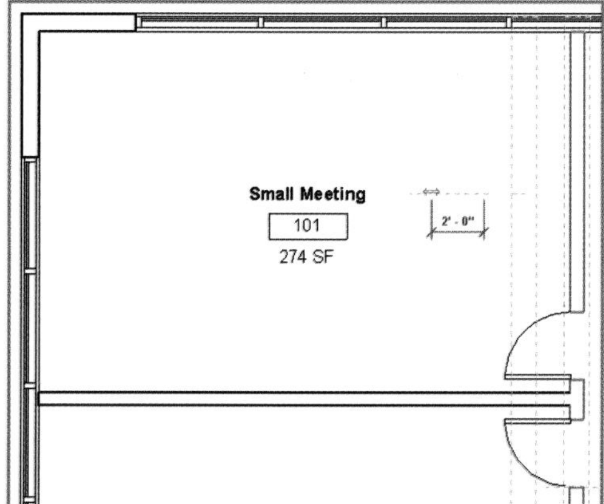

FIGURE 9.6: Moving the wall

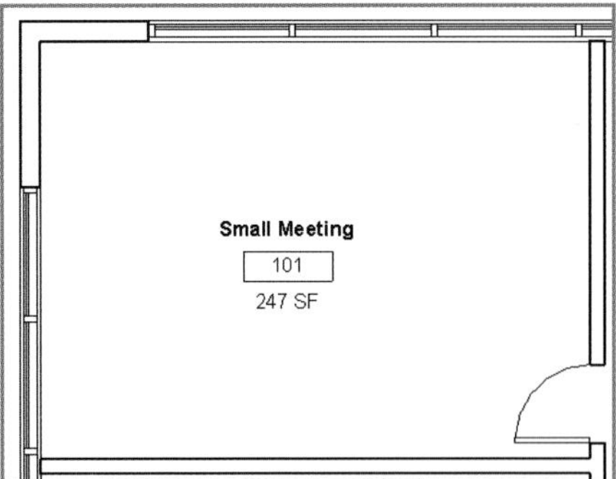

FIGURE 9.7: Updated room space and tag

Continue to add rooms and tags to the Level 1 floor plan as shown in Figure 9.8. The rooms will be numbered as you place them, so place the rooms according to the numeric sequence shown in the figure, starting with room 102.

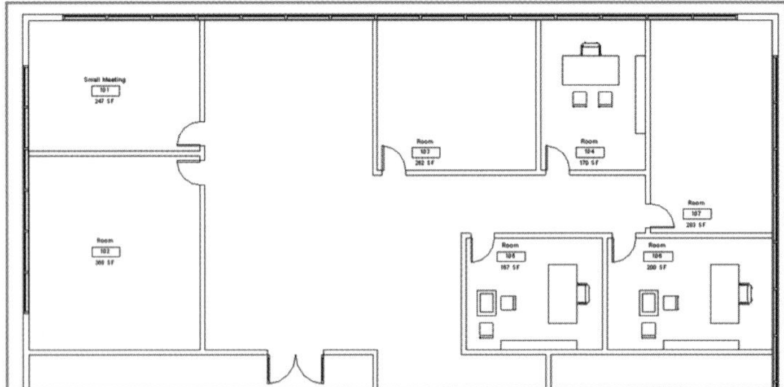

FIGURE 9.8: Adding rooms and tags

Room Separation Lines

As you start to add a tag to the large, central open space, it's obvious that the space will be tagged as a single room (Figure 9.9). But in many cases, open spaces need to be divided into smaller functional areas. You don't want to add walls to carve the large space into smaller areas; fortunately, there's a better option. You can draw spatial dividers known as room separation lines.

Follow these steps to subdivide the open space in the project into three functional spaces:

1. Return to the Room & Area panel in the Architecture tab of the ribbon, and select Room Separator.

2. Draw a line between the wall intersections labeled 1 and 2 in the sample file. These are model lines, and they show up in 3D views. The great thing about them is that they allow you to create spaces without using 3D geometry.

   By default, these lines are thin and black, but you can change the settings to make it easier to distinguish the lines from other elements. You will modify the Room Separator line style to be more visible in a working view, but it will be turned off in your sheet views.

Turn off room separation lines in the Visibility/Graphic Overrides for a view under the Lines category.

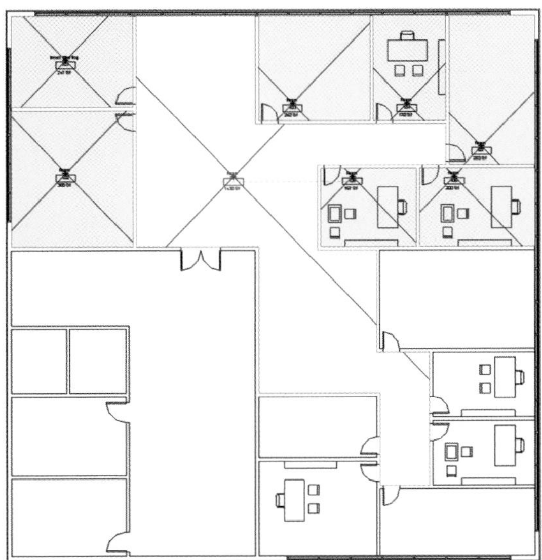

FIGURE 9.9: Tagging a large space

3. Go to the Manage tab ➢ Settings panel ➢ Additional Settings flyout, and select Line Styles. Change the default values for the <Room Separation> lines as follows:

   - Line Weight: 5
   - Color: Blue
   - Line Pattern: Dot 1/32″ (Dot 1mm)

Of course, this is only one way of using the room separators; you may customize these settings as needed.

4. Sketch another room separator in the sample file between the wall intersections labeled 1 and 3. Then add rooms and room tags to the spaces, as shown in Figure 9.10.

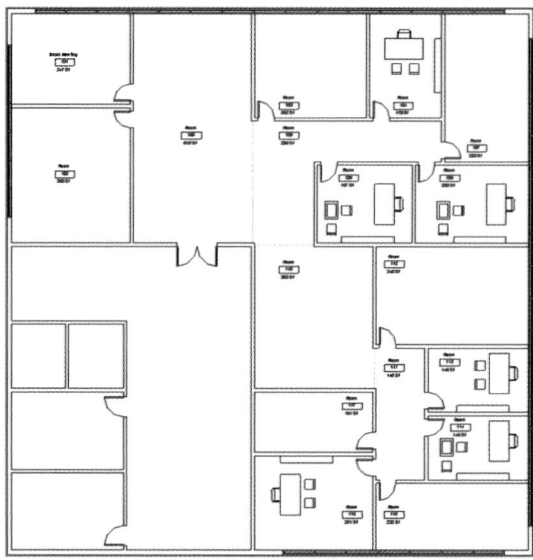

FIGURE 9.10: Adding room separation lines

Deleting Rooms

You have seen that using the Room command, you can place a room and a room tag simultaneously; however, deleting a room completely from a project takes multiple steps. If you simply delete a room tag, the room object remains in the space. You can add another tag later or tag it in a different view.

If you delete a room object, the definition of the room remains in your project until you either place another room using the same definition or delete it in a room schedule. Let's explore this behavior with a quick exercise in which you will delete a room object, observe the unplaced room in a schedule, and then replace the room object in the floor plan:

1. From the Level 1 floor plan, delete the first room you placed in the previous exercise. A warning appears in the lower-right corner of the application. This warning tells you that the room you just deleted will remain in the project until it is deleted from a room schedule.

2. Go to the View tab ➢ Create panel ➢ Schedules flyout ➢ Schedule/Quantities.

3. Select Rooms from the Category list, and click OK.
4. Add the following fields to the Room Schedule in this order:
   - Number
   - Name
   - Area
5. Click OK. One room in the schedule displays Not Placed in the Area column. There are filters in the ribbon to *show*, *hide*, or *isolate* unplaced or unenclosed rooms when you are viewing a room schedule. These filters are useful when you want to perform quality control on your project and quickly clean up unplaced rooms.
6. To replace the room you just deleted, return to the Level 1 floor plan, and start the Room command again. This time, open the Room drop-down on the Options bar. You see any unplaced rooms available in your project (Figure 9.11). Select the unplaced room from the list, and place the room back in the floor plan.

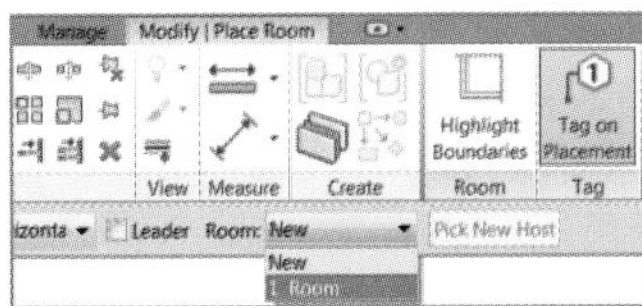

FIGURE 9.11: Place rooms with unplaced room definitions.

Creating a Key Schedule

You could certainly continue editing all the room names manually (and this is regularly done during early design). But in many cases—and particularly on larger projects—the program is very specific about room names and other values given to spaces. Certain types of rooms may also be repetitive and require identical names. If multiple room names need to be edited, this can be a time-consuming and tedious process.

A better option to manage repetitive information is to create what is known as a *key*. A key can be defined to manage as many parameters as you need for a particular object type. In the following exercise, you will define a key to manage the room name. Once the key is established in a key schedule, the key value is then assigned to one or many rooms. If you need to edit the parameter values related to the key, you only need to edit the value in the key schedule, and all the rooms update instantly.

To create a key, you must start with a key schedule. Follow these steps to create a key schedule for rooms:

1. Once again, return to the View tab ➢ Create panel ➢ Schedules flyout, and select Schedule/Quantities.
2. This step is particularly important. In the New Schedule dialog box, choose Rooms from the category list, and select Schedule Keys as the option on the right side (not Schedule Building Components). Then change the schedule name and the key name to **Room Name Key**, as shown in Figure 9.12.

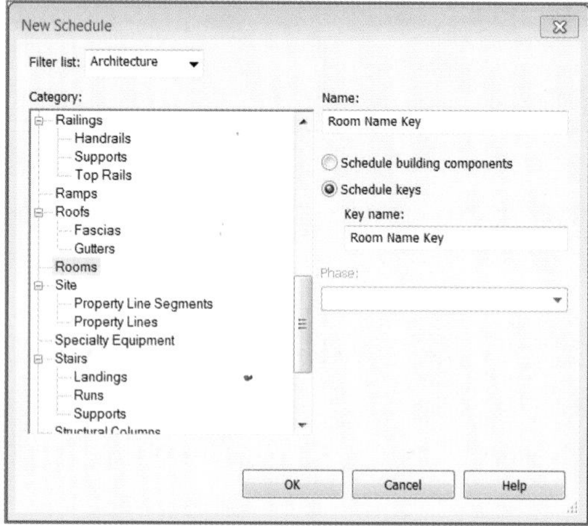

FIGURE 9.12: Creating a schedule key

3. Click OK to close the New Schedule dialog box.
4. In the Schedule Properties dialog box, the Key Name field is already added by default. The only other field you want to add is Name. Select the Name field in the left pane, and click the Add button so Name appears in the Scheduled Fields list on the right (Figure 9.13).
5. Click OK to close the dialog, and you will see no line items. This is because you didn't create a schedule; you created a key schedule. You'll add the key fields in the next section.

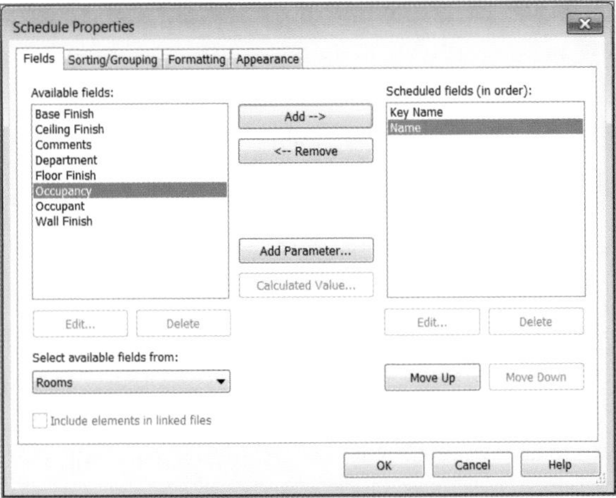

FIGURE 9.13: Adding fields to the room key

Creating Key Fields

The next process is to create the key fields that will populate the associated room properties once a key is applied to a room. Continue the exercise from the previous section by following these steps:

1. Make sure the Room Name Key schedule is still activated. From the Rows panel in the ribbon, select the New option. Now you can add rows to your schedule key.

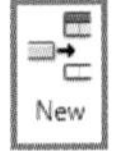

2. Add a total of six rows with the data shown in Table 9.1.

TABLE 9.1: Room Name Key values

Key Description	Name
001 Hallways and Circulation	CIRCULATION
002 Large Meeting Spaces - Formal	MEETING 1
003 Small Meeting Spaces - Informal	MEETING 2
004 Reception and Lobby Spaces	RECEPTION
005 Large Office - Management	OFFICE 1
006 Small Offices - Staff	OFFICE 2

The key description will not show up in your room tag. (Hint: Use a real-world description that helps the design team understand the context of the tag beyond a one-word name.)

3. Go back to the Level 1 floor plan, select room 101, and assign a key value from the Room Name Key drop-down in the Properties palette (Figure 9.14).

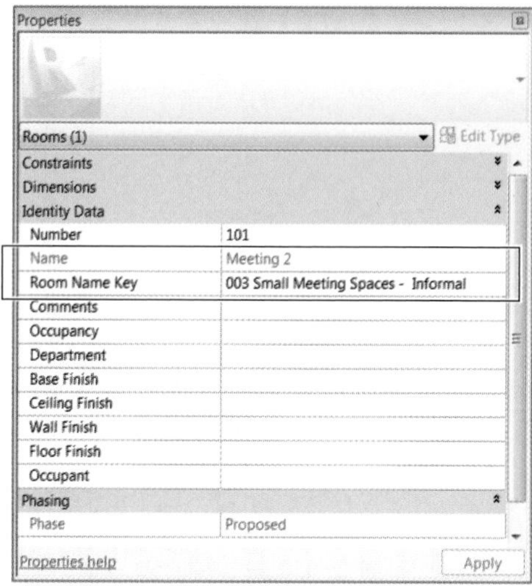

FIGURE 9.14: Assigning a key value to the room

When you assign the Room Name Key parameter to a key schedule, you can no longer edit the room name directly in the room tag.

Notice that the Name value cannot be modified in the Properties palette. This is because after assigning a key to a model component, you must manage the parameters related to the key in the respective key schedule.

4. Continue to place rooms in all the remaining spaces in the Level 1 floor plan. Assign room name keys to all the rooms as well, making sure you apply the same Room Name Key to several rooms.

Modifying Key Fields

When you select a value from the Room Name Key field in the Properties palette, all of the key values are available (Figure 9.15). This helps avoid inconsistencies that come with naming all rooms manually (where spelling and syntax errors can lead to confusion and uncoordinated documentation).

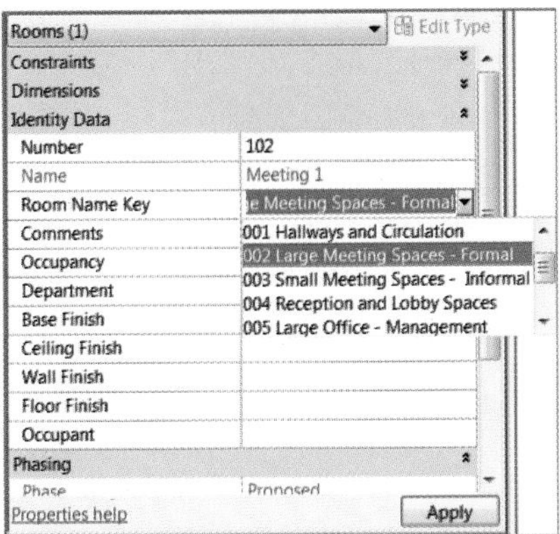

FIGURE 9.15: Key values from the Room Name Key drop-down menu

The great thing about this is that if the room names need to change, you need to change them in only one location—the key schedule. Activate the Room Name Key schedule again and then experiment with changing the room names in the key schedule. Return to the Level 1 floor plan and observe how the room names remain consistent with the changes you made in the key schedule.

Generating Color-Fill Room Plans

Certification Objective

Creating color-fill plans in Revit Architecture is easier to accomplish than most other design applications. Once again, color-fill plans constantly update as existing information is modified or new information is added. This allows you to focus on communicating rather than coordinating your design information—as if resolving your design isn't already hard enough!

Adding a Color Legend

To create a color-fill plan, go to the Annotate tab ➢ Color Fill panel ➢ Color Fill Legend tool. Click anywhere in the Level 1 floor plan, and a dialog opens that allows you to select the space type and color scheme (Figure 9.16). In this case, set Space Type to Rooms and Color Scheme to Name.

You can create any number of color schemas based on various data in your project model. For example, you could create color-fill legends according to department, floor finish, occupancy type, and even ranges in area.

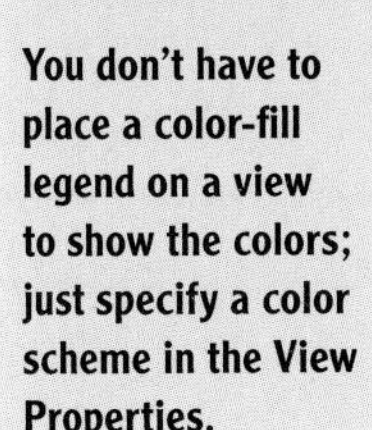

You don't have to place a color-fill legend on a view to show the colors; just specify a color scheme in the View Properties.

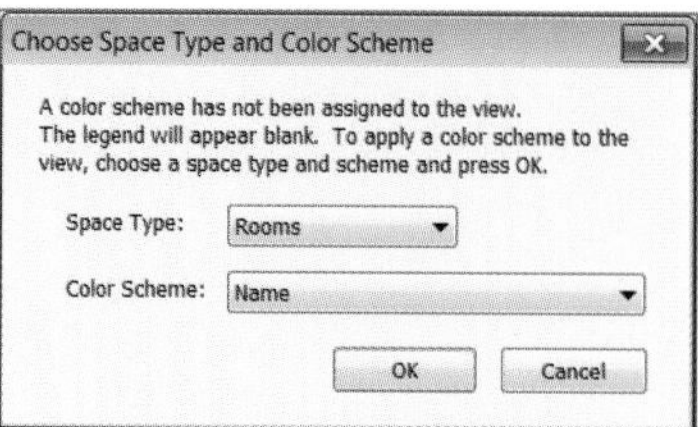

FIGURE 9.16: Defining the color-fill legend

To edit the color assignments, select the color-fill legend in the plan view. You can then select the Edit Scheme tool from the contextual ribbon. You can also access the same settings in the Properties palette for the current view. Just find the Color Scheme property, and click the button in the parameter field.

Selecting the Edit Scheme tool opens the Edit Color Scheme dialog where all the values are available for editing (Figure 9.17). You can edit the color as well as the fill pattern. Changing the fill pattern is helpful if you want to create an analytic fill pattern for a black-and-white or grayscale print.

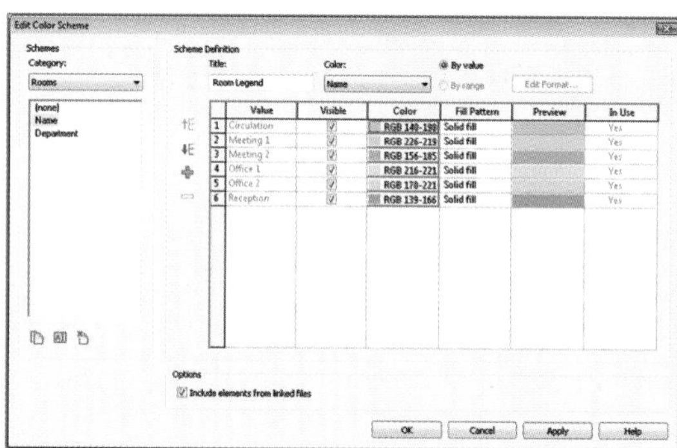

FIGURE 9.17: Edit Color Scheme dialog

Modifying Color Schemes

By default, solid fill colors will be automatically assigned to each unique value in a color scheme. Fortunately, you can completely customize the colors and fill patterns for the scheme. Let's edit the color of the Circulation fill by following these steps:

1. With the Edit Color Scheme dialog box open, select the Color field in the row for Circulation. The Color dialog box opens.
2. Modify the color values to **R 255**, **G 128**, and **B 128**. When you complete the changes, the fill color automatically updates to reflect your changes (Figure 9.18).

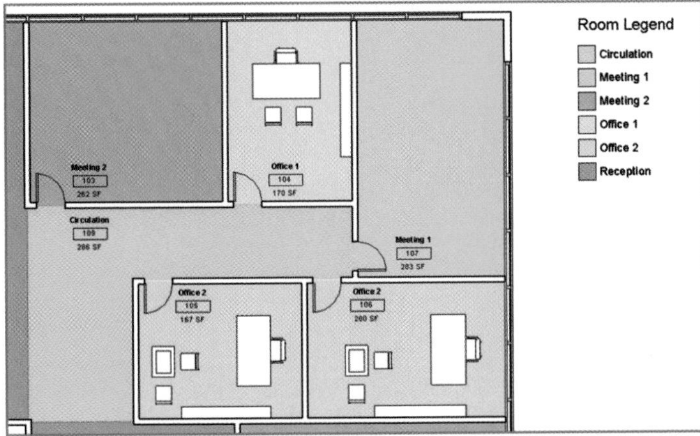

FIGURE 9.18: Resulting color fill

Color fills were automatically created in the project view based on all the assigned room names. What would happen if you created a new room name in the Room Name Key schedule? Well, let's find out.

3. Activate the Room Name Key schedule and add a new room key with the description **007 Director's Office** and the name **Office 3**. In this scenario, you're adding a new key to accommodate another type of room that will be used throughout the project.
4. You need to associate the new room key to at least one of the rooms. Do so by selecting the room for Meeting 2 and reassigning this space to the newly created room key. The color fill is modified immediately on the floor plan, and the new value is added to the color-fill legend (Figure 9.19).

All the room tags and color fills are associated with the elements of your building design. Experiment with this behavior by moving some of the walls. Note how the room areas and color fills automatically adjust as each space changes.

You can also right-click a view reference like a section and select Go To View from the context menu.

Adding Tags and Fill Colors in Section

Room tags and color fills are not just for use in floor plans—they can be utilized in sections as well. Let's examine this functionality with a quick exercise:

1. Activate the Level 1 floor plan. Go to the View tab ➢ Create panel and select the Section tool. Create a section across the project plan view, as shown in Figure 9.20.

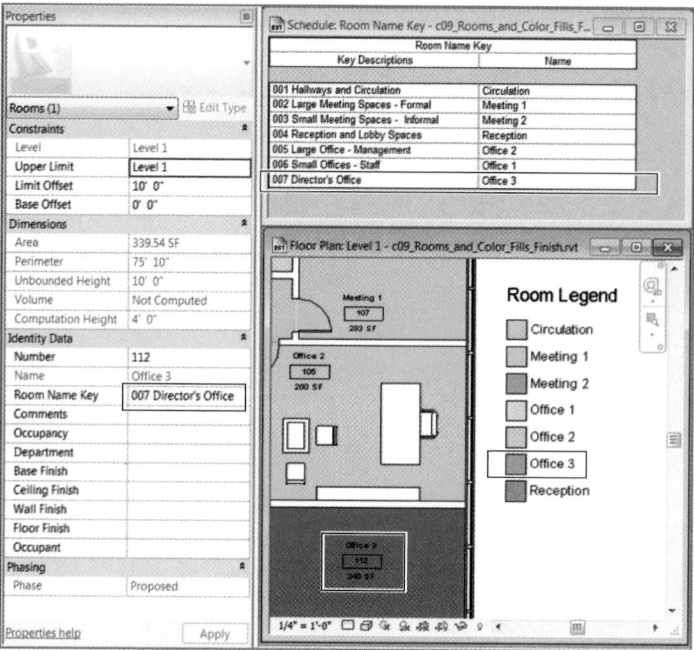

FIGURE 9.19: Updated color fill and legend

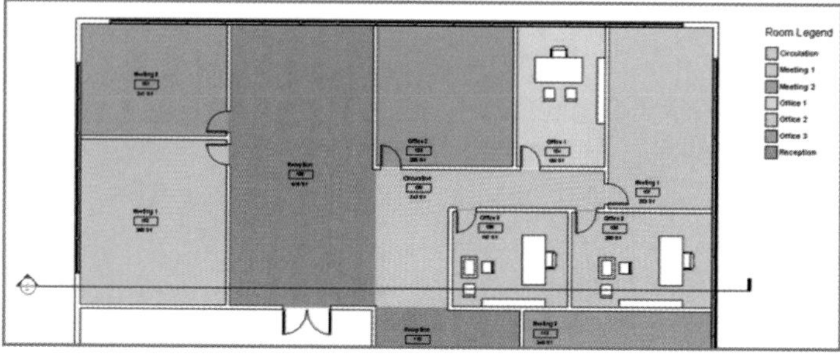

FIGURE 9.20: Creating the building section

2. Press the Esc key to de-select the section you just created. Double-click the section head to open the new view. Figure 9.21 illustrates the new building section. Although all the geometry is shown correctly, it would certainly help to tag the spaces with their room names.

   You have two options to tag the room objects. Room Tag lets you place each tag manually. This approach is fine for a small project, but on a larger project it would take a considerable amount of time. Instead you can use the Tag All Not Tagged command to automatically place tags in the current view.

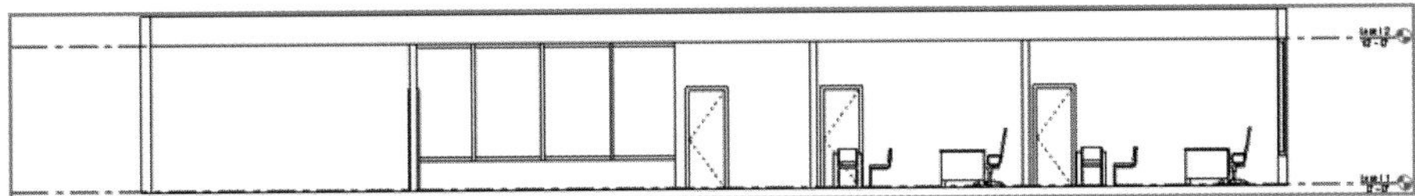

FIGURE 9.21: Resulting building section

3. Select the Annotate tab ➢ Tag panel ➢ Tag All. Doing so opens the Tag All Not Tagged dialog, allowing you to tag numerous element categories in a view simultaneously. You only need to tag rooms in this exercise, so select the Room Tags category as shown in Figure 9.22, and then click OK.

FIGURE 9.22: Adding room tags with the Tag All command

The section view is automatically populated with room tags (Figure 9.23). Keep in mind that the tags will be centered in each room, so you may need to move their location slightly if the tag is overlapping element geometry. To move a tag, click the Modify button in the ribbon (or press the Esc key), select a tag, and drag it using the grip that appears near the selected tag. You can also grab and drag a tag directly without selecting it first.

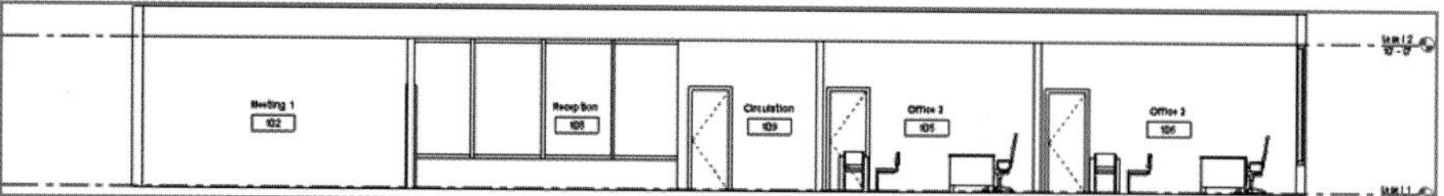

FIGURE 9.23: Room tags shown in section

4. What about the color fills? Return to the Annotate tab ➢ Color Fill panel ➢ Color Fill Legend tool, and place the legend in the section view.

5. Once again, set Space Type to Rooms and Color Scheme to Name. The rooms are filled with the same pattern and color in the section view as the color fill in the plan view, as shown in Figure 9.24. Remember, the color fills in the section view could describe Department or other values, while the room tags displayed the room name.

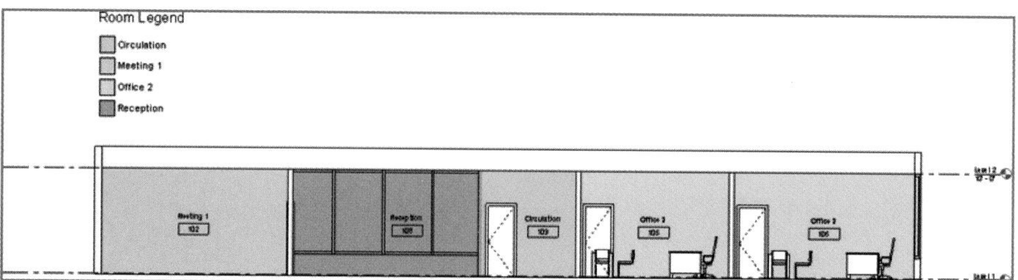

FIGURE 9.24: Room colors in the section view match the plan colors.

Notice in Figure 9.24 that the color fill is obscured by some of the model elements such as doors and furniture. This is because the color fill can be placed as a background or foreground in any view. To change this setting, look in the Properties palette for the settings of the current view, and find the Color Scheme Location parameter. Change this setting to Foreground, and observe how the color-fill display is modified.

The Essentials and Beyond

User-defined parameters can be used to manage room and program data in a way not practical before the Revit Architecture software was available. Even the desired program areas can be added to the room key, allowing you to compare proposed and actual areas. There's a lot of wonderful functionality with regard to rooms, room tags, and color fills that we haven't been able to cover in this brief chapter. Instead, we focused on typical uses to get you up to speed so you can be confident and productive as quickly as possible.

Additional Exercises

- Create a single room, and add a room and a room tag. Now add a wall across the middle of the room. Which side of the room contains the space of the room? What denotes the origin of the room?
- Create a room color fill that uses black-and-white patterns rather than color. Why might this be useful?
- Create a room tag that displays information not visible in the default tag (such as Department).
- Create a room key with desired room areas, and compare them to actual room areas.
- Create a color fill in your own project template.

CHAPTER 10

Worksharing

Understanding multiuser workflow is essential to completing your Autodesk® Revit® Architecture pilot project. There's plenty of work to go around between the design, development, and eventual documentation of a building project.

If you've never used the Revit Architecture software before, you're probably used to CAD. Multiuser workflow in CAD is a very different animal, so you may need to suspend your expectations of what it will be like to use Revit Architecture tools.

Whereas CAD projects are typically divided along the lines of what needs to be drawn (plan, section, elevation at various levels of detail), Revit Architecture envelops you in the entire process. 2D, 3D, schedules, and so on, are in a single database, waiting for the input and direction of your team.

This is a far more elegant and efficient process than manually managing 2D files (which only one person can work on at a time). You can expect a large CAD-based project that would require five or six staff working in CAD to require about half that number working in Revit Architecture.

In this chapter, you learn the following skills:

- **Enabling worksharing**
- **Creating central and local files**
- **Adding worksets**
- **Assigning elements to worksets**
- **Saving to the central file**
- **Creating new elements**
- **Using workset display filters**
- **Using worksharing to work with consultants**
- **Using guidelines for worksharing**

Enabling Worksharing

Certification Objective

The first thing that you'll need to do is open the file from the end of Chapter 9, "Rooms and Color Fill Plans." If you don't have the file, go to the book's web page at `www.sybex.com/go/revit2013essentials` and download `c10_Worksharing_Start.rvt`.

Preparing the Central File

We strongly suggest that before you enable worksharing, you create a new copy of the file in order to back up your old work. For example, you may have been doing some schematic design planning in Revit Architecture, and now it's time to add more people to the project in order to meet a deadline. Creating a copy of your old file (before enabling worksharing) is just good practice in case you need to return to your previous work.

In this case, prepare for this file to be the central file by naming it `c10_Worksharing_Central_Finish.rvt` (Figure 10.1). Then continue with these steps:

1. Open the file, and go to the Collaborate tab ➢ Worksets palette ➢ Worksets tool. This tool lets you enable and access worksets.

   The Worksharing dialog box shown in Figure 10.2 appears, telling you three important things:

   - Worksharing can't be undone and requires careful planning and management (aren't you glad you saved a copy of your file?).
   - Datum is moving to a workset called Shared Levels and Grids.
   - Project content that is not view specific (geometry and rooms) is all being assigned to Workset1.

   All of this is fine and will allow you to enable worksharing. Click OK to continue.

2. The Worksets dialog box shown in Figure 10.3 opens. Your workset username appears in the Owner field. At present, you own everything in the project. No one else can work on the project without your permission.

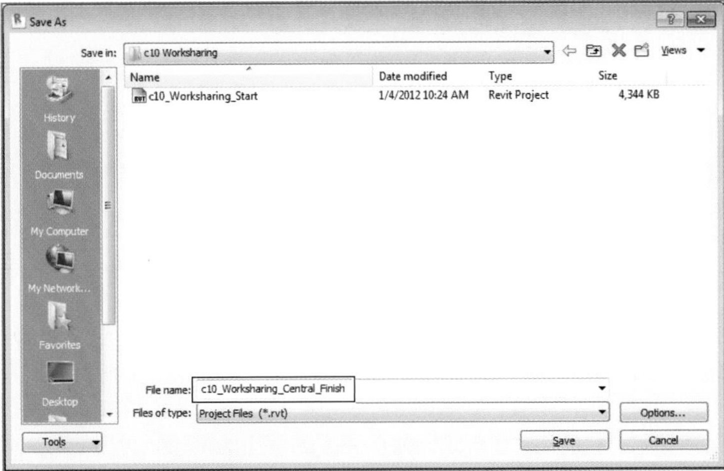

FIGURE 10.1 Saving a copy of the file

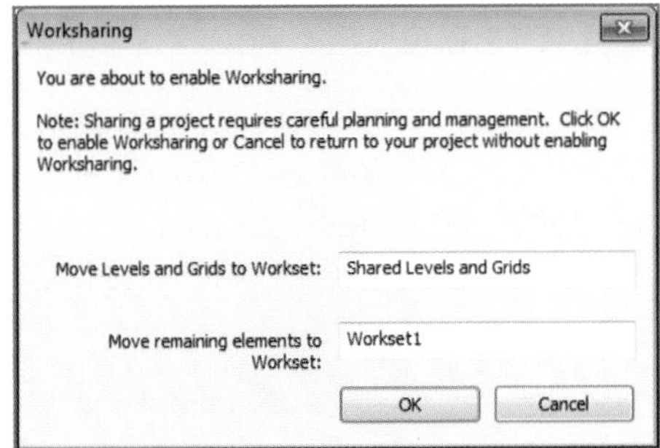

FIGURE 10.2 The initial Worksharing dialog box

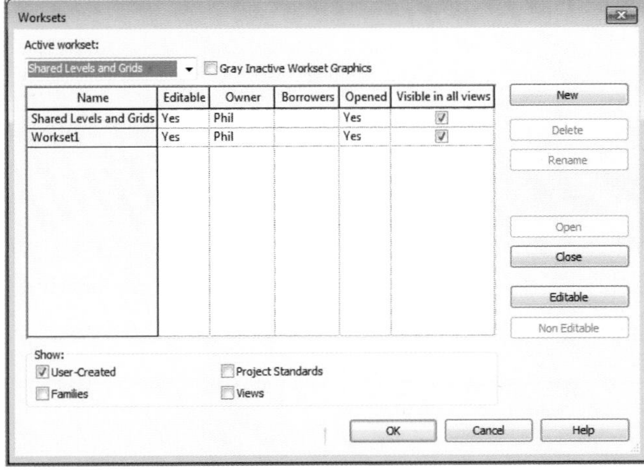

FIGURE 10.3 Worksets dialog box

Creating Central and Local Files

In a real project, you will likely want to save the central file on a local server so your team members can have access to the file. They're not going to work directly in the central file, but they will need to have access to it in order to make their own local copies and so that those local copies can communicate to the central file from a central location.

Creating the Central File

It's a good idea to save the project, which will establish it as the central file. Before you save the file, think about where you want it to be located. Be aware that you can't simply move it after the fact. It's a bit complicated, because moving a central file will create a local copy. We won't get into all the details now—just know that you should save the file in the desired location.

When you save the file, click the Options button in the save dialog. The File Save Options dialog that opens assures you that this will be the central file and provides other options, such as the number of backups that Revit Architecture will maintain for the central file (Figure 10.4).

Close the central file, and let's create a local copy.

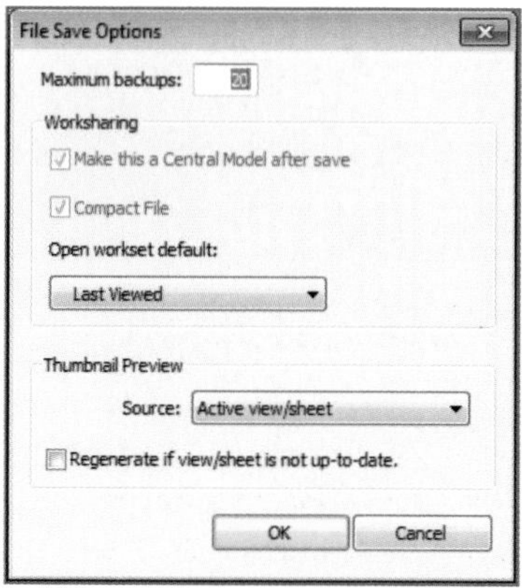

FIGURE 10.4 Saving the central file

Creating the Local File

When you work in Revit Architecture with worksharing enabled, it's unlikely that you'll be working in the central file. Rather, you will work on your own local copy of the central file, as will everyone else. These local copies are constantly communicating and syncing to the central file in order to avoid conflicts.

Click Open from the Application menu or Quick Access toolbar in the Revit Architecture software, and browse to your central file. Select it, but don't double-click. As shown in Figure 10.5, ensure that the Create New Local option is selected. Selecting this option will not open the central file but rather will create a copy of the central file.

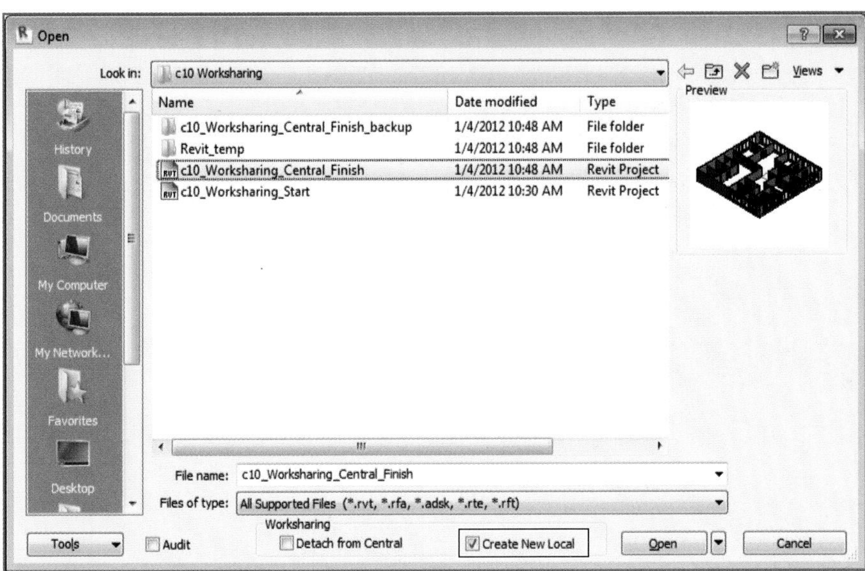

FIGURE 10.5 Creating the local copy

By default, your local copy is placed in your `Documents` folder with a suffix based on your username in Revit Architecture. In this author's case, the username is Phil. So, the local file is saved in the `Documents` folder as `c10_Worksharing_Central_Finish_Phil.rvt` (Figure 10.6).

Now that the local file has been created, you're ready to create some user-defined worksets and then assign geometry to those worksets. Theoretically, other users could also start to access the central file and make their own local copies. But in practice, they'll probably wait until the user-defined worksets are created and the geometry has been properly assigned.

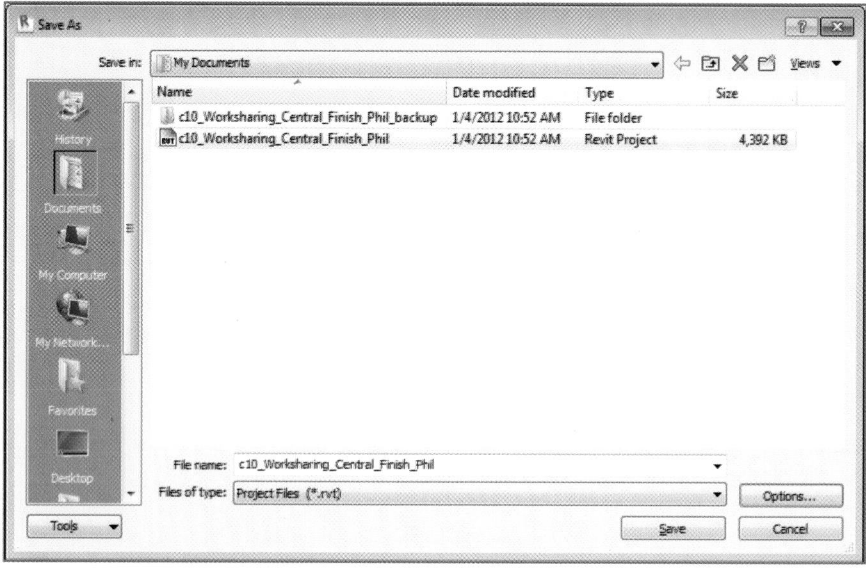

FIGURE 10.6 Saving the local copy

Adding Worksets

To create worksets, follow these steps:

1. Open the Worksets dialog box by using the same Workset tool you used to activate worksharing previously.

2. Click New, and then create three additional worksets, as shown in Figure 10.7. Keep in mind that worksets are not layers, and not much granularity is required. Basically, worksets are for broad collections of objects based on their relationship to the project.

   The project you're using for this exercise is fairly modest. Interior, exterior, and core worksets are sufficient. If this were a multistory project, you would likely create interior worksets for each building level, as well as another workset for the roof and roof-related elements (such as equipment and skylights).

   Once you've created the worksets, click OK.

3. Open the Visibility/Graphic Overrides dialog box for the view (press V+G on the keyboard). As you can see in Figure 10.8, there's an

additional Worksets tab that didn't exist before worksharing was enabled. This tab allows you to turn off elements based on their workset assignment.

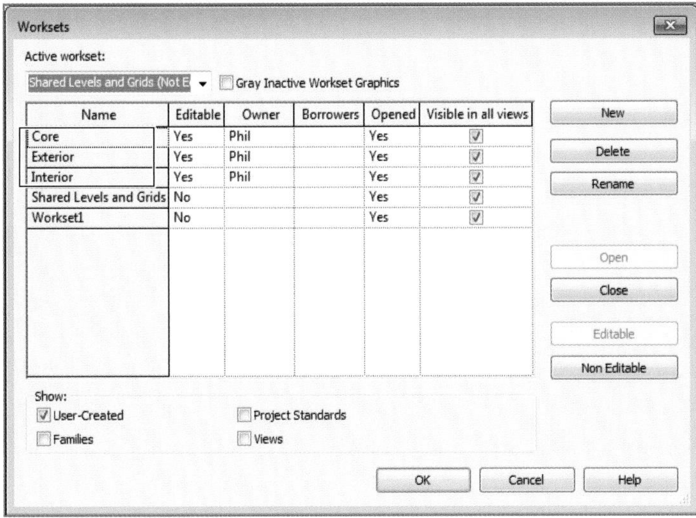

FIGURE 10.7 Creating additional worksets

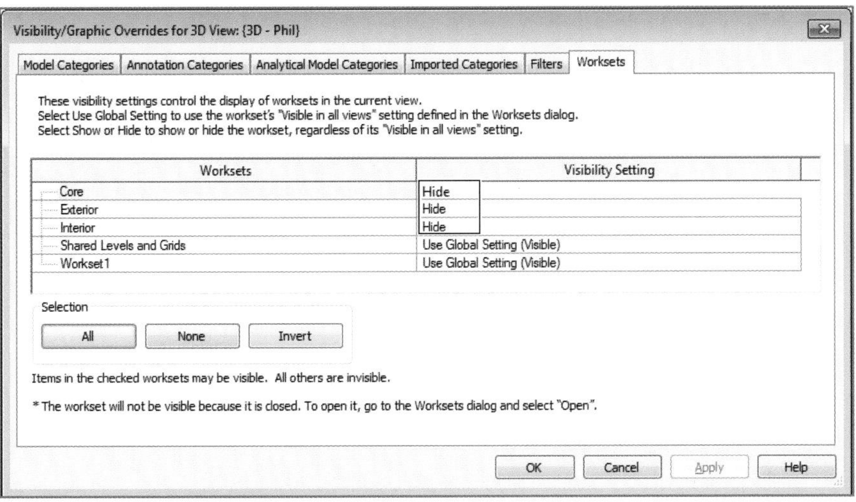

FIGURE 10.8 The Worksets tab

Workset Visibility

You're about to begin assigning portions of the project to your user-defined worksets. As you do this, you want to be able to clear the view of elements that have already been assigned to one of your newly created worksets. Basically, you want to work "subtractively" by removing elements.

To do this, set the Visibility Setting column for the active view to Hide, as shown in Figure 10.8. As geometry is assigned to each of those worksets, it will disappear from view and keep you from accidentally selecting it again.

By the way, don't delete Workset1 from your project. It's a great place to put content when you're not sure which workset something is supposed to belong to. Also, we've encountered many projects that were introduced midstream to staff who had minimal Revit Architecture experience. Rather than have them obsess over which workset should be active as they worked, we told them to put all their work in Workset1 and that we'd move things around later. This also helped us isolate and review their work.

Now you can begin assigning elements to your user-defined worksets.

Assigning Elements to Worksets

Assigning elements to worksets is easily done. Just be sure of what you're selecting. You will often use the Filter tool and may work in more than one view. Except for rooms, it's often easier to select elements in 3D views. But for this exercise, you'll keep it simple by working from the 2D Level 1 floor plan view. Follow these steps:

1. Select the elements shown in Figure 10.9—the walls in the lower-left corner of the plan.

2. On the Properties palette, a field indicates the workset assignment. Change this value from Workset1 to Core. Once you do so, the elements assigned to the core workset are no longer visible in this view. Don't be alarmed! Recall that in the previous section, you turned off the visibility for this (and other) worksets, so this behavior should be expected.

   Now let's select all the interior elements and move them to a new workset rather than selecting one element at a time.

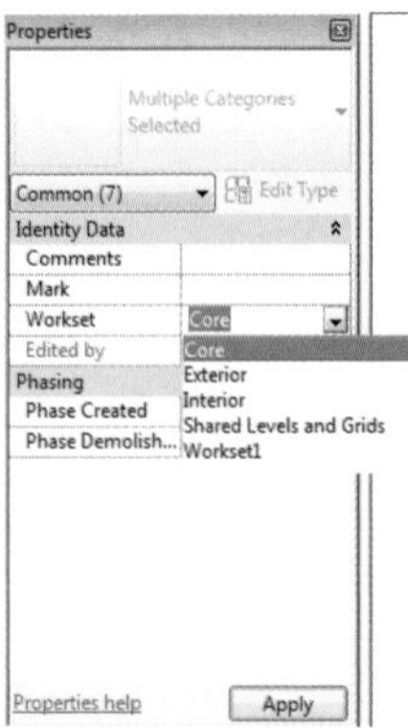

3. To select all the elements described, draw a selection window from lower right to upper left inside the exterior walls. Windowing from this direction will include every element you cross or include within the window you draw. (If you windowed from left to right, it would select *only* the elements fully contained within the selection box.)

FIGURE 10.9 Assigning user-defined worksets

4. Not all of the selected elements can be assigned to user-defined worksets, so you need to use the Filter tool to deselect some of the elements. Choose Modify ➢ Filter. In the Filter dialog box, deselect Room Tags And Views, as shown in Figure 10.10.

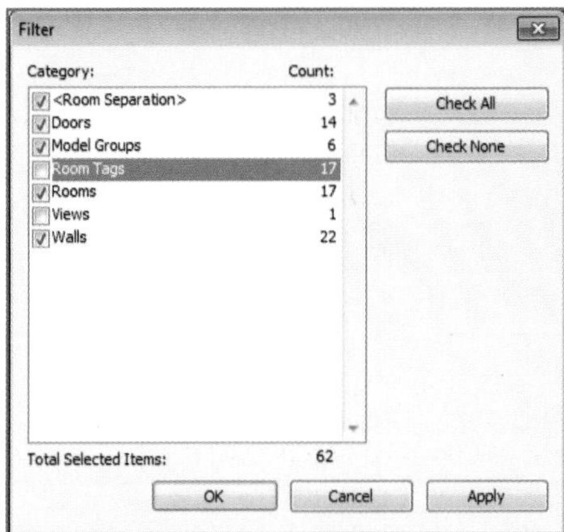

FIGURE 10.10 Deselecting elements with the Filter tool

5. Assign these elements to the interior workset. Once again, don't be alarmed when they seem to disappear.

6. For the final selection, select all the remaining walls that are visible in the view, and then select the Filter tool again. This time, only choose Walls in the Category list (Figure 10.11). Elements such as curtain panels, grids, and mullions automatically belong to their parent workset: walls.

7. None of the geometry or rooms is visible in your project. Open the Visibility/Graphic Overrides dialog box for the view, and reset the visibility settings as shown in Figure 10.12. All the elements once again become visible.

At this point, you can save your project and synchronize it with the central file.

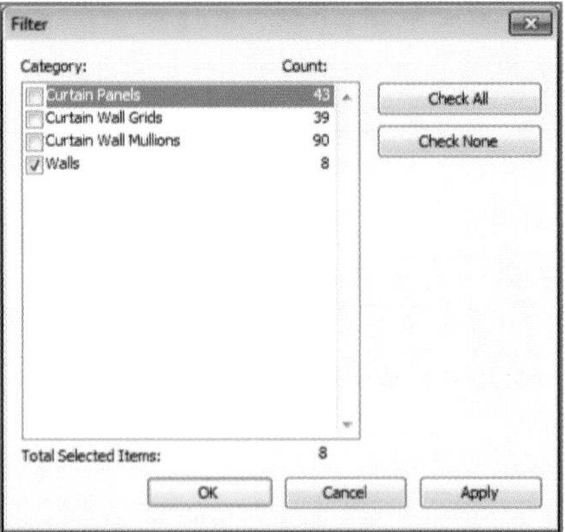

FIGURE 10.11 Isolating walls with the Filter tool

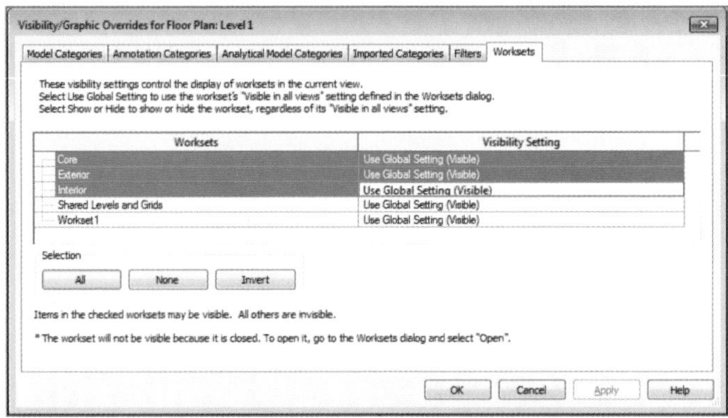

FIGURE 10.12 Resetting the visibility settings

Saving to the Central File

When you want to save your work to the central file, there are a number of options to fit your workflow. The following options are available on the Synchronize panel of the Collaborate tab:

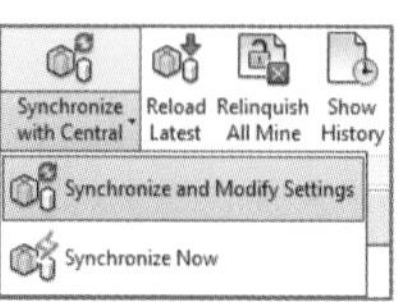

Synchronize And Modify Settings Synchronize And Modify Settings provides more specific control when saving the central file. The dialog box shown in Figure 10.13 gives you options to relinquish worksets, compact the central file, and save your local file after the sync with the central file is complete.

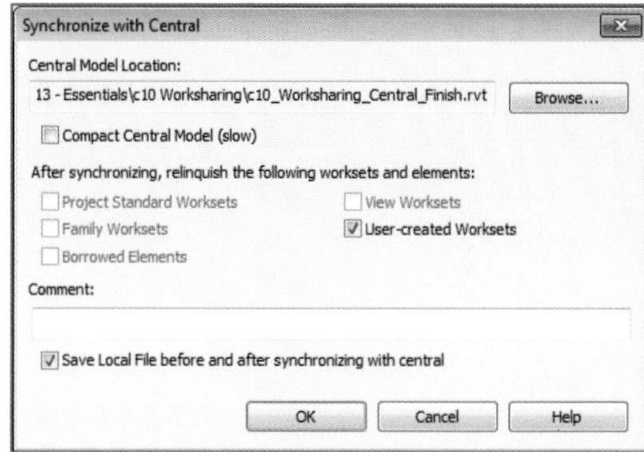

FIGURE 10.13 Synchronize And Modify Settings options

Synchronize Now This option is probably more frequently used than the other options. Consider creating a keyboard shortcut so you don't have to return to this tab as you work and want to save to the central file.

Synchronize Now saves your local copy and syncs with the central file as well as updates your file with any changes from the central file. Any borrowed elements are also relinquished. But if you have any workset checked out or editable, it's not checked back in. It will still be editable by you.

Reload Latest The Reload Latest option lets you reload the latest version of the central file in your local project. However, it doesn't publish any of your work in the central file.

Relinquish All Mine Relinquish All Mine allows you to check back in elements that you may have borrowed but not changed. If you've made changes, you either have to sync them with the central file or discard the changes without saving. You cannot relinquish elements in a file that has been modified.

So, what do you do if you've made changes that you want to get rid of? The only way to do this is to close the file and select the Do Not Save The Project option (Figure 10.14). This will close the project without saving your work or syncing with the central file.

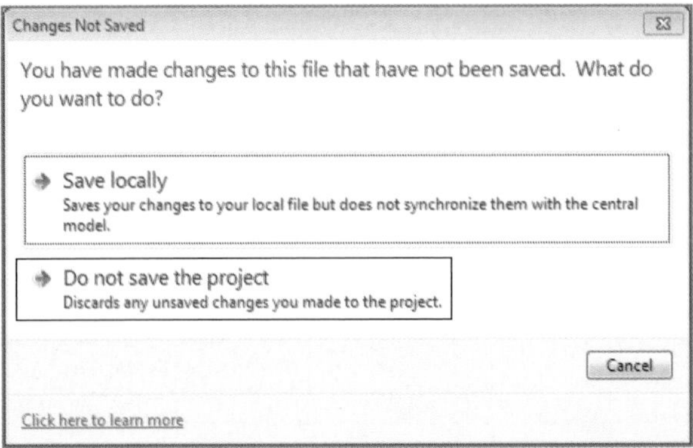

FIGURE 10.14 Closing the file without saving changes

If you select this option, Revit Architecture will ask you what to do with the elements you've borrowed or worksets you have enabled (Figure 10.15). If you relinquish the elements and worksets, other people will be able to modify them in their local files. If you keep ownership, the changes you've made will be lost, but you'll still have the elements and worksets enabled.

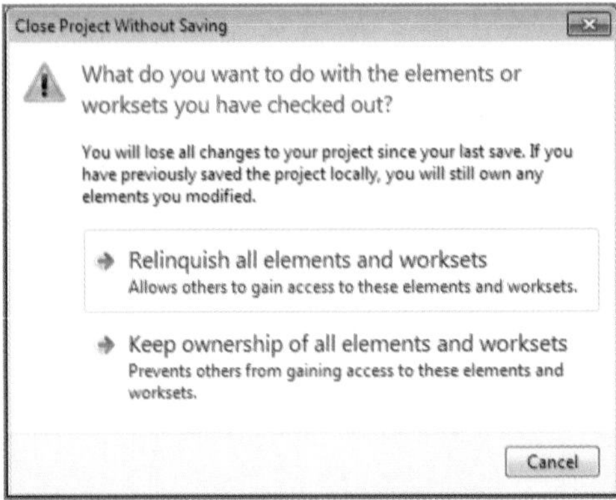

FIGURE 10.15 Relinquishing elements and worksets

When you have no elements or worksets enabled in a project, you can confirm this by opening the Worksets dialog box in Figure 10.16.

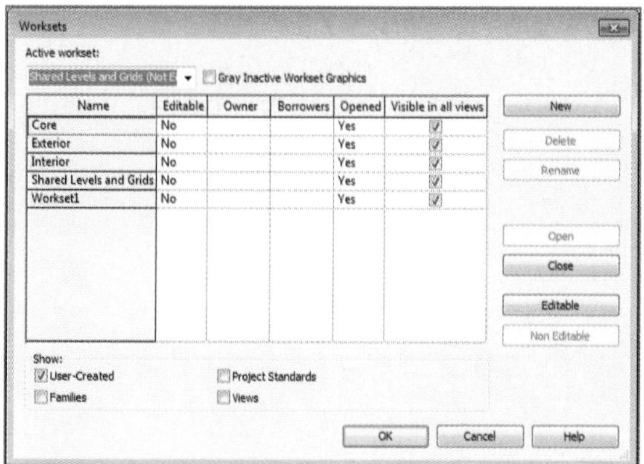

FIGURE 10.16 Relinquished elements and worksets

Let's continue by adding new elements to your local file.

Creating New Elements

When worksharing is enabled, you'll want to make sure that any new geometry or rooms you add are being assigned to the right workset. You're going to add some new furniture to the project, so you need to make the interior workset active. Then follow these steps:

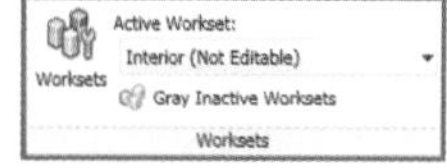

1. Copy a group of furniture from room 105 to room 103, as shown in Figure 10.17. Because the active workset is interior, the elements in the group are assigned to this workset.

   It's not possible to have elements in a workset assigned to a different workset than the group. Revit Architecture automatically assigns the elements within a workset to the same workset as the group.

   Now let's duplicate an existing component, create a new type, and then use this new type in the project.

2. Duplicate the table. In the Project Browser, right-click 72″ × 30″ (180 cm × 75 cm) and choose Duplicate from the context menu (Figure 10.18).

3. To modify the duplicated table, select the table again in the Project Browser, right-click, and choose Type Properties.

   Select the Rename button in the Properties dialog to rename the type to 144″ × 48″ (350 cm × 120 cm).

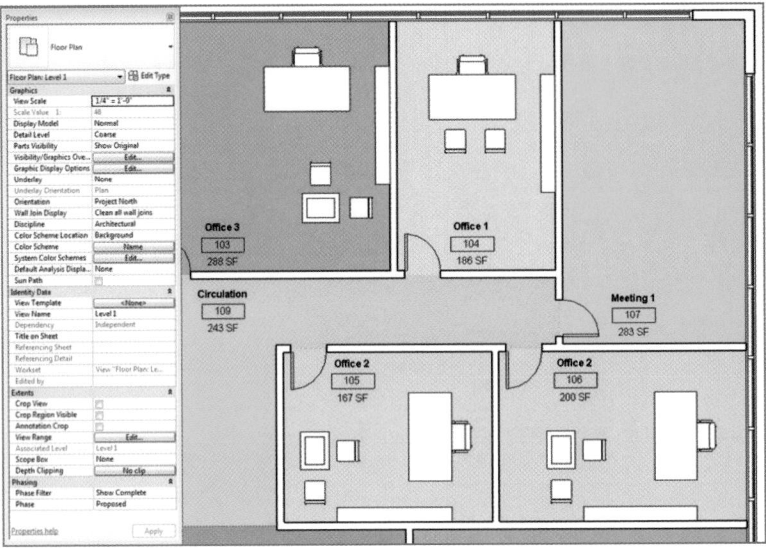

FIGURE 10.17 Copying a group

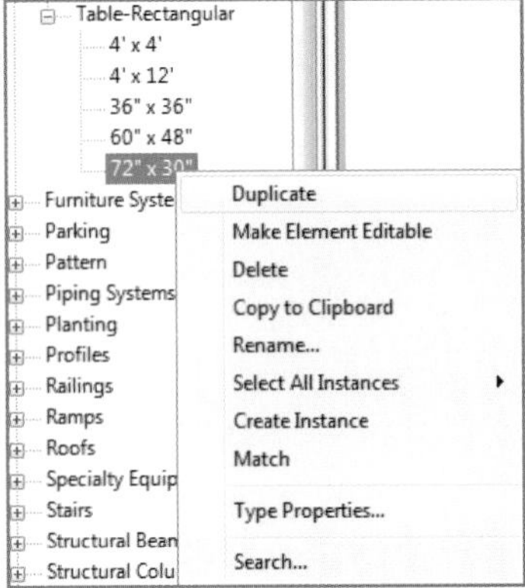

FIGURE 10.18 Duplicating an existing type

4. Modify the dimensional parameters as shown in Figure 10.19, changing the Height, Length, and Width values. Doing so creates a significantly larger table for use in your conference rooms. Click OK to finish editing the family.

5. Place a new instance of the table in the project (Figure 10.20). Again, because interior is the active workset, the table is assigned accordingly.

Type Properties

Family: Table-Rectangular — Load...

Type: 144" x 48" — Duplicate...

Rename...

Type Parameters

Parameter	Value
Materials and Finishes	
Base Material	Wood - Birch
Top Material	Wood - Birch
Dimensions	
Height	2' 6"
Length	12' 0"
Width	4' 0"
Identity Data	
Assembly Code	E2020200
Keynote	
Model	
Manufacturer	
Type Comments	
URL	
Description	
Assembly Description	Furniture & Accessories
Type Mark	
Cost	
Workset	Family : Furniture : Table-Rectang

<< Preview | OK | Cancel | Apply

FIGURE 10.19 Modifying the type parameters

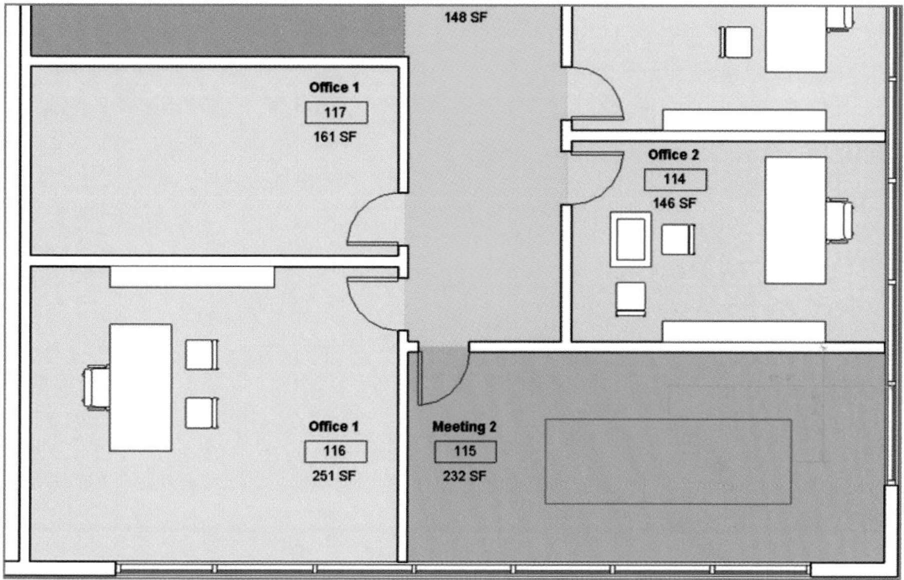

FIGURE 10.20 Adding the table to the project

6. Place chairs around the table, as shown in Figure 10.21.

   This grouping of furniture will be a useful addition to other meeting spaces in the project. But rather than copy them as separate elements, it will be more helpful to create a group and then copy this group in the project.

7. Select all the elements in the furniture group, and then select the Group tool. Name the model group **Large Table and Chairs.** Click OK.

   Note that the group is also assigned to the active workset (Figure 10.22).

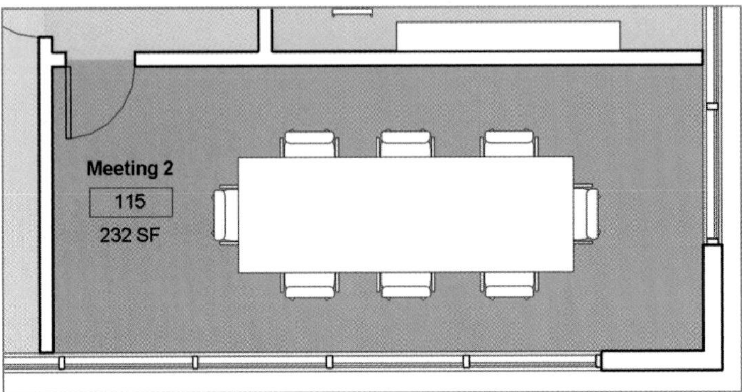

FIGURE 10.21 Adding chairs to the table

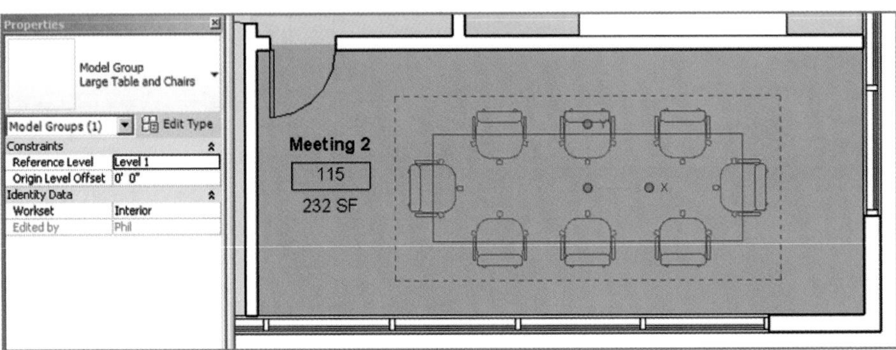

FIGURE 10.22 Workset assignment for the new group

Opening and Closing Worksets

As you work on larger and larger projects (or even very dense small projects), worksets are a great way to help you isolate and focus on what you're trying to accomplish. And although each view has its own visibility settings, when you want to isolate (or hide) elements throughout your project, worksets offer helpful options.

Open the Worksets dialog box, and notice that at the moment all the user-created worksets are set to Opened. This is fine if you need to see everything at once. But for larger projects, or in cases where you want to limit what you're seeing across all project views, you can selectively open and close worksets. Leave the Interior Workset to Yes so that it remains Opened, but set the other worksets to No by selecting the pull-down menu for each workset (or select multiple worksets by holding the Control key and picking each workset and then select the Close button on the right). Click OK to close the dialog box.

The results are immediate (Figure 10.23). Only the interior workset is shown in all your project views (3D, perspective, plan, elevation, section, and so on).

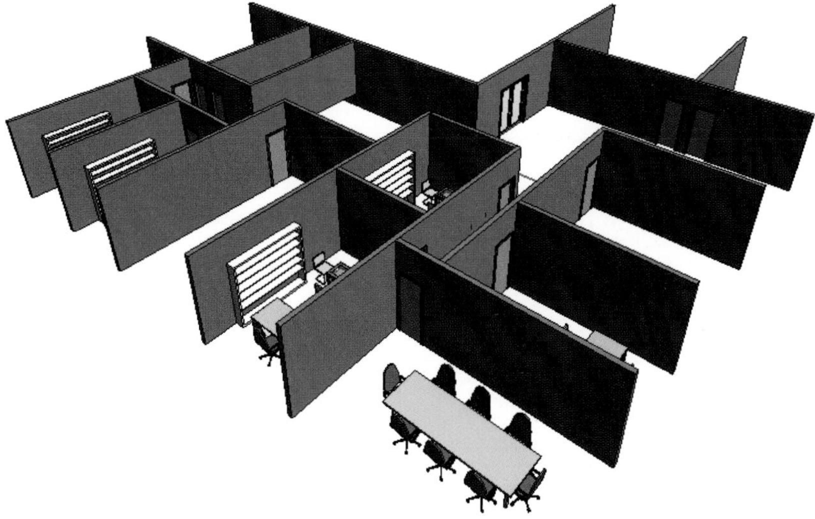

FIGURE 10.23 Interior workset isolated

Now that you have a good understanding of how to place elements on an active workset as well as open and close worksets selectively, let's explore workset display filters.

Using Workset Display Filters

Workset filters are a great way to visually understand many things about your project. To create this scenario, all three authors are accessing this file at the same time. There's a central file on the server, and we're all working from our local copies.

Furthermore, all of us have borrowed elements in the central file. In the past, it was difficult to see who had ownership of certain elements, and this issue often created workflow problems when borrowed elements were modified.

In Figure 10.24, the Worksets dialog box shows that no worksets are editable but that other users have borrowed elements.

Worksets

Active workset:

Shared Levels and Grids (Not E | Gray Inactive Workset Graphics

Name	Editable	Owner	Borrowers	Opened	Visible in all views
Core	No		Phil	Yes	☑
Exterior	No			Yes	☑
Interior	No		Phil	Yes	☑
Shared Levels and Grids	No			Yes	☑
Workset1	No			Yes	☑

New | Delete | Rename

FIGURE 10.24 Borrowed elements in the Worksets dialog box

Now let's look at the worksharing display options settings available for worksharing display in a project: Checkout Status, Owners, Model Updates, and Worksets. These settings are based on the particular parameters in your project (number of worksets, active users, and so forth). To activate any of these settings, click the icon in the lower portion of the Revit Architecture project window, and choose one of the menu items from the list (Figure 10.25).

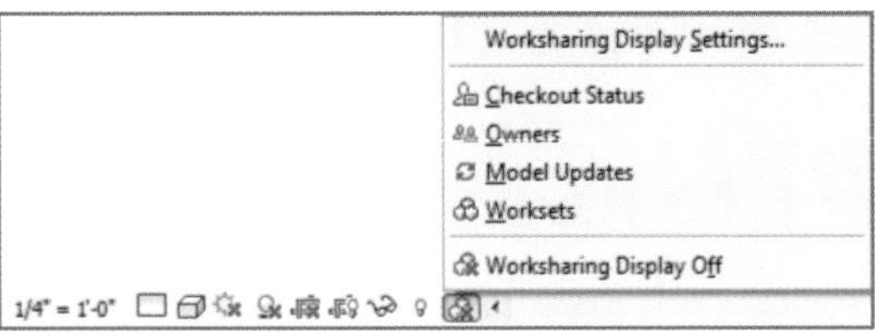

FIGURE 10.25 Worksharing Display Settings options

Selecting the Workshare Display Settings option from the menu toggles your visibility settings and applies an orange border to the view you're in, alerting you that you've engaged the settings. To turn them back off, choose the Worksharing Display Off option from the menu.

Let's make some of these options active one at a time and view the results. Start with the Checkout Status tab. Ownership status helps you distinguish between elements that are owned by you, others, or no one.

Individual owners will help you visualize exactly which elements belong to which users (Figure 10.27).

The Worksets tab helps you visualize elements based on the workset to which they're associated (Figure 10.28).

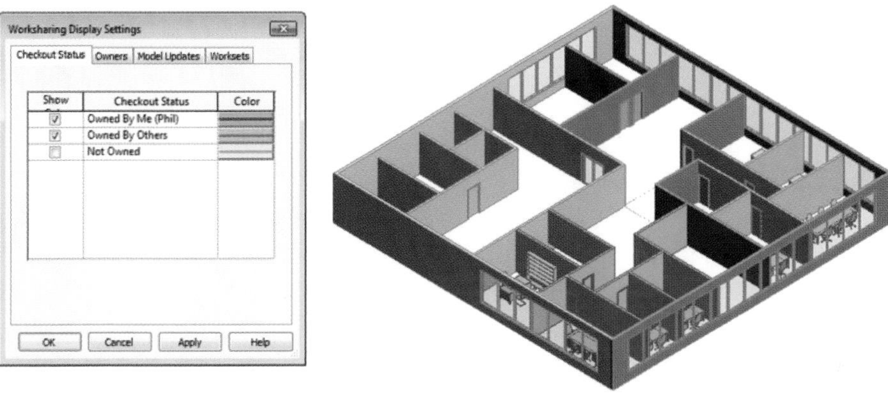

FIGURE 10.26 Checkout Status visibility

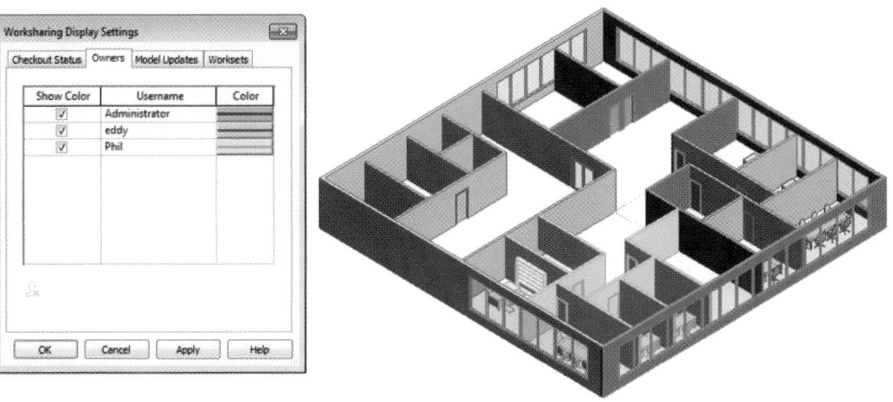

FIGURE 10.27 Owners

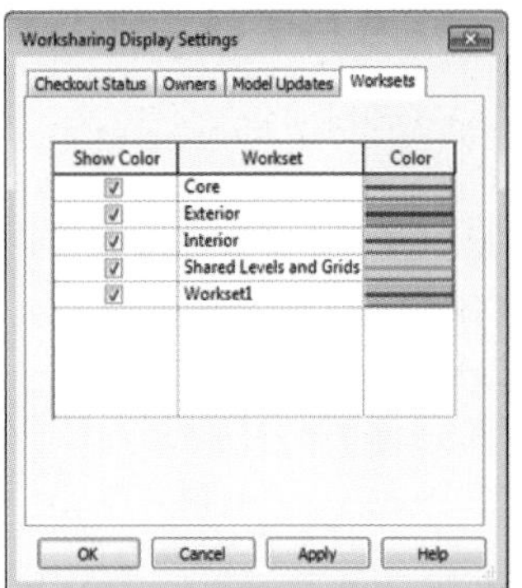

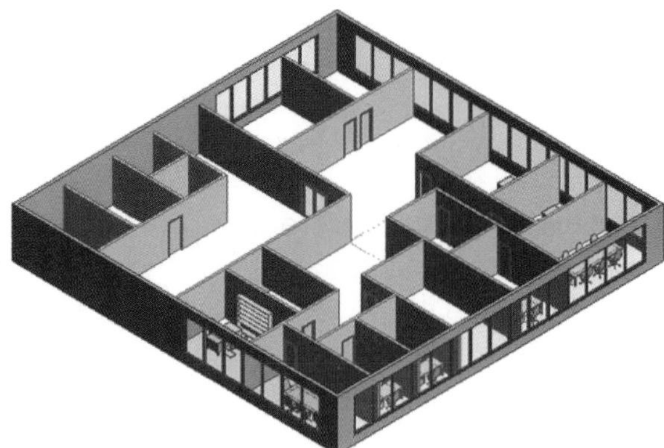

FIGURE 10.28 Worksets

Using Worksharing to Work with Consultants

One of the great benefits of worksharing is sharing your work with others. So far, we've discussed how to do this within your team, but what happens when you want to share with a larger team—like structural or mechanical, electrical, and plumbing (MEP) consultants?

Revit Architecture allows you to link in other Revit Architecture files that we covered earlier in this book. Once those files are loaded into your model, a key tool gives you additional leverage over the information you just linked so you can work more seamlessly with your expanded team. This is called the Copy/Monitor tool.

Certification Objective

Copy/Monitor allows you to create local copies of linked elements for better graphic control of the elements, while maintaining an intelligent bond to the linked elements.

In the project file saved from the previous exercise, go to the Collaborate tab ➢ Copy/Monitor ➢ Select Link. Pick the linked architectural model, and the ribbon will change to Copy/Monitor mode. Click the Options icon to open the dialog box shown in Figure 10.29. Note that the options in the Copy/Monitor tool in Revit Architecture are slightly different from those in the Autodesk® Revit® Structure and Autodesk® Revit® MEP products. For the purpose of this book, we will focus only on the options available in Revit Architecture.

The Copy/Monitor Options dialog box in Revit Architecture is divided into five tabs representing the elements available to be copied and/or monitored. Each element tab has a Categories And Types To Copy list. As shown in Figure 10.30, the Floors tab lists the available floor types in the linked model in the left column and host model floor types in the right column. Notice that for any of the linked types, you can specify the option Don't Copy This Type. This feature can be used for quality control if your project's BIM execution plan states that certain elements are not to be copied. For example, if walls are not to be copied, switch to the Walls tab and set all linked wall types to Don't Copy This Type.

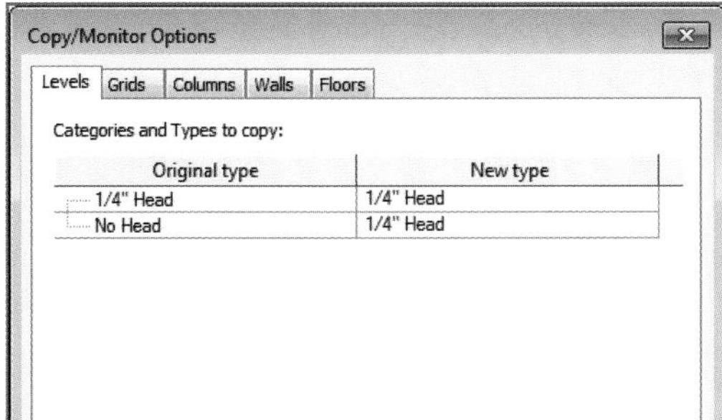

FIGURE 10.29 Element tabs available for Copy/Monitor in Revit Architecture

Levels | Grids | Columns | Walls | Floors

Categories and Types to copy:

Original type	New type
6" Foundation Slab	Don't copy this Type
Generic - 12"	Generic - 12"
Generic - 12" - Filled	Generic - 12"
LW Concrete on Metal Deck	LW Concrete on Metal Deck
Steel Bar Joist 14" - VCT on Concrete	Steel Bar Joist 14" - VCT on Concrete
Wood Joist 10" - Ceramic Tile	Wood Joist 10" - Ceramic Tile
Wood Joist 10" - Wood Finish	Wood Joist 10" - Wood Finish
Wood Truss Joist 12" - Carpet Finish	Wood Truss Joist 12" - Carpet Finish

FIGURE 10.30 Some of the elements you can choose to monitor in the Copy/Monitor Options dialog box

At the bottom of the Copy/Monitor Options dialog box, each element tab has a section called Additional Copy Parameters (Figure 10.31). Note that the additional parameters are different for each element category. For example, when levels are copied and monitored, you can apply an offset and a naming prefix to accommodate the difference between the finish-floor level in a linked architectural model and the top-of-steel level in the host structural model.

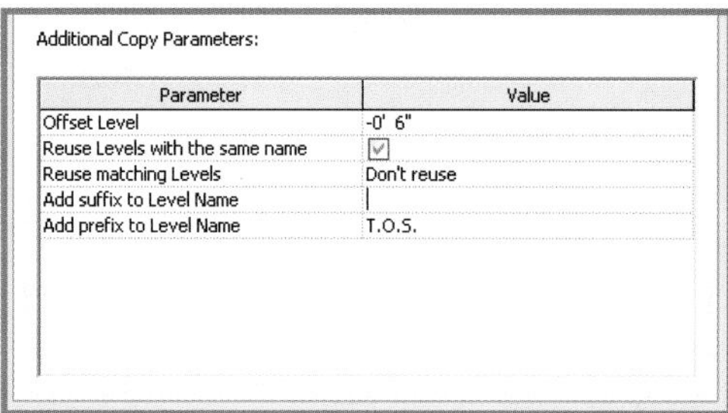

FIGURE 10.31 Additional copy parameters can be applied to each element category.

Let's take a closer look at each of the element category options available for the Copy/Monitor tool:

Levels In most cases, the difference between the location of a structural level and an architectural level may lead to the presumption that you would not want to copy levels between files; however, this is a good case where you can apply additional copy parameters to build in an offset distance. Keep in mind that the offset will apply to all Copy/Monitor selections. Thus, if a structural level needs to be offset by a different value, create the level in the host model and use the Monitor command to create the intelligent bond to the linked model's level. The difference will be maintained through any modifications in the linked model.

Grids Copying in the grids allows you to coordinate important datum between projects. You can use the Options button on the Tool tab to convert the grid bubbles used by the architect into those used by the structural engineer. It is also possible to add a prefix to the grid names from the Grids tab of the Copy/Monitor Options dialog. For instance, you could add the value "S-" in the prefix field, and grid "A" from the architectural model would come into the structural model as "S-A."

Columns The structural engineer can choose to replace any column—architectural or structural—in the architectural model with an appropriate structural column; however, this implies that the architect will maintain an understanding of where differentiating column types would exist. Realistically, the structural elements should exist only in the structural engineer's model and then link into the architectural model. The architect may then choose to either copy/monitor the linked structural columns with architectural columns (which act as finish wrappers) or place architectural columns along the monitored grid lines. In the latter option, architectural columns will move along with changes in grid-line locations but will not update if structural columns are removed in the linked model.

Walls and Floors Because they're so similar, let's consider the Walls and Floors tabs together. Similar to columns, structural walls that are important to the coordination process may be better managed in the structural model and linked into the architectural model. If you decide to use a Copy/Monitor relationship for these types of elements, it is best to create uniquely named wall types for structural coordination. Name such wall types in a manner that makes them display at the top of the list in the Copy/Monitor Options dialog box. You can do so by adding a hyphen (-) or underscore (_) at the beginning of the wall-type name.

Finally, make sure you select the Copy Windows/Doors/Openings check box for walls or Copy Openings/Inserts for floors from the Additional Copy Parameters found in the Walls tab and Floor tab so you also get the appropriate openings for those components in the monitored elements.

Use the Copy/Monitor tools in Monitor mode to establish the relationships of the grids between host and linked models. Doing so will ensure that changes to grids in either model will be coordinated.

Downloading the Completed File

If you want to download this completed file, go to the book's web page at `www.sybex.com/go/revit2013essentials` and download the file `c10_Worksharing_Central.rvt`. Keep in mind that although this is a central file, the copying will automatically create a local copy. To resolve this, open Revit Architecture and browse to the downloaded file. Select the file, and then choose the Detach From Central option from the Worksharing frame at the bottom of the Open dialog. Selecting this option will create a central file rather than an orphaned local copy.

Using Guidelines for Worksharing

Now that you have a general understanding of how worksharing and worksets operate, let's take a moment to consider a few best practices:

Think of worksets as containers. Worksets aren't layers as in CAD. Think of them as containers for majors systems in your building (interior, exterior, roof, core, and so on). You need to manage or be mindful only of stuff that belongs to user-created worksets:

- Datum (levels and grids)
- Geometry (building elements that show up in multiple views)
- Rooms (the spaces that can be tagged)

Be mindful of the active workset. As you're creating Datum, Geometry, or Rooms, be mindful of the active workset. And keep in mind that Revit Architecture manages the worksets for everything else (views, families, and project standards).

Borrow elements on the fly. Don't enable entire worksets by making the entire workset editable. Instead, just borrow elements on the fly. This approach lets you avoid many conflicts that occur when one person needs to modify something you own (but don't really need) in the model. With the interconnected nature of buildings, you don't even need to deliberately make an element editable. The simple act of modifying something that exists (or placing a new element) will borrow it for you.

Associate linked files to their own workset. Associate any linked files to their own workset. Then you can open and close the worksets associated to those links. This strategy is much more predictable than loading and unloading links (which will have an effect on everyone working on the project). Opening or closing a workset affects only your project.

Stay out of the central file. Stay out of the central file—don't move it, and don't rename it (unless you know what you're doing). Opening the central file restricts access by the files that are trying to connect to it. And if you break something in the central file, you'll break the connections that others have from their local copy, which means they may end up losing their work, which means your team will not like you.

Open and close worksets selectively. Selectively opening and closing worksets is a lot faster than opting to modify multiple view-visibility settings or use hide/isolate on a view-by-view basis. If you're supposed to be working only on the core and internal areas of a multistory building, opening only the worksets associated to those areas will save a lot of computing power.

The Essentials and Beyond

Worksets are straightforward once you get down the basics. Larger projects will require more granular workset assignments, but the principles are the same.

Additional Exercises

- Use the previous exercise with a friend or co-worker to access the same project at the same time.
- Link a Revit Architecture project into a file that has worksharing enabled. Assign the linked file to a workset, and then practice opening and closing the workset. What happens to the linked file?
- Create a workset named Entourage, and make it not visible by default. Use this workset for elements that are useful for visualization but not documentation.
- Practice locking the datum (levels and grids) by making the workset editable to you and not relinquishing it. Others will be able to graphically adjust the endpoints, but they won't be able to move or delete the datum.

CHAPTER 11

Details and Annotations

So far, you have used the Autodesk® Revit® Architecture software to create walls, doors, roofs, and floors; to define space; and to bring your architectural ideas into three-dimensional form. In each of these cases, the geometry is typically modeled based on a design intent, meaning that your goal hasn't been to model everything but rather enough to demonstrate what the building will look like. To this end, it becomes necessary to embellish parts of the model or specific views with detailed information to help clarify what you've drawn. This embellishment takes the shape of 2D detail elements in Revit Architecture that you will use to augment views and add extra information.

In this chapter, you learn the following skills:

- **Creating details**
- **Annotating your details**
- **Using legends**

Creating Details

Even when you're creating details, Revit Architecture provides a variety of parametric tools that allow you to take advantage of working in building information modeling (BIM). You can use these tools to create strictly 2D geometry or to augment details created from 3D plans, sections, or callouts. To become truly efficient at using Revit Architecture to create the drawings necessary to both design and document your project, you must become acquainted with these tools.

These view-based tools are located on the Detail panel of the Annotate tab (Figure 11.1). This small but very potent toolbox is what you will need to familiarize yourself with in order to create a majority of the 2D linework and components that will become the details in your project. To better understand how these tools are used, let's quickly step through some of them.

You're going to use the Detail Line, Region, Component, and Detail Group tools, because they will be your most widely used toolkit for creating 2D details in Revit Architecture.

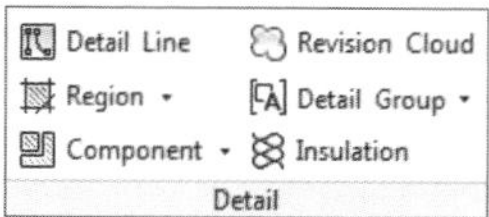

FIGURE 11.1 The Detail panel of the Annotate tab

Detail Line

The Detail Line tool is the first tool located on the Detail panel of the Annotate tab. This tool is the closest thing you'll find to traditional drafting in Revit software. It lets you create view-specific linework using different lineweights, draw different line shapes, and use many of the same manipulation commands you would find in a CAD program, such as offset, copy, move, and so on.

Detail lines are view specific—they appear only in the view in which they're drawn. They also have an arrangement to their placement, meaning you can layer them under or on top of each other or other objects. This feature is especially important when you begin using regions, detail lines, and model content to create details.

Using the Detail Line tool is fairly easy. Selecting the tool changes your ribbon tab to look like Figure 11.2. This new tab has several panels that allow you to add and manipulate linework.

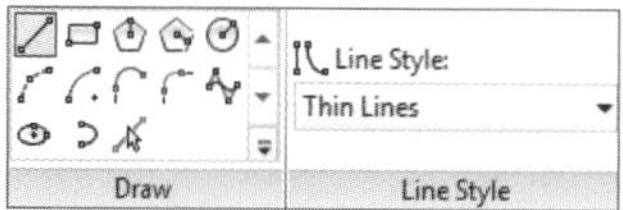

FIGURE 11.2 The Detail Line toolset

This tab primarily contains three panels: Modify, Draw, and Line Style. You've seen the Modify panel before. It contains the host of tools you've used so far for walls, doors, and other elements. Here you can copy, offset, move, and perform other tasks. The Draw panel lets you create new content and define shapes, and the Line Style drop-down allows you to choose the line style you'd like to use.

Region

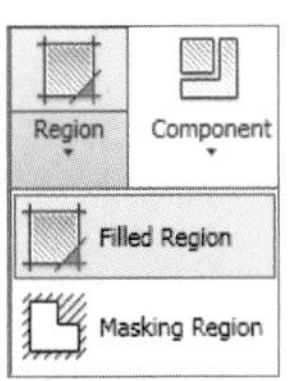

The next tool on the Detail panel of the Annotate tab is the Region tool. *Regions* are areas of any shape or size that you can fill with a pattern. This pattern (much like a hatch in AutoCAD) dynamically resizes with the region boundary. Regions layer just like detail lines do and can be placed on top of, or behind, linework and model objects. Regions also have opacity and can be completely opaque (covering what they are placed on) or transparent (letting the elements show through).

Certification Objective

There are two types of regions: filled regions and masking regions. *Filled regions* allow you to choose from a variety of hatch patterns to fill the region. They are commonly used in details to show things like rigid insulation, concrete, plywood, and other material types. *Masking regions*, on the other hand, come in only one flavor. They are white boxes with or without discernable border lines. Masking regions are typically used to hide or *mask* from a view certain content that you don't want shown or printed.

Component

The Component drop-down menu lets you insert a wide array of component types into your model. These are 2D detail components, or collections of detail components in the case of a repeating detail. Detail components are schedulable, taggable, keynotable 2D families that allow an additional level of standardization in your model. Some examples of when you'd use detail components are blocking in section, steel shapes, and brick coursing in section—just about any replicated 2D element that comes in a standardized shape.

Detail components are 2D families that can be made into parametric content. In other words, a full range of shapes can be available in a single detail component. Because they are families, they can also be stored in your office library and shared easily across projects.

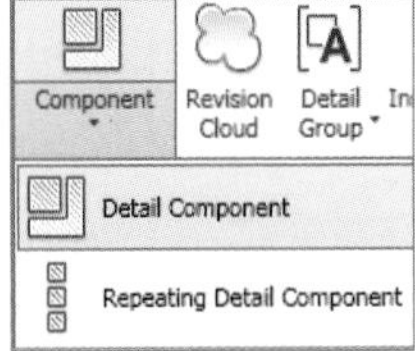

To add a detail component to your drawing, select Detail Component from the Component drop-down list located on the Annotate tab, and use the Type Selector to choose from detail components that are already inserted into the model. If you don't see a detail component you want to insert in the Type Selector, click the Load Families button on the Modify | Place Detail Component tab and insert one from the default library or your office library.

Creating a Detail

Making a detail component is much like creating a 2D family. Let's step through making a simple 2D detail component.

From the book's web page (`www.sybex.com/go/revit2013essentials`), download the `c11-Detail-Start.rvt` file and open the view `Exterior Detl, Typ`, which you'll find in the Sections (Building Section) node of the Project Browser. In the next few steps, you'll create some detail components and regions to get started with a typical window detail:

1. Use the Callout tool on the View tab to create a new detail of the second-floor window sill: create a new callout, and name it **Exterior Window Sill, Typ**. The starting view looks like Figure 11.3.

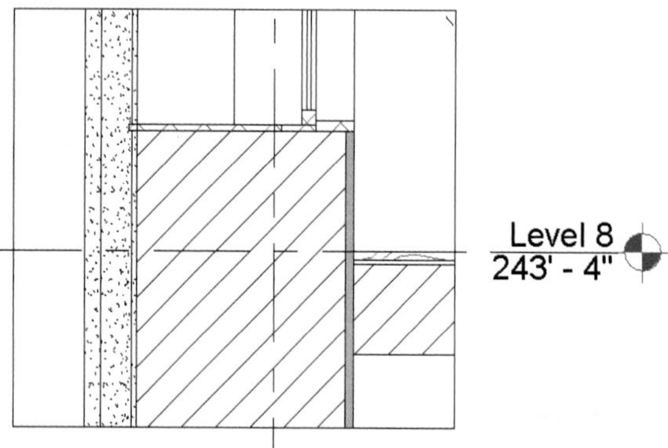

FIGURE 11.3 The window sill detail before embellishment

Certification Objective

Now, let's make the detail. You have some detail elements that can't exist in real-life construction. For example, you'd never run the sheetrock back behind the floor slab, and there's no room for flashing or blocking below the window. You need to modify this view to rectify these conditions. Let's start with the floor slab and fix the sheetrock. To do this, you'll cover a portion of this area with a filled region.

2. Click the Filled Region button on the Annotate tab. Choose Invisible from the Line Style drop-down in the Modify tab, and create a box bounding the floor slab (Figure 11.4).

   Two of the bound lines are on cut planes: the top and bottom edges of the box. Select these edges, and use the Line Style drop-down to change the lineweight to Medium.

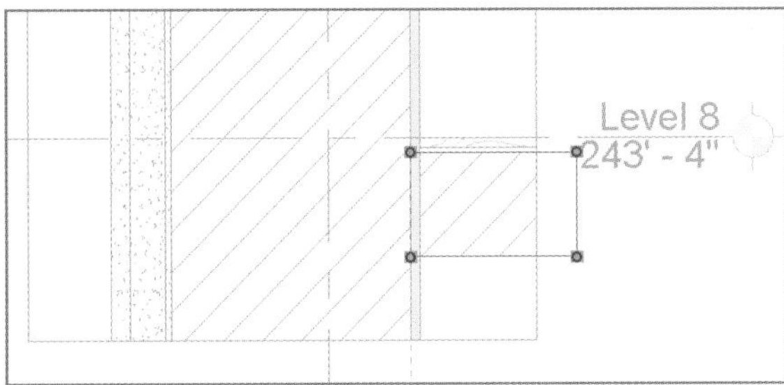

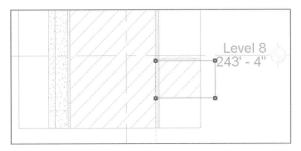

FIGURE 11.4 **Modifying the boundary of the filled region**

3. Click the Edit Type button in the Properties palette to open the Type Properties dialog box. Because there is no defined region type that is identical to existing materials, you need to make one. Click Duplicate, name the new region type **00 Existing**, and click OK.

4. Modify the settings in the Properties palette:

   Fill Pattern: Set this field to Drafting, and choose ANSI31.

   Background: Opaque

   Line Weight: 1

   Color: Black

   Click OK when you're done.

5. Click the green check mark to complete the sketch. Your finished filled region appears highlighted and slightly transparent. Click off the region to see the finished product. When you do this, notice that the invisible line on the left doesn't cover the cut of the wall, and a thinner line remains. To cover the remainder of the existing wall, highlight the filled region again and use the Nudge tool (the arrow keys on the keyboard) to move the region over slightly. The finished region looks like Figure 11.5.

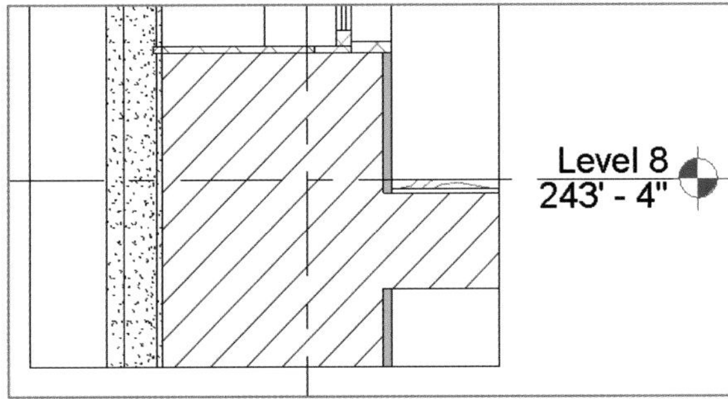

FIGURE 11.5 **Adding the filled region**

As part of the window-sill condition, say you know you have a 1″ (25 mm) gap between the bottom of the window sill and the top of the existing masonry opening. This gap isn't reflected in the window detail currently because the window family was created to cut a square opening just big enough for the window. For this detail, you need to create a masking region under the window sill so you can add some other components, such as blocking.

6. Choose the Masking Region tool from the Region flyout on the Annotate tab.
7. With Line Style set to Thin Lines, create a box 1″ (25 mm) deep under the window sill (Figure 11.6).

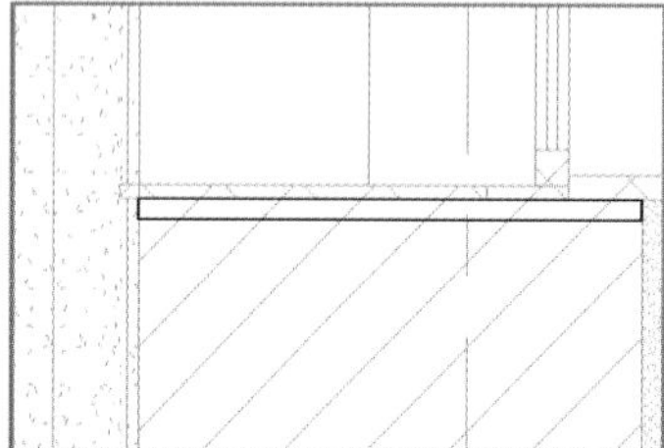

FIGURE 11.6 Adding a masking region

8. Click the green check to complete the sketch. The finished sill looks like Figure 11.7.

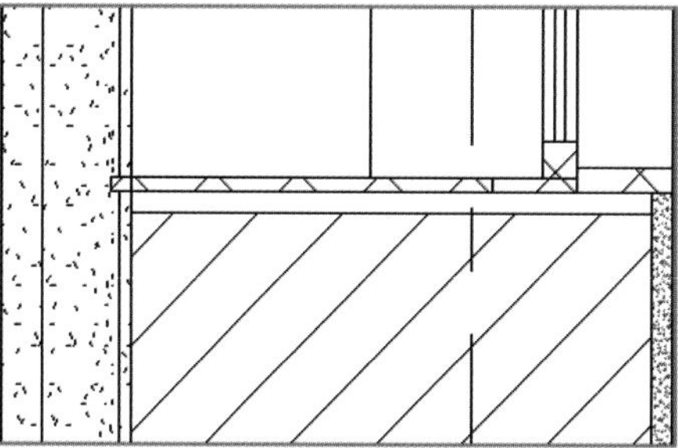

FIGURE 11.7 The completed sketch

The next step is to add some detail components for blocking and trim. Choose Application ➢ File ➢ New ➢ Family, and choose `Detail Item.rft`. When you're creating detail components, as with any other family, you'll start with two reference planes crossing in the center of the family. This crossing point is the default insertion point of the family.

The first family, blocking, is straightforward. You'll use Masking Region instead of the Lines tool so you have a clean, white box that you can use to layer over other elements you might not want to see:

1. Select the Masking Region tool on the Create tab, and draw a box with the lower-left corner at the origin. The box should be 1″ (25 mm) high and 3″ (75 mm) wide. Click the green check to complete the region.
2. On the Create tab, click the Line tool, and draw a line across the box to denote blocking. The family should look like Figure 11.8.

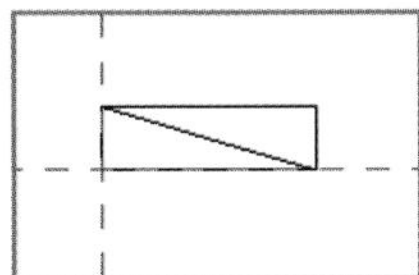

FIGURE 11.8
Creating a blocking detail component

3. Choose Application ➢ Save As ➢ Family, and name the family **06 Blocking**. Place it in a folder with the model.
4. Click the Load Into Project button at the far right on the ribbon to add the family to the model.
5. On the Annotate tab, click the Detail Component button. The component you insert will become the default component; you can see the name 06 Blocking in the Type Selector. Insert a piece of blocking at the left, right, and center of the sill (Figure 11.9).
6. Let's make one more detail component for the baseboard. Create a new detail item using steps 1–5; for this item, use the dimensions 1″ (25 mm) wide by 6″ (150 mm) high, and name the new family **06 Baseboard**. Save the baseboard, click Load Into Project, and place the baseboard at the corner of the gypsum board and finished floor. The detail looks like Figure 11.10.

   You create these elements as families and not just as filled regions so that later in the detailing process you can annotate them using the Keynote tool. Families offer a lot more functionality and versatility down the line for faster documentation.

   You can't complete all the detailing using components. Sometimes, it is easier and more effective to simply use linework to create the necessary features in a detail. For these purposes, you want to create some flashing at the window sill.

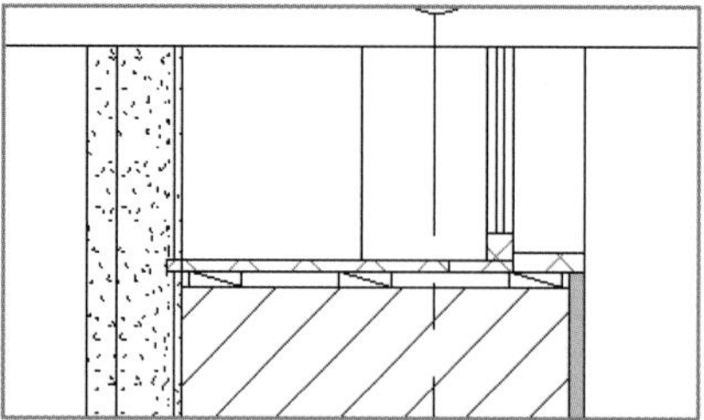

FIGURE 11.9 Inserting and placing the blocking

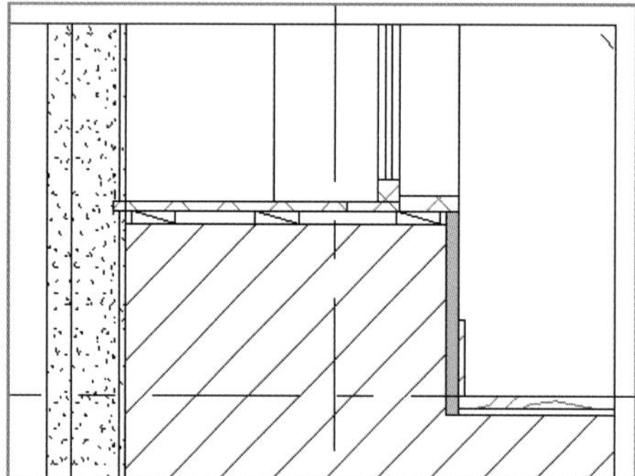

FIGURE 11.10 The sill detail with base

7. Choose the Detail Line tool, and select Medium Lines from the Line Style drop-down menu.
8. Using the Detail Line tool, draw in some flashing for the window sill (Figure 11.11).

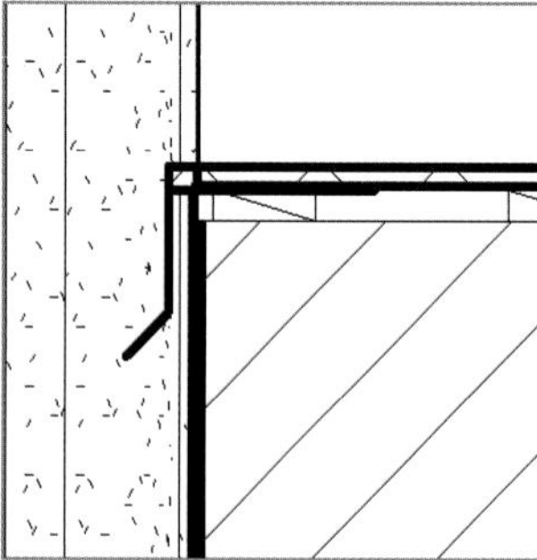

FIGURE 11.11 Adding flashing using detail lines

Arranging Elements in the View

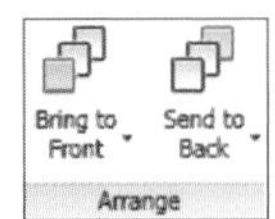

So far, you have created all the content in order and have not had to change the arrangement of any of the elements. However, knowing how to change arrangement is an important part of detailing so you don't have to draw everything in exact sequence. Arrangement allows you to change the position of an element, such as a line or a detail component, relative to another element. Much like layers in Photoshop or arrangement in PowerPoint, Revit Architecture allows you to place some elements visually in front of or behind others. Once an element or group of elements is selected and the Modify menu appears, on the far right you'll see the Arrange panel.

From here, you can choose among four options of arrangement: Bring To Front, Bring Forward, Send To Back, and Send Backward. Bring Forward and Send Backward are available selections using the drop-down arrows next to Bring to Front and Send to Back, respectively. Using these tools will help you get your layers in the proper order.

Repeating Detail Component

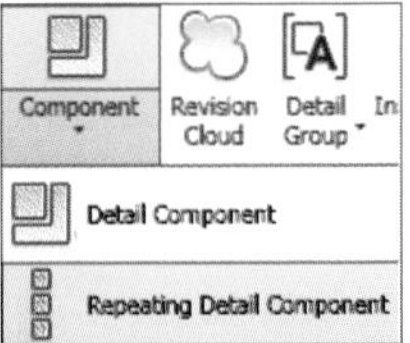

Repeating elements are common in architectural projects. Masonry, metal decking, and wall studs are some common elements that repeat at a regular interval. The Revit Architecture tool you use to create and manage these types of elements is called Repeating Detail Component, and it's located in the Component flyout on the Annotate tab.

This tool lets you place a detail component in a linear configuration in which the detail component repeats at a set interval; you draw a line that then becomes your repeating component. The default Revit Architecture repeating detail is common brick repeating in section. Creating elements like this not only lets you later tag and keynote the materials but also allows you some easy flexibility over arraying these elements manually.

Before you create a repeating detail component, let's examine one such component's properties. Select the Brick component and choose Properties from the Properties palette to open the Type Properties dialog box shown in Figure 11.12.

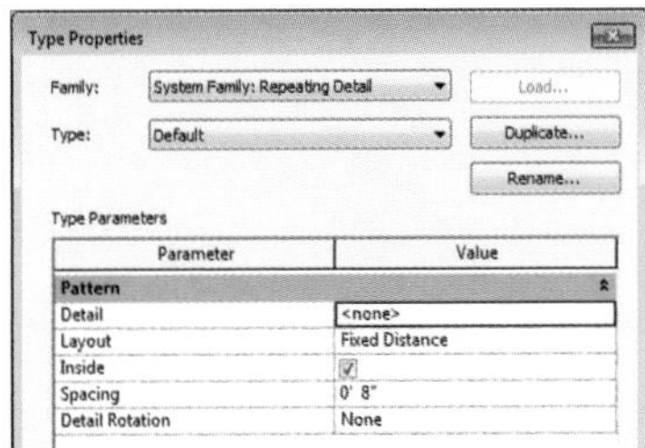

FIGURE 11.12 Type Properties dialog box for a repeating detail

Here's a brief description of what each of these settings does:

Detail This setting lets you select the detail component to be repeated.

Layout This option offers four modes:

> **Fixed Distance** This represents the path drawn between the start and end points when the repeating detail is the length at which your component repeats at a distance of the value set for Spacing.
>
> **Fixed Number** This mode sets the number of times a component repeats itself in the space between the start and end points (the length of the path).
>
> **Fill Available Space** Regardless of the value you choose for Spacing, the detail component is repeated on the path using its actual width as the Spacing value.
>
> **Maximum Spacing** The detail component is repeated using the set spacing, and the number of repeated components is set so that only complete components are drawn. Revit Architecture creates as many copies of the component as will fit on the path.

Inside This option adjusts the start point and end point of the detail components that make up the repeating detail. Deselecting this option puts only full components between start and end points rather than partial components. As an example, if you have a run of brick, selecting the Inside check box will make a partial brick at the end of the run. If you want to see only full bricks (none that would be cut), deselect the option.

Spacing This option is active only when Fixed Distance or Maximum Spacing is selected as the method of repetition. It represents the distance at which you want the repeating detail component to repeat. It doesn't have to be the actual width of the detail component.

Detail Rotation This option allows you to rotate the detail component in the repeating detail.

With these settings in mind, let's create a custom repeating detail for the sill detail you've been working on. The exterior of the building is terracotta brick and will have visible joint work every 8″ (200 mm). Follow these steps:

1. Select a new Detail Component family again. Choose Application ➢ New ➢ Family, and choose `Detail Item.rft` from the list.
2. Create a masonry joint 6″ long and 3/8″ (10 mm) high with a strike on one of the short ends (Figure 11.13) using a filled region. Save the family as 04 Grout, and load it into the project.

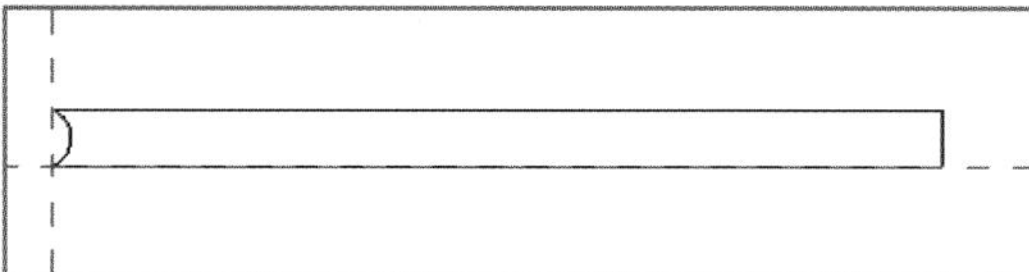

FIGURE 11.13 The grout detail component

3. Back in the project, choose the Annotate tab ➢ Detail panel ➢ Component flyout ➢ Repeating Detail Component tool. Choose Edit Type from the Properties palette, and then click the Duplicate button in the Type Properties dialog. Name the new type **04 Terracotta Grout**, and click OK.

4. You need to change the properties of this new type to reflect the detail component you just created and its spacing. Change the following fields:

   Detail: Set this field to 04 Grout, the family you just created.

   Spacing: Set this value to 8″ (200 mm).

   You can leave the rest of the fields alone. Click OK when you're finished. The Type Properties dialog box looks like Figure 11.14. Click OK when you're done.

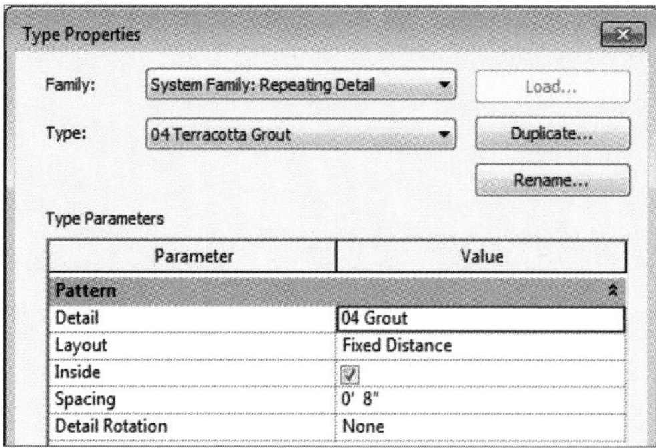

FIGURE 11.14 The repeating detail's type properties

5. Because you're still in the Repeating Detail command, you can begin drawing a line with the repeating detail. Starting at the base of the view, draw a line all the way up the left edge, placing the new joint over the terracotta exterior.

6. You can further finesse the appearance by placing one of the joints directly below the window sill. This appears placed on top of the flashing you drew earlier, so you'll want to move the flashing to the

front. Select the flashing detail line, and choose Bring To Front from the Arrange panel. The completed detail looks like Figure 11.15.

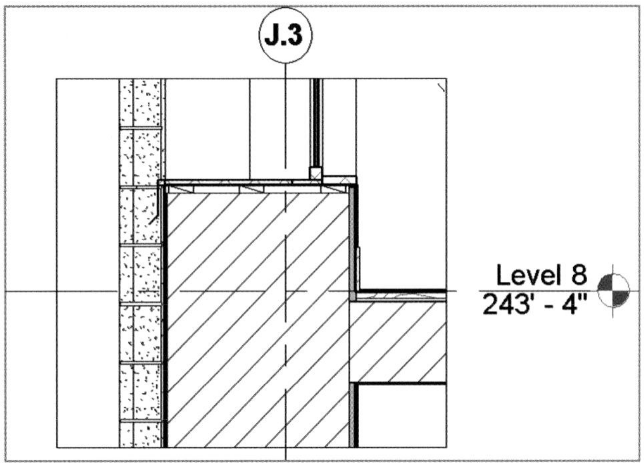

FIGURE 11.15 The finished window-sill detail

Although this detail needs annotations before you can think about placing it onto a sheet, you can begin to see how you have used the 3D geometry of the model and were able to quickly add embellishment to it in order to create a working project detail. For now, save this detail. You'll return to it later in the chapter.

Insulation

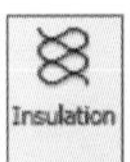

The best way to think of the Insulation tool is like a premade repeating detail. You'll find this tool on the Detail panel of the Annotate tab.

Selecting this tool allows you to draw a line of batt insulation, much like a repeating detail. You can modify the width of the inserted insulation from the Options Bar (Figure 11.16). The insulation is inserted using the centerline of the line of batt, and you can shorten, lengthen, or modify the width either before or after inserting it into your view.

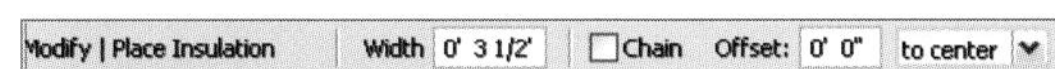

FIGURE 11.16 Modifying the Insulation width in the Options Bar

Detail Groups

Detail groups are similar to blocks in AutoCAD and are a quick alternative to creating detail component families. These are collections of 2D graphics and can contain detail lines, detail components, or any collection of 2D elements. While you will probably want to use a detail component to create something like blocking, if you plan to have the same blocking and flashing conditions in multiple locations, you can then group the flashing and blocking together and quickly replicate these pieces in other details. Like blocks in AutoCAD, manipulating one of the detail groups changes all of them consistently throughout the model.

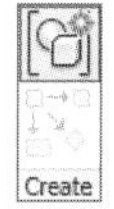

There are two ways to make a detail group. Probably the most common is to create the detail elements you'd like to group and then select all of them. When you do, the Modify context tab appears: click the Create Group button to make the group. When you're prompted for a group name, name the group something clear like **Window Head Flashing** or **Office Layout 1** rather than accepting the default name Revit Architecture wants to give it (Group 1, Group 2, and so on).

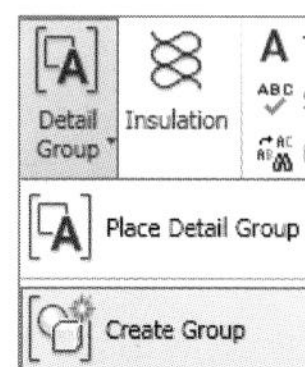

The other way to create a detail group is to go to the Annotate tab ➢ Detail Group flyout and click the Create Group button. You are prompted for the type of group (Model or Detail):

Model Model groups contain model elements (elements that are visible in more than one view). Choose Model if you want elements to be visible in more than one view or if they are 3D geometry.

Detail Detail groups contain view-specific detail elements and are visible only within the view you're in (you can copy or use them in other views). Choose Detail if you're creating a group containing detail lines or other annotations and 2D elements.

You cannot create a group that has both model elements and detail elements.

When you select the elements, you're taken into Edit Group mode. A yellow transparency is overlaid on top of the view, and elements in the view appear gray. To add elements to the group, select Edit Group and then click the Add button (Figure 11.17). You can also remove unwanted elements. When you're finished, click the green Finish check, and your group will be complete.

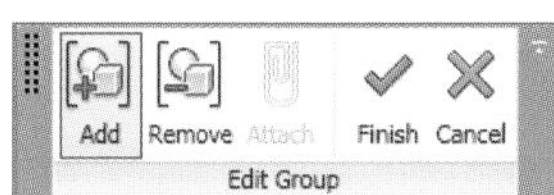

FIGURE 11.17 The Edit Group panel

You can place any group you've already made using the Annotate tab ➢ Detail panel ➢ Place Detail Group button. Groups insert like families, and you can choose the group you'd like to insert from the Type Selector on the Properties palette.

Linework

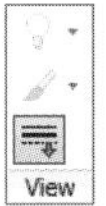

Although not part of the Annotate tab, the Linework tool is an important feature in creating good lineweights for your details. Revit Architecture does a lot to help manage your views and lineweights automatically, but it doesn't cover all the requirements all the time. Sometimes the default Revit Architecture lines are heavier or thinner than you desire for your details. This is where the Linework tool comes in handy; it allows you to modify existing lines in a view-specific context.

To use the Linework tool, go to the Modify tab ➢ View panel and click the Linework button, or use the keyboard shortcut **LW**. You will see the familiar Line Styles Type Selector panel on the right of the tab, and you can select a line style from the list. Simply choose the style you want a particular line to look like, and then select that line in the view. The lines you pick can be almost anything: cut lines of model elements, families, components, and so on. Selecting the line or boundary of an element changes the line style from whatever it was to whatever you have chosen from the Type Selector. Figure 11.18 shows a before and after of the sill detail with the linework touched up.

FIGURE 11.18 Before and after the Linework tool

You can also choose to visually remove lines using this tool. Doing so leaves the line in the view or as a part of the 3D element, but makes it effectively invisible for the sake of the view. Do this by selecting the <Invisible> line type. This is a good alternative to covering unwanted linework with a masking region.

Annotating Your Details

Notes are a critical part of communicating design and construction intent to owners and builders. No drawing set is complete without descriptions of materials and notes about the design. Now that you've created a detail, you need to add the final touches of annotations to communicate size, location, and materiality. The tools you will use for annotations are found on the same Annotate tab that you used to create details. These are the Dimension, Text, and Tag panels shown in Figure 11.19.

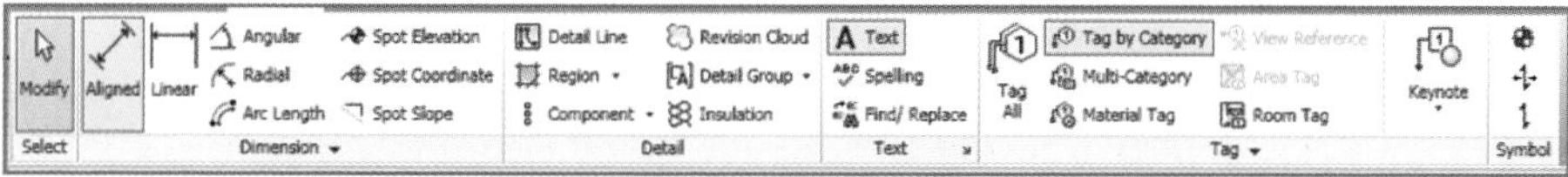

FIGURE 11.19 The Revit Architecture annotation tools

Dimensions

In your detail, you have added aspects to the window family to reflect some of the details needed for construction. Now, with much of the linework and elements in the view, you need to annotate and add dimensions. The dimension tool you will use the most often is Aligned, located on the left side of the Dimension panel and highlighted in Figure 11.19. It can also be found on the Quick Access toolbar. Let's begin by adding dimensions to the detail you just created:

1. Select either of the Aligned dimension tool, and place a dimension string from the grid line to the centerline of the wall, as shown in Figure 11.20.

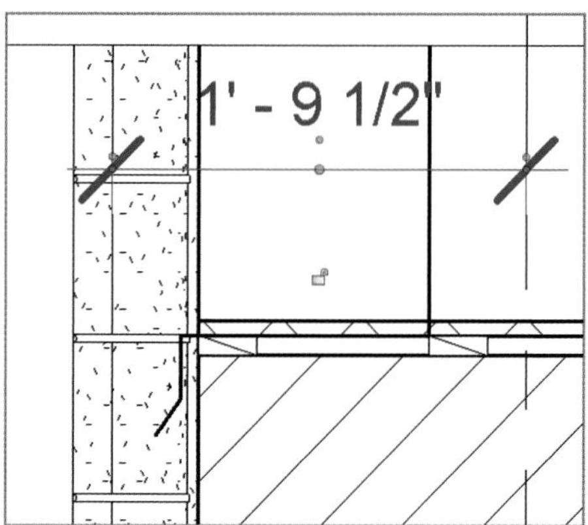

FIGURE 11.20 Adding a dimension string

2. Now that you've placed the dimension, you realize it's in the wrong location: you want the left side at the exterior wall. Dimensions are dynamic in Revit Architecture and easy to relocate. Highlight the dimension string, and you see two sets of blue dots on either side. One set controls the length of the *witness line* (the line that extends

from the actual element you dimensioned to the tick mark), and the other (on top of the tick mark) controls the witness line's location. Select this blue dot that controls the witness line location, and drag it to the exterior of the wall. The dimension automatically updates.

3. Add another dimension string from the grid line to the back of the window jamb.

4. The dimension you just added doesn't read very well because it's located over the window sill. You need the dimension located there, but you can relocate the text. To do so, grab the blue dot under the text and drag the text string to the right. Once the dimension text is outside of the dimension string, Revit Architecture adds an arc associating the text to the dimension (Figure 11.21).

5. Add another dimension that locates the gypsum board relative to the grid line (Figure 11.22). By default, the exterior face of the gypsum board won't highlight to accept the dimension. With your mouse hovering over the right edge of the gypsum board, press the Tab key, and you can place the other side of the dimension string.

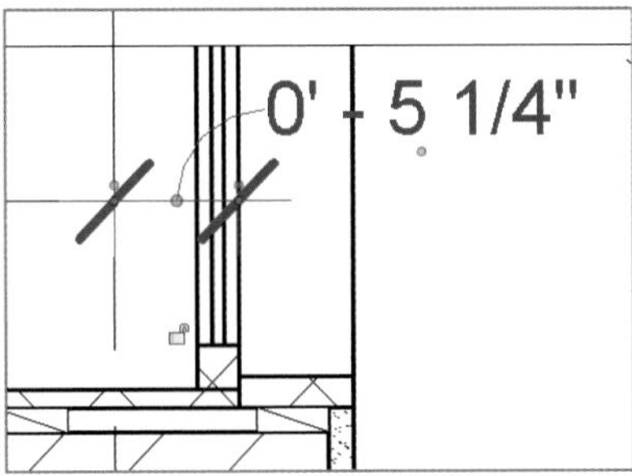

FIGURE 11.21 Modifying the text location

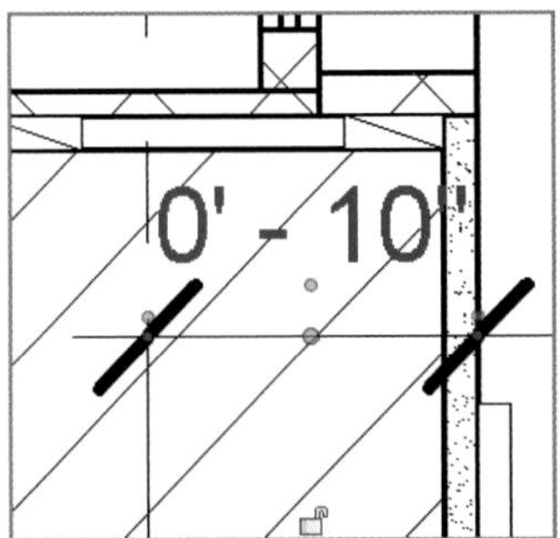

FIGURE 11.22 Dimensioning the wall location

6. In this dimension, the dimension text has a white box similar to a masking region that lies behind the text and covers some of the detail of the sill condition. You can eliminate this box so the dimension string reads clearly and doesn't cover underlying elements. To do this, highlight the dimension by left-clicking it, and select Edit Type from the Properties palette. The Type Properties dialog box for dimensions opens, as shown in Figure 11.23.

   This dialog box allows you to change all the dimension settings: text, color, length of each dimension element, and so forth.

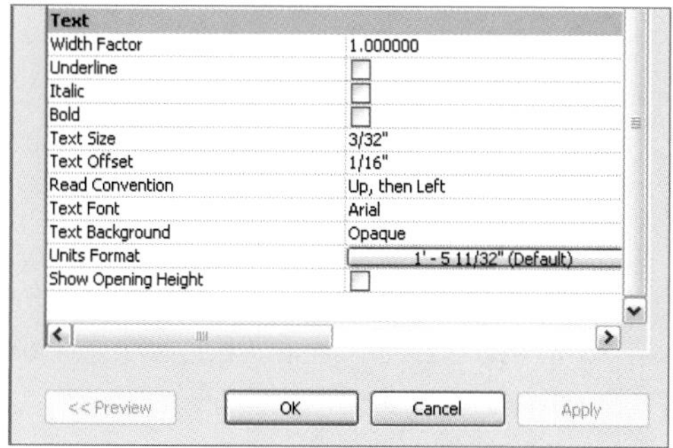

FIGURE 11.23 Dimension type properties

7. Scroll to the bottom to find the Opaque/Transparent setting. This controls that white box behind the dimension. Set it to Transparent, and click OK. The dimension now has a transparent background.

8. Let's add one final dimension string. Add a dimension locating the window sill relative to the floor, as shown in Figure 11.24.

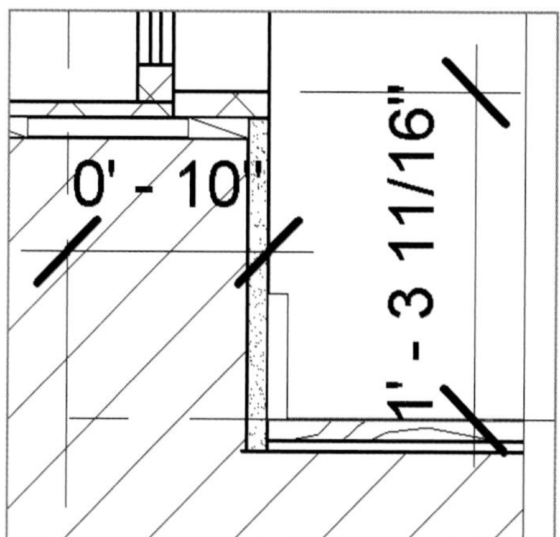

FIGURE 11.24 Dimensioning the window sill

9. This dimension is an awkward length and probably isn't something you want to include in the CD set. Remember that in Revit Architecture, dimensions report the relative location of objects—they cannot be forced with values. So to change the dimension string, you need to change the location of one of the two objects you've dimensioned. The floor probably isn't going to move, but you can reposition the window slightly.

   Select the window. The dimension string turns blue, and the numbers become very small (Figure 11.25).

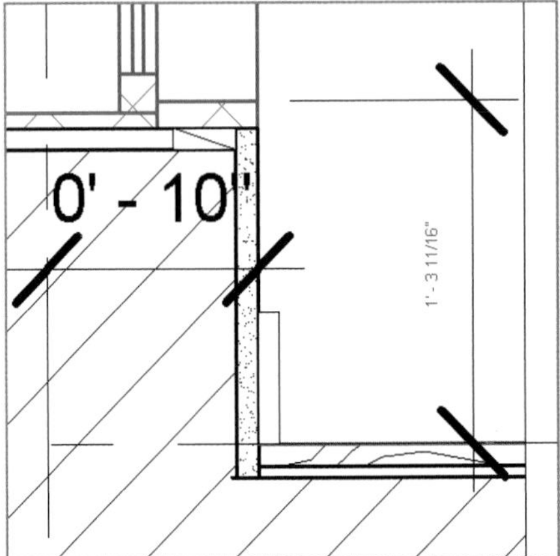

FIGURE 11.25 To change the dimension string value, change the location of the objects dimensioned by selecting the window.

10. You can now key in a more reasonable value. Select the blue text, and type **1 4** (**400 mm**) in the text box (Figure 11.26). Press Enter. The window pushes up just a bit and resets the dimension string.

With all the dimensions on the detail, it should look like Figure 11.27.

Tags

Now that you have embellished and dimensioned the detail, it's time to add some tags. In this detail, you're going to tag the window as well as some of the materials in the detail to help identify these items to the contractor. Material tags can be added through the Annotate tab ➢ Tag panel ➢ Material Tag button. Begin by tagging the window:

1. Choose the Annotation tab ➢ Tag panel ➢ Tag By Category button, and select the window.

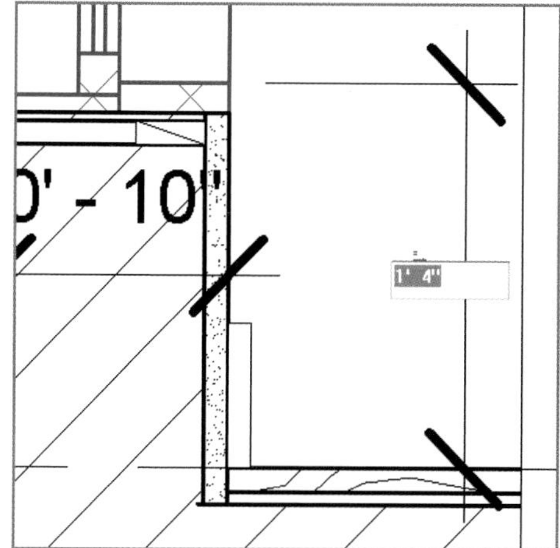

FIGURE 11.26 Keying a value into a dimension string

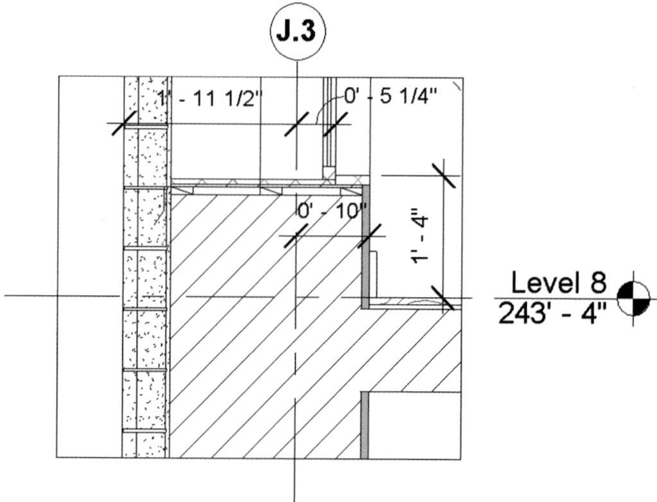

FIGURE 11.27 The dimensioned detail

Revit Architecture displays the warning shown in Figure 11.28. It tells you that Revit Architecture has added a tag but that it has fallen outside of your view. By default, Revit Architecture places tags in the center of the element being tagged. In this case, the tag resides in the middle of the window cut in section, which is above your crop box.

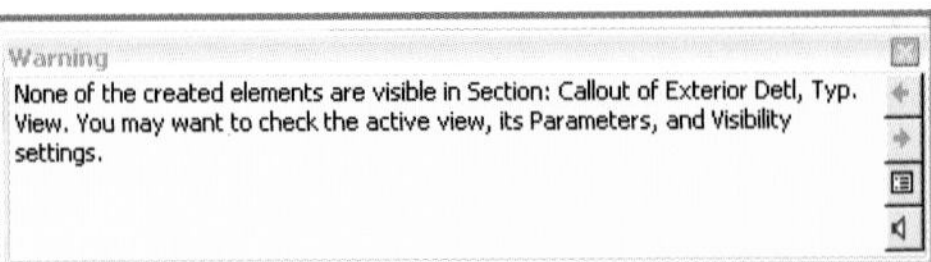

FIGURE 11.28 The tag fell outside of the crop window.

2. To remedy this, select the box that defines the crop region for the detail. Doing so highlights the crop box and also an invisible, dashed box called the *annotation crop box*. This crop window can be turned on and off through the Properties palette.

   Drag the upper limit of the annotation box higher, and you will eventually see the Window tag you placed on the window (Figure 11.29).

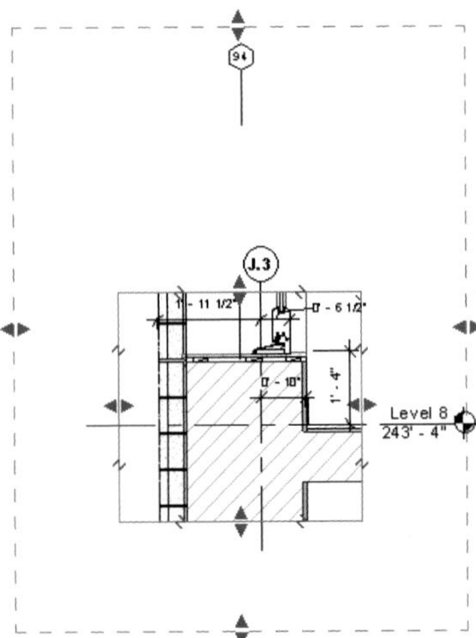

FIGURE 11.29 Extending the annotation crop window

3. The tag has a leader line associated with it. You want to move the tag but also remove the leader line. To do so, highlight the tag, and, in the Options Bar, deselect the Leader check box that is shown checked (Figure 11.30). Doing so lets you drag the tag down—leader free—and place it in the crop region.

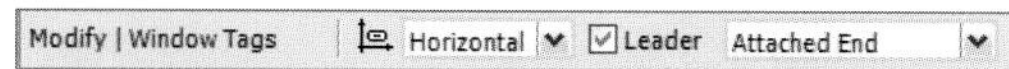

FIGURE 11.30 Removing the leader from the Window tag

4. Now let's add a Material tag. Material tags let you tag materials consistently throughout the model. This means if you tag something like Concrete once in the model, the material will remember the tag you used and show that same tag every time you tag it in any other view.

   To add the tag, choose the Material Tag button from the Tag panel. With the tag selected, mouse over the vertical panel shown in Figure 11.31. The material there has been prepopulated with 5/8″ GYPSUM BD as a tag through the material (from the Manage tab). Select the material, and place the tag.

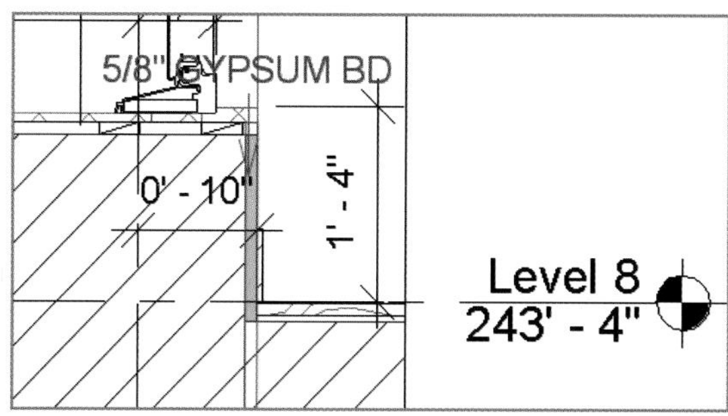

FIGURE 11.31 Using the Material tag

5. Notice that by default the tag has no arrowhead. Select the tag, and choose Edit Type from the Properties palette. Here in the tag's Type Properties dialog, you can assign an arrowhead. Choose 30 Degree Arrow for the Leader Arrowhead property, and click OK (Figure 11.32).

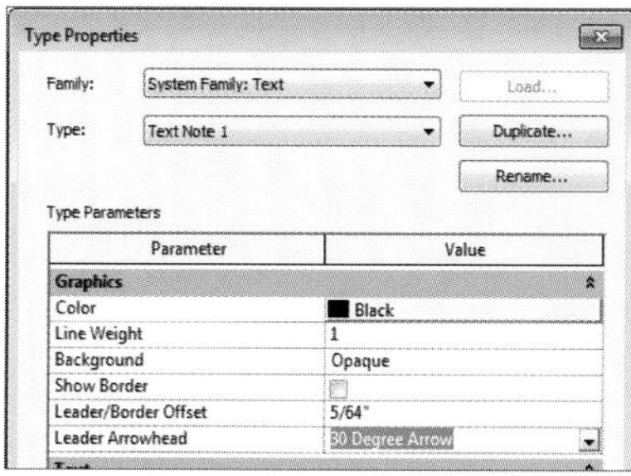

FIGURE 11.32 Adding an arrowhead to the tag

In the same way, you can populate the remainder of the materials in the detail. For materials that aren't already specified, Revit Architecture will display a question mark. Click it, and you can enter the text describing that material; all other materials of that type in the model will automatically show the text you just entered. Changes made to this material will also be broadcast throughout the model.

Text

Not all elements in Revit Architecture have materiality to them, and sometimes tags are not the best way to convey information. In these cases, you can use text. The Text tool is located on the Text palette of the Annotate tab.

When you're using text in your model, it's important to remember that text is not linked to any element or material. If you label something with text or use text to call out notes, the text doesn't dynamically update as elements change in the model.

In your example detail, the shims you placed as part of the window family do not have a way to tag a material and need to be called out using text. Here are the steps:

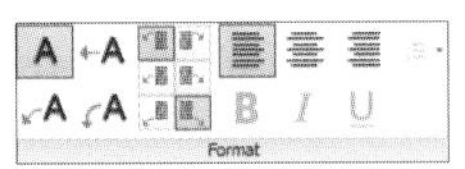

1. Choose the Text command from the Annotate tab. Doing so opens the Modify | Text tab. The tools on the Format panel control the leaders, leader location, justification, and font formats, respectively.

   For now, leave the selections at the defaults, choose a location on the screen, and click the left mouse button. Doing so begins a text box. Type **1/2″ SHIMS** (Figure 11.33).

FIGURE 11.33 Adding text to the detail

2. When you add text to the box, the Modify menu changes. You now have the option to add and remove leaders. To add a leader, click the Add Leader button at upper left in the Format panel.

   Move the text and leader into position with the other notes. In this way, you can complete the annotations on the detail (Figure 11.34) and begin the next one.

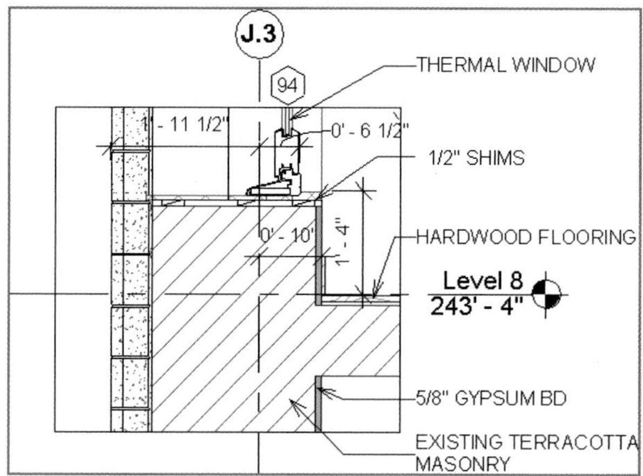

FIGURE 11.34 Finishing the detail

Using Legends

Legends are unique views in Revit Architecture because they are the only view type you can place on more than one sheet. These can be great tools for things like general notes, key plans, or any other view type that you want to be consistent across several sheets. It's important to note that anything you place inside a legend view—doors, walls, windows, and so on—will not appear or be counted in any schedules. Legend elements live outside of any quantities present in the model.

The Legend tool is located on the View tab. You can create two types of legends from this menu: a *legend*, which is a graphic display, or a *keynote legend*, which is a text-based schedule. Both legend types can be placed on multiple sheets, but for this exercise, you'll focus on the legend.

As part of the sample workflow, you may want to present some of the wall types as part of your presentation package to demonstrate the Sound Transmission Class (STC) of the walls and the overall wall assembly. Because these wall types will appear on all the sheets where you use them in the plan, you'll make them using a legend:

1. Choose the View tab ➢ Legends flyout ➢ Legend button. Creating a new legend is much like creating a new drafting view. A New Legend View dialog box opens (Figure 11.35) where you can name the legend and set the scale. Name this legend **WALL LEGEND**, and choose 1″ = 1′-0″ (1:10) for the scale. Click OK to create the legend.

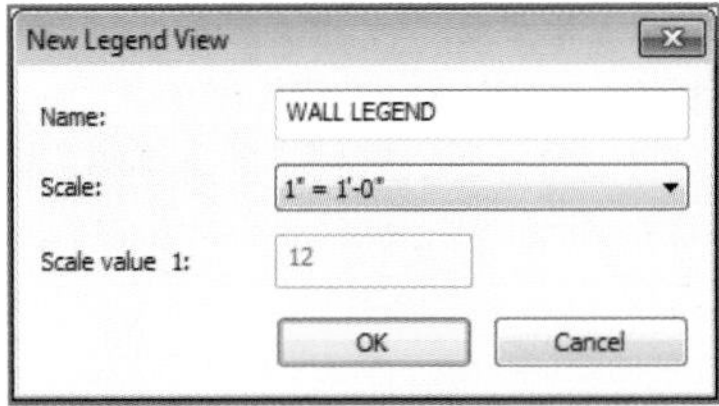

FIGURE 11.35 Creating a legend

The legend you've created looks like a blank view. At this point, it's up to you to add content. The simplest type of legend would include notes such as plan or demolition comments that would appear in each of your floor plans. You could do this by using the Text tool and adding text in this legend view; however, in this example you want to add more than just text.

2. To add wall types or any other family to the legend view, expand the Families tree in the Project Browser and navigate to the Wall family. Expand this node, and then expand the Basic Wall Node. Select the `Interior - Gyp 4 7/8` wall type, and drag it into the view.

3. The family appears in the view as a 3′ (1000 mm) long plan wall. Change the view's detail level in the view's Properties palette from Coarse to Medium or Fine so you can see the detail in the wall. Remember, you can turn off the thicker lines in the view by clicking the Linework button in the QAT. With that done, highlight the inserted wall and look at the Modify | Legend Components settings in the Options Bar (Figure 11.36).

FIGURE 11.36 Select a legend component to access its properties in the Options Bar.

This menu is consistent for any of the family types you insert. It consists of three sections:

Family This drop-down menu allows you to select different family types and operates just like the Type Selector does for other elements in the model.

View The View option lets you change the type of view from Plan to Section.

Host Length This option changes the overall length (or, in the case of sections, height) of the element selected.

4. Let's make some minor adjustments to the wall. Change View to Section, and change Host Length to 1′-6″ (500 mm).

   The wall now looks like a sectional element. By adding some simple text, you can embellish the wall type to better explain the elements you're viewing (Figure 11.37).

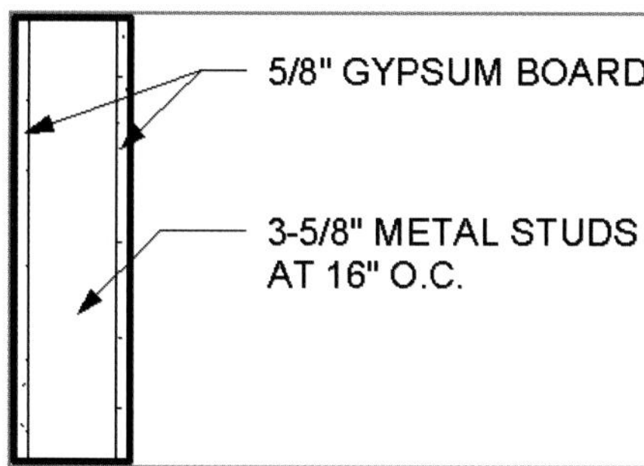

FIGURE 11.37 Add other annotations to embellish the wall-type section.

5. Continue the exercise by adding the `Exterior - Brick` wall type to the legend along with some additional text notes.

The Essentials and Beyond

The process of embellishing a model to reflect the design intent and detailing gets easier with practice. Remember that you won't have all the geometry you need in the 3D model to show the level of detail you'll need for full documentation. By embellishing the callouts and sections with additional information, you can quickly add the detailed information you need to show.

Additional Exercises

- You need to detail the window-head condition for a full set of documents. Using the section you've already created, create a detail view of the window head; and using the same tools and workflow demonstrated in this chapter, add a similar level of detail to the condition. A number of the elements—such as keynotes and some of the filled regions—can be reused from the previous detail, making this effort a bit quicker. Don't be afraid to copy and paste filled regions or other elements from one detail to another.
- In this chapter, you added a level of detail to the window family by including some CAD details. Replicate the same level of detail in the head condition. You can reuse the information in the sill to expedite the process.

CHAPTER 12

Creating Drawing Sets

While the industry continues to move toward a building information model as a contract deliverable, today we still need to produce 2D documents for most construction and permitting purposes. Using the Autodesk® Revit® Architecture software, you can create these sets with more accuracy and dependability than in the past.

In this chapter, we're going to introduce a scenario that will mimic what might happen on a real project in preliminary design. You'll be using the `c12-Residence.rvt` model from the book's web page (`www.sybex.com/go/revit2013essentials`) in the Chapter 12 folder.

Here's the story. You have recently completed some design work in advance of your upcoming pricing package for a residential design project. You will need to present the plans, elevations, and perspectives on some sheets for the package. But you want to help the contractor by providing some quantities, so you will also include schedules.

In this chapter, you will learn the following skills:

- **Creating schedules**
- **Placing views on sheets**
- **Printing documents**

Creating Schedules

Schedules are lists of elements and element properties in the model. They can be used to itemize building objects such as walls, doors, and windows; calculate quantities, areas, and volumes; and list elements such as the number of sheets, keynotes, and so on. They are yet another way to view building objects in a model. Once created, they are dynamically kept up-to-date with any changes that occur to the model itself.

Understanding Schedules

In a project workflow, creating schedules of model elements, areas, or other objects is usually one of the most laborious tasks for architects. When this process is performed manually, it can take a very long time and typically results in errors requiring much checking and rechecking of the information. In Revit Architecture, all the elements have information about their properties defined in the model. For example, doors have properties such as size, material, fire rating, and cost. All this information can be scheduled and quantified. As those doors are changed, the properties update in the schedule.

Because Revit Architecture is a bidirectional parametric modeling program, you are also able to make changes to element properties in a schedule—updating the model and all other views automatically. Continuing with the door example, you can change the material of a door in the door schedule, and the material tags and rendering view will be instantly updated.

DOOR SCHEDULE					
		DOOR PANEL			
ID	DESCRIPTION	WIDTH	HEIGHT	THK	COMMENTS
Level 1					
101	Double-Glass 2	5' - 8"	7' - 0"	0' - 2"	Exterior Door
103	Overhead-Rolling	8' - 0"	6' - 6"	0' - 2"	
104	Single-Flush	3' - 0"	6' - 8"	0' - 2"	Standard
105	Single-Flush	3' - 0"	6' - 8"	0' - 2"	Standard
109	Single-Panel 3	3' - 0"	6' - 8"	0' - 2"	Metal panel door
110	Sliding-Closet	5' - 8"	6' - 8"	0' - 2"	
111	Sliding-Closet	5' - 8"	6' - 8"	0' - 2"	
112	Single-Glass 2	3' - 0"	6' - 8"	0' - 2"	
Level 2					
201	Double-Panel 1	6' - 0"	7' - 0"	0' - 2"	
202	Single-Flush	3' - 0"	6' - 8"	0' - 2"	Standard
203	Single-Flush	3' - 0"	6' - 8"	0' - 2"	Standard
204	Single-Glass 2	3' - 0"	6' - 8"	0' - 2"	
205	Single-Glass 2	3' - 0"	6' - 8"	0' - 2"	
206	Single-Glass 2	3' - 0"	6' - 8"	0' - 2"	
207	Sliding-Closet	5' - 8"	6' - 8"	0' - 2"	
Grand total					

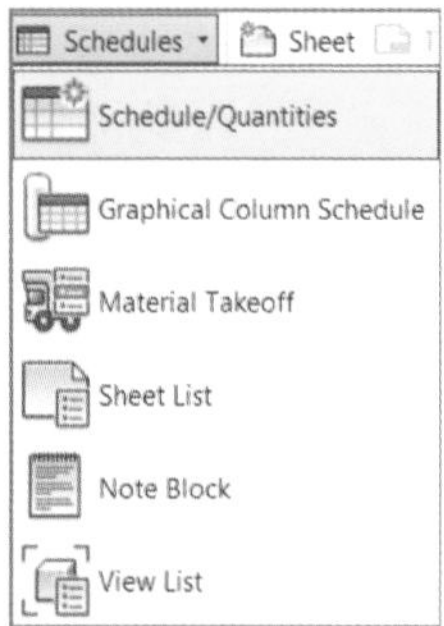

There are several types of schedules that can all be accessed from the Create panel of the View tab. Let's look at each of the six primary types of schedules:

Schedule/Quantities This is the most commonly used schedule type, allowing you to list and quantify any element category. You can use this type to make door schedules, wall schedules, window schedules, and so on. These schedule types are usually limited to scheduling properties in the same category; however, you can create a multi-category schedule or use some fields from other elements. For example, many model elements can refer to the properties of the room in which they are placed.

Graphical Column Schedule This schedule is different from the other schedule types and is commonly used by structural engineers. Structural columns are displayed according to their grid intersections, indicating top and bottom constraints as well as offsets.

Material Takeoff This type of schedule lists all the materials and subcomponents of any family category. You can use a material takeoff to measure any material that is used in a component or assembly. For example, you might want to know the volume of concrete in the model. Regardless of whether the concrete is in a wall or floor or column, you can tell the schedule to report the total amount of that material in the project. Material takeoffs report material properties across multiple categories.

Sheet List This schedule allows you to create a list of all the sheets in the project.

Note Block This tool creates a unique schedule that lists the properties of a generic annotation symbol used in a project.

View List This schedule shows a list of all the views in the Project Browser and their properties. A view list can be a valuable tool to help you manage your project's views efficiently.

Choosing a Schedule Category

Each of these schedule types has a host of categories that you can mix and match to track elements in the model. You can adjust several aspects of these schedules to build and customize your schedules to meet your needs. Let's step through these aspects and see how they can be used.

Go to the View tab ➢ Create tab ➢ Schedules flyout ➢ Schedule/Quantities. The New Schedule dialog box appears, allowing you to select a category to schedule (Figure 12.1).

If there aren't enough categories for you to choose from to create a schedule, there is a venue to add additional options. At the top of the New Schedule dialog box is a Filter List drop-down that gives you the ability to schedule elements from the mechanical, electrical, and plumbing (MEP) and structural categories. This option can be useful when those disciplines are supplying model files to you and you are linking them into your architectural model.

You also have the opportunity to create schedules that span multiple categories. The first option in the Category list in Figure 12.1 is Multi-Category. You might want to schedule all the casework and furnishings in a project simultaneously. Or perhaps you want to schedule all the windows and doors if they are being ordered from the same manufacturer. One of the limits of this schedule type is that you cannot schedule host elements such as walls, floors, and ceilings.

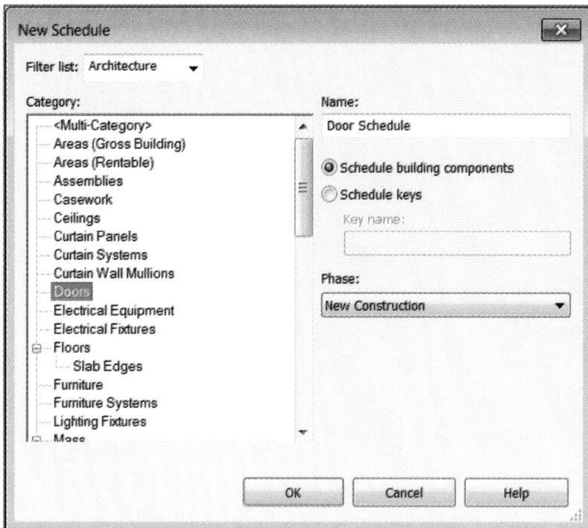

FIGURE 12.1: Creating a new schedule

Customizing Schedules

With this description in mind, let's look at the other options when creating a schedule. Choose Walls from the Category list, and click OK. Doing so opens a new dialog box called Schedule Properties. Here you can set the various properties of a schedule that define not only how it looks but also what information it reports.

Five tabs appear across the top: Fields, Filter, Sorting/Grouping, Formatting, and Appearance. Each of these controls different aspects of the schedule. Let's step through these tabs and see how they affect the look and reporting of the schedule:

Fields The Fields tab lets you select the data that will appear in your schedule. For the wall schedule, it shows all the properties available in the wall category. The list of available fields on the left will vary based on the category you chose to schedule. If you've added any project-based parameters to a category, they will be available here as well. Also notice in the lower-left corner the option Include Elements In Linked Files. Enabling this option allows you to schedule across multiple files; it can be a great tool on larger projects. Choose Family And Type, Type Mark, and Volume, and add them to the Scheduled Fields list on the right by clicking the Add button (Figure 12.2). Note that the order of the items in the Scheduled Fields list from top to bottom will be the order of the columns in your schedule from left to right.

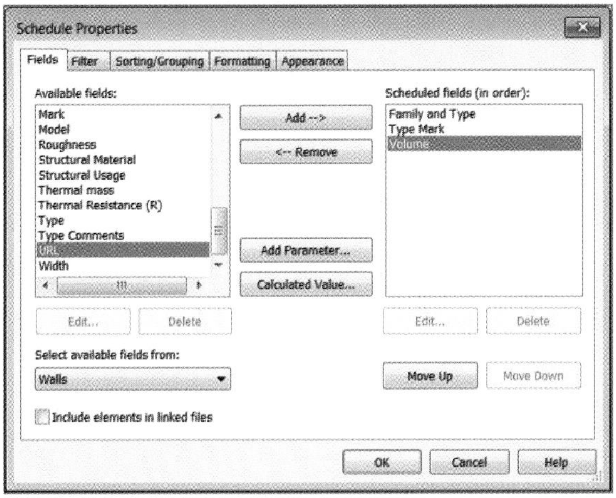

FIGURE 12.2: The Fields tab

Filter On the Filter tab (Figure 12.3), you can filter out the data you don't wish to show in your schedule. Filters work like common database functions. For example, you can filter out all the sheets in a set that don't begin with the letter *A*. Or you can filter a material list so that it shows only materials containing the word *Concrete*. In Figure 12.3, we have created a filter that will exclude walls that have *X* in the Type Mark property. Note that to create a filter, you can only use fields added to the Scheduled Fields list.

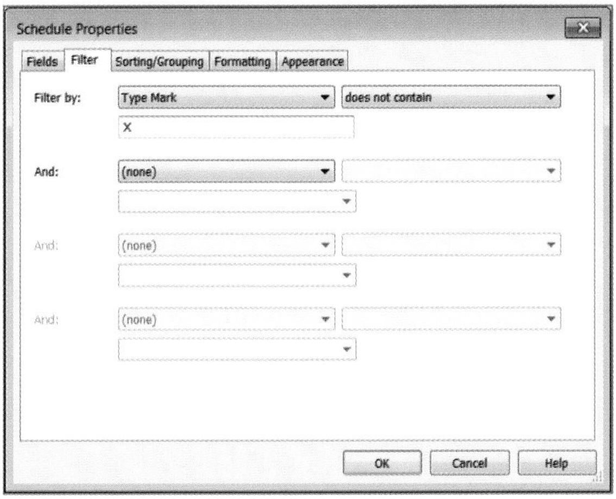

FIGURE 12.3: The Filter tab

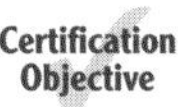

Sorting/Grouping The Sorting/Grouping tab (Figure 12.4) lets you control the order in which information is displayed and which elements control that order. For instance, if you are creating a sheet index, you can choose to sort by Sheet Number or Sheet Name, depending on how you'd like the information displayed. You can also decide whether you want to show every instance of an item or a roll-up of common items using the Itemize Every Instance check box at the bottom. Set the Sort By value to Family And Type, and select the Itemize Every Instance option. Also select the Grand Totals option, and set the adjacent drop-down menu to Totals Only.

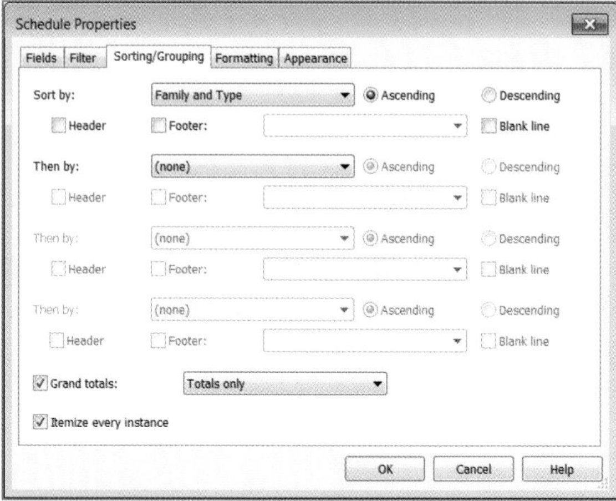

FIGURE 12.4: The Sorting/Grouping tab

Formatting The Formatting tab (Figure 12.5) controls the display of each field and whether the field is visible on the schedule. You can modify various properties of each field such as alignment, heading, and orientation of the header. You can also modify the format of measurement properties. For example, the default unit of measurement for volume on your project might be cubic feet, but you may want to show the volume of walls in cubic yards rounded to the nearest full unit (no decimals). The Calculate Totals option in the Formatting tab is important. This option must be selected for the Grand Totals to function at the bottom of the schedule. Pick Volume from the Fields list, and select the Calculate Totals option. Click the Field Format button, and the Format dialog box opens. Deselect the Use Project Settings option, set Units to Cubic Yards, set Rounding to 0 Decimal Places, and select the Use Digit Grouping option.

Appearance The Appearance tab (Figure 12.6) controls the graphical aspects of the schedule, such as font size and style of text for each of the columns and headers in the schedule. It also allows you to turn the schedule grid lines on and off, as well as modify the line thickness for the grid and boundary lines.

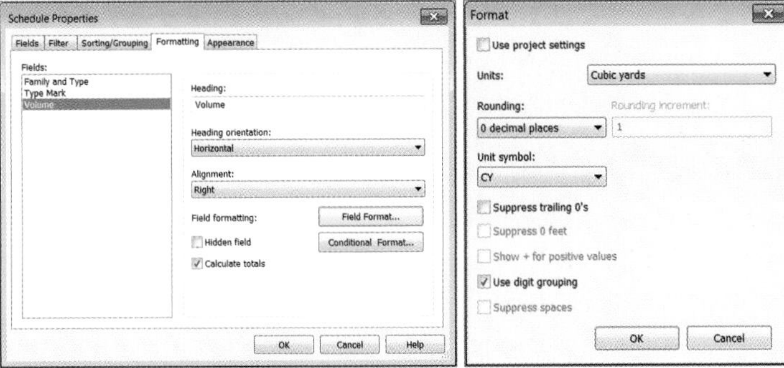

FIGURE 12.5: The Formatting tab

FIGURE 12.6: The Appearance tab

Once you've established the fields and look of your schedule, click OK to view the working schedule. This layout can be modified at any time, but it gives you a basis from which to begin. To modify the schedule, use the buttons in the Properties palette to access any of these five tabs. You will see the final graphic formatting of the schedule only when it is placed on a sheet. We'll get to that later in this chapter.

Using Ribbon Commands in a Schedule

Schedules have their own special tab on the ribbon that is active when you are viewing the schedule outside of a sheet. The tab (Figure 12.7) allows you to select the properties, add and delete rows, and show or hide columns in the schedule.

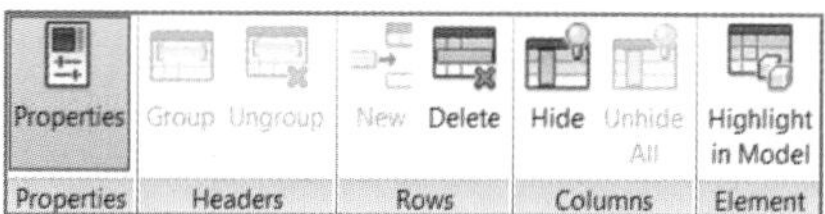

FIGURE 12.7: The Schedule tab buttons

Another key feature of this menu bar is Highlight In Model. This button allows you to select any element in the schedule and locate that element in the model. Let's say you want to locate a particular wall segment from your wall schedule. Highlight the wall in the schedule, and click the Highlight In Model button; you will be taken to a different view with that wall instance highlighted.

Now that you have an idea of the elements that compose a schedule, let's return to the demonstration workflow and create a window schedule, a room schedule, and a sheet list.

Making Schedules

Continue using the `c12-Residence.rvt` model from the book's website. You'll notice that several views and sheets are already created. This model is a work in progress—it's a private residence of 1,230 square feet. The project is a renovation of an 1890s two-story brick house. In the design, all the interior walls have been eliminated and put on a demo phase, which keeps the 19′ (6 m) clear span as open as possible. All new interior walls have been added, and the entire interior has been refreshed in the historic shell. Because the renovation is so substantial, the designer chose to replace all the existing original windows with new insulated, wood windows.

Creating a Window Schedule

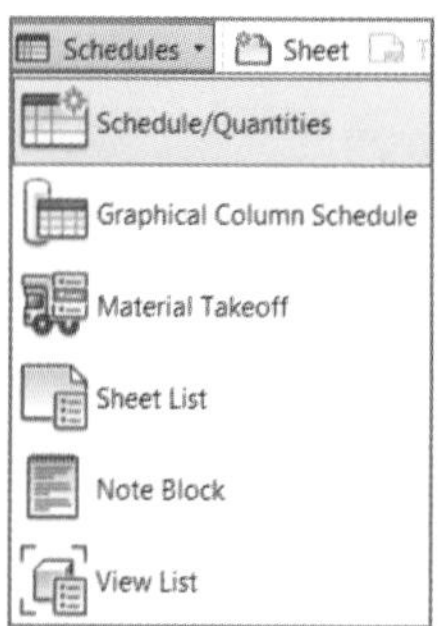

To assist the window manufacturer with the custom sizes, you need to create a window schedule. To begin, go to the View tab ➢ Create panel ➢ Schedule flyout ➢ Schedule/Quantities button. The New Schedule dialog box (shown earlier in Figure 12.1) opens. Here you'll make a series of selections to create the schedule. Follow these steps:

1. From the Category list, select Window at the bottom. Because this project has multiple phases, you want to make sure the phase is set to New Construction—you don't need to schedule the windows you're removing. Note that a particular phase filter will need to be set in the Properties palette for the schedule. We will get to that after progressing through the Schedule Properties tabs. Click OK to continue.

You'll now step through the five tabs in the Schedule Properties dialog box to format the schedule and choose what you'd like to see. Note that you can freely switch between tabs in this dialog box without clicking OK each time.

2. Switch to the Fields tab, and add the following fields to the Scheduled Fields list (in order):
   - Type
   - Type Mark
   - Width
   - Height
   - Count
3. Choose the Sorting/Grouping tab. From the Sort By drop-down, choose Type. Uncheck the Itemize Every Instance option.
4. Choose the Formatting tab, and select Count from the Fields list on the left. Change the Alignment setting to Right. Select the Type Mark field, and change Alignment to Center so all the letters will align nicely.
5. To leave the rest of the schedule at the defaults, click OK and the schedule will display as shown in Figure 12.8. Note that you can also change any of the heading names by simply typing inside the box. Because this example is using the type name to describe the unit size, we have changed the first heading to OPENING SIZE and Type Mark to TYPE.
6. With the window schedule still active, look in the Properties palette for the Phase Filter parameter. Set it to Show New. In step 1, you set the phase to New Construction; however, the phase setting alone does not customize the display of elements in a view. The Show New filter setting excludes model elements that were demolished in a previous phase.

WINDOW SCHEDULE				
OPENING SIZE	TYPE	WIDTH	HEIGHT	COUNT
18" x 54"	D	1' - 6"	4' - 6"	1
18" x 64.75"	H	1' - 6"	5' - 4 3/4"	1
18" x 82"	FF	1' - 6"	6' - 10"	1
28" x 63.5"	C	2' - 4"	5' - 3 1/2"	1
29" X 48"	F	2' - 5"	4' - 0"	1
29" x 60"	E	2' - 5"	5' - 0"	6
29" x 64 3/4"	G	2' - 5"	5' - 4 3/4"	1
32" x 82"	A	2' - 8"	6' - 10"	5
34" x 82"	B	2' - 10"	6' - 10"	2
36" X 12"	J	3' - 0"	1' - 0"	2

FIGURE 12.8: The Window schedule

Creating a Room Schedule

Certification Objective

Creating other schedule types is fairly simple if you follow the guidelines we just went over and step through the tabs in the Schedule Properties dialog box. You have one schedule under your belt, so let's try another—this time, you'll create a room schedule. Let's try a different method for starting a new schedule. In the Project Browser, right-click Schedules/Quantities, select New Schedule/Quantities, and then follow these steps:

1. Choose Rooms from the Category list in the New Schedule dialog box, set the phase to New Construction, and click OK.
2. In the Fields tab, add the following fields from the Scheduled Fields list in order:
    - Number
    - Name
    - Floor Finish
    - North Wall
    - East Wall
    - South Wall
    - West Wall
    - Area
    - Comments
3. On the Sorting tab, sort by Number, and select the Itemize Every Instance option.
4. On the Formatting tab, select the Area field, and set the alignment to Right. Click OK to get the schedule you see in Figure 12.9.

Notice that some of the fields already contain data. This is because some of this information is generated automatically (such as room areas) and some of it was added earlier in the process by adding room numbers to the plans or room names. Remember, schedules are just a tabular way of viewing the model—changes to the schedule will alter what you see in the model.

Now let's do something slightly different with this schedule. Because four of the columns are dealing with wall finishes, let's add a header to those columns so you can group them under one header:

1. Select the four headers as shown in Figure 12.10. Grab one with your mouse and, holding down the left mouse button, drag across to select all four. Note that the first one you select does not highlight in black.

Room Schedule								
Number	Name	Floor Finish	North Wall	East Wall	South Wall	West Wall	Area	Comments
100	LIVING ROOM	WOOD					307 SF	a
101	DINING ROOM	WOOD					99 SF	a
102	OFFICE	WOOD					71 SF	a
103	1/2 BATH	WOOD					25 SF	a
104	KITCHEN						134 SF	
200	BEDROOM 1	WOOD					161 SF	a
201	BATH 1						39 SF	
202	BEDROOM 3	WOOD					121 SF	a
203	BATH 2						41 SF	
205	HALL	WOOD					95 SF	a
206	Room						7 SF	
207	Room						15 SF	
208	Room						7 SF	
209	Room						22 SF	
210	Room						12 SF	

FIGURE 12.9: Room schedule

Room Schedule					
Floor Finish	North Wall	East Wall	South Wall	West Wall	Area
WOOD					307 SF
WOOD					99 SF
WOOD					71 SF
WOOD					25 SF

FIGURE 12.10: Selecting the wall finishes

2. With the four columns selected, click the Group button in the Headers panel in the ribbon. This gives you a new row above your existing headers.

3. Type **Wall Finishes** to complete your schedule (Figure 12.11).

Creating a Sheet List

The last kind of schedule type we'll talk about is a sheet list, which allows you to create a customized list of drawing sheets in your project and place it on a sheet for printing. This can be especially useful on larger projects where the sheet list can get long. This tool is also located on the Create panel of the View tab in the Schedules flyout.

Room Schedule									
			Wall Finishes						
Number	Name	Floor Finish	North Wall	East Wall	South Wall	West Wall	Area	Comments
100	LIVING ROOM	WOOD					307 SF	a.
101	DINING ROOM	WOOD					99 SF	a.
102	OFFICE	WOOD					71 SF	a.
103	1/2 BATH	WOOD					25 SF	a.
104	KITCHEN						134 SF	
200	BEDROOM 1	WOOD					161 SF	a.
201	BATH 1						39 SF	
202	BEDROOM 3	WOOD					121 SF	a.
203	BATH 2						41 SF	
205	HALL	WOOD					95 SF	a.
206	Room						7 SF	
207	Room						15 SF	
208	Room						7 SF	
209	Room						22 SF	
210	Room						12 SF	

FIGURE 12.11: The Room schedule

This schedule has a feature that allows you to create placeholders for sheets that are not yet created or will not be a part of your discipline's drawings. You can use this feature to create full-sheet schedules including all consultant drawings. It also lets you create placeholder entries in the sheet schedule before you've created your own sheets.

In the sample workflow, you have created several sheets and you now need to add a sheet list to your drawings:

1. Select the Sheet List tool from the Schedules flyout. The Sheet List Properties dialog box appears, starting with the Fields tab. Add the Sheet Number and Sheet Name fields from the list on the left to the column on the right (Figure 12.12).

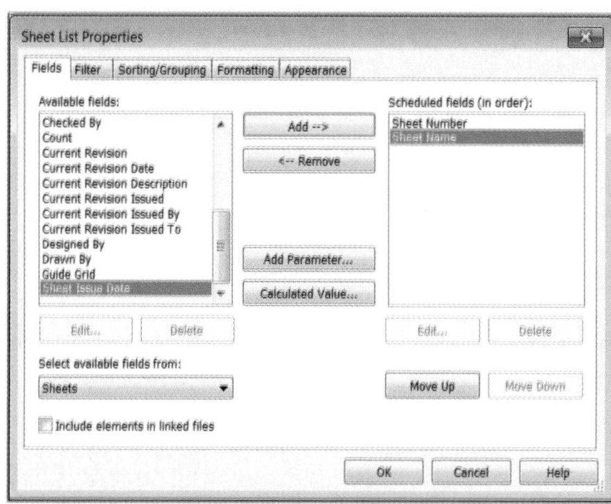

FIGURE 12.12: Creating the sheet list

2. On the Sorting/Grouping tab, choose to sort by Sheet Number, and make sure the Itemize Every Instance check box is selected.

   Because you're creating a sheet index for a specific set of sheets, you need to create a filter. In this exercise project, the only sheets you need to schedule are the A-series sheets.

3. On the Filter tab, choose to filter by Sheet Number. From the next drop-down, choose Begins With. In the third field, enter the letter A. (Be sure to use an uppercase *A*, because queries in Revit Architecture filters are case-sensitive.) The filter should look like Figure 12.13. When you're done, click OK to close the dialog box.

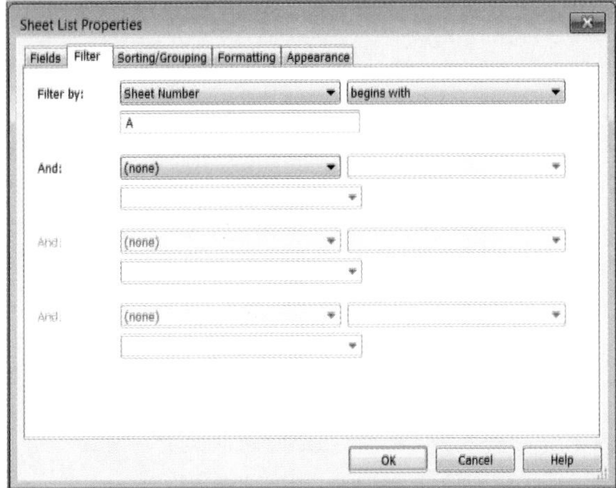

FIGURE 12.13: Creating a filter for specific sheets

You should have a schedule with only sheet numbers that begin with the letter *A*. Now you need to populate the rest of the sheet list.

At this point, it is critical to understand the two methods you can use to create new sheets in your project:

- Create new sheets from the View tab in the ribbon or by right-clicking the Sheets heading in the Project Browser.
- Add sheets by adding rows to a sheet list. These become placeholders until you create an actual sheet in your project. If you have placeholders in a sheet list, when you create a new sheet, you can select a placeholder from the New Sheet dialog box.

Although you can use either method with similar efficacy, let's continue the exercise by first adding placeholders and then creating the respective sheets.

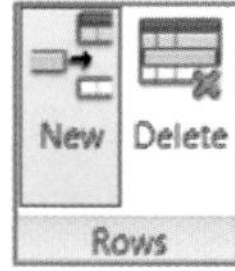

4. With the sheet list still active, click the New button in the Rows panel of the ribbon. You should see a row appear with a sheet name defined as Unnamed. Change the number to **A100** and the name to **FLOOR PLANS**.

5. Click the New Sheet button in the ribbon. In the New Sheet dialog box, choose the 22 × 34 Sheet CD - C1 titleblock, and select A100 - FLOOR PLANS from the list of placeholder sheets (Figure 12.14). Click OK to close the dialog box and create the new sheet.

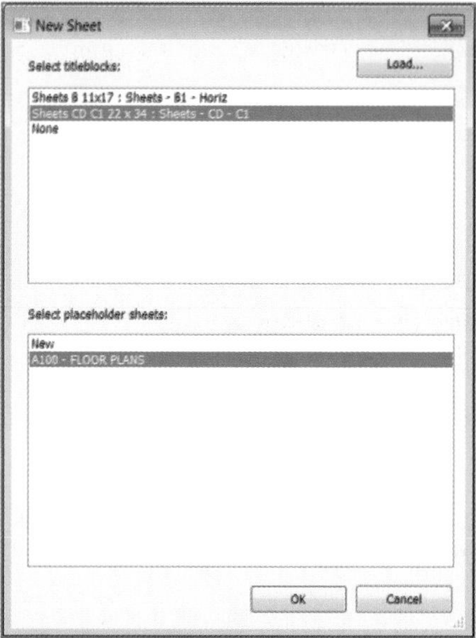

FIGURE 12.14: Adding sheets using a placeholder

You'll notice in the new sheet that the sheet number and sheet name have been automatically populated based on the information you added to the sheet list as a placeholder. This workflow is useful for larger projects where the index of drawings may be planned in advance and entered into a sheet list. As the design progresses and sheets are created, the design team only needs to pick from the list of placeholders. Also remember that additional parameters can be added to the sheet list in addition to the number and name.

Placing Views on Sheets

Throughout this book, you have created several different kinds of views, from plans to elevations to perspectives. Eventually, you will need to lay out those views onto sheets so they can be printed or converted to PDF and sent to clients or team members for review.

Creating sheets in Revit Architecture is very easy. As you've already seen, they can be created through a Sheet List schedule. You can also create sheets by right-clicking the Sheet node in the Project Browser and selecting New Sheet from the context menu. Regardless of which method you use to create them, let's walk through laying out these views on sheets and see how each view can be further manipulated once it's placed on a sheet.

Adding Floor Plans to the Sheet

Certification Objective

Because a series of views has already been created in the exercise file, let's use the sheet you just made for placing some views. You place a view on a sheet by dragging the view out of the Project Browser and placing it on the sheet. Let's practice this with another exercise:

1. Open the A100 – Floor Plans sheet by double-clicking it in the Project Browser.
2. Under the Views heading in the Project Browser, find Floor Plans, and expand the tree to locate the plan named Basement. Holding down the left mouse button, drag the Basement floor plan out of the Project Browser and onto sheet A100. Release the left mouse button, and the outline of the view displays with a view title. This outline represents the extents of the view at the appropriate view scale.
3. Click once more on the sheet to complete the placement of the view. Remember, you can adjust the location of the view on the sheet at any time. Figure 12.15 shows the view placed on the sheet.
4. You have space left on the sheet, so let's add other views. Add Level 1 and Level 2 by dragging and dropping them from the Project Browser onto the sheet.

   When you're placing the second and third views on the sheet, you're presented with an outline of the plan view with a dashed line in the center of the view. This is an alignment tool; Revit Architecture is assuming that you want the plans to align on the sheet, and it is intelligent enough to aid you in this process. You can casually drag the views around on the sheets enough to find the alignment lines and to ensure that all your plans line up (Figure 12.16). Your sheet full of views should look like Figure 12.17.

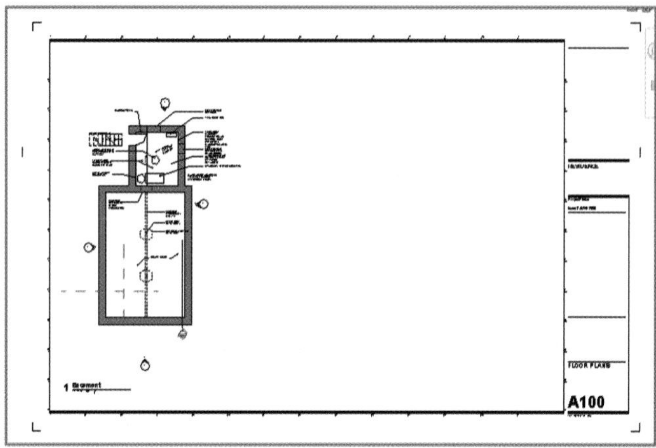

FIGURE 12.15: Placing the view on a sheet

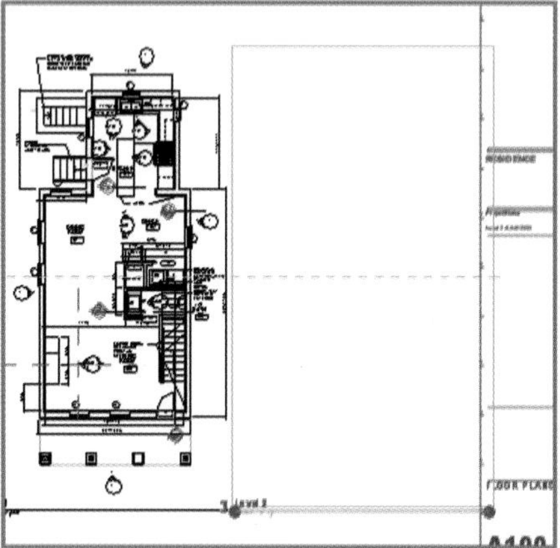

FIGURE 12.16: Aligning views on a sheet

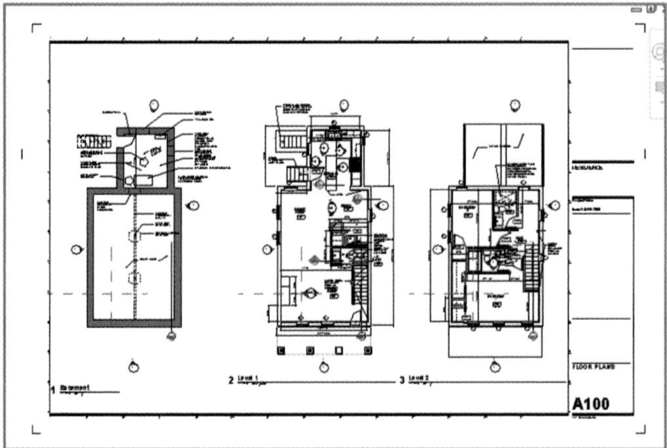

FIGURE 12.17: All the views placed on the sheet

Once the views are placed on a sheet, you'll inevitably want to do a bit of cleanup to the drawings to place everything properly. First, the view tag is placed in roughly the same place for each view; however, the default location might not be the location you desire. Revit Architecture also numbers the views sequentially (1, 2, 3, …) in order of placement.

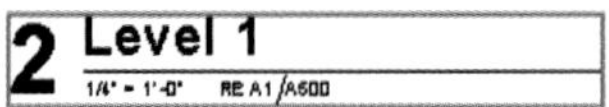

Let's adjust the view tags on the sheets. To adjust the text in the tags, start by selecting the view itself—*not the tag*:

1. Select the Basement floor plan view placed on the sheet. The view tag highlights in blue. You want to change two things on the tag: the number and the length of the line.
2. Select the number 1, and change it to **A1** to reference the ConDoc drawing system—letters vertically along the side of the sheet and numbers across the bottom of the sheet. Move the detail to the location on the lower-left corner of the detail on the drawing sheet.
3. Using the blue grips on the view tag line, drag the right grip closer to the end of the Basement text. The tag looks like Figure 12.18.
4. Let's move the view tag to a better position. Click off the tag, anywhere on the sheet, to deselect the tag. You can also press the Esc key twice or select the Modify arrow at the upper left. Then, select the tag

itself. It highlights blue again, but without the grips on the line. Hold the left mouse button, and drag the tag to any location on the sheet (Figure 12.19).

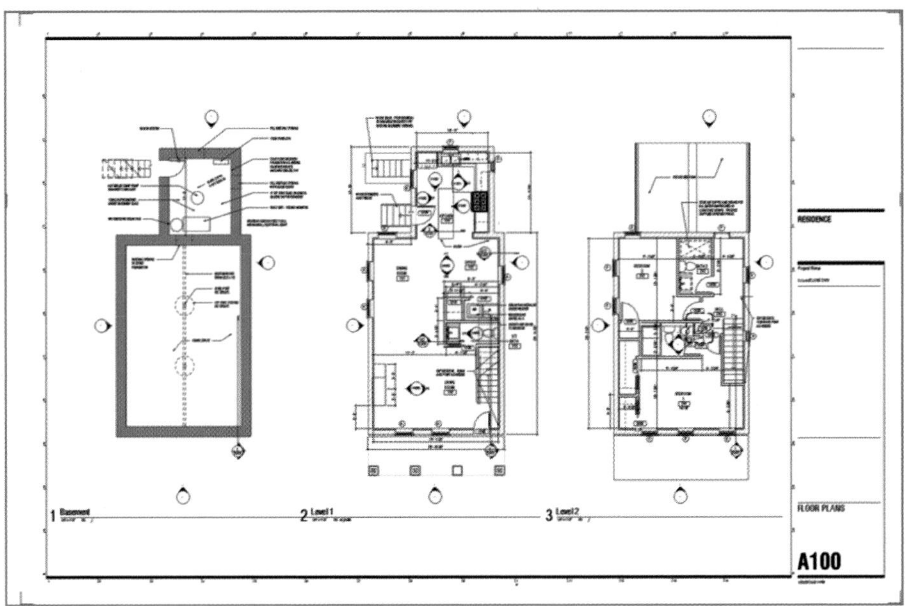

FIGURE 12.18: The edited view tag

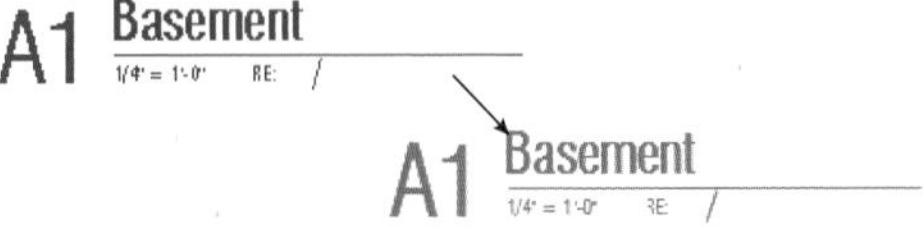

FIGURE 12.19: Moving the view tag

5. Do the same to the other two views. Renumber Level 1 to **A6** and Level 2 to **A11** to match their location on the sheet as shown, shortening the view-tag lines to a more appropriate length (Figure 12.20). Notice that the view tags align with other view tags on the sheet, similar to the way the plans did.

   To finish organizing your sheet, let's add a few lines to divide the views. You can do so easily by using the Detail Line tool, which is on the Annotate tab.

Detail Line

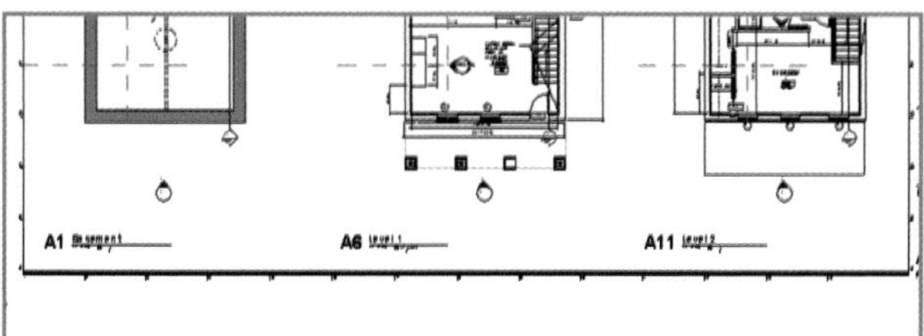

FIGURE 12.20: Laying out the rest of the sheet views

6. On the Annotate tab, choose Detail Line from the Detail panel. Doing so activates the Modify | Place Detail Lines context menu. From the Line Style panel at far right, choose Wide Lines from the drop-down.

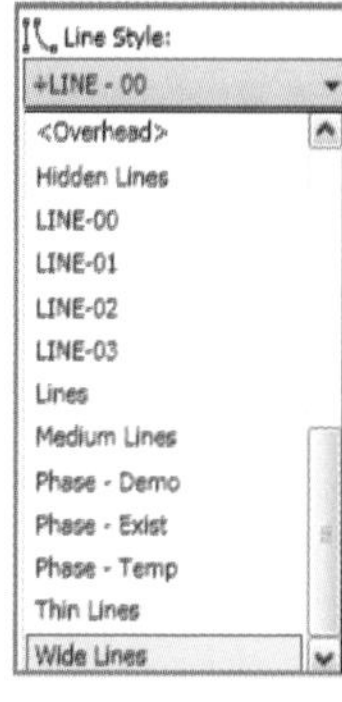

7. You're ready to start drawing lines, and by default, the straight-line tool is active. You can select one of the nodes on the sheet between views and draw a vertical line between the Basement and Level 1 plans and again between the Level 1 and Level 2 plans (Figure 12.21).

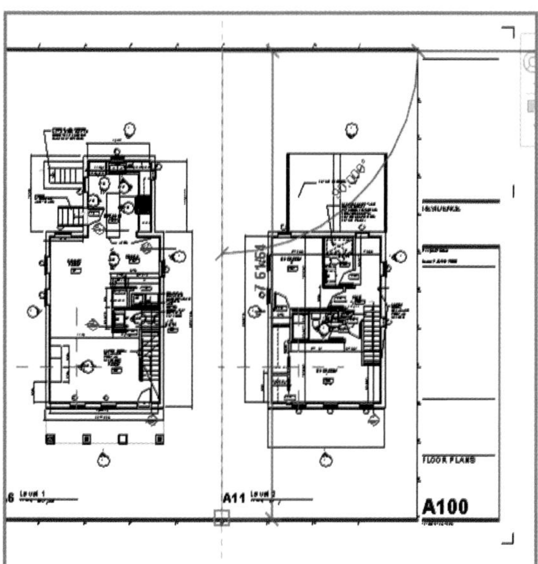

FIGURE 12.21: Adding lines to the sheet

With these dividing lines in place, you may notice that one of the text annotations in the Basement view is a little too close to the dividing line you added to the sheet (Figure 12.22). Let's adjust it.

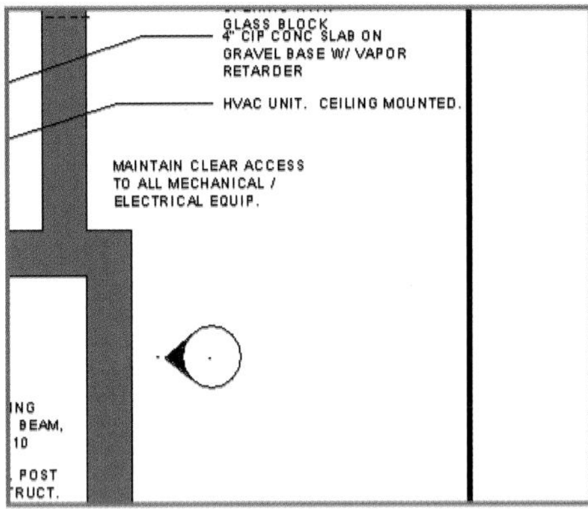

FIGURE 12.22: Text to be adjusted in the sheet view

To adjust the text object on the floor plan view, you could simply open the view and adjust the text box, but you wouldn't have the sheet and the dividing line as a reference. Instead, you're going to use a command called Activate View.

Activating a view is like working in a model-space viewport while in paper space using AutoCAD. You're working on the actual view, but you're doing so while it is placed on the sheet. This approach allows you the benefit of seeing how changes to the view affect the layout of the view on the sheet:

1. Right-click the plan view, and choose Activate View from the context menu (Figure 12.23).

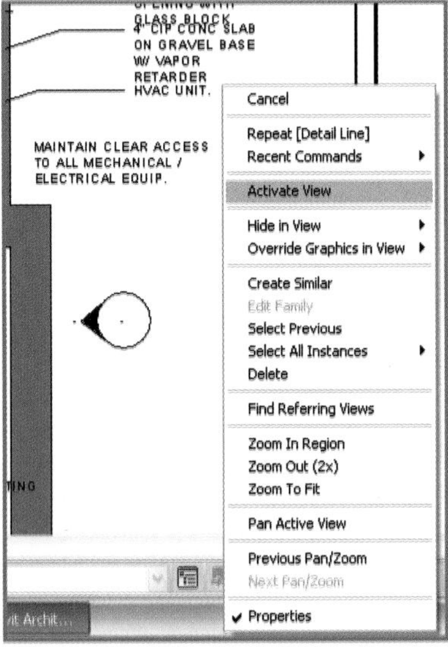

FIGURE 12.23: Activating the view

2. With the view activated, notice that the other views have become grayed out. Only the elements you can currently edit remain active in the view. Select the text box you've identified, and drag the right grip inward so the text wraps as shown in Figure 12.24.

3. To complete your edits, you need to deactivate the view. Right-click anywhere outside the view, and choose Deactivate View from the context menu.

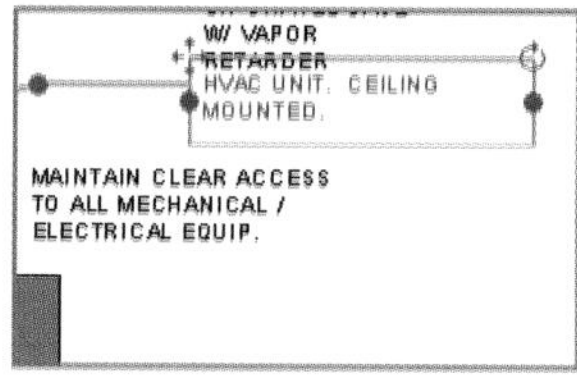

FIGURE 12.24:
Modifying the text box

Adding the Schedules

With your sheet of floor plans configured and ready to print, you can quickly finish the sheet set by adding the window schedule you created earlier. Adding a schedule is just like adding any other view—you drag and drop it from the Project Browser onto the sheet:

1. Open the sheet named G000 - COVER SHEET by double-clicking it in the Project Browser.

2. Grab the window schedule from the Project Browser, and drag and drop it onto an open area on the sheet.

3. Repeat this process for the room schedule and the sheet list.

Once the schedules are on the sheet, they may need a bit of adjustment. You can redefine the column spacing and even split larger schedules directly on the sheet to make them easier to read. Such adjustments do not change the actual schedule—just its appearance on the sheet.

To adjust a schedule placed on a sheet, highlight the schedule by selecting it. The schedule turns blue, and a few new grips appear that you can use to make changes (Figure 12.25). The blue inverted triangles at the top of each column allow you to modify the column widths. Grab one, and drag it left or right to change the column sizing.

You'll also notice a blue cut symbol . This cut symbol lets you break the schedule into parts while on the same sheet. This can be especially handy if you have a long schedule, such as a room or door schedule, that has too many rows to fit on your sheet vertically. Selecting this tool breaks the schedule in half (and you can break it into half again and again) so you can take advantage of the horizontal real estate on your sheet. If you choose to separate your schedule in this fashion, it retains all the necessary information, and all the portions continue to automatically fill themselves dynamically as a single schedule would. You can also change the overall height of the schedule once it is broken up by grabbing the grips at the bottom of the schedule and dragging up or down.

With your schedule on the sheet and the columns properly formatted, you can drag the schedule around on the sheet until it's located where you'd like to have it. To do so, click the schedule and hold down the left mouse button. As you move the schedule on the sheet, it behaves like other views: it aligns with the other schedules on the sheet and displays a light green dashed line to help with alignment. Your finished sheet should look like Figure 12.26.

WINDOW SCHEDULE				
OPENING SIZE	TYPE	WIDTH	HEIGHT	COUNT
18" x 54"	D	1' - 6"	4' - 8"	1
18" x 64.75"	H	1' - 6"	5' - 4 3/4"	1
18" x 82"	FF	1' - 6"	6' - 10"	1
28" x 63.5"	C	2' - 4"	5' - 3 1/2"	1
29" X 48"	F	2' - 5"	4' - 0"	1
29" x 60"	E	2' - 5"	5' - 0"	6
29" x 64 3/4"	G	2' - 5"	5' - 4 3/4"	1
32" x 82"	A	2' - 8"	6' - 10"	5
34" x 82"	B	2' - 10"	6' - 10"	2
36" X 12"	J	3' - 0"	1' - 0"	2

FIGURE 12.25: Modifying the schedule on the sheet

FIGURE 12.26: The finished cover sheet

Printing Documents

You will eventually need to get the sheets out of Revit Architecture and into a printed format. If you've been working in the Windows environment, you'll find that printing from Revit Architecture is straightforward because the process resembles that used in other Windows-based applications.

The Print Dialog Box

To begin printing, you do not need to be in any particular view or sheet. Select Application ➢ Print ➢ Print to open the dialog box shown in Figure 12.27. All the features for printing are found here. Let's step through this dialog box and explore each element.

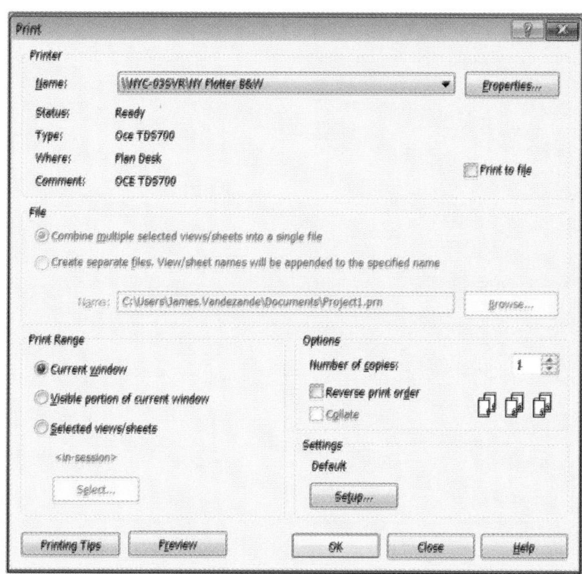

FIGURE 12.27: Print dialog box

The drop-down menu at the top of the Print dialog box allows you to select the printer or plotter to which you wish to print. This can be a physical printer or a virtual one (such as Adobe Acrobat Distiller). You can add printers to this list using your Windows Printer control panel.

Most of the controls you need to use can be found at the bottom of this dialog box in the Settings section on the right and the Print Range section on the left.

Print Settings

In the Print dialog box, click the Setup button under Settings to open the Print Setup dialog box (Figure 12.28). Here you can customize the print settings including paper size, zoom, and orientation. You can save these settings with a name so that you can reuse them in later work sessions. We recommend creating saved setups based on a printer type—not for one specific printer. For example, if your office has several plotters of the same make and model, it is sufficient to create one setup named Full Size B/W Plot.

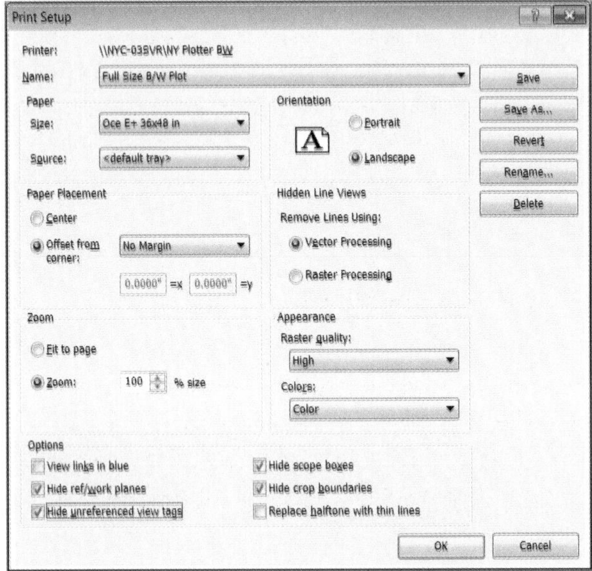

FIGURE 12.28: The Print Setup dialog box

The print settings can also be transferred to other project files if necessary, using the Transfer Project Standards tool located on the Manage tab in the ribbon. Let's take a look at some of the important printing options available to you.

Hidden Line Views

Views in Revit Architecture can be displayed in several graphic modes: Wireframe, Hidden Line, Shaded, Consistent Colors, and Realistic. The most commonly used type is Hidden Line. You'll choose this mode for most floor plans, sections, and elevations, and sometimes even for 3D.

You have the option to print this type of view with vector processing or raster processing of the hidden lines. Vector is faster; however, you need to be aware of some nuances when working with hidden-line views. For example, transparent materials (such as glass) print transparent with raster processing but opaque with vector processing.

Zoom

If you're looking for the ability to print a view to a specific scale (the way you would in Autodesk® AutoCAD®), it's actually much simpler in Revit Architecture. Remember that every view is assigned a scale factor; therefore, printing a view is always determined as a percentage of that assigned scale. For example, if a floor plan is assigned a scale factor of 1/4″=1′-0″ (1:50) and you would like to generate a quick print of the plan at 1/8″=1′-0″ (1:100), simply set the zoom to 50 percent. Sheets should be printed at 100 percent for full-size or 50 percent for a half-size set.

Options

The Options pane is at the bottom of the Print Setup dialog box. The pane includes these options:

View Links In Blue View links are hyperlinked tags that lead you from one view to another. They appear blue in the views and print black by default, but you can specify that they should be printed in blue, mimicking their on-screen appearance. This option is useful when you are creating an electronic print in a format such as DWFx or PDF.

Hide Ref/Work Planes, Hide Scope Boxes, and Hide Crop Boundaries These three check boxes let you decide whether to print various elements that are usually used only while working in the software.

Hide Unreferenced View Tags During the course of a project, you may create a lot of elevation tags, section flags, or detail callouts for working purposes that you don't wish to be printed in the final documents. If the corresponding views are not placed on any sheets, these view tags are referred to as *unreferenced,* and you have the option not to print them.

Replace Halftone With Thin Lines If you experience trouble with printing linework that is configured as halftone (gray shade), you can select this option to temporarily convert any halftone lines to solid black thin lines.

When all your options are set, you can save the settings so you can reuse them on future prints. Because everyone's system printer configurations will be somewhat different, we won't ask you to create a specific setting configuration. Instead, use the information we just reviewed to create your own printer setup configuration. Note that you can change settings temporarily by selecting the <in-session> setting from the Name drop-down. Then, click OK to close this dialog box and return to the Print dialog box.

Print Range

The other important part of the Print dialog box is Print Range. In this section, you can define exactly what areas, sheets, or views you want to print. It includes these options:

Current Window This option prints the full extent of the open view, regardless of what extents of that view are currently visible on your screen.

Visible Portion Of Current Window This option prints only what you see in the frame of the open window framed for the sheet size you've selected.

Selected Views/Sheets This option allows you to define a reusable list of views, sheets, or any combinations of views and sheets. This way, you can essentially batch-print a job by sending large quantities of sheets to the printer in one shot and save these selections for future print jobs.

You can pick any view or sheet to include in the view/sheet set. If you want to include only sheets in a set, use the Show options at the bottom of the View/Sheet Set dialog box to shorten the visible list. Doing so allows you to select only sheets or only views if you choose.

This is a great tool to help define print lists. Some examples of using these selections would be a 100 percent construction document package or a specific set of presentation sheets.

In the exercise project, suppose you want to print the A-series sheets and the G000 cover sheet. Follow these steps:

1. In the Print dialog box, choose the Selected Views/Sheets option, and click the Select button.
2. In the resulting View/Sheet Set dialog box, deselect the Views check box at the bottom. Revit Architecture displays only the sheets you've created to date.

3. From the list, select the A-series sheets and the G000 cover sheet (Figure 12.29).

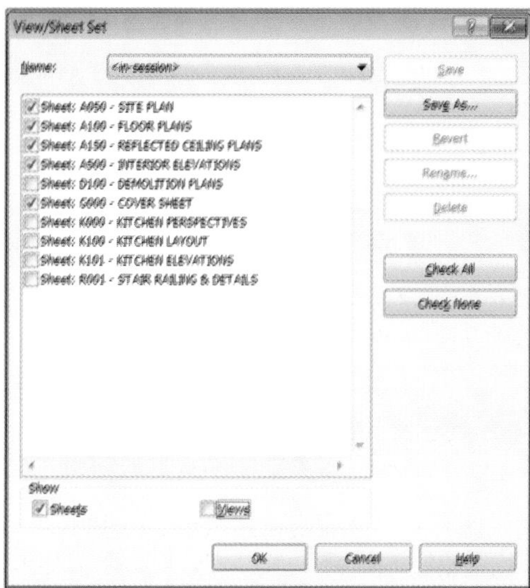

FIGURE 12.29: Selecting the desired sheets

4. Because you will more than likely want to print this set again, click the Save As button and name the set **Presentation Set 1**. Doing so will keep your current collection of sheets together, and if you want to reprint this set, you can grab the set name from the Name drop-down menu in the View/Sheet Set dialog box.

   Remember, if you add more drawings to the set, by default they won't be added to this print set. You'll need to revisit this dialog box, add the sheets, and click the Save button. For now, click OK to close this dialog box.

4. Clicking OK in the Print dialog box prints the selected drawings to the printer listed at the top. Clicking Close saves your print setup and closes the dialog box without printing.

The Essentials and Beyond

In this chapter, you learned how to quantify the elements in the model by using schedules. You used the same Schedule tool to create a standard window schedule, a room schedule, and a sheet list. You also learned how to place views onto sheets and print them.

Additional Exercises

- Create a door schedule, and add the following fields:

  Mark

  Type

  Width

  Height

  Thickness

  Material

  Finish

  Comments

- Lay out this new schedule on sheet G000; be sure to align it with the schedules you already placed on that sheet. Change the schedule's Sorting/Grouping options by including the Count field and toggling the Itemize Every Instance setting. Observe the differences in scheduling every door compared to a rolled-up schedule showing only individual door types, and how many of each exist in the project.

CHAPTER 13

Workflow and Site Modeling

Understanding the Autodesk® Revit® Architecture software and how to use it is not a difficult challenge. The real challenge is determining how using Revit Architecture and building information modeling (BIM) changes your organization's culture and your project's workflow—especially if you're coming from a CAD-based environment. Revit Architecture can be more than just a different way to draw a line. In this chapter, we'll focus on what those changes are and provide some tools to help you manage the transition.

In this chapter, you learn the following skills:

- **Understanding a BIM workflow**
- **Modeling a site**
- **Detailing in Revit Architecture**
- **Performing quality control on your Revit Architecture model**

Understanding a BIM Workflow

Regardless of the workflow you have established, moving to Revit Architecture is going to be a change. You'll need tools to help transition from your current workflow to one using Revit Architecture. To begin, we'll cover some of the core differences between a CAD-based system and a BIM-based one.

Moving to BIM is a shift in how designers and contractors look at the design and documentation process throughout the entire life cycle of the project, from concept to occupancy. In a traditional CAD-based workflow, represented in Figure 13.1, each view is drawn separately with no inherent relationship between drawings. In this type of production environment, the team creates plans, sections, elevations, schedules, and perspectives and must coordinate any changes between files manually.

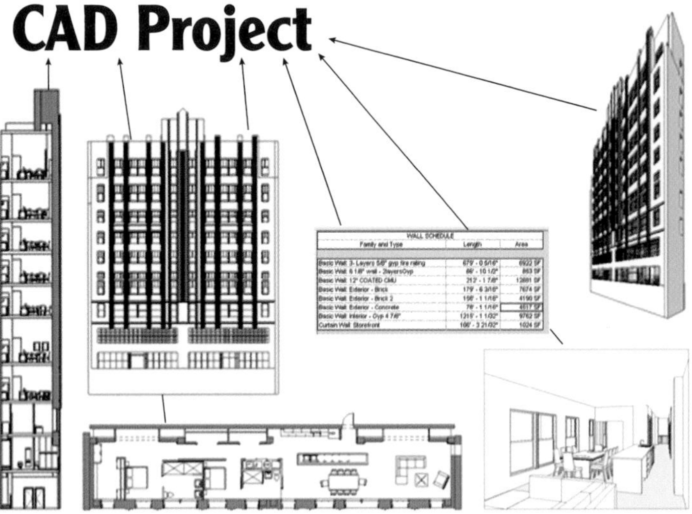

FIGURE 13.1 A CAD-based workflow

In a BIM-based workflow, the team creates a 3D, parametric model and uses this model to automatically generate the drawings necessary for documentation. Plans, sections, elevations, schedules, and perspectives are all byproducts of creating an embellished BIM model, as shown in Figure 13.2. This enhanced documentation methodology not only allows for a highly coordinated drawing set but also provides the basic model geometry necessary for analysis such as daylighting studies, energy, material takeoffs, and so on.

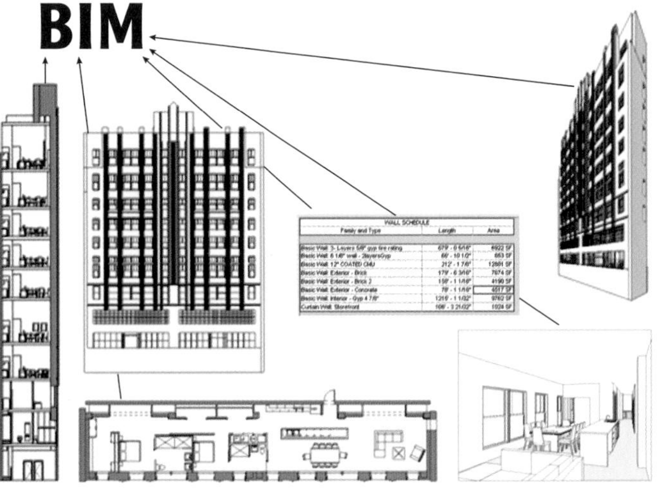

FIGURE 13.2 A BIM workflow

Using Revit Architecture becomes more than a change in software; it becomes a change in workflow and methodology. As various design specializations interact and create the building model (Figure 13.3), you can see how structure, mechanical, energy, daylight, and other factors inform design direction. You can also draw relationships between some of these elements that might not have been as obvious in a more traditional approach. Although some of these specialties (such as structure and mechanical) are historically separate systems, by integrating them into a single design model, you can see how they interact in relation to other systems within a building.

Analysis such as daylighting can inform your building orientation and structure. Depending on your glazing, it can also affect your mechanical requirements (as solar gain). You can see some of these effects through a computational fluid dynamics (CFD) model (used to calculate airflow). Geographic information system (GIS) data will give you your relative location globally and allow you to see how much sunlight you will be receiving or what the local temperature swings will be during the course of a day. As you can see, all of these variables can easily affect building design.

Staffing a BIM Project

As you rethink the process of design and documentation, one of the semantic changes you will need to address is staffing. A common misconception of project management when teams are first moving from CAD to BIM is that staffing the project will be the same in both workflows. This couldn't be further from the truth. When the workflow changes, staffing allocations, time to complete tasks, and percentage of work by phase are all affected as a byproduct of the change of method.

In a CAD-based project, the level of effort during each of the phases is fairly well known. The industry has been using some metrics over the past several years that should be fairly familiar. There is modest effort and staffing in the conceptual design and schematic design phases, and this effort builds until it crescendos during construction documentation. At this phase, a CAD project can greatly increase the number of staff in an effort to expedite the completion of the drawing set. This staff increase can be effective because the CAD drawings are typically separate files, and moving lines in one drawing won't dynamically change another.

In a BIM-based framework, there is still a gradual increase of staffing and effort through conceptual design and into the schematic phase, but the effort during schematic design is greater using BIM than in CAD. During schematic design and design development, the project team is still performing all the same tasks that occur in any design process: testing design concepts, visualizations, or design iteration. The increase in effort during the early design phases lets the team use the parametric nature of the model to significantly reduce the effort later during construction documents, allowing for a decrease in the overall effort over the project cycle.

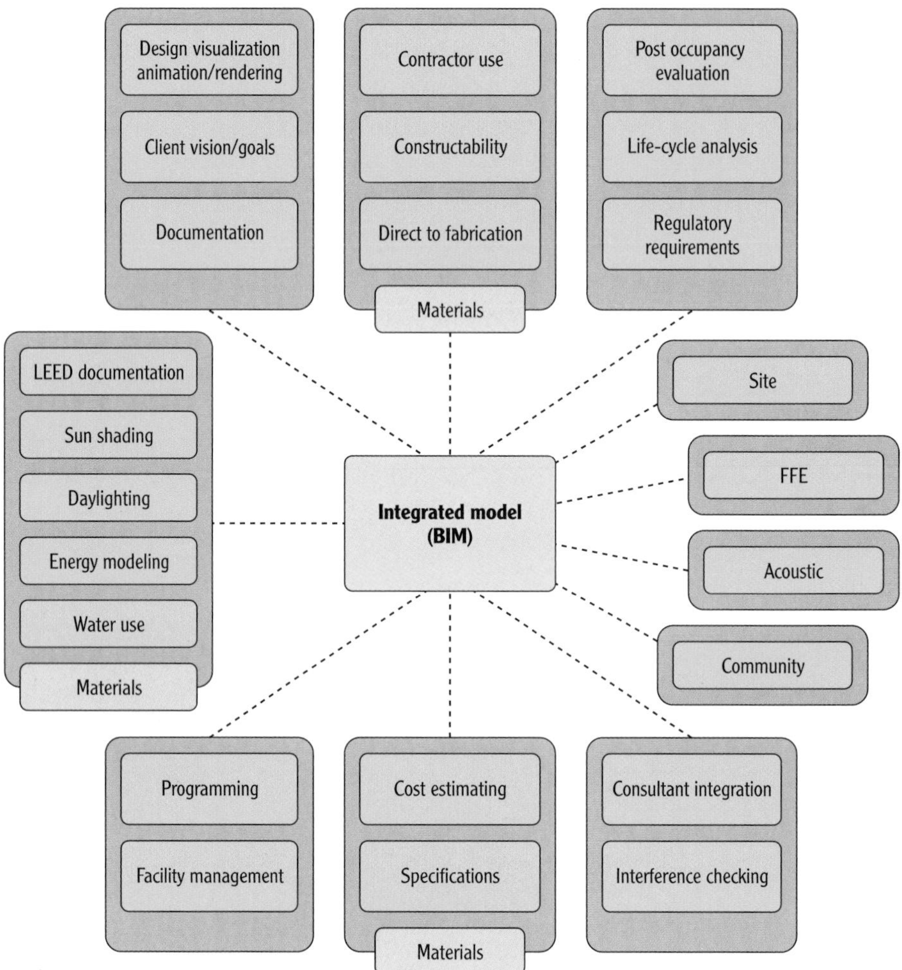

FIGURE 13.3 The integrated design model

Project Roles Using Revit Architecture

With such a significant change in the effort behind a BIM-based project flow, it's also important to understand how this can change the various roles and responsibilities for the project team. The changes in traditional roles can become a barrier to many projects successfully adopting BIM. Project managers need to be able to predict staffing and time to complete tasks throughout the project phases and have relied on past precedent of staff and project types to do this. Because a BIM-based project can significantly alter the project workflow, many of the historic timetables for task completion are no longer valid. However, a BIM-based project can be broken down into a few primary roles that will allow you some level of predictability through the various project phases. Although the specific effort and staffing will vary between offices (and even projects), some general roles will need to be accounted for on every project.

There are three primary roles on every BIM project:

Architect Deals with design issues, code compliances, clear widths, wall types, and so on

Modeler Creates content in 2D or in 3D

Drafter Deals with annotations, sheet layout, view creation, and detail creation

These roles represent efforts and general tasks that you need to take into account on any Revit Architecture project. On a large project, these roles could also represent individual people, whereas on a smaller project they might be all the same person, or one person might carry multiple roles. We'll now cover each of these in a bit more detail and discuss how these roles interact with the project cycle.

Architect

The role of the architect is to deal with the architectural issues revolving around the project. As the model is being created, you will naturally have to solve issues like constructability and wall types, set corridor widths, deal with department areas, and deal with other issues involving either codes or the overall architectural design. This role will be the one applying standards to the project (as in wall types, keynotes, and so on) and organizing the document set. This role will need to be present on the project from the beginning to ensure consistency of the virtual building creation and isn't necessarily limited to only one person.

This role also might or might not be a "designer." Although it is possible to do early design in Revit Architecture, many project teams prefer to utilize other tools such as Google SketchUp or even pencil and trace paper. The job of the architect is steering the creation of the building in Revit Architecture. Tasks for this role include the following:

- Leading the creation of massing (if used) and major architectural elements and building from within the model
- Designing around code requirements and other building logistics
- Constructability and detailing aspects of the design

Modeler

The role of the modeler is to create all the 2D and especially the 3D content needed in the project. This content includes all the parametric families for elements such as windows, doors, casework, wall types, stairs, railings, and furnishings. Typically, this role is the responsibility of less experienced staff, who might not be able to fulfill the role of architect. These less experienced positions tend to have longer periods of undisturbed time, making them better suited to deal with some of the longer, more involved tasks in modeling content. Finally, they also tend to have some 3D experience coming out of school. They might not have worked with Revit Architecture directly but possibly with Autodesk 3ds Max or Google SketchUp, and are thereby familiar with working in a 3D environment. Tasks for this role include:

- Exchanging any generic elements used during early design stages for more specific building elements
- Creating and adding new family components, and modifying existing components in the project
- Regularly reviewing and eliminating project warnings

Drafter

The role of the drafter is to create sheets and views and embellish those views with annotations or other 2D content. This role will be doing the bulk of the work needed to document the project. In earlier stages of the project, this role is typically assumed by either the architect or the modeler, but as documentation gets moving into high gear, it can quickly become the role of multiple people on a larger project. Tasks for this role include the following:

- Keynoting
- Dimensioning
- Setting up sheets and views
- Creating schedules

For a staffing-planning purpose, we are discussing the ideal times to bring in some of these various roles into the project. At the inception of a project design, a modeling role will be of the best use. This person can help create the building form, add conceptual content, and get the massing for the building established. If you're using the conceptual modeling tools, the modeler can even do some early sustainable design calculations.

Once the design begins to settle down, you'll need an architect role to step into the project. Since the design is more resolve, it's a good time to begin applying specific materials and wall types and validating spatial requirements and the owner's program. The process of moving from the general "what" something is and "where" it is to the more specific "how" something is going to be assembled isn't new. It's the same process that was used to create both traditional and modern buildings (Figure 13.4).

FIGURE 13.4 Traditional and modern designs

During schematic design, you'll need to include the role of the drafter to begin laying out sheets and creating views. These sheets and views don't have to be for a construction document set yet, but you'll have to establish views for any schematic design submittals. If these views are set up properly, they can be reused later for design development and construction-document submittals as the model continues to gain a greater level of detail.

What you'd like to avoid for your project staffing, if possible, is adding staff during the construction-document phase. In a BIM/Revit Architecture workflow, this can sometimes cause more problems than it solves and slow down the team rather than get work done faster.

Adding Team Members to Fight Fires

In many projects, there comes a time when the schedule gets tight and project management wants to add more staff to a project to meet a specific deadline. In a 2D CAD environment, new team members would be added to help meet a deadline and would have the burden of trying to learn the architecture of the building, the thoughts behind its design, and how its various systems interact. In a Revit Architecture project, they have that same obligation, but they have the additional task of learning how the *model* goes together. The model will have constraints set against various elements (such as locking a corridor width) as well as various digital construction issues (such as how floors and walls might be tied together, what the various family names are, or workset organization). This ramping-up period consumes additional time.

Regardless of planning, deadlines escape the best of architects and project managers. It's a good idea to know when and how you can staff to make sure you meet deadlines. Keeping in mind that any team members new to the project have to learn about *both* the design and the model they have been thrown into, follow these suggestions so new staff can help production and don't accidentally break anything along the way:

Create content, content, content. You will find that you are making model families or detail components until the end of the project. This process will help get the newbie engaged in a specific part of the project and also isolate them until they learn more about how the model has gone together.

Put them into a drafting role. Even if this isn't their ultimate role on the project, having staff new to the design help create views and lay out sheets will get them familiar with the architecture while still allowing the team to progress on the document set.

Start them to work on detailing. Every project can always use someone who knows how to put a building together. If you have someone new to the project and possibly even new to Revit Architecture, let them embellish some of the views already created and laid out on sheets. These views can be layered with 2D components, linework, and annotations.

Modeling Site

In the previous sections of this chapter, you learned about the fundamental roles and workflow for your project team. Now let's talk about some other less frequently used tools. Another set of tools you should become familiar with are the site tools. They allow you to create a context in which your building models can be situated. For example, a toposurface will create a hatched area when you view your building in a section, and it will function as a hosting surface for site components such as trees, shrubs, parking spaces, accessories, and vehicles (Figure 13.5).

FIGURE 13.5 A toposurface can host components such as trees, entourage, and vehicles.

The site tools in Revit Architecture are intended only to be used for the creation of basic elements, including topography, property lines, and building pads. Although editing utilities are available to manipulate the site elements, these tools are not meant to be used for civil engineering like the functionality found in Autodesk® AutoCAD® Civil 3D®.

In the following sections you'll learn about the different ways to create and modify a toposurface, how to generate property lines with tags, and how to model a building pad in a toposurface.

Using a Toposurface

Certification Objective

As its name suggests, a toposurface is a surface-based representation of the topography context supporting a project. It is not modeled as a solid in Revit Architecture; however, a toposurface will appear as if it were a solid in a 3D view with a section box enabled (Figure 13.6).

FIGURE 13.6 A toposurface appears as a solid in a 3D view only if a section box is used.

You can create a toposurface in three different ways: by placing points at specific elevations, by using a linked CAD file with lines or points at varying elevations, or by using a points file generated by a civil-engineering application. You'll create a site from an imported CAD file in the following exercise.

A common workflow you may encounter involves the use of CAD data generated by a civil engineer. In this case, the engineer must create a file with 3D data. Blocks, circles, and contour polylines must exist in the CAD file at the appropriate elevation to be used in the process of generating a toposurface in Revit Architecture.

In the following exercise, you will download a sample DWG file with contour polylines. You must link the file into your Revit Architecture project before creating the toposurface. Here are the steps:

1. Create a new Revit Architecture project using the `default.rte` or `DefaultMetric.rte` template.
2. Download the file `c13-Site-Link.dwg` from this book's web page.
3. Activate the floor plan named Site in the Project Browser.

4. Go to the Insert tab in the ribbon, and click the Link CAD button. Select the `c13-Site-Link.dwg` file, and set the following options:
    - Current View Only: Unchecked
    - Import Units: Auto-Detect
    - Positioning: Auto - Center To Center
    - Place At: Level 1

5. Click Open to close the dialog box and complete the insertion of the CAD link. Open a default 3D view to examine the results (Figure 13.7).

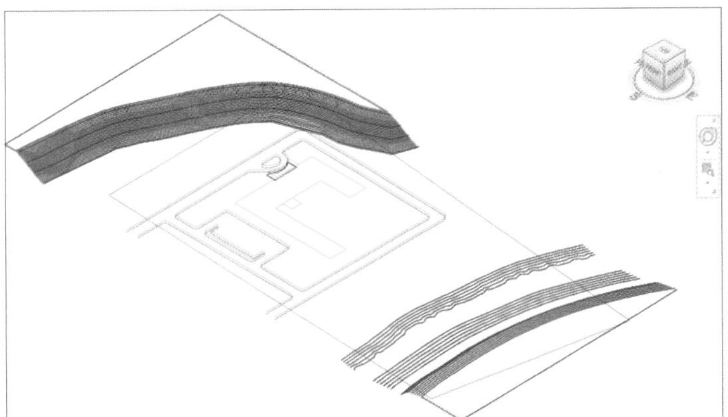

FIGURE 13.7 Linked CAD file as seen in a 3D view

6. From the Massing And Site tab in the ribbon, click the Toposurface button. In the Tools panel on the Modify | Edit Surface ribbon, select Create From Import and then Select Import Instance.
7. Pick the linked CAD file, and the Add Points From Selected Layers dialog box appears (Figure 13.8). Click the Check None button, and then select the layers C-TOPO-MAJR and C-TOPO-MINR.
8. Click OK to close the dialog box. Revit Architecture may take a few seconds to generate the points based on the contour polylines in the linked file, but they will appear as black squares when they have all been placed.

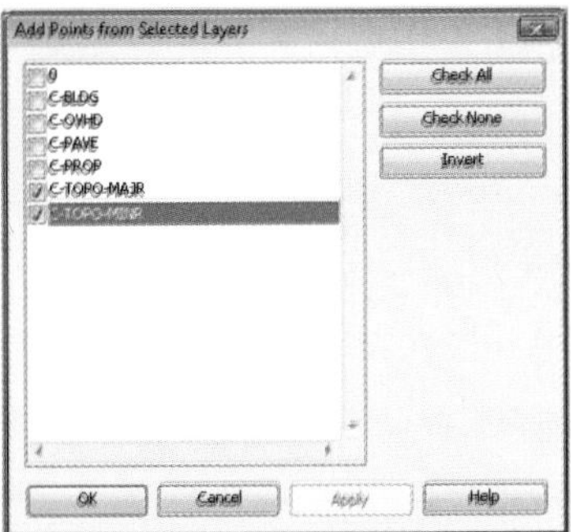

FIGURE 13.8 Select only the layers containing 3D contour information.

9. If you would like to use fewer points to define the toposurface, click the Simplify Surface button in the contextual ribbon, and enter a larger value such as 1′-0″ (250 mm).

10. Click the Finish Surface button in the contextual ribbon to complete the toposurface. Change the visual style of the view to Consistent Colors to examine your results.

Creating a Building Pad

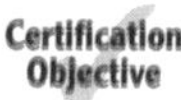

A *building pad* in Revit Architecture is a unique model element that resembles a floor. It can have a thickness and compound structure, it is associated with a level, and it can be sloped using slope arrows while you're sketching its boundary. The building pad is different from a floor because it will automatically cut through a toposurface, defining the outline for your building's cellar or basement.

The process to create a building pad is virtually identical to that of creating a floor. Let's run through a quick exercise to create a building pad in a sample project:

1. Open the file `c13-Site-Pad.rvt`, which you can download from this book's web page.

2. Activate the floor plan named Site in the Project Browser. You see an existing topographic surface and a property line. Notice that reference planes were created to demarcate the required zoning setbacks from the property line. Foundation walls have been created in these reference planes.

   Note that you don't have to create a property line and walls before creating a building pad. You might create a building pad before any other building elements. Just realize that you can use the Pick Walls mode to associate the boundary of the building pad with the foundation walls.

3. Activate the Cellar floor plan from the Project Browser.

4. Go to the Massing And Site tab in the ribbon, and click the Building Pad button. In the Properties palette, change the Height Offset From Level value to 0.

5. Switch to Pick Walls mode in the Draw panel of the contextual ribbon, and then pick the inside edges of the four foundation walls. You can use the Tab-select method to place all four lines at once.

6. Click the Finish Edit Mode button in the contextual ribbon to complete the sketch, and then double-click the section head in the plan view to examine your results. Notice that the top of the building pad is at the Cellar level and the poche of the topographic surface has been removed in the space of the cellar (Figure 13.9).

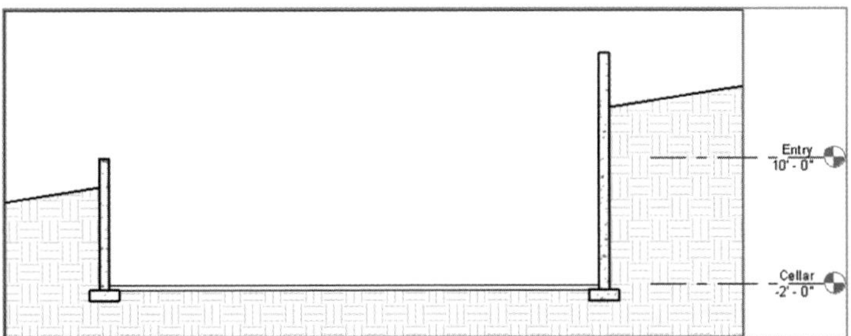

FIGURE 13.9 **This section view illustrates how the building pad adjusts the extents of the topographic surface.**

ADJUSTING THE SECTION POCHE FOR TOPOGRAPHIC SURFACES

If you would like to customize the settings for the fill pattern and depth of the poche, click the small arrow at lower right on the Model Site panel in the Massing And Site tab of the ribbon to open the Site Settings dialog box shown here:

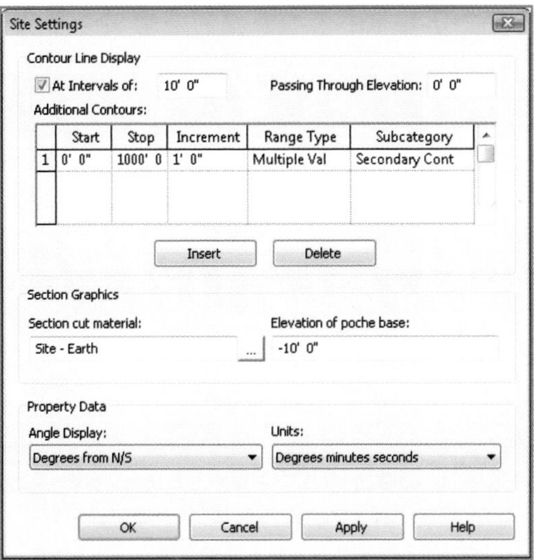

Keeping an Eye on File Size

Watch the size of your file. It's a good metric for general file stability. A typical Revit Architecture file size for a project in construction documents will be between 100 MB and 250 MB—250 MB is on the high side of file sizes. Beyond that, you will find that the model will be slow to open and hard to rotate in 3D views; and other views, such as building elevations and overall plans, will also be slow to open.

Should your file become large or unwieldy, you have several ways to trim the file down and get the model lean and responsive again.

Purging Unused Families and Groups

On the Manage tab is a command called Purge Unused. This command removes all the unused families and groups from your model by deleting them. Many times in a design process you will change window types or wall types or swap one set of families for another. Even if those elements are not being used in the project, they are being stored in the file, and therefore when the file is opened, they are being loaded into memory. Depending on the stage of your project, you should periodically delete these elements from the model to keep your file size down. Don't worry—if you find you need a family you've removed, you can always reload it.

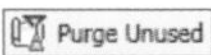

Select the Manage tab, and choose Purge Unused from the Settings panel. Depending on the size of your model and how many families you have loaded, it might take Revit Architecture a few minutes to complete this command.

After Revit Architecture is done thinking, it will provide you with a list of all the families and groups in the file that are not actively in a view (Figure 13.10). At this point, you have the option to select the elements you want to delete or to keep and remove the rest.

We don't recommend that you use this command in the early stages of design, mainly because your file size won't be that large early on and purging at this stage would eliminate any preloaded families that you might have included in your template. During schematic design and design development, you are typically going through design iteration and will likely be adding and removing content regularly. It can become a hassle to have to constantly load or reload families into the model. If your model is not suffering from performance issues or the file size isn't unruly, it's not necessary to perform a Purge Unused.

Cutting Down on the Number of Views

The ability to quickly create views in a model is one of the fast and easy benefits of using Revit Architecture. This ability can also be a detriment, though, if it is not managed. Beyond the hassle of having to sort through many views to find the one you need, having too many views in Revit Architecture can also impact your performance and file size.

Obviously, a number of views are needed in the model to create the construction documentation. In addition, you will find yourself creating views to study the design, deal with model creation, or view the building or project from a new angle. These types of working views will never make it to the sheet set, and some will be used only for brief periods.

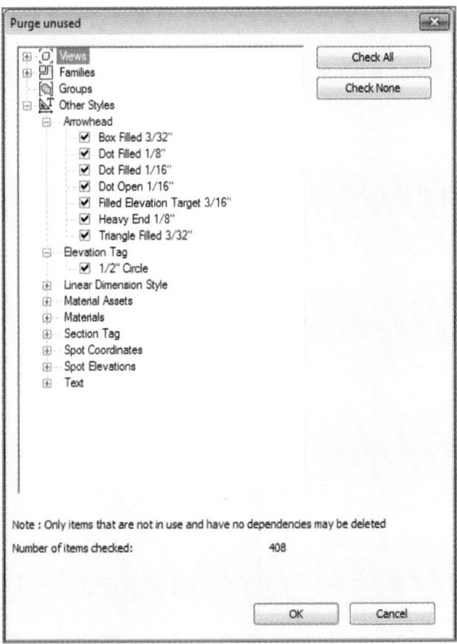

FIGURE 13.10 The Purge Unused dialog box

How Many Working Views Is Too Many?

How many working views is too many to have in your model? The obvious answer is that when performance begins to suffer, you need to start looking at ways to make the model lean and speed up response times. We had a project team new to Revit Architecture, and they were complaining about the file being slow to open and manipulate. When we reviewed their model, the file size was around 800 MB! We were surprised that they were able to do any work at all.

One of the first things we did to get the file size down was look at all the views that were not on sheets. More than 1,200 views were not being used. Deleting those views, paired with a File ➢ Save (with the Compress check box selected), reduced the file size to 500 MB. Although the result was still high, you can see the impact that keeping too many views has on file size.

Dealing with Warnings

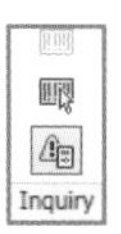

A really important way to troubleshoot your model is to use the Warnings tool. This tool will do very little to affect your overall file size, but it will alert you to problems in the model. Warnings should regularly be addressed to ensure file stability. To open the Warnings dialog box, shown in Figure 13.11, click the Warnings button on the Inquiry panel of the Manage tab. The dialog box lists all warnings still active in your project file.

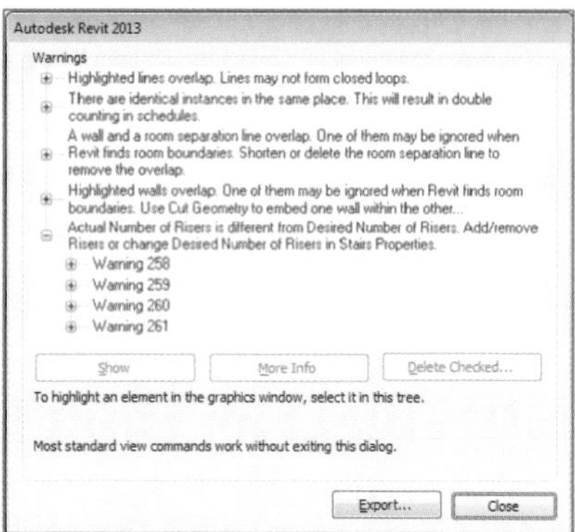

FIGURE 13.11 The Warnings dialog box

Errors and warnings are all essentially types of issues Revit Architecture has when it tries to resolve geometry, conflicts, or formulas that do not equate. Things that appear in this dialog box include instances of multiple elements sitting directly on top of each other, thereby creating inaccurate schedule counts; wall joints that do not properly clean themselves up; wall and room separation lines overlapping; stairs that have the wrong number of risers between floors; and so on. This dialog box shows you all the times the yellow warning box appeared in the bottom-right corner of the screen and you ignored it. Errors that go unchecked can compound to create other errors and can also lead to inaccurate reporting in schedules or even file corruption. Check the Warnings dialog box regularly as part of your periodic file maintenance, and try to keep the number of instances to a minimum.

Notice that the Warnings dialog box has an Export feature. Use this feature to export your error list to an HTML file so you can read it at your leisure outside the model environment (Figure 13.12). You can also pull this list into a Microsoft Word or Excel document so you can distribute the errors across the team to be resolved.

In the example shown in Figure 13.12, using the Jenkins model, the file has 261 errors and warnings. How many errors in a file are too many? Much of that

depends on your model, your computer's capabilities, the error types, and your deliverable. For instance, if you are delivering a BIM model to your client or to the contractor, you might have a zero-error requirement. In that case, no errors are acceptable. If you are still actively in the design phase of the project, however, you will always have some errors—it is an inescapable part of the iteration process. As you refine the drawings, errors will be resolved; and as you add new content to the model that is in need of resolution, new errors will be created.
If you are not worried about a model deliverable, you can get away with having fewer than 1,000 errors in the project without too much trouble. That said, the cleaner the model, the smoother it will run.

JenkinsMusicBldg-Cntrl-Eddy Error Report (1/3/2012 11:51:07 AM)

Error message	Elements
Highlighted walls are attached to, but miss, the highlighted targets.	Exterior and Structure : Floors : Floor : CIP Concrete : id 263090 Exterior and Structure : Walls : Basic Wall : 12" COATED CMU : id 613698
Highlighted walls are attached to, but miss, the highlighted targets.	Exterior and Structure : Floors : Floor : CIP Concrete : id 263090 Exterior and Structure : Walls : Basic Wall : Exterior - Brick 2 : id 693453
Highlighted walls are attached to, but miss, the highlighted targets.	Exterior and Structure : Floors : Floor : CIP Concrete : id 269226 Interiors : Walls : Basic Wall : Interior - Gyp 4 7/8" : id 605102
Highlighted walls are attached to, but miss, the highlighted targets.	Exterior and Structure : Walls : Basic Wall : Exterior - Brick 2 : id 325781 Exterior and Structure : Floors : Floor : CIP Concrete : id 334468
Highlighted walls are attached to, but miss, the highlighted targets.	Exterior and Structure : Walls : Basic Wall : Exterior - Brick 2 : id 325861 Exterior and Structure : Floors : Floor : CIP Concrete : id 334468

FIGURE 13.12 Exporting errors and warnings

The Essentials and Beyond

This chapter focused on understanding some essential but atypical things about Revit Architecture and a BIM workflow. We discussed how you can best transition from a 2D CAD environment to a Revit Architecture BIM workflow, and how to incorporate some of the lesser-used (but just as important) tools such as site work and creating pads. We also discussed how to manage the Revit Architecture file itself. Good file management will help to ensure that your Revit Architecture projects are quick and responsive. Using Revit Architecture means understanding BIM as a workflow and process at all levels in your office and at all phases on your project. Being prepared for a process change as well as a software change will help you become successful as you move into BIM.

(Continues)

THE ESSENTIALS AND BEYOND *(Continued)*

Additional Exercises

- Diagram your project or office's historical workflow using CAD or hand drafting. Consider the hours used in each phase of the project and the number of staff needed to complete a given phase. Track your first Revit Architecture project so you can compare the two.
- Revit Architecture is a great tool, but it is also one of many that you will use in your projects. Discuss with your design teams how they would like to transition from design tools (such as SketchUp and trace paper) to Revit Architecture.

CHAPTER 14

Tips, Tricks, and Troubleshooting

This chapter provides tips, tricks, and troubleshooting ideas to help keep your project files running smoothly. We provide pointers to keep you from getting into trouble, as well as a sampling of time-savers and other great ideas.

In this chapter, you learn the following skills:

- **Optimizing performance**
- **Using best practices**
- **Fixing file corruption**
- **Learning tips and shortcuts**
- **Finding additional resources**

Optimizing Performance

It should make sense that a smaller file on a good network will run the fastest. Autodesk® Revit® Architecture files can range anywhere from 10 MB to over 300 MB. Much of that variation depends on the level of detail in the model itself, the presence of imported geometry (2D CAD files, SketchUp, and so on), the number of views, and the overall complexity of the model geometry. Obviously, your hardware configuration will also be a factor in determining the performance of your models.

You can optimize your hardware in a number of ways to get the most out of your configuration. You should first look at the minimum hardware specifications for a computer running Revit Architecture. Autodesk has published those requirements on its website, and they are updated with each new version of the application. You can find the current specs at `www.autodesk.com/revit`; choose System Requirements under the Product Information heading. Beyond the default specifications, you can do a number of things to help keep your files nimble. Here are some other recommendations:

Use a 64-bit OS. Revit Architecture likes RAM, and the more physical RAM it can use, the more data you can cache into active memory. Windows now offers several versions of a 64-bit OS. Windows XP, Windows Vista, and Windows 7 all have 64-bit capability. This allows you to bridge the 32-bit limit of Windows XP and earlier. The older operating systems were limited to only 2 GB of RAM per application, but a 64-bit OS allows you to use as much as you can pack into your machine.

If you have a 32-bit OS, use the 3 GB switch. If you have a 32-bit OS such as Windows XP, need to get your project done, and don't want to deal with the upgrade, use the 3 GB switch. This setting allows you to grab an extra gigabyte of RAM from your computer, for a maximum of 3 GB. To take advantage of this switch, you'll need to load Windows XP Service Pack 2 and follow the instructions found on the Autodesk support site at `www.autodesk.com/support`; choose Autodesk Revit Architecture from the list of applications, and search for the term **3 GB switch**. Of course, you need more than 2 GB of RAM in your workstation.

Figure out how much RAM your project will need. Before you email your IT department requesting 12 GB of RAM, figure out how much you're actually going to use on your project. Your OS and other applications like Microsoft Outlook will use some of your RAM, but you can calculate how much RAM Revit Architecture will need to work effectively. The formula is as follows:

Model Size in Explorer × 20 + Linked File Size(s) × 20 = Active RAM Needed

Let's look at a couple of examples to demonstrate how this works. You have a project file with no linked files, and the file size on your server is 150 MB. So, 150 × 20 = 3,000 MB, or 3 GB of RAM to operate effectively.

In another example, you have a 120 MB file, a 50 MB structural model linked in, and four CAD files at 1 MB each:

(120 × 20) + (50 × 20) + (4 × 20) = 3,480 MB, or 3.5 GB of RAM

Once you've put as much RAM into your workstation as is practical, your next recourse for improving model performance is to reduce your file size so you're not using as much RAM. Here are some tips to do that and thereby improve your file speed:

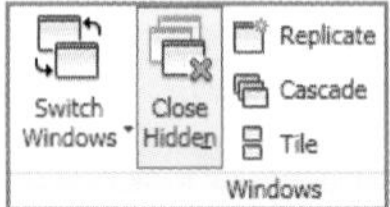

Manage your views. You can do two things using views to help improve performance. First, close windows you're not using to help minimize the drain on your resources. It's easy to have many views open at once, even if you're concentrating on only a few views—and the more views you open, the more information you will load into active RAM. You can always close all the windows but your active one, using the Close Hidden Windows tool: on the View tab, click the Close Hidden button (it's also conveniently located in the Quick Access toolbar [QAT]). You can also assign this command to a keyboard shortcut such as XX.

The other way to manage your views is to remove from your project the ones you don't need. You can make views in your model quickly and easily, and this feature can lead to an abundance of views (possibly hundreds) that you aren't using in your document set and don't plan to use. Adding too many views can raise your overall file size even if you haven't added any geometry. Get rid of those unused views—typically views that are not on sheets—to help keep your file running smoothly. An easy way to manage this is to create a View List including the Sheet Number parameter. In other words, if the Sheet Number parameter for a view is empty, that view has not been placed on a sheet. Select rows in a View List, and use the Delete button in the ribbon; or select multiple views in the Project Browser, and use the Delete command on the right-click command menu.

Delete or unload unused CAD files. Many times in a project process, you'll want to load content from another source as a background. This could be a client's CAD as-built drawings or a consultant's mechanical, electrical, and plumbing (MEP) design. You might link or import these files into your drawing and forget about them during the busy course of the project. As you've seen from the earlier tips on RAM use, all these small files add up. Getting rid of them can speed up your file and is good housekeeping. If the file is linked, you can unlink it using the Manage Links button on the Insert tab. If it is inserted, right-click an instance of the file and choose Select All Instances from the context menu. Clicking Delete will then remove all the instances in the entire model as opposed to only in the active view.

Don't explode imported CAD files. When imported into a family or project, a CAD file is a collection of objects that is managed as a single entity. If you explode a CAD file, the single object immediately becomes many objects—and they all take up space in the file, requiring more resources from the application to track and coordinate them.

If you're importing DWG files, leave them unexploded as much as possible. If you need to hide lines, use the Visibility/Graphic Overrides dialog box to turn layers on and off. Explode *only* when you need to change the imported geometry, and start with a partial explode to minimize the number of new entities. The margin illustration shows the tools available in the Options Bar when you select an imported or linked DWG file. Also note that lines smaller than 1/32″ (1mm) are not retained when CAD files are exploded.

A better workflow than importing your CAD files directly into the project is to import them into a family and then load that family into the project. This approach will also aid in keeping accidents from happening, such as a novice user exploding the file.

Turn on volume computation only as needed. Calculating the volumes on a large file can slow down your model speed immensely. Volume calculations are typically turned on when exporting to gbXML, but sometimes teams forget to turn them back off again. Volumes will recalculate each time you edit a room, move a wall, or change any of the building geometry. Turn off this option using the Area and Volume Computations dialog box found below the Room and Area panel on the Architecture tab (Figure 14.1).

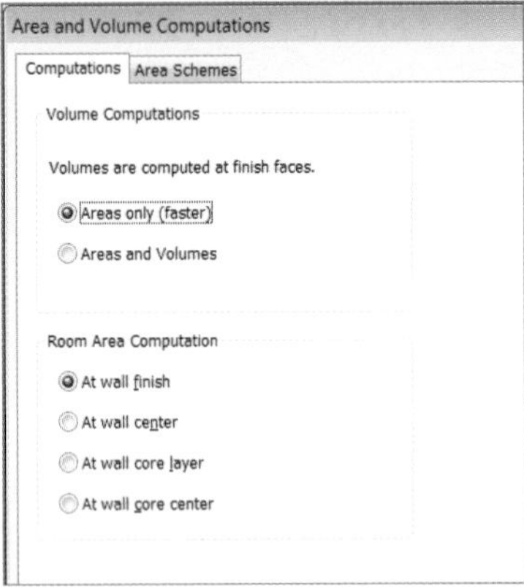

FIGURE 14.1 Choose the area calculations to minimize unneeded computations.

Using Best Practices

Good file maintenance is critical to keeping your files running smoothly and your file sizes low. Here are some best practices and workflows identified in other areas of the book but consolidated in this section as a quick reference:

Manage the amount of information shown in views. In our daily lives, we all suffer from TMI (too much information) from time to time. An overload of information in views not only will make them look cluttered but will also adversely affect project performance. Show only what you need to show in a view. Do this by minimizing the level of detail, view detail, view depth, and view content. Here are some simple tips to keep your individual views working smoothly:

Minimize the level of detail. Set your detail level, found in the View Control Bar, relative to your drawing scale. For example, if you're working on a 1/32′ = 1′-0″ (1:100) plan, you probably don't need Detail Level set to Fine. Doing so will cause the view to have a higher level of detail than the printed sheet can show, and you'll end up with black blobs on your sheets and views that are slow to open and print.

Minimize view detail. Make sure you're not showing more detail than you need. For instance, if you have wall studs shown in a 1/16″ (1:200) scale plan or the extruded aluminum window section shown in a building section, chances are it will not represent correctly when printed. Turning off those elements in your view will keep things moving more smoothly as well as printing more cleanly.

Minimize view depth. View depth and crop regions are great tools to enhance performance. As an example, a typical building section is shown in Figure 14.2. The default behavior causes a regeneration of all the model geometry to the full depth of that view every time you open the view. To reduce the amount of geometry that needs to be redrawn, drag the section's far clip plane (the green dashed line when you highlight the section) in close to the cutting plane.

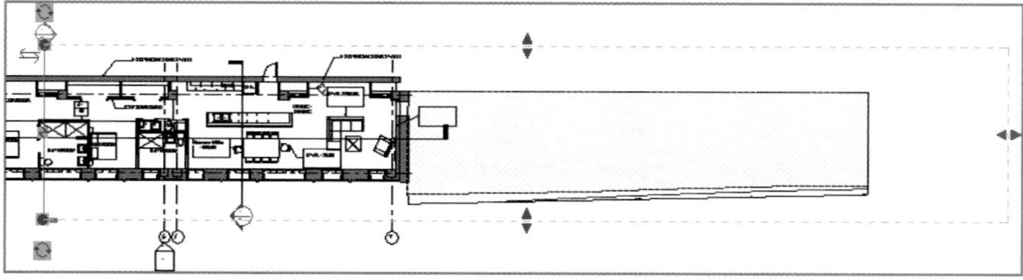

FIGURE 14.2 Minimizing the view depth

Minimize view content. Another best practice is to limit the amount of visible content to only what is necessary in a view. For example, in an exterior 3D view of an entire building, perhaps you can turn off complete categories of detailed interior content such as electrical fixtures, plumbing fixtures, and furniture.

Model only what you need. Although it is possible to model to a very small level of detail, don't fall into the trap of over-modeling. Be smart about what you choose to model and how much detail you show. If it's not conveying information about the project, maybe it's not needed. The amount of information you do or do not model should be based on your project size and complexity, your timeframe, and your comfort level with the software.

When trying to decide how much detail to put into a model or even a family, you can use the following three very good rules of thumb to help you make the right decision for the element you're looking to create:

Scale At what scale will this detail be seen? If it's a very small-scale detail, it might be simpler to just draw it in 2D in a drafting view.

Repetition How many times will the element appear in the drawing set? If it will appear in only one location or only one time, it might be easier to draft it in 2D rather than try to model the element. If it will appear in several locations, modeling is probably the better solution. The more exposure an element has in the model (the more views it shows in), the more reason you have to model it. For example, doors are good to model; they show in elevations and plans all over the sheet set.

Quality How good at modeling families in Revit Architecture are you, honestly? Don't bite off more than you can chew. If you're new to Revit Architecture, keep it simple and use 2D components. The more projects you complete, the better you'll understand the BIM workflow.

Don't over-constrain. Embedding user-defined constraints into families and the model helps keep important information constant. However, if you don't need to lock a relationship, don't do it. Over-constraining the model can cause problems later in the project process when you want to move or modify locked elements. Constrain only when necessary. Otherwise, let the model be free.

Watch out for imported geometry. Although you have the ability to use geometry from several other file sources, use caution when doing so. Remember that everything you link into your model takes up about 20 times the file size in your system's RAM. So, linking a 60 MB NURBS-based ceiling design will equal 2 GB of RAM and more than likely slow down your model. Deleting unused CAD files, using linking rather than importing, and cleaning up the CAD geometry before insertion will help keep problems to a minimum.

Purge unused files. You won't use every family and every group you create in your model. The Purge Unused tool lets you get rid of those unused elements to help keep your file sizes at a reasonable level. This too can be found on the Manage tab on the Settings panel. If a file is very large, the tool can take several minutes to run, but eventually you'll be presented with a list (Figure 14.3) of all the unused elements in your file.

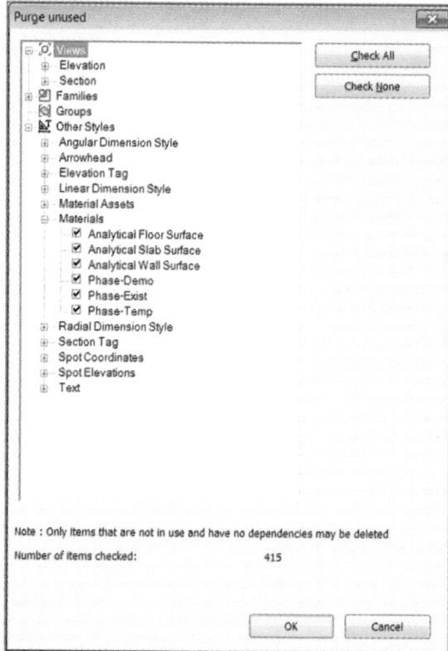

FIGURE 14.3 Use the Purge Unused dialog box to reduce file size.

Using this tool is typically not recommended at the beginning of a project while you are still iterating various design solutions and file sizes tend to be fairly small.

Model correctly from the beginning. As you refine your design, it's critical to model correctly from the beginning, not taking shortcuts, so you don't have to fix things later. If you can begin by thinking about how your project will be assembled, it will save you a lot of time later in the process. It's good practice to plan ahead, but remember that you can make major changes at any stage in the process and still maintain coordination. If you are in the early phase of design and do not know an exact wall type, use generic walls to capture your design intent; changing them later will be simple.

Manage workshared files. When you're employing worksharing on a project, there are additional tools and tips you'll want to follow:

> **Make a new local copy once a week.** In a workshared environment, your local copy can begin to perform poorly or grow in file size while the central file remains small and nimble. If this is the case, it might be time to throw out the old local copy for a new one. As a general practice, if you're accessing a project on a daily basis, it's a good idea to make a new local copy once a week.
>
> **Divide your model.** For larger projects or campus-style projects, you can break up the model into smaller submodels that are linked together. You can also do this on a single large building. Dividing a model helps limit the amount of information you are loading into a project at one time.

If you decide to divide your project, make your cuts along lines that make sense from a holistic-building standpoint. Don't think of the cuts as you would in CAD, but consider how the actual assemblies will interact in the building. For example, don't cut between floors 2 and 3 on a multistory building unless you have a significant change in building form or program. Here's a list of some good places to split a model:

- At a significant change in building form or massing
- At a significant change in building program
- Between separate buildings on the site
- At the building site

Fixing File Corruption

From time to time, your project files may begin to experience duress and possible corruption. This can happen for any number of reasons: network problems, file size, too many errors, or gremlins. If your file begins crashing, don't panic. There are a few things you can do before contacting Autodesk Support. Here are some suggestions to help get you back on track:

Review warnings. Each time you create something that Revit Architecture considers a problem, a warning is issued. Warnings will accumulate if left unresolved. Think of all these errors as unresolved math calculations. The more there are, the more your computer will have to struggle to resolve them, and eventually you will have performance issues or file instability. To review the warnings, click the Warning button on the Manage tab. You'll get a dialog box like the one in Figure 14.4, which will allow you to search for and resolve the problem objects.

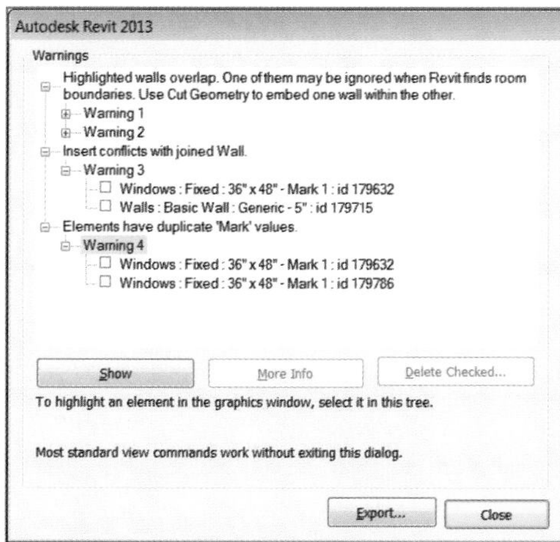

FIGURE 14.4 Resolving errors

Reduce your file size. Sometimes when file corruption occurs, it's due to a file that has grown beyond the capacity of the machines using it. Reduce your file size using the previous tips to make the model more manageable and resolve some of the errors.

Audit the file. Another way to deal with file corruption is to perform an audit on your file. You can find this tool in the lower-left corner of the File Open dialog box (Figure 14.5). Auditing a file will review the data structures and try to correct any problems that have occurred. When the audit is completed, ideally you will have a fully functioning file again.

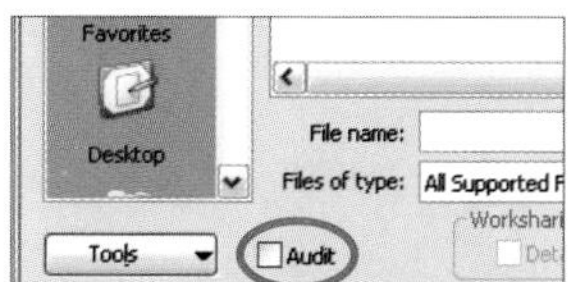

FIGURE 14.5 Auditing a file

You can audit either a local file or the central file. Whenever you audit a file, make a new central copy and have all of your project team members create new local copies. The last thing you want is for someone with file corruption in a local copy to synchronize those problems back to your newly fixed central file.

Learning Tips and Shortcuts

In addition to all the things you can do to hone your Revit Architecture skills, you will begin to learn tips and shortcuts as your experience grows using the software. Here is a compilation of some of those tips and tricks:

Let Revit Architecture do the math. Revit Architecture is like a big calculator, and it's very good at doing math correctly. Don't want to spend the time figuring out what the room size is after you subtract a 3 5⁄8″ and 5⁄8″ piece of gypsum board from an 11′-2″ room? Then don't. If you need to modify a dimension, simply add an equal sign and a formula (Figure 14.6), and the value will be calculated for you.

Dimensions	
Thickness	=4' 5" - 2 13/16"
Height	7' 0"
Trim Projection Ext	0' 1"
Trim Projection Int	0' 1"

FIGURE 14.6 Performing calculations in Revit Architecture

Add a sloped ceiling. Suppose you want to add a gypsum soffit to the bottom of a stair, or you want a sloped ceiling. Well, you can't do that with the Ceiling tool. But you can with a ramp. Make a gypsum board ramp and align it to the bottom of your stair or angle it to create your sloped ceiling plane.

Make elevators visible in your plans. Suppose you want to create a shaft that will penetrate all the floors of your building and put an elevator in it that will show in all your plans. You could do this with an elevator family and cut a series of holes in the floors by editing floor profiles, but sometimes those holes stop aligning on their own recognizance. Fortunately, you can do both things at once using the Shaft tool found on the Opening panel of the Home tab. Here, not only can you cut a vertical hole through multiple floors as a single object, but also you can insert 2D linework to represent the elevator in plan view (Figure 14.7). Every time the shaft is cut, you're certain to see the elevator linework.

Orient to view. Creating perspective views of isolated design elements can be quick and easy in plan view or in section view, but let's say you want to see that same element in 3D to be able to work out the details:

1. Create a callout or section cut isolating the area in question. If you're using a section, make sure to set your view depth to something practical.
2. Open the default 3D view or any other 3D orthographic view of the project.

3. Right-click the ViewCube, select Orient To View, and select the callout or section from the context menu.
4. Your 3D view looks identical to your section or plan region, but by rotating the view, you can see that portion in 3D.

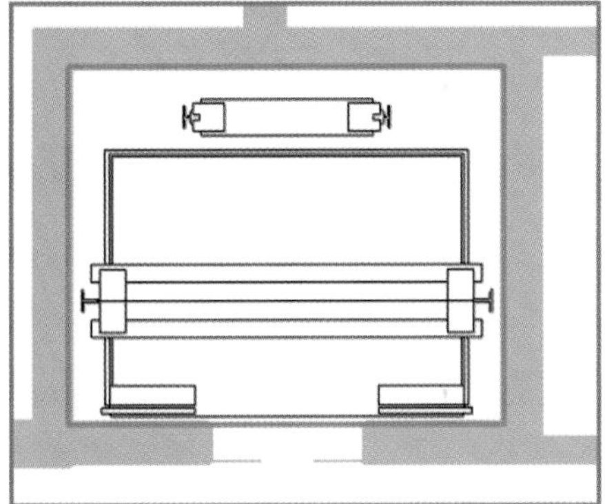

FIGURE 14.7 Adding elevators to a shaft

Tune your shortcuts. You can now edit your keyboard shortcuts without the hassle of searching through your hard drive for a TXT file. To edit your shortcuts, choose Application ➢ Options. Choose the User Interface tab, and then click the Customize button. You can also access this command from the View tab in the ribbon under the User Interface flyout button. The Keyboard Shortcuts dialog box (Figure 14.8) allows you to edit those shortcuts. Consider making common shortcuts the same letter. So, instead of pressing VG to get to your Visibility/Graphic Overrides dialog box, make the shortcut VV for quicker access.

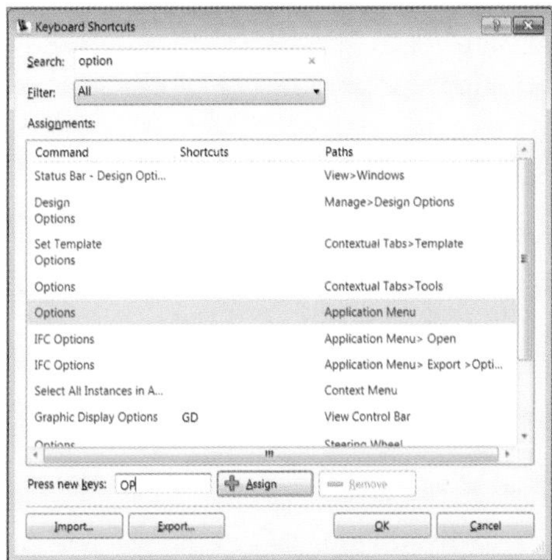

FIGURE 14.8 Editing your keyboard shortcuts

Drag and drop families. Suppose you need to load a family into a project, the Explorer window is open, and you know where the family is, but you don't want to go through the laborious effort of navigating across your office's server environment to get there. No problem. You can drag and drop families from Explorer directly into the project file.

Copy a 3D view. Suppose you made the perfect 3D view in your last project, and you can't figure out how to get it into your current project. Fortunately, there's a way to copy views from one project to another. Open both files in the same instance of Revit Architecture, and then do the following:

1. In your perfect view, right-click the 3D view in the Project Browser, and choose Show Camera from the context menu.
2. Press Ctrl+C to copy the selected camera.
3. In your new model, press Ctrl+V to paste the camera. The view and all its settings are now there.

Use a quick-cut poche. Want to change everything that's cut in a view without having to select every family and change its properties? A quick-cut poche is, well, quick:

1. Open the view you want to modify.
2. Using a crossing window, select all the elements in the view.
3. Right-click, and choose Override Graphics in View ➢ By Element from the context menu. As shown in Figure 14.9, you can choose any filled region in the project and assign it to anything that is cut in the current view.

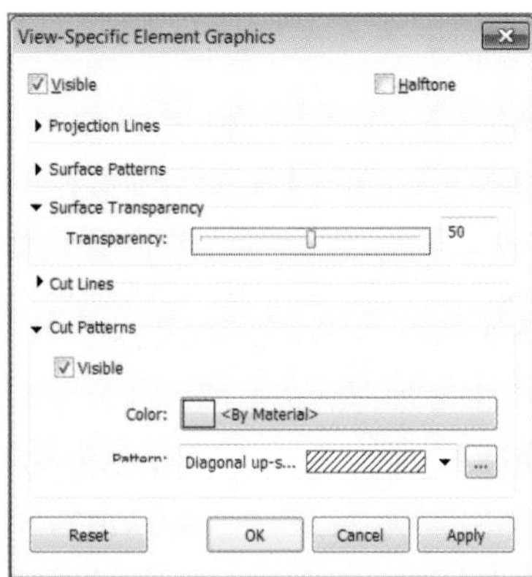

FIGURE 14.9 Using View-Specific Element Graphics for a quick poche

Move your ribbon. Did you know that you can reorganize the tabs on the ribbon and place them in any order you'd like? To do so, hold down the Ctrl key, and select a tab (such as Manage). You can drag it left or right to change the order in which it appears.

Finding Additional Resources

A number of resources are available to help you along the way and improve your use of the software, help you solve problems, and assist you in creating new content. In our digital age, there is a wealth of information online to help you learn or communicate with users far and wide. So, before you spend hours trying to solve a particularly challenging problem on your own, you might check some of these tools:

Revit Architecture Help Menu Open the Revit Architecture Help menu by clicking the question-mark icon in the upper-right corner of the application. This tool will give you a basic synopsis of all the tools, buttons, and commands available in the application. It is also available as an online wiki at `http://wikihelp.autodesk.com/Revit`.

Subscription Support If you have purchased Revit Architecture on subscription, Revit Subscription Support offers web-based support. Their responses are speedy, their advice is top-notch, and chances are they've seen your problem before. Subscription Support can be accessed online at `http://subscription.autodesk.com`.

AUGI Autodesk User Group International (AUGI) is a source for tips and tricks as well as excellent user forums. The forums are free to participate in, and it's a great place where you can ask questions, find answers, and discuss project workflows. AUGI is located online at `www.augi.com`. Once you're there, look for Revit Architecture.

Revit City Looking for content or families? Revit City offers another free online resource and has a growing database of families posted by users; see `www.revitcity.com`. On our blog, we have also compiled a list of websites where various Revit Architecture content is available: `www.architecture-tech.com/2011/12/bim-content-for-revit.html`.

YouTube Here's a great reason to tell your IT department you need access to YouTube. Autodesk has its own channel with great free content: `www.youtube.com/user/autodesk`. It has hundreds of short videos showing how to perform specific tasks in Revit Architecture.

AECbytes AECbytes is a website dedicated to following the trends in the AEC industry, with a strong focus on BIM, technology, and the direction of the industry. The site is put together by Lachmi Khemlani; see www.aecbytes.com.

Architecture-Tech The authors of this book (Phil, Eddy, and James) maintain a popular blog at www.architecture-tech.com. A variety of posts related to Revit Architecture, other BIM software, and fun topics are available on a regular basis. You can also find links to many other blogs from industry experts.

The Essentials and Beyond

Whew! You made it to the end of what would be three days of Revit Architecture training. You should know enough by this point to be valuable to your project teams and ready to start your first Revit Architecture project. In this chapter, you learned some of the tips and tricks that seasoned users employ every day. High fives all around! While you bask in the glow of your new knowledge, you might be wondering, "Where do I go from here?" If you're looking for additional resources beyond what we've listed, join the larger Revit Architecture community:

- Reading our blog, www.architecture-tech.com, is a great place to start.
- Check out the AUGI forums. Many a Revit Architecture user has found helpful hints there.
- If you truly learned from what you read here and want to take the next step, we recommend the ***Mastering Revit*** book series, which you can find at www.sybex.com/go/masteringrevit2013, www.amazon.com, or wherever fine Revit Architecture titles are sold.

Autodesk Revit Architecture 2013 Certification

Autodesk certifications are industry-recognized credentials that can help you succeed in your design career, providing benefits to both you and your employer. Getting certified is a reliable validation of skills and knowledge, and it can lead to accelerated professional development, improved productivity, and enhanced credibility.

This *Autodesk Official Training Guide* can be an effective component of your exam preparation. Autodesk highly recommends (and we agree!) that you schedule regular time to prepare, review the most current exam preparation roadmap available at `www.autodesk.com/certification`, use *Autodesk Official Training Guides*, take a class at an Authorized Training Center (find ATCs near you here: `www.autodesk.com/atc`), and use a variety of resources to prepare for your certification—including plenty of actual hands-on experience.

Certification Objective

To help you focus your studies on the skills you'll need for these exams, the following tables show objectives that could potentially appear on an exam and in what chapter you can find information on that topic—and when you go to that chapter, you'll find certification icons like the one in the margin here.

Table A.1 is for the Autodesk Certified Associate Exam and lists the section, exam objectives, and chapter where the information is found. Table A.2 is for the Autodesk Certified Professional Exam. The sections and exam objectives listed in the table are from the Autodesk Certification Exam Guide.

These Autodesk exam objectives were accurate at press time; please refer to `www.autodesk.com/certification` for the most current exam roadmap and objectives.

Good luck preparing for your certification!

TABLE A.1 Certified Associate Exam sections and objectives

Topic	Learning Objective	Chapter
User Interface: Definitions	Identify primary parts of the user interface (UI): tabs, application menu, InfoCenter, ribbon, Elevation tag, Status bar, View Control bar, Project Browser, context/right-click menus.	Chapter 1
User Interface: UI Navigation/ Interaction	Name the key features of the ribbon. Define how a split button works. Demonstrate the three ways the ribbon can be displayed: Full Ribbon, Min to Panel Tiles, Min to Tabs. Demonstrate how to detach a panel and move it on the screen.	Chapter 1
	Describe the hierarchy in the Project Browser for a new project.	Chapter 1
	Define what "context" means when right-clicking in the drawing window.	Chapter 1
	Name the tools found on the Application menu (Save, Plot, Export, Print).	Chapter 1
	Demonstrate how to add items to the Quick Access toolbar.	Chapter 1
	Describe why the Options Bar changes.	Chapter 1
	Describe the function of the status bar.	Chapter 1
	Describe what pressing the Escape key does.	Chapter 1

Topic	Learning Objective	Chapter
User Interface: Drawing Window	Describe what double-clicking an elevation view marker does.	Chapter 1
	Demonstrate how to turn on/off the 3D Indicator.	Chapter 1
	Demonstrate how to change the view scale.	Chapter 1
User Interface: Navigation Control	Describe the functionality of the ViewCube.	Chapter 1
	Describe what the ViewCube home icon does.	Chapter 1
User Interface: Zoom	Describe how to zoom using the Navigation bar.	Chapter 1
	Describe the quickest way to zoom in or out.	Chapter 1
	Describe the quickest way to pan.	Chapter 1
File Management: Definitions	Define the acronym BIM and why it is important to Revit users.	Introduction
	Define a template file.	Chapter 13
File Management: Project Files	Identify the file extension of a project file (`.rvt`).	Chapter 1
	Identify the file extension of a template file (`.rte`). Create a template file for later project use.	Chapter 13
	Identify the file extension of a Revit family file (`.rfa`).	Chapter 6

(Continues)

TABLE A.1 *(Continued)*

Topic	Learning Objective	Chapter
File Management: Open Existing Revit Project	Locate the Recent File window.	Not Covered
	Demonstrate how to open a Revit file through Projects ➢ Open and through Application menu ➢ Open Documents icon.	Chapter 1
File Management: Create New Revit Project	Demonstrate how to create a new Revit project folder and file through Application menu ➢ New ➢ Project.	Chapter 1
	Change to a metric drawing.	Not Covered
	Add project information to a new drawing set.	Chapter 12
	Change system settings to create a new dimension style. Change arrows to architectural tick (obliques).	Chapter 11
Views: View Control and Properties	Navigate and change views using the View Control bar.	Chapter 2
	Understand the view range of plan views and be able to change it.	Not Covered
	Understand the purpose of view templates.	Not Covered
	Change object visibility using temporary hide, hide category, and hide element.	Chapter 1

Topic	Learning Objective	Chapter
Views: View Types	Create section views including segmented ones.	Chapter 9
	Modify, crop, and place elevation views on a sheet.	Chapter 12
	Create and navigate 3D views.	Chapter 3
	Create callouts for details.	Chapter 11
	Create and annotate a drafting view.	Chapter 11
	Use the section box to create a cutaway 3D view.	Chapter 4
Views: Cameras	Create a camera view, and modify its orientation.	Not Covered
	Create and edit a walkthrough.	Not Covered
Levels: Definitions	Describe a level. Describe a use of a non-story level.	Chapter 1
	Understand how levels interact with intersecting views.	Chapter 1
	Create new levels.	Chapter 1
	Understand level properties and characteristics.	Chapter 1
Walls: Home Tab ➢ Wall	Describe how to place walls.	Chapter 3
Walls: Options Bar	List options available when placing and modifying walls: Height, Location Line, Chain, Offset, Radius.	Chapter 3
Walls: Openings	Create a floor-to-ceiling opening in given wall.	Chapter 3

(Continues)

TABLE A.1 *(Continued)*

Topic	Learning Objective	Chapter
Walls: Join	Demonstrate a join on crossing wall elements.	Chapter 3
Walls: Materials	Create a new wall style, and add given materials.	Chapter 3
Doors: Home Tab ➢ Door	Describe how to place doors.	Chapter 3
Doors: Options Bar	Describe door options: Vertical/Horizontal, Tag on Placement, Leader, Leader Attachment Distance.	Chapters 3, 6
Doors: Model in Place	Edit existing doors. Use Align to position a door.	Chapters 3, 6
Windows: Home Tab ➢ Window	Describe how to place windows.	Chapter 3
Windows: Options Bar	Describe window options: Vertical/Horizontal, Tag on Placement, Leader, Leader Attachment Distance.	Chapters 3, 6
Windows: Model in Place	Edit existing windows.	Chapters 3, 6
Component: Options Bar	List options available when placing a component.	Chapter 6
Component: Component Host	Describe how to move a component to a different host.	Chapter 6
Component: Families	Navigate to find component families and load them.	Chapter 6
	Edit a family file and save.	Chapter 7

Topic	Learning Objective	Chapter
Columns and Grids: Definitions	Identify the uses of a grid.	Chapter 2
Columns and Grids: Home Tab ➢ Grid	Create an equally spaced grid pattern.	Chapter 2
Columns and Grids: Grid Properties	List the options available when placing and modifying grids.	Chapter 2
Columns and Grids: Home Tab ➢ Column	Place columns on a grid.	Not Covered
Columns and Grids: Column Properties	List the options available when placing and modifying columns.	Not Covered
Columns and Grids: Modify	List the tools you can use to modify columns and grids.	Not Covered
Stairs and Railings: Stair Types and Properties	Set the stair type.	Chapter 5
	Change the stair tread depth.	Chapter 5
Stairs and Railings: Stair Placement Options	Add a stair.	Chapter 5
Stairs and Railings: Railing Types and Properties	Set the railing to rectangular.	Chapter 5
	Set the railing properties.	Chapter 5

(Continues)

TABLE A.1 *(Continued)*

Topic	Learning Objective	Chapter
Stairs and Railings: Railing Placement Options	Add a railing.	Chapter 5
Roofs and Floors: Roof Types and Properties	Create a roof.	Chapter 4
	Modify the roof properties.	Chapter 4
Roofs and Floors: Roof Elements	Create a fascia, a soffit, and a gutter.	Not Covered
Roofs and Floors: Floors Types and Properties	Set the floor type (Sloped and Tapered). Create a floor.	Chapter 4
Sketching: Geometry	Sketch geometry and profiles using all sketching tools: Lines, Arcs, Polygons, Rectangles.	Chapter 3
Sketching: Fillet, Trim	Fillet objects.	Chapter 3
	Trim objects.	Chapter 3
Sketching: Snaps	Describe the benefits of using snaps.	Chapter 3
	List the shortcuts to toggle osnap on and off.	Not Covered
Annotations: Text	Add model text to a floor plan.	Not Covered

Topic	Learning Objective	Chapter
Annotations: Dimensions	Add a dimension to a given floor plan. Create a wall section.	Chapter 11, 12
	Add a spot slope to a roof on a given plan.	Not Covered
Annotations: Tags	Add tags.	Chapter 11
	Tag untagged elements in a given floor plan.	Chapter 9
Schedules: Schedule Types	Create a door schedule.	Not Covered (while there is no specific coverage of a door schedule, creating schedules is in Chapter 3)
	Create a window schedule.	Chapter 12
	Create a room schedule.	Chapter 12
Schedules: Legends	Create legend	Chapter 11
Schedules: Keynotes	Add keynotes.	Chapter 12, 13
Construction Document Sets: Sheet Setup	Create a title sheet with a sheet list.	Chapter 12
Construction Document Sets: Printing	Create view/sheet sets for printing.	Chapter 12
	Print in scale. Print with percentage.	Chapter 12
Construction Document Sets: Rendering	Render.	Not Covered
	Place generic lights.	Not Covered
	Set the solar angle.	Not Covered

TABLE A.2 Certified Professional Exam sections and objectives

Topic	Learning Objective	Chapter
Collaboration	Copy and monitor elements in a linked file.	Not Covered
	Use worksharing.	Chapter 10
	Import DWG files into Revit.	Not Covered (although the same process using PNG files is covered in Chapter 2)
Documentation	Create and modify filled regions.	Chapter 11
	Place detail components and repeating details.	Chapter 11
	Tag elements (doors, windows, and so on) by category.	Chapter 11
	Use dimension strings.	Chapter 11
	Set the colors used in a color-scheme legend.	Chapter 9
Elements	Change elements within a curtain wall: grids, panels, mullions.	Chapter 3
	Create compound walls.	Not Covered
	Create a stacked wall.	Not Covered
	Differentiate system and component families.	Chapter 6
	Create a new family type.	Chapter 7
	Modify an element's type parameters.	Chapter 3
	Use Revit family templates.	Chapter 6

Topic	Learning Objective	Chapter
Modeling	Assess or review warnings in Revit.	Chapter 14
	Create a building pad.	Not Covered
	Define floors for a mass.	Chapter 2
	Create a stair with a landing.	Chapter 5
	Create elements such as floors, ceilings, or roofs.	Chapter 4
	Generate a toposurface.	Not Covered
	Model railings.	Chapter 5
	Work with phases.	Chapter 8
	Edit a model element's material: door, window, furniture.	Chapter 3
	Change a generic floor/ceiling/roof to a specific type.	Chapter 4
	Attach walls to a roof or ceiling.	Chapter 4
Views	Define element properties in a schedule.	Chapter 12
	Control visibility.	Chapter 1
	Use levels.	Chapter 1
	Create a duplicate view for a plan, section, elevation, drafting view, and so on.	Not Covered
	Create and manage legends.	Chapter 12

(Continues)

TABLE A.2 *(Continued)*

Topic	Learning Objective	Chapter
	Manage the view position on sheets.	Chapter 12
	Move the view title independently of the view.	Chapter 12
	Organize and sort items in a schedule.	Chapter 12

INDEX

Note to the Reader: Throughout this index **boldfaced** page numbers indicate primary discussions of a topic. *Italicized* page numbers indicate illustrations.

A

B

C

D

E

F

M

Q

R

S

U

V

W

Y

Z